BEFORE PECOS

Settlement Aggregation

at Rowe, New Mexico

BEFORE PECOS

Settlement Aggregation at Rowe, New Mexico

by Linda S. Cordell

including the 1917 Rowe Field Diary of Carl C. Guthe
transcribed by Jean Bagalah

WITH CONTRIBUTIONS BY
Linda Mick-O'Hara
Carol Raish
Mollie S. Toll

AND ILLUSTRATIONS BY
Eden A. Welker

Maxwell Museum of Anthropology
Anthropological Papers No. 6

This book is dedicated to the memory of
Albert C. Sandoval

Contents

Figures

Tables

Acknowledgments

The work reported here would not have been undertaken and could not have been completed without the assistance of the students and staff of the University of New Mexico and New Mexico State University Field Schools. Their names are given on page 4 of this report. To Mark Lycett and Kathleen Morrison I owe special thanks for continuing to work on the Rowe material in San Francisco. The family of the late Albert C. Sandoval of Rowe, New Mexico, were gracious hosts, helpmates and extremely patient friends of the project. None of this would have been possible without them and their interest in archaeology. They have my most sincere gratitude.

I am grateful to Richard Reycraft of the University of New Mexico for assistance in compiling climatological and excavation data and to Willow Roberts of the Museum of New Mexico for providing access to and help with Guthe's field notes and photographs. Walter Wait was the inspiration for the Rowe field work and Isolde Wait for the transcription of Guthe's notes that Jean Bagalah accomplished. The staff at Pecos National Monument graciously permitted me to copy field notes and records on more than one occasion and Douglas Schwartz allowed me summer use office space at the School of American Research. I am indebted to June-el Piper for her organizational and editorial skills as well as her good humor, to Ron Stauber for last-minute work on the figures and camera-ready manuscript, to Emmy Ezell for desk-top publishing, and to Michael Adler and Kate Spielmann for their useful comments on the manuscript. I accept full responsibility, however, for the interpretations made in the report. I am pleased to acknowledge Garth Bawden and Bruce Huckell for assistance with publication.

Partial financial support for field work and analysis was made possible by grants from the National Endowment of the Humanities (RS-1144-79) to Walter Wait and Larry Nordby and the National Science Foundation (BNS-831981) to me, Fred Plog and Steadman Upham. I thank my colleague Stead Upham for his common sense, patience and humor in the field and for co-hosting most of our many visitors. I thank those who visited the site as well, particularly Dee F. Green, Mark Harlan, Mollie Toll, Frances Levine, R. S. "Scotty" MacNeish, Lewis R. Binford, Brian M. Fagan, George Gumerman, and Eric Devor. Among those who did not live to see this report, the late Harry Basehart, Elizabeth Garrett, and Florence H. Ellis were not only visitors to the site but important contributors to the research. My late friend and colleague Fred Plog was the impetus for the joint field school and most of the research direction. His was also the enthusiasm and energy that made the project work. His untimely death deprived all of us of a colleague, mentor and friend. Finally, this book is dedicated to the memory of Albert C. Sandoval, who chose to make his home next to the site of Rowe Pueblo. He cared deeply about the ancient village and brought the archaeologists to help reveal its story.

LINDA S. CORDELL
Boulder, Colorado

Part I
ROWE RUIN

INTRODUCTION

THIS VOLUME CONCERNS EXCAVATIONS AND SITE surveys carried out in 1980, 1983, and 1984 at and in the vicinity of Rowe Ruin (LA 108), located in the Upper Pecos River Valley, San Miguel County, New Mexico. Rowe Ruin lies about 7 km southeast of the ruins of Pecos Pueblo, Pecos National Monument. The site itself consists of masonry roomblock quadrangles set around three plazas arranged north-south along the left bank of a small tributary of the Pecos (Bandelier 1892:125; Wait and Nordby 1979). The work at Rowe Ruin in 1980 was a collaborative project, under my direction, among the University of New Mexico Summer Field School in Archaeology; the landowners, Mr. and Mrs. Albert C. Sandoval; and Walter K. Wait and Larry Nordby, of the National Park Service, with partial funding provided by a grant from the National Endowment of the Humanities (RS-1144-79) to Wait and Nordby administered by Southern Illinois University. With my assistance, Wait prepared a preliminary report of the summer work and filed it with both NEH and SIU.

During the summer of 1983, a three-week field season at Rowe Ruin was undertaken jointly by the University of New Mexico Summer Field School in Archaeology, again under my direction, and the New Mexico State University Summer Field School in Archaeology led by the late Fred Plog with assistance from Steadman Upham. During the second half of the 1983 season students worked on a completely separate project, in south-central New Mexico, under the supervision of Margaret C. Nelson (see Nelson 1984).

The field season in 1984 was again a joint summer field school project of the University of New Mexico and New Mexico State University. The work was partially funded by a National Science Foundation grant (BNS-831981) to me, with subcontracts to Fred Plog and Steadman Upham. The 1984 field school took place be-tween June 6 and July 20, the normal seven-week field school session. I submitted a preliminary report of the 1984 work to NSF in 1987.

The artifacts excavated from Rowe Ruin are curated on site by the Sandoval family. Human remains excavated by the field schools were returned to the Sandovals for reburial at the site. Artifacts collected in the course of the field school surveys in 1980 and 1984 were deposited with the superintendent at Pecos National Monument, as requested by the late Buddy Fogelson, then owner of the Forked Lightning Ranch, where the surveyed sites are located. Field maps and descriptions of the sites recorded by the surveys were filed with the superintendent at Pecos Monument and entered into the NMCRIS (formerly ARMS) file at the Museum of New Mexico, Santa Fe.

This volume consists of four major sections. The first (Part I) is a discussion of Rowe Ruin, including a brief characterization of the current environmental setting, a history of research at the site, the research problem addressed in 1984, and summaries of technical studies, including paleoenvironmental data relevant to the research design. A final, short narrative uses the information derived from the preceding sections to comment on the process of site aggregation in the Upper Pecos, especially comparisons with other localities in the general Northern Rio Grande area.

The second section of this volume (Part II) is a transcription of the field notebook of Carl Guthe, who excavated at Rowe in 1917. The original notebook is on file in the archives of the Laboratory of Anthropology at the Museum of New Mexico. The transcription was prepared by Ms. Jean Bagalah, while she served as a volunteer at the Department of Anthropology at the California Academy of Sciences in San Francisco, where I was Irvine Curator and Department Chair.

The technical appendices in Part III consist of studies of the botanical remains, fauna, and ceramics. The final section of this volume (Part IV) concerns the site surveys done in 1980 and 1984. The results of the site surveys provide the basis for discussion of the history of settlement and land use in the Upper Pecos region from the Archaic period through the early twentieth century.

I am indebted to the students and staff of the field schools at Rowe and to the staff of the Laboratory of Anthropology at the Museum of New Mexico for their assistance facilitating my use of archival and site file records.

STUDENTS AND STAFF 1980, 1983, 1984

1980

Staff

Acklen, John (T.A.)
Anschuetz, Kurt (T.A.)
Binford, Martha (T.A.)
Cordell, Linda (P.I.)
Earls, Amy (R.A.)
Raish, Carol (T.A.)
Rowlands, Kathy (T.A.)
Sandoval, Juanita (Cook)
Wait, Walter (Co-P.I.)

Students

Alley, Margaret
Boss, Marian
Cisco, Barbara,
Côté, Robyn
Gafney, James
Gregg, Nancy
Heidke, James
Hill, Amy
Johnson, Byron
Kram, Brian
Morales, William
Morton, Nancy
Nelson, Norman
Rapson, David
Piper, Mary June-el
Reineback, Kathy
Saavadra, Anita
Savage, Annie
Seyfarth, Jill
Speyer, Patricia
Stefan, Heather
Van Tatenhove, Jane

Volunteers

Sandoval, Alby
Wait, Heike

1983

Staff

Carrillo, Charles (T.A.)
Cordell, Linda (P.I.)
Douglass, Amy (T.A.)
Plog, Fred (P.I.)
Sandoval, Juanita (Cook)
Sebastian, Lynne (T.A.)
Upham, Steadman (P.I.)

Students

Alexander, Therese
Backer, Anna
Baldwin, Sy
Kneebone, Ron
Larcombe, Claudia
Lycett, Mark
McBride, Terri
Morrison, Kathleen
Nordstrom, Carl
Rossignol, Jacqueline
Schwenn, Bernadette
Stark, Miriam

1984

Staff

Boston, Richard (Survey)
Cordell, Linda (P.I.)
Douglass, Amy (T.A.)
Kauffman, Barbara (Survey)
Korsmo, Thomas (R.A.)
Lycett, Mark (T.A.)
Mick, Linda (T.A.)
Morrison, Kathleen (T.A.)
Newton, Richard (T.A.)
Plog, Fred (P.I.)
Sandoval, Juanita (Cook)
Upham, Steadman (P.I.)

Students

Adams, Kim
Alexander, Zibby
Cooper, Kelt
Cutter, Jeff
Farrell, David
Galvin, Carol
Hart, Jeannie
Herberger, Tianna
Hollenberg, Ilana
Jones, Chris
Jones, Stephanie
Kelly, Bebe
Kimmelman, Lewis
McCuller, Bryan
Mitchell, Annie
Morales, Thomas
Null, Kitty
Olsen, Nancy
Peterson, Melissa
Reed, Paul
Reiter, Joanne
Robbins, Helen
Prahalis, Fabiola
Shaw, Dan
Simpson, Bill
Stephens, Lorie
Stone, Nancy

THE NATURAL AND CULTURAL SETTING

Rowe Ruin lies at an elevation of 2,072 m (6,800 ft) above sea level at the base of the Upper Pecos River Valley, and at the southern edge of the Sangre de Cristo Range, the southernmost extension of the Rocky Mountain system. At Rowe, the valley floor is relatively flat and wide, with a slope of less than 5% and a width of three to four kilometers, on average. In the vicinity of Rowe Ruin, the Pecos River is deflected about 2.5 km to the eastern edge of the valley by a limestone ridge. The ridge itself borders Rowe Ruin on the east. South and southwest of Rowe Ruin, the scarps of Glorieta and Rowe mesas rim the valley. Glorieta Mesa is a dramatic landform composed of Permian sandstone and shale. Talus at the base of Glorieta Mesa lies at an average elevation of 2,130 m. The flat top of Glorieta Mesa is between 2,230 m and 2,250 m in elevation. Small drainages run north-northeast from the mesa top to Glorieta Creek, an important tributary of the Pecos, which it joins about 3 km north-northwest of Rowe (Figure 1).

The Upper Pecos Valley is part of an important pass from the Great Plains to the Rio Grande Valley. Along with Glorieta Pass, it formed a natural conduit between the buffalo-hunting tribes of the Plains and the Pueblo farming villages of the river valleys. Between 1821 and 1880, wagon traffic moved between Independence, Missouri, and Santa Fe along the Santa Fe Trail, which followed the Upper Pecos Valley and Glorieta Pass. The same route served the main line of the Santa Fe Railroad and today is followed by Interstate 25, the major highway between Santa Fe and Las Vegas, New Mexico (Southerland and Montgomery 1975). The primary topographic characteristic of the area, the pass through the southern Sangre de Cristos between the Rio Grande Valley and the Plains, figures prominently in several explanations for both the development of ancient Pueblo settlements at and near modern Pecos as well as their eventual demise.

Compared with some other locales in the Southwest, the Upper Pecos Valley is relatively well-watered but still marginal for dependable maize agriculture. Climatic records have been maintained at the Pecos District Ranger Station of the USDA Forest Service since 1949. These records show an average annual precipitation of 38.6 cm (15.19 inches), with a standard deviation of 11.68 cm (4.60 inches). Minnis (1981:197) cites studies indicating that modern hybrid maize requires about 45 cm (17.7 inches) to 60 cm (23.6 inches) of precipitation a year. Moisture stress at key times in maize growth, such as the tasseling and/or silking stage, can reduce yields between 25% and 50% (Classen and Shaw 1970; Minnis 1981:197). Today, precipitation follows the biannual pattern that is noted for the eastern Colorado Plateaus in general (Dean 1988: 124–125), with about half falling in summer and half in winter. The records also indicate that, although spring is the driest season, no season has averaged less than 5 cm (1.96 inches) of precipitation over the period that records have been kept. While varieties of maize grown by the indigenous Pueblo people may have been more tolerant of moisture deficiencies than modern hybrid maize, periodic lack of adequate precipitation would have been a risk.

The length of the growing season in the vicinity of Rowe Ruin might also have been problematical for Puebloan farmers. David Snow (1991) discusses a variety of difficulties in determining whether or not ancient varieties of maize were at risk because of short growing seasons above 6,000 ft (1,828 m) in the Rio Grande region. Among these problems for researchers are a lack of knowledge of frost tolerance of the maize, variability in the methods used to measure either the "frost-free" or "growing"

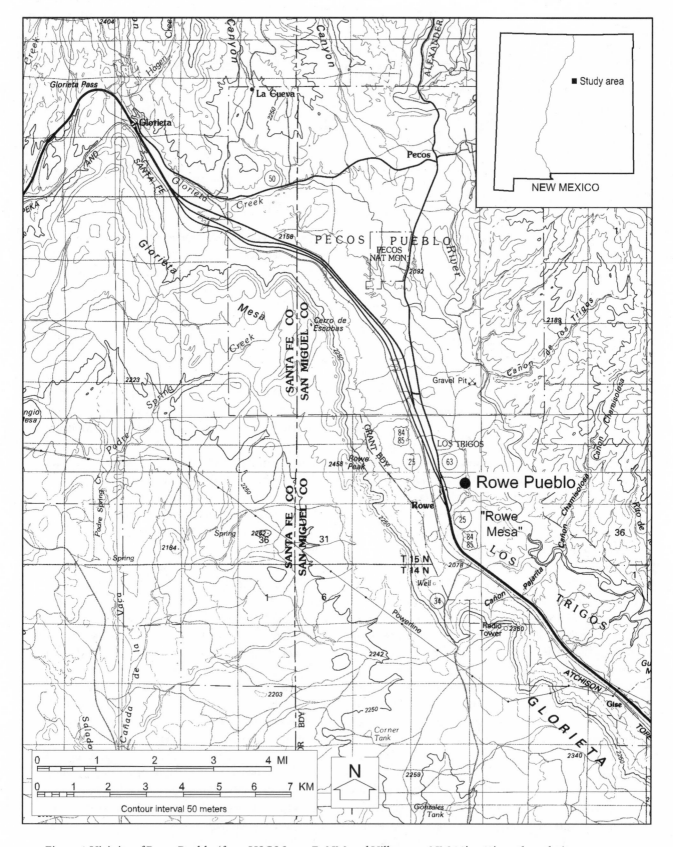

Figure 1.Vicinity of Rowe Pueblo (from USGS Santa Fe NM and Villanueva NM 30' × 60' quadrangles)

season, and the fact that the U.S. Weather Bureau does not record temperatures at soil level. Snow (1991:83) concludes that "given the risks involved in corn production and the frequent references to the use of green corn—both from archaeological sites and in the ethnographic record—immature corn was harvested more often than not in areas above 6,000 feet and in more northerly latitudes."

Rowe is situated on the Los Trigos Land Grant, one of several Spanish community land grants established in the first part of the nineteenth century (Meining 1971:30; Earls 1980). The name Los Trigos means the "wheat fields" (Pearce 1965:93), which suggests that wheat was the preferred, or perhaps more dependable, crop. Of course, land use cannot be inferred reliably from the name. Nevertheless, the initial surviving petition for the grant, dated May 26, 1814, requested land to "establish our small stock ranches to pasture animals toward some betterment of our standard of living, to clear and plow a few pieces of land for planting, whether it be wheat or maize" (Kessell 1979:443).

By 1880, the six farms on the Los Trigos grant averaged twenty-one acres per farm. Agricultural production was primarily for home use or for the local market, because the two potential larger markets, Santa Fe and Las Vegas, were served by communities that were closer to them. Fifty-two percent of acreage at Los Trigos was devoted to wheat, 31% to corn. Yields of 1.73 bushels of wheat and 1.5 bushels of corn per acre are reported (Earls 1980), again suggesting that wheat may have been the more dependable crop.

Cultivated crops never made up the entire inventory of Pueblo diet. Wild plant food and game were important dietary components. At times of poor yields, they may have been the crucial supplementary foods that prevented severe malnutrition or even starvation. The Upper Pecos Valley and its bordering mountains encompass an area with abundant game, conifer forests, alpine meadows, and majestic 4,160 m (13,000 ft) peaks (Southerland and Montgomery 1975:11). In the vicinity of Pecos and Rowe are areas of grasslands, desert shrubs, forbs, and cacti. Along the Pecos River itself, cottonwood *(Populus fremontii),* willows *(Salix* spp.) rabbitbrush *(Chrysothamnus nauseosus),* and reeds *(Scirpus* spp.) are abundant. Dense woodlands that include oak *(Quercus* spp.), pinyon pine *(Pinus edulis),* and juniper *(Juniperus scopulorum)* give way to ponderosa pine *(Pinus ponde-*

rosa), douglas fir *(Pseudotsuga menziesii glauca),* and aspen *(Populus tremuloides)* at higher elevations. At the highest elevations, grassland meadows and forbs dominate the vegetation. Floral taxa recovered archaeologically from Rowe include pinyon, juniper, American plum *(Prunus americana* type), wild grasses, prickly pear *(Opuntia* sp.), and a variety of useful weedy plants, such as pigweed *(Amaranthus* sp.) and goosefoot *(Chenopodium* sp.) (Toll 1981).

Game animals recorded historically in the area include bighorn sheep *(Ovis canadensis),* elk *(Cervus elaphus),* mule deer *(Odocoileus hemionus),* and pronghorn *(Antilocapra americana).* Bison *(Bison bison)* played an important role in the historical economy of Pecos Pueblo but most likely were found primarily east of the Pecos River. Alfred V. Kidder (1932) reported an abundance of bison bones recovered in the excavations at Pecos, but because skulls and pelves were rarely found, he suggested that the animals were killed and butchered some distance from the site. Smaller animals included beaver *(Castor canadensis),* porcupine *(Erethizon dorsatum),* jackrabbits *(Lepus californicus),* and cottontails *(Sylvilagus* sp.). Carnivores were represented by bears *(Ursus* sp.), mountain lion *(Felis concolor),* wolf *(Canis lupus),* fox *(Vulpes* sp.), coyote *(Canis latrans),* bobcat *(Lynx rufus),* and badger *(Taxidea taxus).* The importance of wild plant and animal foods in the diets of the inhabitants of Rowe Ruin is discussed later in this volume in regard to models of population aggregation and site abandonment.

The Upper Pecos Valley is part of the Northern Rio Grande Pueblo area. This categorization provides cultural context only in the most general sense. Although the inhabitants of the Upper Pecos Valley are considered "Anasazi" (part of the Basketmaker– Pueblo tradition that is ancestral to the modern Rio Grande Pueblo Indians, the Hopis, and the Zunis), workers generally use the Wendorf and Reed (1955) chronological scheme because it is more appropriate than the Pecos Classification (Kidder 1927). There is some irony in the fact that the Pecos Classification, which was developed at the first Pecos Conference held at Kidder's field camp at Pecos Pueblo in 1927 and meant to describe the cultural development of the Anasazi, is not used with reference to the history of occupation of the Upper Pecos Valley or the Northern Rio Grande region. The focus of archaeological research in the area has long been on Pecos Pueblo itself and on interaction between the inhabitants of Pecos Pueblo and

Plains peoples. That research history is discussed in the following section. Here, it is important to point out that most of the research effort has been on the more recent periods of Pueblo history with little systematic discussion of antecedent conditions. In addition, despite the intensive archaeological interest in the area, and although Kidder excavated at Pecos Pueblo, the Upper Pecos Valley has been neglected relative to other areas of Anasazi development. A very brief sketch of cultural development in the Upper Pecos Valley, as traditionally described, is given here (Figure 2).

The cultural sequence outlined by Wendorf and Reed (1955) divides the Northern Rio Grande tradition into five chronological periods: Preceramic, Developmental, Coalition, Classic, and Historic. In the Upper Pecos Valley, the Preceramic (ca. 15,000 BC to AD 600) is documented by surface finds of fluted projectile points (Anschuetz 1980; Nordby 1981; Wendorf and Miller 1958). Nordby (1986:6) suggests that these artifacts represent Clovis use of the Upper Pecos Valley and the Sangre de Cristo Mountains. Stanford and Patten (1984) have reported on three Folsom and four Cody sites located above the Sapello River near Las Vegas. No Archaic age sites (ca. 5500 BC to AD 200) have been excavated in the Upper Pecos Valley, although such sites have been studied at similar latitudes and elevations in the Jemez Mountains (Ford 1975; Traylor et al. 1977) and in the Upper Cimarron (Cordell 1979; Steen 1955) and four are described in Part IV of this report. Nordby (1981:7) notes that Archaic-style projectile points have been recovered from the Upper Pecos Valley by private landowners (and see Wendorf and Miller 1958).

The Rio Grande Developmental period (AD 600 to 1200), as described by Wendorf and Reed (1955), encompasses quite a long segment of time and considerable diversity in remains. Early in the period, settlements consist of rare, small, pithouse "villages" (Wendorf and Reed 1955). Later, especially after AD 900, villages become larger and more numerous, with some sites containing ten to twenty surface structures and from one to four kivas. LA 835, a Developmental period site 15 miles north of Santa Fe, reportedly had a Great Kiva (Wendorf and Reed 1955). The diagnostic ceramic type is Kwahe'e Black-on-white, a mineral-painted ware considered a cognate of "Chaco II" and reflecting some affiliation between the San Juan Basin and the northern Rio Grande, but with the Rio Grande being decidedly marginal to the San Juan at this time (Wendorf and Reed 1955).

Until 1977, no pithouse occupation had been documented for the Upper Pecos Valley. Then, two pithouses were located and excavated at Pecos Monument (Nordby 1981). There had been no surface indications of these structures; they were encountered in the course of laying sewer pipe. The houses were roughly circular, and large (about 10 m in diameter), with central fire and heating pits, storage bins along part of the wall, and two roof support posts near the central axis of the room. The two tree-ring dates from the structures (AD 801r and 832r) indicate that they were in use in the ninth century. The pottery from the pithouses consisted of undecorated jar forms similar to those reported by Michael Glassow (1980) from the Ponil Drainage on the Cimarron (Figure 2). Consequently, it is the house form and the tree-ring dates that establish the Developmental period placement of these structures rather than the ceramic assemblage. No painted pottery was recovered that would suggest affiliation with the San Juan Basin. Obsidian from the Jemez region was recovered in the pithouse excavations. Nordby (1981:7) views this as evidence of interaction with the Rio Grande region proper. According to Nordby (1981:7), "following the initial pithouse occupancy between AD 800 and 900, there is virtually no evidence for people in the upper reaches of the valley for two hundred to four hundred years" until the Rio Grande Coalition period.

Wendorf and Reed (1955) describe the Coalition period (AD 1200 to 1325) as consisting of two sequential phases. The first, the Pindi phase (AD 1200 to 1250), named after Pindi Pueblo near Santa Fe, is characterized by a shift throughout most of the Rio Grande area from mineral-based to carbon-based black pigment in pottery designs (Santa Fe Black-on-white) and by the retention of round, subterranean kivas. The Late Coalition period (from AD 1250 to 1325) is regionally variable but generally marked by a dramatic increase in the number of sites, interpreted as population increase; construction of aboveground kivas that are incorporated into roomblocks; and the production of Galisteo Black-on-white pottery that closely resembles Mesa Verde Black-on-white (Wendorf and Reed 1955).

In the Upper Pecos Valley, two quite large pueblos, Dick's Ruin (LA 276) and Forked Lightning Pueblo (LA 672), were probably built around AD 1200 (Nordby 1981:8). Both Forked Lightning, which was excavated by Kidder (1926), and Dick's Ruin, the subject of a small

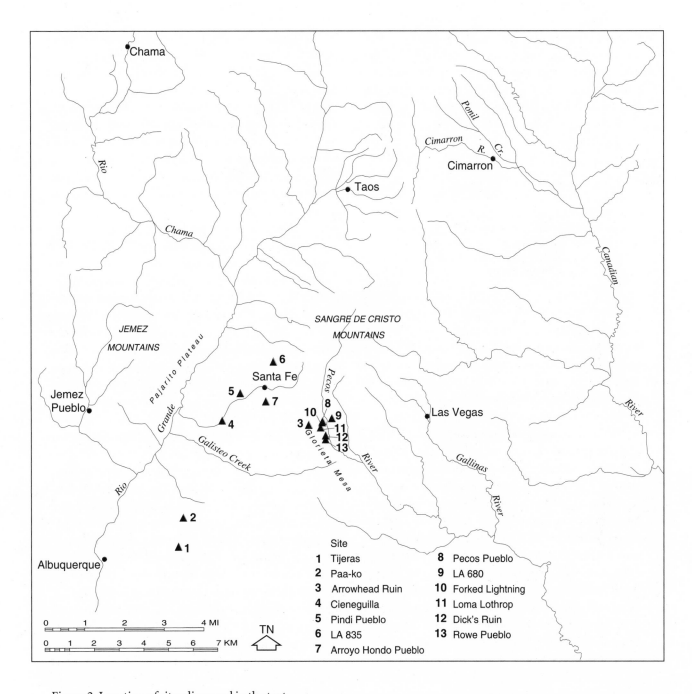

Figure 2. Location of sites discussed in the text

amount of testing (Nordby 1981) that remains unpublished, were constructed of coursed adobe. Neither the extent nor the nature of these sites was apparent from surface remains. Bandelier (1892) had noted abundant ash and sherds where Forked Lightning was eventually discovered, and Kidder established his field camp directly on top of the site from 1922 to 1926. As Kidder explains,

> no housewalls could be found, and as there were no mounds, nor any fallen building-stone on the surface, we concluded that although the site had evidently been occupied for a long time, the houses upon it must have been small and scattered, and that it had never borne a large compact building of the pueblo type (Kidder 1926:1–2).

Eventually, more than one hundred rooms were excavated at Forked Lightning Ruin. Variation in room size and room orientation, in addition to wall bonding and abutment patterns, suggested to Kidder (1926) that Forked Lightning Ruin had been occupied for a long period of time and had grown primarily by accretion.

The accidental discovery of Forked Lightning Pueblo and Kidder's remarks concerning the configuration of its rooms are significant in terms of proposed population dynamics in the Upper Pecos Valley. First, it is entirely likely that some Upper Pecos Classic period sites are located on top of coursed adobe pueblos. We were able to corroborate Guthe's (1917) inference that this was the case at Rowe Ruin. Second, the accretive nature of the construction, as well as the reuse of specific locations for building, suggests that the population was indigenous to the area. Four tree-ring dates, on wood charcoal, were later obtained for Forked Lightning Pueblo. These dates range from AD 1113 to 1120. Kidder (1958:42–46) believed these dates were too early. Four tree-ring dates are far too few to securely date a site as large as Forked Lightning Ruin, especially since it was built over time. Importantly, if ruins of coursed adobe pueblos have been obscured and therefore underestimated in accounts of the settlement history of the Upper Pecos Valley, our estimates of the timing of the period of major population increase could be in error by 100 or 200 years. Then the population increase could have occurred in the 1200s rather than the 1300s as is often suggested. Nevertheless, in contrast to Nordby's (1981:7) assertion (quoted above), there seems to have been a Puebloan population in the Upper Pecos Valley between AD 800 and 1300.

The ceramics from Forked Lightning also suggest a pre-1300 date. They are not Galisteo Black-on-white, the cognate of Mesa Verde pottery. Rather, Forked Lightning ceramics are within the general Santa Fe Black-on-white genre, which quite consistently dates to AD 1200. There is no indication that Forked Lightning was built as late as, or after, AD 1300. Together, these observations suggest that the Coalition period population in the Upper Pecos Valley may have been considerably larger than is generally credited, and it may have been made up of people local to the valley rather than migrants from the Mesa Verde–northern San Juan region.

Rowe Ruin, with its visible masonry construction, is considered a "Galisteo phase" Coalition period site. Unlike at other Late Coalition period sites, however, the characteristic ceramics at Rowe Ruin are Santa Fe and Rowe Black-on-white rather than Galisteo Black-on-white. Considerable ceramic diversity is represented within the Rio Grande white wares, as is characteristic of the Late Coalition period in general (Wendorf and Reed 1955; Habicht-Mauche 1993).

In fact, much of the research history discussed below, as well as more recent work at Rowe Ruin, has been concerned with attempting to establish the origins or "cultural affiliations" of the founders of the Coalition period pueblos of the Upper Pecos Valley, in part because these sites differ one from another in layout, material of construction, number of kivas, and characteristic ceramics. The eight large sites of the Upper Pecos Valley that were occupied in or before 1300 are Arrowhead Ruin (LA 251; Holden 1955), Loma Lothrop (LA 277), Pecos Pueblo (LA 625), Forked Lightning (LA 672), Dick's Ruin (LA 276), Rowe Ruin (LA 108), LA 267, and LA 680. Excavations and testing indicate that not all of them were occupied at the same time; Forked Lightning and Arrowhead represent earlier and later ends of this occupation. However, by sometime after AD 1325, only Pecos Pueblo remained inhabited.

Another aspect of the early research attempted to verify traditional accounts obtained from the descendants of those who left Pecos Pueblo in 1838 and joined the community of Jemez Pueblo. For example, the survivors from Pecos Pueblo are said to have moved to Jemez to join their linguistic relatives. Today, Jemez is the only Towa-speaking village. If, as is generally believed, the Pecos inhabitants also spoke Towa, then these communities are more distant geographically than most other Pueblo language clusters. Exceptions would be Hano, at the Hopi First Mesa, and other Tewa speakers in the Rio Grande Valley, and the Northern and Southern Tiwa–speaking villages. The founders of Hano came from the Galisteo Basin and settled at Hopi in the context of the Pueblo Revolt and Reconquest as part of the tremendous population displacements that resulted from the Spanish conquest. Northern and Southern Tiwa, now at least dialectically differentiated, are believed to have become separated by precolumbian population movements out of the San Juan Basin (Ford, Schroeder, and Peckham 1972).

Finally, the Rio Grande Classic (AD 1325–1600) is described as a period of "cultural expansion and florescence" with large aggregated communities and elaborate material culture (Wendorf and Reed 1955:153). Among the diagnostic artifacts are decorated pipes, elaborate axes, carved bone tools, stone effigies, mural paintings, and variety in vessel forms. The key change in ceramics over much of the general Northern Rio Grande region, and the Upper Pecos Valley specifically, is the introduction of red-slipped, glaze-decorated ceramics. The Rio Grande glazes were produced until about 1700 and were widely traded within the Rio Grande region and to Plains groups to the east. The Rio Grande glazes are thought to have been inspired by earlier western trade wares, such as St. Johns and Heshotauthla polychromes. The technology of the glazes was studied by Shepard (Kidder and Shepard 1936; Shepard 1942, 1965) and more recently by Warren (1970, 1977, 1979). The Rio Grande glazes are especially important in the history of Rio Grande archaeology, because they formed the backbone of Kidder's (in Kidder and Shepard 1936) chronological ordering of construction at Pecos Pueblo and hence of the Classic and Early Historic periods of the Rio Grande in general. Shepard's (1936, 1942:137–138) technological studies, which Kidder did not use when he developed his sequence, showed that Glaze I Red, Glaze I Yellow, and Glaze VI (Glaze A and F in Mera's 1940 scheme) excavated from Pecos Pueblo contained tempering material that was not available there. Pecos Pueblo produced glaze ware between about AD 1400 and 1600—during Glaze II through Glaze V (B through E) times—but the types included what Kidder and Shepard recognized as a local "degenerate" Glaze I Red (Kidder 1936:72–73; Shepard 1936:520). Both before and after this period, Pecos Pueblo seems to have imported glaze ware from villages in the Galisteo Basin to the southwest.

The Historic period in the Upper Pecos Valley is the post-contact history of Pecos Pueblo, known in considerable detail. That history begins with Francisco Vasquez de Coronado's 1540 *entrada,* chronicled by Castañeda (Winship 1896), and ends in 1838 when the seventeen Pecos survivors (seven men, seven women, and three children) gave up their home and trekked eighty miles west to join Jemez Pueblo (Hayes 1974:18; Kidder 1962:87; Riley 1987:251–284). This history is known from translations of Spanish chronicle accounts (e.g., Hammond and Rey 1940), Anglo-American travelers' accounts (e.g., Gregg 1954), scholarly histories (Kessell 1979), and traditional histories (Hewett 1904; Parsons 1925). Yet for several reasons, I suspect, it is difficult for archaeologists to work with the written and narrated accounts. As Polzer (1989), among others, has noted, only some of the vast amount of archival documents relating to the Spanish Empire in the Americas have been transcribed or translated. In addition, archaeologists are generally not trained in historiography, so we lack insights into the cultural norms and biases of the sixteenth and seventeenth Spaniards and their systems of recording (Wilcox and Masse 1981). We are generally also ignorant of Native American historiography (e.g., Malotki 1993), which would give us the tools Native Americans use to evaluate traditional narratives, and few ethno-historic studies are available for New Mexico, particularly the Rio Grande Pueblos (Riley 1987).

Another problem is not often discussed by archaeologists. In essence, most historical narratives (written or not) are accounts of events at a scale of precision that is not available to archaeologists. For example, with respect to time, historical accounts detail events that may be counted in hours, days, weeks, seasons, or sometimes years and decades. Archaeologists generally believe that they have tight chronological control if they can discern centuries. It is true that because of the availability of tree-ring dating in the Southwest, there is a sense of greater precision. Yet, in most cases, we do not "see" nor can we apply that greater precision to the sites we excavate. For example, only under relatively unusual circumstances can we determine how much of a site was occupied over what number of years, though we often make estimates based on recorded information. With respect to the spatial dimension, historical accounts generally describe activities that took place on landscapes that include built and natural features, when neither the activities nor the built features are available to the archaeologist. Archaeology is not the ethnography of the past. The scenarios archaeologists develop are at a longer, larger, and far less precise scale. Thus Kidder's (1958:316) comment: "Unfortunately, we have no first-hand account of what the Pecos were actually like. As a matter of fact, we really know very little beyond the most obvious externals, of the still extant Pueblos."

What archaeology does have to offer, of course, is an understanding of patterns of long-term stability and change and of large-scale spatial patterning. This archaeological perspective is extremely valuable and is generally not available from other sources. Archaeologists themselves often sell their own view short by emphasizing the poor quality or incomplete nature of archaeological data. I believe resolution of this problem will take place in the context of discussions within the international archaeological community. It certainly cannot be resolved in the context of a site report. Nevertheless, it is worth remembering the different scales of resolution in archaeological vs. ethnographic and historical data when we review the history of research at Rowe Ruin, which itself goes back more than a century.

HISTORY OF RESEARCH

Virtually all of the research conducted at Rowe Ruin has been concerned with its place in the pre-contact history of the Upper Pecos Valley, a setting dominated by the eventual influence and singularity of Pecos Pueblo. From about 1540 to 1680, Pecos was one of the largest and easternmost of the pueblos, and it was the only Indian pueblo in the Upper Pecos Valley to remain occupied after the European *entradas.* Pecos was also a center of exchange and more formal trade between semi-"nomadic" Indians of the buffalo Plains and the "sedentary" Pueblos. The story of the abandonment of Pecos Pueblo concerned increasing attacks by Plains Indian raiders, epidemics of European diseases, and intra-Pueblo disputes (Kessell 1979).

In investigations of Rowe Ruin, researchers have sought the tribal, linguistic, or ethnic origins of its occupants and their temporal and social distance from the inhabitants of Pecos Pueblo. Scholars have examined the possibility that Rowe also was a location of Pueblo-Plains exchange. They have tried to understand how people came to be aggregated at the settlement of Rowe and how and why Rowe was eventually abandoned, its inhabitants presumably joining the larger village of Pecos on the Mesilla del Pueblo to the northwest.

Rowe Ruin was first described in print by Adolph F. Bandelier (1892), who had visited it in the early 1880s as part of his general survey of the ruins of the Upper Pecos Valley. According to him, the site was called "Ku-uang-uala" by the past inhabitants of Pecos Pueblo. Bandelier described the site as consisting of "three quadrangles connected with one another, with only two entrances," no apparent kivas, and pottery that seemed quiet ancient because it lacked even "coarsely glazed specimens" (Bandelier 1892:125). Bandelier noted that although the compact arrangement of the site was well designed for defensive purposes, the setting of the ruin

at the foot of a wooded mesa afforded no view and had been selected "on account of the proximity of wood and water" (Bandelier 1892:125).

In 1904, Edgar L. Hewett cited Rowe Ruin to exemplify a class of ruined "communal houses" composed of two to three hundred rooms as well as smaller, ten- to fifty-room sites that were scattered over Pecos territory from Anton Chico in the south to the Cañon de Pecos on the north (Hewett 1904). Hewett called the site "Ton-ch-un," a name obtained from former Pecos Pueblo residents then living at Jemez Pueblo. Hewett published a sketch map (Figure 3) of Rowe Ruin and described the pueblo as being almost 1,400 ft (325 m) long, containing more than three hundred rooms (Hewett 1904:433). He noted that the roomblocks around the central and south plazas were two stories high but those around the north plaza were of one story, as were the detached segments shown in his sketch. Hewett did not excavate the site, but he did write that no burial mounds had been discovered in which there might have been whole pottery vessels; erosion by the arroyo probably destroyed whatever trash mounds had existed on the east side of the ruin.

Hewett was interested in the Upper Pecos Valley because it offered one of those relatively rare situations in which a combined ethnographic, archaeological, and historical study of a people would be possible, comparable to those done among the Classical cultures of the Old World and to the studies of the Hopi that attempted to link migration legends and archaeological sites (i.e., Fewkes 1900). Hewett (1904) reported both from his own notes, and those made by F. W. Hodge (1907), that occupants of Jemez Pueblo had much traditional information regarding the pueblo they called Ton-ch-un. According to this traditional knowledge, Ton-ch-un had not been a farming village of Pecos but had been occu-

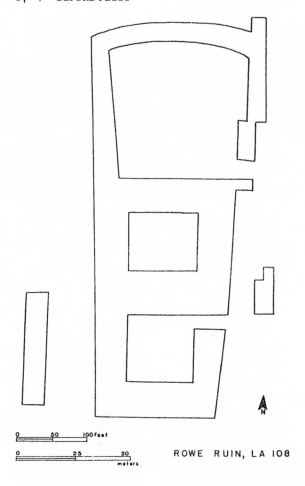

ROWE RUIN, LA 108

Figure 3. Hewett's 1904 sketch map

pied year-round by a group that had entered the Upper Pecos Valley from the west and were originally of Jemez stock. Sites to the south of Ton-ch-un were said to have been peopled from the Mesa Jumanes ("Gran Quivira") and the Manzano Mountain area, whereas the first occupants of Pecos Pueblo were said to have come from the north. The notion that the Upper Pecos Valley pueblos were from different ethnic, tribal, or linguistic origins was later pursued in the research proposal Wait and Nordby (1979) submitted to NEH and in the 1980 field season at Rowe (discussed below).

An additional notion derived from traditional history and recorded by Hewett (1904) was that prior to the arrival of the Spaniards, predatory tribes from the Plains forced abandonment of the settlements south of Pecos and the ultimate concentration of population at Pecos Pueblo. According to these reported traditional

accounts, Ton-ch-un was the last to give way. This idea was discounted by Kidder (1958), who considered Arrowhead Ruin and Loma Lothrop to have been inhabited later than Rowe Ruin on the basis of surface ceramics. Kidder's inference was supported by excavations carried out at Arrowhead Ruin (Holden 1955).

Following Fewkes's (1900) discussions of the Hopi region, Hewett suggested that a new system of social relations would have emerged in the context of population aggregation, such as "the integration of clan legends and religious practices." Further, successful competition of one clan for supremacy in the organization "would depend largely on the extent to which it could apparently influence supernatural powers by invocatory, propitiatory, or divinatory methods, the exercise of these magic powers taking shape in ritual and finding graphic expression in pictography. Thus the highest development of the ceramic art, particularly its richest symbolic ornamentation, is found in the ruins occupied by tribes in the early stages of this epoch of concentration" (Hewett 1904:437–438).

Although Hewett did not pursue further research in the Upper Pecos Valley, the opportunity to integrate historical, ethnographic, and archaeological data was among the reasons Kidder selected Pecos Pueblo for a major research commitment beginning in 1915 (Kidder 1924). Kidder worked at Pecos in 1915 and 1916, suspended activity there during World War I, from 1917 to 1919, and resumed again in 1920. In 1917, after one field season at Pecos as Kidder's assistant, Carl Guthe led the Pecos Expedition on reconnaissance in the Upper Rio Grande and then, from August 27 through October 6, conducted the first excavations at Rowe Ruin. Guthe published a brief report of this work in 1917. His transcribed field notes are included here (as Part II), and his observations about the architecture of Rowe and its artifact assemblage are discussed throughout this volume.

Guthe's intention was neither to excavate the entire site nor to work out its plan of rooms and physical organization. Rather, his purpose was "to find enough material to be able to ascertain from it what an unadulterated 'Black on White' culture consisted of, from the point of view of pottery, stone and bone implements" (Guthe 1917). Guthe's excavations were limited to the south plaza and its surrounding roomblocks because it was the most compact of the three quadrangles. Guthe extended a trench from the east side of the eastern roomblock of the south quadrangle to about midway across the northern roomblock of the same quadrangle. He then turned the trench south across the south plaza. He continued this trench across the southern roomblock of the south quadrangle and outside its outer wall. In all, Guthe excavated 12 rooms, a portion of the south plaza, and a small extramural area south of the ruin. He recovered 17 burials and more than 300 objects of stone, bone, and pottery.

Guthe observed that there was a great deal of pottery, faunal remains, and other debris in the south plaza. To show the abundance of this material and the relative numbers of sherds, lithic artifacts, and fauna, he collected a sample of all these materials excavated in one day and cached them at the end of the season at the western end of the plaza trench (Guthe's notes, October 8, 1917). As corroborated by more recent faunal analyses of Rowe materials, more than half of the catalogued objects were bone. The Rowe faunal assemblage is generally larger and richer in medium to large body-size animals than are those of contemporary Pueblo ruins in the Rio Grande area (Mick-O'Hara 1987). Despite the depth of the deposits and the multiple architectural components Guthe discovered, which would suggest a lengthy occupation, the ceramic assemblage appeared quite homogeneous, generally indicative of a rather brief occupation. Guthe (1917) reported that black-on-white and corrugated ceramics predominated in all three components. The rare pieces of red ware were generally found in association with black-on-white sherds. Further, in his notes he indicates a lack of apparent change within the black-on-white pottery that might have suggested a long period of occupation (Guthe's notes, October 5).

Guthe hoped that work would continue at Rowe Ruin so the culture of the Indians "who congregated at the site of the big Pecos Ruin" (Guthe 1917) could be better known. Guthe suggested that the ceramics from Rowe Ruin might enable scholars to trace the development of design and shape in black-on-white pottery. In fact, though, Rowe Ruin was not investigated further by Guthe or the Pecos Expedition. Instead, the expedition excavated Forked Lightning Ruin, and that site became the "type site" for black-on-white period sites in the Upper Pecos Valley (Kidder 1926, 1958). In Kidder's (1958) view, Forked Lightning dated to an earlier period than Rowe Ruin. Some of the pottery from Rowe was included in the analyses of ceramics that featured so prominently in the cultural reconstructions of the Pecos Expedition

(Kidder and Amsden 1931; Kidder and Shepard 1936). Finally, the boxed sherds, lithic artifacts, and fauna that Guthe buried in the south quadrangle (Figure 4) were re-excavated in 1977–1978 by Wait, Nordby, and the Sandovals and became part of the study collection used prior to the 1980 season.

Guthe's work provided invaluable information on the architectural extent, complexity, and depth of Rowe Ruin. Prior to excavation, the site appeared to be a single-component ruin. However, Guthe discovered evidence of three distinct periods of building in portions of the south quadrangle rooms, although not in others. During all three building episodes, masonry walls were constructed that were similar in form and used little adobe mortar. The building episodes were distinguished on the basis of the color of the adobe mortar and whether the walls were offset or laid across one another. The walls of rooms I through VI, some of which were exposed on the slope along the arroyo, were identified with the middle component since they were under, and offset from, the walls of rooms VII and VIII (Figure 5). Yet another series of walls was discovered west of room IX. In this last area, the excavation was extended to a depth of 14 ft [4.6 m] until undisturbed ground was reached. Walls of the earliest component were not encountered under rooms on the south side of the plaza. On this side, there was evidence of the middle and late building episodes only.

Guthe noted an apparent gateway in the east roomblock of the south quadrangle (Guthe's notes, September 5). Additional observations about the structure included locating ash lenses above the room walls in the area of rooms I–IV. This post-occupational layer was particularly thick over the corner of room III and contained many "animal bones" (Guthe's notes, August 30). In addition, underlying sections of the room IX wall in that area were apparently sections of an adobe wall, but they were not followed. Finally, outside the outer walls of room XII, in the southern extension of the trench, Guthe discovered a "mass of lumps of earth, ashes, charcoal and much pottery. . . . at least seven bowls" (Guthe's notes, October 5) and "a section of hard earth . . . from which the earth chipped as if from a floor." Guthe had this area reburied in expectation of returning to it the following year—an expectation that was not met.

A single dendrochronological specimen was obtained from Rowe Ruin in 1953 by Stanley Stubbs. It yielded a non-cutting date of 1306 (Smiley, Stubbs, and Bannis-

Figure 4. Animal bone and pottery "rejects" excavated by Guthe and reburied at the site. These sherds were exhumed and used as the type collection for the site during field school analysis (Neg. 537, Kidder/Pecos Collection, Archives of the Laboratory of Anthropology, Museum of Indian Arts & Culture, Santa Fe)

ter 1953:22). After Guthe's work, however, no systematic excavation was conducted at Rowe Ruin until 1977. Highway salvage archaeology in the vicinity of the village of Rowe and Rowe Ruin was conducted in 1963 in conjunction with widening the roadway now called Interstate 25. Four masonry "farming structures," dating from the 1500s to the 1600s and considered related to Pecos Pueblo land use, were excavated by the Laboratory of Anthropology and reported by Gerald Wood (1963).

In 1977, limited testing at Rowe Ruin was begun by Wait in cooperation with the Sandoval family. Initially, the goal was to recover information from disturbed areas of the site and to provide the Sandoval family with a grounding in archaeology and the preservation ethic. Another result of this work was development of a research design for a grant proposal to the National Endowment for the Humanities.

Excavations under the auspices of Wait and Nordby in 1977–1978 were directed toward resolving three general research questions that related Rowe to Pecos Pueblo

and to ancient interactions among populations of the Upper Pecos Valley and those of the Plains to the east. First, according to the traditional history related by Hewett (discussed above), the population of Pecos Pueblo derived from different geographic areas, with that of Rowe specifically originating in the Jemez area to the west. For this reason the excavators sought identification of a western origin or affiliation. Second, any information about the social interactions among the several Upper Pecos Valley sites antedating Pecos would facilitate understanding how population aggregation had occurred at Pecos Pueblo in the fourteenth century. Third, in view of Pecos Pueblo's importance in Pueblo-Plains trade in the eighteenth century, the researchers would also search for indications that this trade was long-standing.

All three general research questions depended upon substantiating the chronological placement of Rowe Ruin prior to about 1325, when the major aggregation occurred at Pecos Pueblo. Since Guthe's work indicated considerable architectural complexity and depositional depth at Rowe Ruin, Wait and Nordby (1979) suggested that the occupation might date back to the late 1100s or early 1200s. Obtaining dates from Rowe Ruin and establishing a chronology for the building sequence would be the baseline for further interpretations of architectural and artifactual evidence related to the more general research problems.

Working with members of the Sandoval family and other volunteers, Wait and Nordby tested areas on the east roomblocks of the central and south quadrangle where walls had been exposed through erosion. They also excavated four previously disturbed rooms in the east roomblock of the north quadrangle (Figure 5). This initial work was both preliminary and limited. Excavations in the midden indicated deposits of about 1.4 m of fill above a culturally sterile red clay substrate. The four rooms excavated in the north quadrangle confirmed Guthe's observation that the north quadrangle was different from the central and south quadrangles primarily in that there was no fill or evidence of remodeling below the excavated rooms, and room fill was hard, homogeneous, and virtually devoid of artifacts. Pollen and flotation samples submitted for paleobotanical studies also lacked vegetal remains (Toll 1981). Wait submitted five tree-ring specimens from north plaza room W1 to the Laboratory of Tree-Ring Research at the University

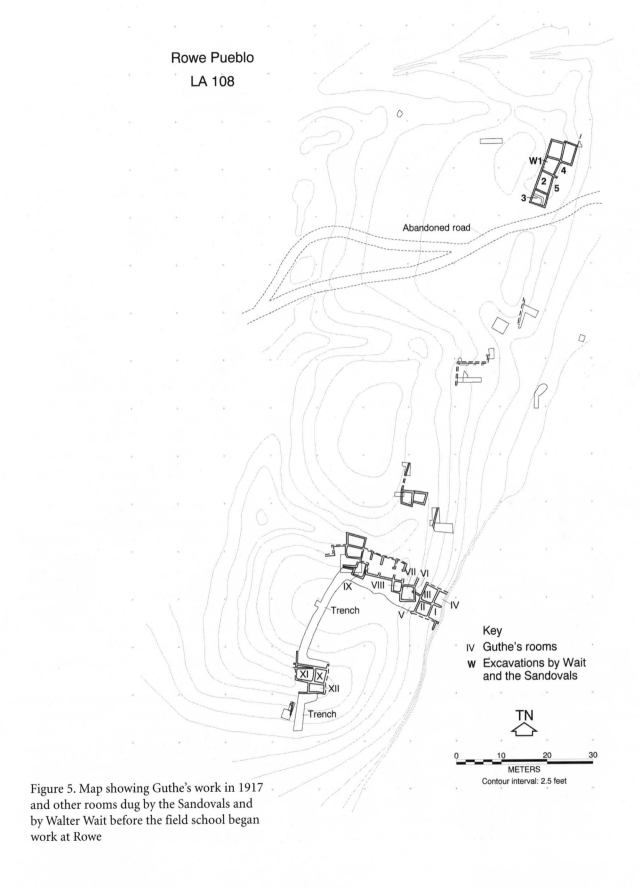

Rowe Pueblo
LA 108

Abandoned road

W1

4

2

5

3

VII VI

IX

VIII

III

IV

Trench

V

II

I

Key

IV Guthe's rooms

W Excavations by Wait and the Sandovals

XI X

XII

Trench

TN

0   10   20   30
METERS
Contour interval: 2.5 feet

Figure 5. Map showing Guthe's work in 1917 and other rooms dug by the Sandovals and by Walter Wait before the field school began work at Rowe

of Arizona, but all five had too few rings to establish cross-dating (letter from William J. Robinson to Walter Wait, 17 March 1980).

Shortly after their request for funding from NEH had been approved, Wait and Nordby invited the University of New Mexico field school, then under my direction, to join the project. Consequently, the seven-week field school season in 1980 was conducted at Rowe Ruin. The 1980 Rowe Ruin project thus represented an unusual example of cooperative research involving the Sandoval family, federal archaeologists Wait and Nordby, and university archaeologists. From the field school perspective the cooperation provided facilities and assistance it might not otherwise have had, such as a renovated, on-site, field laboratory; use of a microcomputer in the field; the assistance of National Park Service personnel; and financial support for field school staff to pursue analysis and write-up during the 1980–1981 academic year. From the perspective of Wait and the Sandoval family, the participation of the field school allowed the project to complete a great deal more work at the site than might otherwise have been accomplished and provided some new perspectives on how the research design might be implemented. The focus of the field school work continued to be the three broad questions framed in the NEH proposal: "(1) what is the chronology of the site; (2) what is the origin of the site's population; and (3) was there any evidence of an active Plains trade?" (Wait 1981). In addition to excavations, the 1980 field school also conducted a reconnaissance survey of archaeological sites in the immediate vicinity of Rowe Ruin. Discussion of the site survey is deferred to a later section of this volume (Part IV). A brief summary of the excavations conducted at Rowe Ruin is presented here.

Excavations were conducted in rooms in each of the three quadrangles and in the extramural plaza, midden, and other areas. Within roomblocks, excavations were conducted in room pairs in an attempt to determine how space in a set of rooms was used and how rooms might be related to plaza surfaces. All excavated rooms and other hand-excavated units are shown in Figure 6. Rooms 10 and 11 were excavated in the eastern roomblock of the north quadrangle. This roomblock was apparently built as a unit and at one time, with major load-bearing walls running north-south and east-west cross walls added to define rooms. All walls were constructed of overlapping blocks of locally available limestone and schist laid flat. Chinking was abundant. In the excavated area the roomblock was only two rooms wide, with the east wall of room 11 also being the outer wall of the pueblo. This outer wall was only 20 cm thick. Despite the narrowness of the roomblock and of the outer wall, the height of excavated standing walls (up to 1.6 m) and the abundance of wall fall suggested either a very high ceiling or two stories. (Room dimensions are given in the architecture section, below). Room 10 was completely excavated but room 11 was only partially excavated. Neither room rested on previous construction or cultural deposits. No rebuilding or remodeling was noted in either room, but interior doorways in this roomblock had been sealed. Access to these rooms was apparently through hatchways in the roof. Several flat, shaped stone slabs; fire-reddened and blackened stones; and a probable hatch cover were distributed through several layers of fill in room 10, suggesting an upper level. Roofing material and wood for beams were absent. Three holes had been made in the outside wall of room 11 (and thus of the roomblock) by displacing stones to the outside of the pueblo. The three holes were subsequently filled in. As noted, artifact density was low. Archaeomagnetic samples taken from a burned area on the floor of room 11 yielded a date of ABOUT AD 1395. Guthe (field notes) had indicated a magnetic anomaly in the north quadrangle that we also experienced as difficulty in taking accurate compass readings. We suspected that the problem might affect the accuracy of the archaeomagnetic dates.

Extramural test excavations in the north quadrangle were designed to determine if apparent gaps in the wall of the east roomblock were entrances or if they were the result of postoccupational disturbances. The latter was found to be the case when a metal lid was encountered under rock fall. This area of the pueblo had sustained considerable damage during construction associated with building the railroad and the station at Rowe, in 1876. An additional stratigraphic test was excavated in a potential midden east of the north quadrangle. The midden proved to be much shallower (only 60 cm) than those associated with either the central or south quadrangles. Finally, a test in a slight depression in the northeast quadrant of the north plaza was excavated to explore for a possible kiva. None was found, but extensive deposits of roadbed cinders again indicated recent disturbance.

Room 20 in the southern roomblock of the middle quadrangle was selected for excavation as a pair to room

30 in the north roomblock of the south quadrangle. Room 30, in turn, had been selected because its southern wall appeared to be curved, suggesting that the room might have served as a "corner kiva" similar to those excavated at Forked Lightning Ruin, Dick's Ruin, and Arrowhead Ruin (Kidder 1958:37–50). Although neither room 20 nor 30 was constructed on culturally sterile ground, we did not locate walls or define rooms beneath them. The patterns of wall bonding and abutting demonstrated that rooms 20 and 30 had been constructed at the same time, although they may not have been inhabited continuously or abandoned simultaneously. The doorway between the two rooms was sealed. Room 20 lacked floor features that might have indicated a specific function. Laminated deposits on the floor suggested that the room had been left open and had deteriorated before the roof collapsed. A single tree-ring date of AD 1344r was obtained from a wood sample in a fill layer above roof fall and floor levels in room 30 and therefore cannot be used to date the construction of either room 20 or 30. Room 30 was also devoid of floor features that might have indicated its function as a kiva or as a living room. Nevertheless, excavation of the southwest and southeast corners of room 30, undertaken to determine if the south wall of the room was indeed curved or if it had buckled, showed that although the southeast corner of room 30 was square, the southwest corner had been intentionally curved. Both rooms 20 and 30 were two-story constructions, as Guthe had suggested for this area of the site. Although no kiva features were located in room 30, the second-story fill contained a turquoise pendant, a miniature ceramic dipper, and 36 very small clay balls, an unusual set of artifacts for the site. These artifacts are similar to those described as evidence of ritually closed kivas in Western Pueblo sites (Walker 1996).

Rooms 21 and 22, located in the eastern room-block of the middle quadrangle, had also been selected to provide a room pairing. These rooms were found to be badly deteriorated, shallow, and underlain by the offset walls of two older rooms designated rooms 23 and 24. Floors in rooms 21 and 22 were poorly defined and lacked features. Time did not permit excavation of complete floor levels in either room 23 or 24. No floor was located in room 23, but a poorly preserved floor was found in room 24. Preservation of structural wood was better in this part of the site than elsewhere, and of the 11 tree-ring dates obtained from Rowe, nine came from rooms 21, 22, and 23. The wood samples from rooms 21 and 22 were all from a subfloor test (T1) and therefore can be related to roof fall of underlying rooms 23 and 24. The dates are 1319vv, 1323vv, 1326vv, 1334vv, 1340vv, 1346vv, and 1351vv from below room 21 (hence room 23), and 1349vv from subfloor room 22 (hence room 24). A single date from room 23, as excavated, is 1343vv. Although none are cutting dates, they do cluster nicely in the middle decades of the 1300s and are congruent with the date of 1344r from room 30.

Excavations in the southern quadrangle included room 30, discussed above, and two test units immediately south of the southern roomblock (T303 and T304, Figure 6). The test units were excavated to locate the extramural area of hard-packed earth with the "ashes, charcoal and much pottery" Guthe described in his notes (October 5, 1917). Although the tests did not yield the abundance of charcoal and ceramics Guthe had found, they did locate extramural work surfaces and underling structural remains of adobe. In the areas tested, 20 to 60 cm of dense midden overlay adobe wall stubs resting on stone foundations, a hard-packed adobe floor, and, below that, a flagstone floor underlain by an adobe floor and additional layers of midden. The wall stubs continued north toward the south side of the southern roomblock of the south quadrangle, but excavations were not undertaken to expose the nature of the articulation of these underlying walls with walls of the south quadrangle rooms.

Finally, remains of three individuals that had been previously excavated were brought to the Osteological Laboratory at the University of New Mexico for analysis. Adequate provenience and burial information were not available for any of them. One burial consisted of a partially complete skeleton of an adolescent female (13 to 15 years of age). The two others were both adult females, one more than 50 years of age and the other between 40 and 45 years of age. The osteological report indicates that the two adults, while having female pelvic girdles, were otherwise of masculine appearance, with regard to features of the skull and particularly rugosity of muscle attachments. The muscle attachments suggested performance of strenuous labor somewhat unusual for ancient Pueblo female skeletons (London 1980). The robust qualities of the skulls, however, do not relate to division of labor but are characteristic of

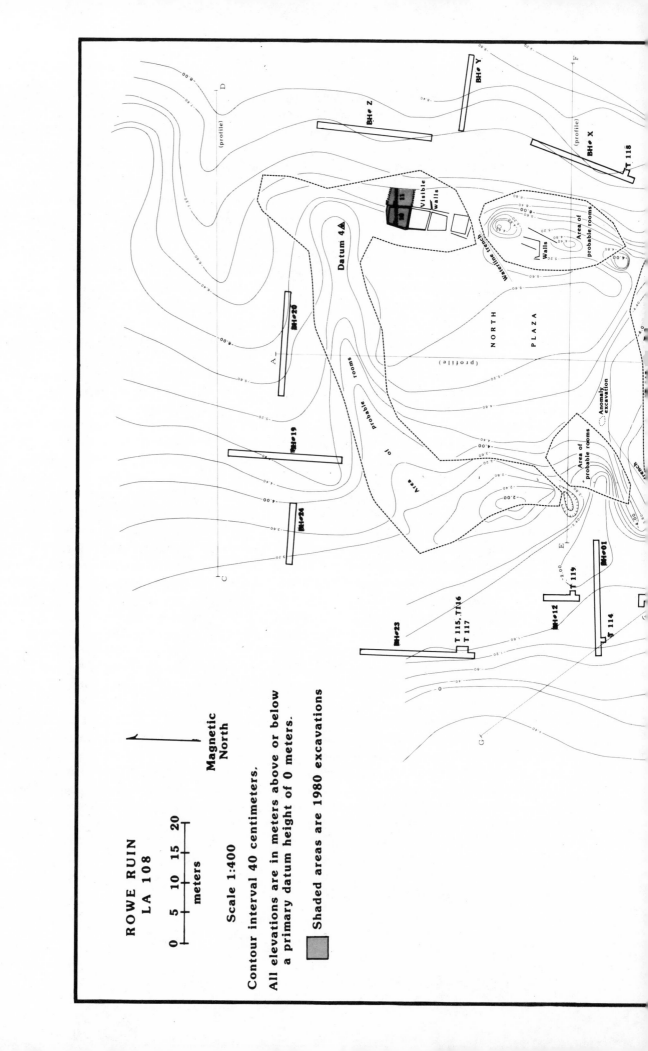

ROWE RUIN
LA 108

0 5 10 15 20
meters

Magnetic
North

Scale 1:400

Contour interval 40 centimeters.

All elevations are in meters above or below
a primary datum height of 0 meters.

▨ Shaded areas are 1980 excavations

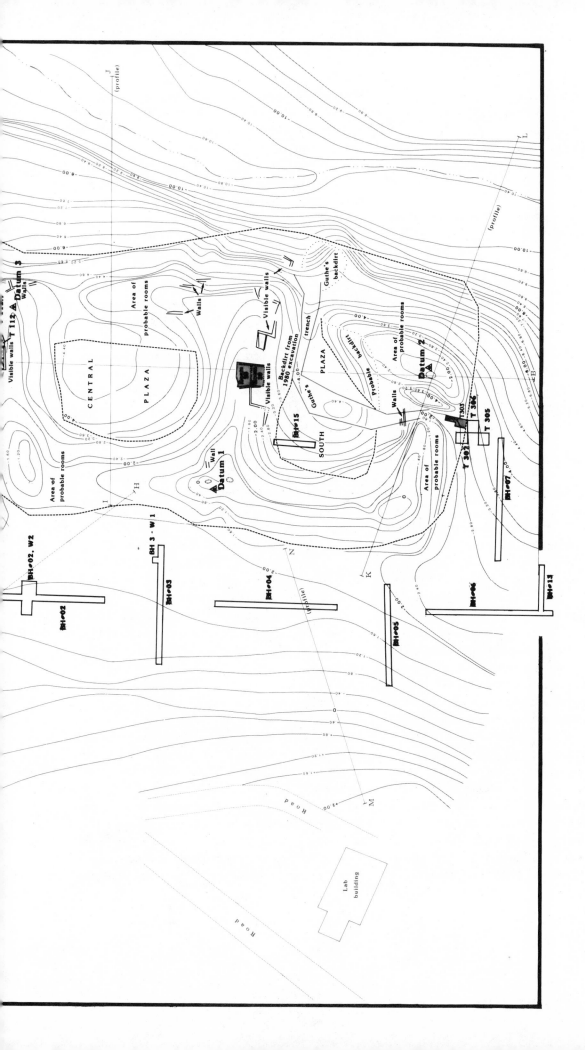

Figure 6. UNM field school map showing excavated rooms, trenches, and test units

remains excavated from Pecos Pueblo (E. Trinkaus, personal communication, 1983) and originally analyzed by Hooten (1930).

A large number of artifacts was recovered in 1980. The excavations at Rowe Ruin yielded 25,360 artifacts of which 11,408 (45%) were ceramics, 6,933 (27%) were fauna, and 6,852 (27%) were lithic artifacts. Less than 1% (158) of the assemblage was composed of ground stone, and less than 0.1% (9) was metal recovered from disturbed areas of the site. A report of the 1980 work at Rowe Ruin was filed with NEH (Wait 1981). The preliminary ceramic report is appended to this volume. Detailed discussion of this and other technical reports is deferred to later sections of this volume, but results related to the specific research questions posed by Wait and Nordby (1979) are presented here.

No specific geographic origin for the inhabitants of Rowe could be stated with any certainty. Wait and Nordby (1979) had been particularly concerned with the possibility of corroborating the traditional information reported by Hewett (1904) that the population of Rowe derived from Jemez Pueblo. According to the field school ceramic analysis, some types among the Rowe ceramic assemblage were found to contain temper of volcanic origin (fine pumice or tuff) that might have come from the Jemez region, but might as easily have derived from the Tesuque Formation of the Española Basin (Habicht-Mauche 1993). Whether these vessels were imported by the original occupants or were types commonly obtained through exchange could not be discerned. Similarly, although some design characteristics of the Rowe pottery (principally ticked rims) also occur on pottery from the Jemez area, they are a widespread horizon marker of Upper Rio Grande and Upper Pecos pottery of the early fourteenth century. Obsidian artifacts from Rowe Ruin were found to be made of Obsidian Ridge materials from the Jemez. These artifacts were few in number, however, and were thought to have been obtained in trade.

Progress toward understanding the relationships among Rowe and the other Upper Pecos Valley sites, including Pecos Pueblo, required quite precise chronological placement of Rowe Ruin. Particularly important to determining how Rowe was abandoned and whether or not its inhabitants had moved to Pecos Pueblo would be a 1325 (or so) abandonment date for Rowe. Specifying the 1325 date indicates acceptance of this date for the major aggregation at Pecos Pueblo. The tree-ring and archaeomagnetic dates obtained indicate that Rowe Ruin continued to be inhabited until late in the fourteenth century. Although Wait and Nordby suggested that the occupation of Rowe might date back into the late 1100s or early 1200s (Wait and Nordby 1979), no chronometric dates relating to these centuries were obtained during the 1980 season. On the other hand, the deposits at Rowe were as deep as Guthe had originally described, and finding the extramural work surfaces and underlying adobe walls at the southern margins of the site supported the suggestion that the occupation dated to earlier than 1300 and perhaps earlier than 1200.

No specific evidence of interaction with Plains nomadic groups was obtained. No ceramic types that had been suggested as being of Plains origin were located; no stone tools of a form that might have been Apache or pre-Apache were noted, and no identifiable Plains lithic sources (i.e., Alibates chert) were represented in the Rowe chipped stone tool assemblage. Finally, although medium to large body-size fauna were abundant, only a very few bison bones were recovered, and these few bones were not thought to substantiate regular exchange relationships with Plains people.

No further work was conducted at Rowe Ruin by University of New Mexico field school staff until 1983. In that year, three weeks of field work at Rowe were designed to evaluate the potential of the site for a somewhat different set of research questions and a field school structure that combined the University of New Mexico and the New Mexico State University field schools. On the basis of the work accomplished during the short 1983 season, a research proposal was submitted to the National Science Foundation for work in 1984. This proposal was funded. Because the 1983 field season was both short and preliminary to the 1984 work, the research results of both seasons are reported together here. A detailed, two-volume report was submitted to the National Science Foundation in 1987 (Cordell 1987) and is on file at the University of New Mexico's Clark Field Archive.

The central focus of the 1983–1984 work was to begin to evaluate proposed relationships among population aggregation in the Southwest, increased regional variation in rainfall, and the development of regional systems of exchange. During the 1970s, several important projects attempted to evaluate the idea, first suggested by Longacre (1966), that pre-contact population aggregation in the Southwest had been a response to deteriorating climate and decreasing crop yields. Although this proposition was examined in a number of cases (see Orcutt 1991), the major instance of population aggregation that was the focus of research conducted in the 1970s was tenth- and eleventh-century developments in Chaco Canyon (Judge et al. 1981). One of the mechanisms that had been proposed to explain the rise of the Chacoan system was a decline in crop yields over parts of the San Juan Basin and the subsequent redistribution of crops that would "even out" shortfalls experienced in some localities. The redistribution model suffered a major setback when paleoenvironmental reconstructions, based on tree-rings and geomorphological studies of ground water levels, showed that the Chacoan system arose and flourished when conditions in the San Juan Basin were at their most favorable for agriculture whereas growth of the system ceased at a time that was coincident with a major drought (Dean et al. 1985; Sebastian 1990, 1991).

Fred Plog and Steadman Upham had recently completed a major project at the Chavez Pass site (Nuvoquwewotekka), a very large aggregated ancestral Hopi site. On the basis of tree-ring data (Dean et al. 1985; Gumerman 1988), Plog was able to correlate periods of population aggregation in the Southwest to times during which there was high spatial variability in rainfall. His observation was that, whether above or below normal, at times the distribution of rainfall throughout the Southwest was quite homogeneous. For example, in AD 1190 there was a decrease in precipitation that affected most of the Colorado Plateaus area. At other times, greater than average precipitation might occur across this large region. At still other times, rainfall distributions were highly varied from one locality to another. Thus, precipitation might be above normal at Black Mesa and Chaco Canyon and below normal at Mesa Verde and the Rio Grande drainage.

Plog suggested that large villages, which might coordinate labor to facilitate exchange or generate craft items that might function in regional exchange networks, would be at a considerable advantage during periods of regional, *spatial,* heterogeneity in precipitation. At those times, large villages could facilitate movement of goods that would even out shortfalls in some areas with overproduction in others. Specifically, for the period between about AD 1260 and 1400, Plog noted a correlation between the formation of large, aggregated sites over much of the Colorado Plateaus and high spatial variability in rainfall. Although paleoenvironment was seen as a key factor, the model developed by Plog and others (e.g., Dean et al. 1985) indicates that this "solution" has considerable social cost and would occur under circumstances when regional population densities were high enough to preclude or discourage population movement from areas with declines in environmental productivity to areas where production was increased. Mobility was seen as a socially less costly option.

Objectives proposed for the research at Rowe included obtaining precise dating for the site to see if aggregation there, and perhaps also at Pecos Pueblo, correlated with the AD 1260 to 1400 peak in spatial variability in rainfall, and gathering refined data that would allow specification of how population aggregation occurred and how aggregated communities functioned. There was an explicit assumption that the paleoenvironmental model was too mechanical and would require modification in light of social and organizational considerations.

Factors important to social inferences about aggregated communities relate to their social complexity, to exchange, and perhaps to differential access to material goods. The term *social complexity* has been used with a variety of referents in recent southwestern archaeological literature (Cordell et al. 1991). In this instance, it refers to two different situations. The first is the simultaneous coexistence of, and perhaps interaction among, groups of people who are relatively sedentary and dependent upon intensive agriculture and more mobile groups who are primarily foragers using limited horticulture. The second notion of social complexity, which may also include the first, refers to the presence in one society of social hierarchies, generally including some form of "managerial elite" and "non-elite" others. The argument linking spatial variability in rainfall with a managerial elite states that "it appears that exchange was one means elected to counter the increasingly high spatial variability. Exchange of some magnitude may have led to 'managerial' roles, large central settlements from which the exchange was coordinated, higher population densities in some localities, and agricultural intensification" (Cordell et al. 1983:2).

One way in which social hierarchies might be manifested archaeologically is in differential distributions of certain ceramic types. In southwestern archaeology, ceramic types are viewed almost entirely as temporal markers. Some scholars, however, working primarily with late Western Pueblo sites in Arizona, have argued that those ceramic types that required more labor to produce than other types used for the same or similar functions might also be distributed differentially on and in settlements that were occupied simultaneously. In this situation, some individuals might have had special access to these kinds of pottery whereas other individuals did not. It might also be proposed that the production and distribution of these kinds of pottery marked the formation of alliance systems linking individuals, from several communities or villages, who shared relatively high social status. This interpretation is elaborated most fully in discussions of Chavez Pass Pueblo and other Anderson Mesa sites in Arizona (Upham 1982; Upham and Bockley 1989).

Among the reasons for looking for such patterning in the Upper Pecos included the observation that Rowe, Loma Lothrop, Arrowhead, and other Upper Pecos Valley "Class II" (Hewett 1904) sites, along with early Pecos Pueblo, might have been occupied at the same time. In addition, excavations at Pecos Pueblo yielded abundant early and middle Rio Grande glaze pottery that Shepard's (1936) petrographic studies indicated had not been made at Pecos. It therefore seemed reasonable to examine the idea that these glaze types might have been a trade item restricted to occupants of Pecos Pueblo and not used by residents of Rowe and other contemporary Class II villages. If this were found to be the case, then the archaeological practice of using these ceramics exclusively as temporal markers would be erroneous.

To explore these issues, the field research addressed four questions: (1) What is the temporal relationship between Rowe and other large sites in the area? (2) What is the nature of the exchange relationships that existed between Rowe and the surrounding area, and how did these change over time? (3) What is the nature of the settlement pattern in the area surrounding these late, Upper Pecos Valley sites? And (4) were the inhabitants of Rowe involved in any processes of craft specialization? (Cordell et al. 1983). Although the work accomplished during 1983

and 1984 was structured by these questions, we did not expect to be able to answer them on the basis of only a few weeks of additional field work. Rather, the questions would help to organize research in the future.

During the brief 1983 season, the project made a detailed map of Rowe Ruin using an EDM (laser-based Electronic Distance Meter). This site map (Figure 6) is more accurate than any previous attempt, at least in part because the EDM could be set up at a considerable distance from the magnetic anomaly known to distort compass readings in the north plaza. The source of the anomaly was found to be a break in a water pipeline underlying the north quadrangle plaza. The line itself was most likely installed in 1876 when the railroad station was built at Rowe.

Because of the unexpected discovery of extensive extramural features south of the southern roomblocks, additional work was conducted to search systematically for extramural features and underlying rooms. During the 1983 season, a proton magnetometer survey and mapping of about 6,000 square meters of non-roomblock space (plaza areas and areas north, west, and south of the main roomblocks) was accomplished. The magnetometer work revealed more than 24 dipole anomalies, which typically identify subsurface cultural features (Weymouth 1981). Some of them were quite large, suggesting either roomblocks or kivas. Others were small, indicating pits, hearths, or small activity areas.

The dipole anomalies suggested, but did not demonstrate, the existence of these features. In order to test the usefulness of the magnetometer work, a series of backhoe trenches was excavated during the 1984 season. Half of these trenches were located over previously mapped anomalies; the other half were positioned away from mapped anomalies to provide a check on the locations of extramural features the magnetometer may have failed to locate. Twenty-one backhoe trenches and one hand-dug trench were excavated (Figure 6). The hand-excavated trench (called "backhoe trench" 15) was dug in the south plaza, where the fragile masonry walls made it desirable not to use heavy equipment.

The testing aspect of the excavation program yielded abundant evidence of extramural features, some of which seem to antedate construction of the masonry roomblocks composing the three plaza-oriented quadrangles at Rowe Ruin. Three excavation units (T305, T306, and T307) were placed south of the southern roomblock of the south quadrangle to explore the extramural features first identified in 1980. These 2 by 2 m units confirmed evidence of an earlier adobe structure; an outside work area or surface, possibly covered by a ramada; burning of these features; subsequent remodeling; and trash deposition. Of particular interest is the sequence of levels and features in T307 that indicated a trash pit sealed below an adobe-walled room. The room appears to have been an interior room that had been remodeled once and had eventually burned. The room area was then trash-filled once again, probably when the masonry roomblock of the southern quadrangle was built. A single radiocarbon date of AD 1170 ± 70 (Beta-18799) was obtained from wood charcoal from the lowest, sealed trash pit below the adobe structure. Two radiocarbon determinations, on corn from trash pits in T306, yielded dates of AD 1010 ± 100 (Beta-18791) and AD 1370 ± 70 (Beta-18789). Burned daub chunks which appear to be part of the roof fall were also encountered in the north wall of backhoe trench 7. This was the southernmost evidence of the underlying adobe structure.

Evidence of additional structures not physically connected to the masonry quadrangles was obtained in the backhoe trenches. Trench 2 had been positioned over a magnetic anomaly mapped in 1983. The trench encountered a masonry wall, a compact clay floor, two hearth and ash dump areas, a possible sipapu, and two loom holes at a depth of 1.70 m below ground surface. A tree-ring date of 1305vv was acquired from pinyon associated with the masonry wall. One archaeomagnetic date was obtained from each hearth. The sample from hearth 1 dates to AD 1000–1015 or AD 1325 to post-1425 (Archaeomagnetic Laboratory, Colorado State University, LA 108-1; 1984 letter report on file, Maxwell Museum of Anthropology, UNM). The sample from hearth 2 produced an archaeomagnetic date of AD 1000–1020 or 1225–1425 (LA 108-2). If the wood that produced the tree-ring date was indeed structural and the masonry wall is associated with the floor and hearths, the later archaeomagnetic dates would be the more probable and the interpretation of the masonry-walled structure as a kiva associated with the main occupation of Rowe Ruin likely. Other observations, discussed below, lend support to the interpretation that the masonry wall and wood sample are part of a later component, perhaps one of the outlying roomblocks mapped by Hewett (Figure 3).

Neither the backhoe trench nor subsequent excavation uncovered evidence of a physical articulation of the clay floor and the masonry wall. If the masonry wall was not associated with the floor and hearths, the earlier of the archaeomagnetic dates would be likely, suggesting that the hearths and floor may have been part of an earlier pithouse.

Additional evidence of occupation encountered in the backhoe trenches consists of a trash pit in backhoe trench 1; two trash pits and a burial pit, with one adult and one infant burial, in backhoe trench 2; a hearth within a pitstructure in backhoe trench 3; two trash pits and a burial pit in backhoe trench 4; a refuse pit and a burial pit exposed in the south wall of backhoe trench 7; and an ash lens with trash in backhoe trench 12. Trench 15, which was excavated by hand in the south plaza, uncovered a slightly curving masonry wall, plaza surfaces, and a burial. Backhoe trench X was cut through suspected midden deposits to define their depth and spatial extent. Culturally sterile soil was encountered in the northern half of this trench. The remaining excavated backhoe trenches—5, 6, 13, 19, 20, 23, Y, and Z—were devoid of artifacts or features. Dipole anomalies may have appeared above some of these trenches because of a natural disconformity between a gray silty layer and a red clay substrate.

Following excavation and profiling of trench X, T118, a 1 by 1 m unit, was excavated in the deepest portion of the midden, as revealed in the backhoe trench X profile. Forty-eight centimeters of midden deposit were excavated in natural levels. Botanical and faunal remains were well preserved in this midden area. Two radiocarbon dates were obtained (from corncobs): AD 1290 ± 90 (Beta-18793) and AD 1160 ± 80 (Beta-18795).

In 1983, excavation was begun in room 112 (Figure 6) in an area that appeared likely to enable definition of the extent of the southern roomblock of the north quadrangle. This room and the adjacent room 113 were completely excavated in 1984. Room 113 was found to have been constructed on culturally sterile ground and to be architecturally tied to the central quadrangle. A female effigy of unfired clay was found 87 cm above the gray to black adobe floor of this room in a matrix of ash and adobe slump. The floor of the room lacked features, but a broken corrugated vessel was found in the northeast corner. Fourteen large masonry blocks were apparently randomly placed in the room when it was abandoned.

Room 112, also tied to the central quadrangle, had underlying masonry walls and appeared to be a later addition that had been "tacked on." The floor of R112 was hard-packed orange sandy clay and brown clay and it lacked floor features or associated artifacts, except for unmodified rocks. The evidence from excavation of these rooms suggests that the north quadrangle roomblocks, which were virtually devoid of cultural fill, were not architecturally linked to the other two quadrangles at Rowe Ruin.

Human skeletal remains from 31 individuals were excavated in 1984. Most of the remains were exceedingly fragmentary, having been found in the backhoe trenches. Of the 31 individuals, 12 were represented by only one or two fragmentary elements. All human remains were analyzed at the Osteological Laboratory at the University of New Mexico (Curran 1985) and returned to the landowner for reburial at the site. Of the 19 somewhat better represented individuals, eight are infants or children less than 4 years old, four are children about 5 to 10 years old, three are adolescents between 10 and 18 years old, and four are adults. The adults are one woman more than 50 years old, a woman between 15 and 20 years old, a woman between 30 and 35 years old, and one man somewhat older than 40 years. Those skeletons complete enough for some analysis manifest the same muscular rugosity noted in the assemblage discussed previously (see the section on Mortuary Data, below).

As stated above, most of the human remains were found in backhoe trench excavations, all but three in trench 2 and its extensions. This trench is between the central quadrangle of rooms and a roomblock sketched on Hewett's (1904) map and subsequently heavily colluviated. Therefore, it is not possible to associate the skeletons with either of the two structures with complete certainty. There is no indication, however, that the remains are other than those of the aboriginal occupants of Rowe Ruin. The highly fragmentary nature of the burials was, in part, the result of an administrative decision rather than a reflection of the condition of the burials themselves. We decided not to extend the trenches to excavate the human remains fully. Rather, only those skeletal parts that were fully exposed in the trench were removed for analysis.

Three of the burials (one aged ca. 10 to 15 years, one male aged 9 to 18 months, and one adult of indeterminate sex) were found in a single pit located in the east wall of backhoe trench 2. A girl about 6 to 8 years old was buried under large stone slabs stratigraphically beneath the pit burial just noted. A man aged greater than 50 years and a child of indeterminate sex aged 5 to 7 years had been buried in a slightly bell-shaped pit that was also found in trench 2. Two more burials from backhoe trench 2, a boy aged 9 to 10 years and a possible girl aged 5 to 7 years, were located within a layer of rock and rubble that may be wall fall associated with the structure encountered in the trench. The burial of an infant, possibly a girl, one-half to one year of age was found in trench 15, in the south plaza. The burial was on its left side with its head facing south. A shell necklace was around its head and what appeared to be a disintegrated mat was wrapped around the body. This burial was 22 cm above the floor of the structure located in backhoe trench 15.

Two burials were excavated in T305, south of the southern roomblock of the south quadrangle. Both were located under a loose alignment of small stones. The first burial was the torso of a child of indeterminate sex, aged 3 to 6 years. The anomalous, incomplete fusion of the halves of the sacral neural arches is consistent with spina bifida occulta (Curran 1985). The second burial, a woman 30 to 35 years of age, had been placed in an oval pit along with a bone awl, a piece of turtle carapace, and a mano fragment. In addition to degenerative pathologies associated with age, two fractured and healed ribs, and a healed neck injury, the cranium displayed several destructive lesions consistent with treponemal infection (Curran 1985).

Rowe Ruin continued to yield an abundance of artifacts. During the brief, three-week 1983 field season, 5,046 artifacts were recovered. Of these, 1,972 (39%) were sherds, 1,486 (29%) were lithic artifacts, 1,582 (31%) were animal bones, and 6 (less than 1%) were ground stone artifacts. During the regular seven-week season in 1984, a total of 31,279 artifacts was recovered from the site: 11,918 (38%) sherds, 9,258 (30%) lithic artifacts, 9,866 (31%) animal bones, and 147 (less than 1%) ground stone objects. Macrobotanical, flotation, pollen, tree-ring, radiocarbon, and obsidian hydration samples were also obtained.

ON THE ARCHITECTURE OF ROWE RUIN

THE VISIBLE PORTION OF ROWE RUIN CONSISTS OF three contiguous rectangles made up of roomblocks enclosing open plazas. The rectangles are aligned north to south. The separate roomblock to the west, as mapped by Hewett (Figure 3), was no longer visible in 1980. It had been covered by thick aolian deposits and the unpaved drive leading to the field cabin. The main part of Rowe Ruin is constructed of masonry made almost entirely of the locally available limestone, probably quarried from the small ridge just east of the site. Table 1 provides basic descriptive measurements of the quadrangles.

In his summary of the architecture of Pecos, Kidder (1958:55) used the term *quadrangle* to refer to "a compact, four-sided, multistoried pueblo . . . built around a spacious courtyard." By this minimal definition, Rowe might be described as being composed of three quadrangles, and for this reason I use the term here. For Kidder (1958:59–63), however, "quadrangle" also specifically referred to the easily defended Glaze III structure at Pecos. He further describes this structure as manifesting a rigid adherence to a transverse linear arrangement of rooms consisting of self-contained units that he called "sections," of three or, more often, six ground-floor rooms connected to each other by doorways but without access to neighboring rooms. Kidder (1958:55–59) calls the long linear arrangement of non-interconnecting rooms "tiers," a descriptor in general use among southwestern archaeologists. The quadrangle at Pecos was seen as a novel architectural concept for Glaze III times. This novel way of building included "designing the building in advance and constructing it as a unit" (Kidder 1958:63).

"The town at Rowe," Kidder (1958:59) noted, "with its three rectangular units gives more the impression of having been planned than does any other early building in the Pecos country, but it was not sufficiently laid bare

for Guthe to be sure how it had developed." Our subsequent excavations at Rowe indicate that much of the pueblo was planned and constructed as a unit, but we could not demonstrate this for all parts of the site. Further, we did not expose enough of the site to reveal whether or not a rigid plan of sections and tiers had been used. Nevertheless, I refer to the three separate plaza and building units at Rowe as quadrangles. They are here designated as the north, middle and south quadrangles, each surrounding a plaza—also north, middle, and south.

The mounds at Rowe Ruin are the remains of masonry rooms arranged in roomblocks. Most of the roomblocks were two stories tall. The obvious differences in mound elevation (Figure 7; also see Figure 6) are primarily a reflection of modification and rebuilding. Despite the fact that Rowe Ruin's three-quadrangle, three-plaza plan gives it the appearance of a single-component site, the appearance is misleading in the extreme. Guthe discovered evidence of two and, in some places, three distinct periods of masonry construction in some portions of the south quadrangle rooms. Kidder (1958:4) acknowledged that the visible site was built over older ruins. The architecture at Rowe Ruin is even more complicated than Guthe or Kidder knew.

The masonry rooms at Rowe Ruin are underlain by adobe-walled rooms in at least one and perhaps other parts of the site. The best exposure of adobe structural elements was outside the southern roomblock of the south quadrangle. Although we hoped to define the extent of the adobe ruin and to date its period of use, our excavations were not extensive enough to be able to do so. Within the masonry pueblo there is some variation among the rooms in each of the quadrangles. These differences are described in the detailed discussions that follow. First, however, a general statement about the

Table 1. Rowe Ruin: Quadrangle Data

Dimension	Quadrangle		
	North	Middle	South
Plaza length (north-south)	43 m	16 m	15 m
Plaza width (east-west)	31 m	23 m	17 m
Approximate plaza area	1333 m²	368 m²	255 m²
Rubble mound (maximum height)	2.8 m	3.8 m	4 m
Maximum length (north-south)	52 m	42 m	38 m
Maximum width (east-west)	55 m	42 m	45 m
Total area	2860 m²	176 m²	1710 m²
Estimated living area	1527 m²	1877 m²	1455 m²

rooms and features at Rowe is provided here, with some comparisons with Pecos and other sites in the area.

The masonry at Rowe generally compares favorably with the early and, according to Kidder, better-quality masonry in the old structures at Pecos (Kidder 1958:55). In fact, one of the photographs included in the description of the early masonry structures at Pecos is of Rowe (Kidder 1958:Fig. 19e). Wall elements at Rowe are longer than they are wide and wider than they are thick, averaging about 30 cm long by 20 cm wide by 5 cm in thickness. These stones were laid in mud mortar with their long axis parallel to the long axis of the wall. The smoother sides of the wall stones faced the room interior and were often shaped by some chipping and pecking. Wall interiors were either left as is or covered with mud plaster.

Walls at Rowe are generally one or very occasionally two elements thick. In addition to mud mortar, small chinking stones are abundant. These stones are of the same local limestone as the wall elements and average about 5 cm in length by 3 or 4 cm in width by 2 cm in thickness. In at least one instance, the east wall of middle quadrangle room 20 (Figure 6), vertical posts were set between the two rows of masonry elements. Sometimes a trench was excavated for the wall foundations at Rowe. In other cases, the first course of wall stones was set vertically and jutted out from the horizontal wall stones of the lower courses of the wall, forming a kind of shelf.

We found three kinds of room floors at Rowe Ruin. In some cases, such as the back rooms of the north roomblock of the middle quadrangle, floors are of adobe similar in color and texture to the clay substrate and only

a few centimeters thick. As at Forked Lightning, these floors are difficult to define (Kidder 1958:24). In a few cases at Rowe, such as rooms 20 and 30, the floor is highly polished, very dark adobe, more like floors in the later structures at Pecos and other large Pueblo IV ruins in the Rio Grande area (cf. Kidder 1958:24; Jeançon 1923:14). At Rowe, adobe floors were laid after the walls had been constructed. These floors abut or turn up against interior wall surfaces, and wall foundations are consistently below the floor.

A single flagstone floor at Rowe was identified by the university crews. This floor, made of thin flagstones of micaceous schist, was associated with the adobe structure south of the south quadrangle (T303, Figure 6). Kidder (1958:24) noted that floors paved with unshaped sandstone slabs were infrequent but occurred at Forked Lightning Ruin and at the early structure at Pecos in room B-IV (Kidder 1958:Fig. 19f). Lambert (1954:13) notes that flagstone floors in the precolumbian portions of Paa-ko were generally associated with construction that was transitional between coursed adobe and stone masonry or with masonry rooms. At Tijeras Pueblo, a flagstone floor was associated with the earlier occupation (ca. AD 1313–1360) of that site (Cordell 1977).

Finally, Guthe described "an elaborate formation" in room VII, where one might have expected a floor. There, about 39 cm above the base of the walls, was a layer of small stones laid together in material resembling lime. Above this was a layer of yellow earth that appeared to be decayed wood.

Few intact firepits or hearths are known for Rowe. A sketch map of room W3, a room excavated by volunteers

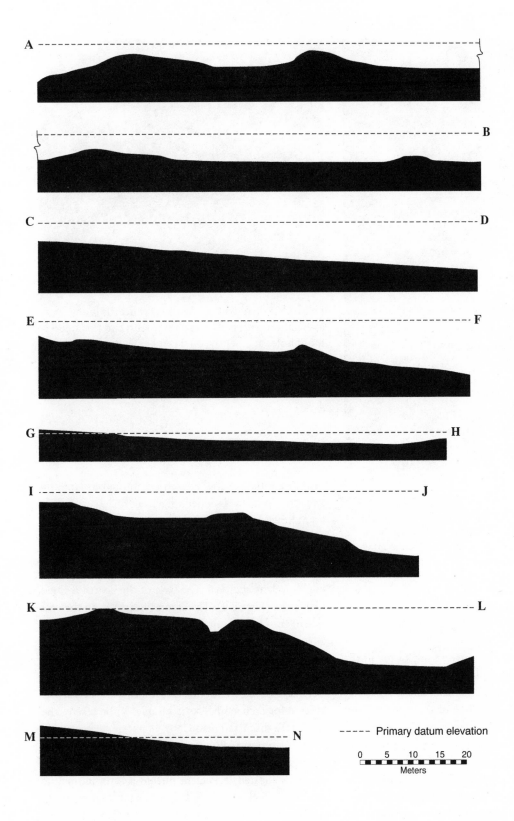

Figure 7. Elevations (see Figure 6 for profile locations)

Figure 9. Ash-filled rectangular clay hearth found in association with a prepared floor with two possible loom holes at a depth of 1.51 m below the ground surface in backhoe trench 2. An archaeomagnetic sample from this hearth yielded a date of AD 1000 to 1020 or 1225 to 1425.

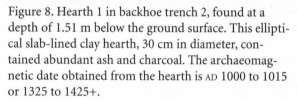

Figure 8. Hearth 1 in backhoe trench 2, found at a depth of 1.51 m below the ground surface. This elliptical slab-lined clay hearth, 30 cm in diameter, contained abundant ash and charcoal. The archaeomagnetic date obtained from the hearth is AD 1000 to 1015 or 1325 to 1425+.

and Wait in 1978 or 1979 on the east side of the north quadrangle, shows a circular hearth, partially ringed by stones. The hearth is 50 cm in diameter and slightly off-center to the west of the midline of the room. In the field school excavations of quadrangle rooms, no intact formal hearths were uncovered. The north quadrangle rooms contained burned areas on the ill-prepared adobe floors and evidence of fallen hearths from second-story rooms. Kidder encountered this same situation at Forked Lightning. "Fires, either for warmth or for cooking could normally be maintained only in chambers with unencumbered roofs. The great rarity of firepits, save in kivas,

therefore indicates that Forked Lightning was largely a two-story pueblo" (Kidder 1958:25).

At Rowe, two formal firepits were excavated in structural remains encountered in backhoe trench 2 (Figure 6). Hearth 1, at the west wall of the trench, is an elliptical, clay hearth, about 30 cm in diameter and containing abundant charcoal. The base of the hearth is lined with slabs (Figure 8). The second hearth is on the east side of the trench, 2 m south of the first hearth. Hearth 2 is a rectangular, clay hearth with raised adobe coping (Figure 9) associated with a floor; additional floor features indicate that this structure was a kiva. Both hearths were 1.51 m below ground surface and were sufficiently burned for archaeomagnetic samples to be taken. The results are discussed below.

In his notes, Guthe did not record finding formal firepits in the center of rooms, which is where they are generally located in ancient pueblo rooms. Rather, he described "pockets" of ash and/or charcoal in some room corners, inferring that these were fireplace locations. If indeed they were "fireplaces," they are unusual if not unique in location for precolumbian pueblos.

No intact roofs were located at Rowe; however, in many instances roofing material consisting of wood, twig fragments, and daub (either burned or unburned) was found in room fill. The wall that rooms 20 and 30 shared in common (the south wall of room 20, north wall of room 30) had three viga sockets located about 80 cm apart. Each socket was about 15 cm in diameter. In room 112, the orientation of wood samples taken for tree-ring dating also indicated that primary beams were oriented north-south while smaller pieces of wood were lying east-west. Even though all structural wood recovered from Rowe has been identified as pinyon, obtaining wood adequate for tree-ring dating was a continuing problem because most specimens had an inadequate number of rings.

Doorways were located in many walls at Rowe, although no instances were found of doorways that had not been sealed in precolumbian times. Table 2 provides locations of the sealed doorways recorded.

One of the reasons we selected Rowe Ruin for study was the apparent lack of kivas. We suspected that Rowe Ruin might have been one member of a site cluster, in which case the residents could have maintained their ceremonial obligations at another community in the cluster. None of the descriptions of Rowe—from Bandelier to Guthe—indicates the presence of kivas. Guthe extended his trench through the south plaza because he noted an area in which the grass appeared thicker than elsewhere and suspected that this might have been indication of a kiva. This was not the case. In 1980 a similar observation prompted us to place a trench in the north plaza, with the same negative results. We also excavated room 30 in the south quadrangle, in part, because it had one curved wall and might have been similar to the "corner kivas" described at Forked Lightning and Dick's Ruin (Kidder 1958:35–42). As discussed below, this again proved not to be the case. Room 30 lacked diagnostic kiva floor features but did produce evidence suggesting ritual closing (Walker 1996). The only structure at Rowe Ruin that did have kiva features is the one encountered and only partially exposed in backhoe trench 2. Discussion of additional questions about kivas at Rowe, as well as the chronology of construction and relationships among the quadrangles and other structures, is deferred to the section following descriptions of the architectural features of each quadrangle and the backhoe trenching tests.

The North Quadrangle

The north quadrangle extends 52 m north-south and 55 m east-west. This quadrangle covers a larger area than either of the other two, and it has a more open appearance, in part because the rubble mounds that are the remains of roomblocks are lower than those surrounding the other two plazas (see Figure 7). Before excavation, these low mounds suggested that the north quadrangle roomblocks might be single-story constructions. This conclusion was not supported; results of excavation indicated two-story construction. At Rowe, the differences in height of the rubble mounds relate to the amount of modification and rebuilding rather than the number of stories (see discussion of the middle quadrangle, below).

The interior plaza of the north quadrangle is nearly square, measuring 43 m by 31 m. Prior to the late 1970s, no authorized excavation had been done in the north quadrangle. The southern end of the west roomblock of the quadrangle had been visibly disturbed by road construction, probably associated with the railroad station at modern Rowe village.

The outlines of rooms W1 through W5 were exposed in 1978 by Wait and Nordby and their volunteer crew. Of these rooms, W1, W2, W4, and W5 were excavated. Rooms 10 and 11 were excavated by the University of New Mexico crew in 1980. Room 10 was completely excavated and room 11 was partially excavated. Table 2 presents all recorded room dimensions. Some excavations had been undertaken before 1978 by members of the landowner's family in parts of rooms W1 through W5. Thus, Wait and Nordby were salvaging information from a disturbed part of the site and instructing the family in excavation techniques and recording. Although only an incomplete set of notes from the 1978 excavations is now available, it contains information valuable for interpreting the northern quadrangle.

The notes for room W1 indicate that a mano, a shaped stone slab, and a 50 cm by 3 cm lens of fine gray ash were located above the roof fall layer, suggesting the room had a second story. In addition, the presence of two floor levels separated vertically by 6 cm suggests that the room had been modified or refurbished. A human burial was excavated from room W2. According to the notes, the remains represented a man aged 30 to 40. Bone preservation was judged to be poor. Before the 1978 work, a

Table 2. Room Characteristics (rooms excavated in 1978–1984)

Room	Dimensions (m)		Floor area (m²)	Maximum wall		Number of prepared floors	Floor features	Subfloor	Doorways	Year excavated
	North-south	East-west		height (m)	thickness (cm)					
NORTH QUADRANGLE										
W1						2?			west wall	1978
W2										1978
W3	3.8	2.8	10.64			2?	1 hearth		east wall ?	1978
W4										1978
W5	2.63	2.97	7.81							1978
10	3.41	2.72	9.27	1.6		1	none	sterile	south wall	1980
11	4.00	2.33	9.32	1.6	30		burn area	sterile	none	1980
MIDDLE QUADRANGLE										
20	4.0	2.05	8.20	2.40	30	2	none	46 cm of fill	south wall	1980
21	2.26	2.56	5.78	0.61	31	none	none	fill, room 23	none	1980
22	3.18	2.27	7.22	1.20	30	1	none	fill, room 24	none	1980
23	unknown	2.90	unknown	1.80	unknown	1	none	fill	unknown	1980
24	unknown	2.14	unknown	1.44	25	none	none	fill	south wall	1980
112	3.23	2.42	7.81	2.19	20	2	none	fill, wall stub	none	1983, 1984
113	2.52	2.19	5.52	2.38	20	1	none	fill	none	1984
SOUTH QUADRANGLE										
30	2.11	2.29	4.83	2.76	27	2†	none	fill	north wall	1980

† The two floors in room 30 are from two different stories; the multiple floors in other rooms are from the same story.

pair of lightning stones had been recovered from the doorway in the west wall of the room. No other information on room W2 is available. A sketch map of room W3 shows a hearth partially ringed by stones, 50 cm in diameter and slightly off-center to the west of the midline of the room.

Excavation in rooms 10 and 11 by the 1980 field school confirmed a comment by Wait that in the east roomblock of the north quadrangle the north and south walls were continuous, with east and west cross-walls abutting them. The floors in rooms 10 and 11 had blackened clay surfaces that gradually blended into the sterile, red clay substrate. In room 10, ground stone and fire-blackened, shaped stones were distributed throughout several levels above the floor. Along with the observations that the room contained abundant wall fall and standing walls remained up to 1.6 m in height, this evidence indicates that, as in room W1, there had been a second story. The south wall of room 10 had a filled-in doorway. A small hole, possibly for ventilation, had been set in the west wall.

In room 11, two manos were found next to a burned area of the floor. The floor was sufficiently burned for an archaeomagnetic sample, and 16 cubes were taken, yielding a date of AD 1395 ± 17. Room 11 had no apparent doorways, but three large (50 by 50 cm) irregular holes had been punched through the eastern (outer) wall of the room and later had been filled in. A smaller hole, possibly for ventilation as in room 10, was found in the north wall. Room 11 also contained fill that suggested a second story. This was a heterogeneous mix with concentrations of decomposing adobe and charcoal in a matrix of hard-packed clay with sandy pockets, caliche, and charcoal mixed with thin black layers suggestive of a floor surface. An exploratory trench (T104) was dug east of room 11 for a distance of 3.85 m without encountering any suggestion of cross-walls. Room 11 was therefore an outer room, and its east wall, though only 20 cm thick, was the outside wall of the pueblo at this location.

The construction methods used in the east roomblock of the north quadrangle were observed and recorded most completely in rooms 10 and 11. At the base of the walls, beneath the floor, a course of large, shaped limestone blocks was set upright, jutting out about 7 cm from the courses above them. Blocks in the basal course averaged 40 by 10 cm. Above the foundation the walls were made of shaped limestone blocks laid either side by side

or overlapping one another. Element size ranged from 10 by 17 cm to 35 by 6 cm. Elements were flattened by chipping the surface that faced the room interior. Limestone chinking was used generously, but these rooms had less adobe mortar between wall elements than did rooms in the central and southern quadrangles. Limestone spalls, evidently debris from shaping the wall stones, were found in trenches excavated outside the rooms.

On the southern end of the east roomblock, a low area indicating an opening into the plaza, also shown on Hewett's map (Figure 3), could be either another instance of railroad-related disturbance or an original entryway into the north plaza. In 1980, three trenches were excavated to resolve whether or not the gap in the east wall of the north quadrangle had been an entry or later disturbance in conjunction with the roadbed. One of the trenches located the outer wall of the pueblo, established its base and followed it south to the gap. The wall ended in a jumble of stone without turning a corner, and a modern metal can lid was found in the test trench, suggesting that the gap was the result of later disturbance rather than an entrance. However, since the trenches were both narrow and rather shallow and Hewett's map was clear in indicating an entrance, the question was not resolved. Another pair of well-formed lightning stones was found in this exploratory trench as it turned west (Figure 10).

An additional exploratory trench was excavated in 1980 inside the north plaza in its northeast corner, where a slight depression suggested the presence of a kiva. Artifact density in this area was extremely low, as it was elsewhere in the north quadrangle, and the area was heavily disturbed. The evidence of disturbance consisted of lumps of coal, cinders, and metal, including a cartridge casing. No plaza kiva was found, but the trench was excavated to a depth of only 40 cm. Finally, in 1984 a test pit was excavated in the north plaza to determine the cause of the 5.5 magnetic anomaly that had distressed Guthe and all subsequent investigators trying to map the site. The magnetic anomaly was strongest in the north plaza. In 1984, a proton magnetometer was used to pinpoint the anomaly as closely as possible. The excavated test revealed that a pipeline, most likely associated with the railroad, had extended through Rowe Ruin and far beyond in both directions and had been broken at some time in the past precisely in this area, which could very well account for the anomaly.

Unlike the middle and south quadrangles, the north

quadrangle lacks an associated roomblock, or tier of rooms, on its southern end. Rooms 112 and 113 were excavated, in part, to explore the architectural connection between the northern and middle quadrangles. Both rooms, however, were found to be part of the back tier rooms of the northern roomblock of the middle quadrangle (see below).

In general, the north quadrangle at Rowe is unusual. In terms of its size and openness, it more closely resembles the plazas at Paa-ko (Lambert 1954) than either of the other two plazas at Rowe or those at Pecos (Kidder 1958). A portion of Paa-ko dates to the Spanish period; however, the pre-contact plaza areas at Paa-ko measure about 46 m north-south by 30 m east-west. At Rowe, the north plaza measures 43 m north-south by 31 m east-west (Table 2). Also, Lambert (1954) noted that in parts of the pre-contact Northeast Communal House at Paa-ko there was evidence of second story, although the clues had been missed by the technical staff during the first weeks of excavation. She lists the following evidence: many more ground-story store rooms than living rooms, an abundance of wall fall, fallen hearths in room fill as evidenced by ash pockets, manos and metates in room fill, and adobe chunks containing roofing impressions in fill below ash deposits. (In the pre-contact portions of Paa-ko there was an architectural transition from adobe to masonry and adobe and finally to masonry walls.) Similar evidence was used to establish the presence of multiple stories at Pindi Pueblo (Stubbs and Stallings 1953). Too few rooms have been excavated in the north quadrangle at Rowe to allow estimates of how many were store rooms rather than living rooms. Otherwise, the indicators of second-story rooms are much the same as at Paa-ko and Pindi Pueblo.

The Middle Quadrangle

The plaza of the middle quadrangle at Rowe extends 16 m north-south and 23 m east-west, slightly less than one-quarter of the area of the north plaza. The maximum height of the rubble mounds surrounding the plaza is 3.8 m, compared with 2.8 m for the north quadrangle. Work conducted in the middle quadrangle in 1980, 1983, and 1984 demonstrates that the height of the rubble mounds primarily reflects the amount of modification and rebuilding and only secondarily the

Figure 10. Pair of quartz "lightning stones" found 10 cm below the surface (16.18 bd) in T102, an exploratory trench on the east side of the north quadrangle, as the trench was turned to the west. It is the second of two pairs found in the same trench. They are 20 cm and 24 cm in length. Unmodified massive quartz occurs among the Pecos River gravels.

number of stories. Excavation of rooms in the middle quadrangle revealed that they differ in size and in construction style from those in the north quadrangle and that this portion of the pueblo underwent repeated episodes of rebuilding, dismantling, and change.

Rooms in the north quadrangle average slightly over 9 m^2. Those in the middle quadrangle average 7.36 m^2. Wall stones in the north quadrangle had been shaped and set more regularly than those in the middle quadrangle, and although chinking stones were plentiful in all walls at Rowe Ruin, mud or adobe mortar was more abundant in middle quadrangle rooms than in the north. As in the north quadrangle, wall element sizes varied considerably. Wall stones in one wall ranged from 13 by 3 cm to 44 by 12 cm. Interior surfaces were shaped or naturally flat.

In part because of the rebuilding of middle quadrangle rooms, the fill in this part of the site was less compact and had a greater abundance of charcoal flecks and artifacts and ecofacts than fill in the north quadrangle rooms. As in the north quadrangle, our strategy was to excavate room pairs in order to determine how space was used and how sets of rooms related to the plazas.

During the 1980 field season, excavation was conducted in rooms 21 and 22 in the east roomblock of the middle quadrangle. Both rooms were shallow and badly deteriorated. The 80 cm of fill removed from room 21 consisted of wall and roof fall material. The bases of the north and east walls of the room were encountered without any evidence of a floor. The roof fall material in room 21 provided seven tree-ring samples that yielded dates, more than any other provenience at Rowe Ruin. The dates obtained are 1319vv, 1323vv, 1326vv, 1340vv, 1344vv, 1346vv, and 1351vv. They are discussed further in the section on the chronology of Rowe Ruin. Forty-four centimeters of fill were excavated from room 22, which adjoins room 21 on the north. Strata defined in the fill were a layer of wall rubble, mixed roof fall and wall rubble, an ash pocket that may have been a deteriorated hearth, and a badly disturbed floor surface. The roof fall yielded a single tree-ring date of 1349vv, also a noncutting date.

Fill continued beneath the bases of the walls exposed in both rooms 21 and 22. Under room 21, an off-set west wall was associated with a continuation of the south wall of room 21. The new room was labeled room 23. Strata in room 23 included roof fall, a floor, and an eolian deposit. A single noncutting tree-ring date of 1343vv was obtained from a viga fragment in room 23. Excavations were terminated at the end of the 1980 field season before reaching culturally sterile soil, a lower floor, or the north and east walls of room 23. The room under room 22 was designated room 24. The east, west, and south walls of this room were defined. The north wall of room 24 was not located, nor did excavation reveal a floor. A sealed doorway was located in the south wall of the room.

Room 20 was excavated to provide information about an interior room in the west roomblock of the middle quadrangle. It was chosen to pair with room 30 in the south quadrangle to see if (and how) the middle and south quadrangles were connected. In contrast to the situation of rooms 21-22 and 23-24, the excavation of room 20 was quite straightforward. Fill reached a depth below surface of 2.35 m. The strata within the fill included rubble, roof fall, segments of a broken second-story floor, additional roof fall, an eolian lens, and the room floor. A subfloor test pit failed to reach culturally sterile ground.

No floor features were encountered in room 20, but nine other architectural features provided important information about the structural integrity of the site.

Two upright posts were found within the east wall of the room, serving as architectural components of that wall. The south wall of room 20 served as the north wall of room 30. Four viga sockets were located in this south wall, and a sealed doorway was found near the base of the center of the wall between rooms 20 and 30. Two postholes were found in the north wall. The east and west walls of room 20 alternately bonded and abutted with the south wall from bottom to top (25 courses for the east wall and 32 courses for the west wall), demonstrating that rooms 20 and 30 had been constructed at the same time. Unfortunately, no tree-ring dates were obtained for room 20; however, a cutting date of 1344 for wood from room 30 supports the inference of contemporaneity of the middle and south quadrangles.

In 1983 and 1984, rooms 112 and 113 in the north roomblock of the middle quadrangle were excavated. These rooms form part of the back tier of the roomblock, and they abut the southern edge of the north plaza. At least in the vicinity of these rooms, the north quadrangle has no southern roomblock. The walls of rooms 112 and 113 were constructed like those in other parts of the middle quadrangle. The limestone blocks were minimally shaped and laid with their long axes parallel to the long axis of the wall. Mud mortar was abundant, as were chinking stones. No plaster was apparent. In corners where walls still stand for many courses, the walls alternately bond and abut over several courses; the west and south walls of room 112 provide good examples, with 22 courses of the south wall standing intact. Rooms 112 and 113 share a common wall; the east wall of room 112 is also the west wall of room 113.

Room 112 was built on fill over a dismantled section of wall running north-south under the west wall of the room. Room 113 was also constructed on fill. Neither room contained floor features, nor were doorways present. Although roofing material from room 112 was submitted to the tree-ring lab, no dates were obtained.

The middle quadrangle at Rowe revealed a complex architectural history. Excavations in 1980, 1983, and 1984 enabled examination of seven rooms. None had been constructed on sterile ground. Although room 20 had evidence of a second story, the height of the rubble mound for the quadrangle as a whole seems largely to be the result of multiple building episodes.

The limited extent of excavation did not allow us to tie building episodes together from one roomblock to another. Clearly, rooms 22 and 23 were built in a construction event that preceded the building of rooms 20 and 21. Tree-ring dates suggest only that room 20 in the east roomblock (because it is architecturally linked to room 30) and the excavated west roomblock rooms were constructed during the latter two-thirds of the fourteenth century. Additional information on the chronological placement of the middle quadrangle is derived from excavation data from the south quadrangle, discussed below.

The total plaza area of the middle quadrangle is 368 m^2, a space much smaller than that of the north plaza (Table 2) or the pre-contact plazas at Paa-ko (Lambert 1954). The middle plaza is also small compared with early ruins at Pecos. At Pecos, the plaza at the early ruins north of the South Pueblo is about 936 m^2 (Kidder 1958:60–61, Fig. 20).

The South Quadrangle

More of the south quadrangle has been excavated than of the other two quadrangles at Rowe. Most of this work was undertaken by Carl Guthe in 1917. Guthe directed the excavation of a single long trench extending from outside the east side of the east roomblock of the south quadrangle, continuing along the south side of the north roomblock of the south quadrangle to the approximate east-west midpoint of the north roomblock, then making a right-angle turn south to extend across the south plaza (Figure 5). The trench was then extended across the south roomblock of the south quadrangle and south outside the masonry portion of the village proper, where a burned area with a mass of broken and burned pottery was exposed. In the course of excavating this trench, Guthe and his crew cleared all or part of twelve rooms (Table 3). University of New Mexico crews excavated room 30, a back room in the north roomblock of the south quadrangle, in 1980. In that season, an exploratory trench south of the south roomblock of the south quadrangle uncovered part of an adobe structure underlying the masonry pueblo. That adobe structure was further explored in 1983 and 1984.

Room 30 was selected for excavation for two reasons. First, it formed a pair with room 20 in the middle quadrangle, and excavation revealed that in this part of the site, the two roomblocks were built at the same time (see

above). Second, the south wall of room 30 curved outward, which suggested that the room might have been a "corner kiva" like rooms at Forked Lightning Ruin and Dick's Ruin (Kidder 1958:29–47; see above). The three corner kivas at Forked Lightning and the single corner kiva at Dick's Ruin were surface rooms with floor-level ventilators facing east and both fire and ash pits, one or both of which had copings of adobe or adobe and sandstone blocks (Kidder 1958:35–47). Another clear example of a corner kiva is kiva 14-6 at Arroyo Hondo (Creamer 1993:92–93). This kiva also had a circular, adobe-coped hearth in a line with a basin, deflector, and ventilator, but in this case oriented north-south.

As noted above, the north wall of room 30 is also the south wall of room 20. A sealed doorway and four viga sockets were located in this wall. The bottom of the sealed door was 58 cm above the floor of room 30 but only 20 cm above the floor of room 20, suggesting that the doorway may have been a functional part of room 20 rather than room 30. Portions of the foundation stones for the north and west walls of room 30 were exposed. The foundation elements are set vertically in both cases. The rest of the walls of the room are constructed of limestone blocks laid horizontally in wet mortar with minimal shaping of the flat surfaces that face the room's interior. Wall elements average 33 by 12 cm in the 35 exposed courses. Chinking stones and mud/adobe mortar are extensive. Above the viga sockets, the north wall of room 30 abuts the west wall of the room. Below the viga sockets, the west wall of room 30 abuts the north wall. This change in abutment pattern indicates that the two walls were constructed at the same time, further supporting the conclusion that rooms 20 and 30 were built simultaneously. The only cutting date obtained from a tree-ring specimen submitted from Rowe is from room 30. A cutting date of 1344 came from pinyon that was part of a roof fall layer in room 30.

No floor features were located in room 30. The room was therefore not a "corner kiva" like the Forked Lightning, Dick's Ruin, or Arroyo Hondo cases. On the other hand, the west and south walls of room 30 were built as one continuous, and markedly curved, wall. The east and south walls were bonded in a normal corner. Although the lack of floor features disqualifies room 30 as a "corner kiva," like those described above, excavations in this room yielded some of the more esoteric items recovered by the field school crews. These consisted of small

Table 3. Room Characteristics (rooms excavated in 1917 by Guthe)

Room	Dimensions (m) North-south	Dimensions (m) East-west	Floor area (m²)	Maximum wall height (m)	Maximum wall thickness (cm)	Number of prepared floors	Floor features	Subfloor	Doorways	Year excavated
W1						2?			west wall	1978
I	2.87	2.03	5.826	1.16	22	none	none	sterile below wall base, NW corner	?	had been vandalized
II	2.43	2.59	6.29	1.22	?	1 stone	burned area, hearth	fill	east wall ? north wall	
III	3.65	2.84	10.36	1.72	?	indefinite	circular charcoal pocket	sterile under wall	south wall	
IV	2.89	1.93	5.77	1.31	?	1	none	fill for 12 cm, then sterile	none	
V	3.73	unknown	unknown	unknown	?	?	?	?	?	not completely dug
VI	2.64	1.57	4.14	unknown	?	?	?	?	?	not completely dug
VII	2.74	2.49	6.82	1.21	?	1	2	fill	none	
VIII	1.98	1.82	3.60	2.36	?	1?	none	ash in NE corner, then sterile	east wall	
IX	ca. 1.82	ca. 2.89	5.25	2.36	?	>1?	none	fill	none	
X	2.64	2.38	6.28	unknown	24.5	1?	none	fill	none	
XI	2.41	3.55	8.55	1.21	?	1?	none	fill, wall stub	south wall	
XII	1.82	3.32	6.04	1.44?	?	1?	none	fill, wall stub	none	

pieces of sheet selenite, five small clay balls, and a fragment of *Olivella* shell. All were found in fill above the floor level. The floor level of room 30 yielded a partial stone ax, a possible lightning stone, a small projectile point, a shaped stone slab, and dispersed ceramics, lithic artifacts, and faunal remains. These items suggest that room 30 was "ceremonially closed" in a fashion consistent with other instances of kivas being taken out of use (Walker 1995). It is possible that room 30 had kiva features at one time and was subsequently remodeled into a living room, as was corner kiva 5 at Forked Lightning (Kidder 1958:37). The subfloor test in room 30 indicates that the room had been constructed on fill. However, the bases for the room walls were exposed in the subfloor tests, and there was no indication of a previous floor associated with the walls.

The rooms excavated in 1917 by Guthe are shown on Figure 5. Table 3 converts the dimensions of these rooms given in Guthe's notes to the metric system. Guthe's notes (Part II of this volume) should be consulted for more detail. His meticulous records are invaluable to the task of unraveling the complex architectural history of Rowe Ruin. Rather than reiterate the information on the map and in Table 3, the following comments focus on a few architectural details Guthe recorded that were not observed in later work at the site.

As mentioned above, Guthe did not find formal circular firepits or hearths, which are commonly located near the center of ancient pueblo rooms. Rather, at Rowe, Guthe noted "pockets" of ash or charcoal in some room corners and interpreted them as fireplace locations (e.g., in rooms II, III, and VII). Also, in room VII Guthe located the "elaborate formation" rather than a floor. About 39 cm above the base of the walls was a layer of small stones laid together in material that resembled lime. Above this was a fine layer of yellow earth that appeared to be decayed wood. In 1984, similar "formations" of small stones, decayed wood, and caliche or decayed lime were found south of the south quadrangle in association with burials (but not in a room context). In 1980, in the floor along the south wall of room 30, a line of squared wall stones was exposed. The stones, both local limestone and green schist, extended 3 cm above the floor but were not set into material resembling either decayed limestone or caliche.

In rooms excavated by the field school crews, walls did not evidence any plaster. Guthe noted some wall plaster in room X, and possibly in room XI. Both rooms are in the southern roomblock of the south quadrangle, an area not excavated by later workers. Guthe, like others working at Rowe, found most room floors unexceptional or very poorly defined. In room II, by contrast, he located a floor made of "wall stones" laid flat. Despite careful examination, no clay floor was found above the stones, so this floor had a rather irregular surface.

Guthe excavated human skeletons from several rooms: skeleton 1 from room I; skeleton 2 from room III; skeletons 4, 5, and 6, from room VI; skeletons 7 and 10 from room VIII; skeleton 11 from room IX; and skeletons 16 and 17 from room 10. The field school crews excavated several burials, but none from room contexts.

Guthe noted a layer of charcoal and ash that extended through several rooms. First encountered in the northwest corner of room I, the deposit was also found in rooms III, IV, VI, and VII, where it occurred at or near the base of walls. No similar deposit was located by later crews working in other parts of the ruin.

Guthe (1917) also describes an unusual feature in his notes on room VII. He comments that in the northwest corner of room VII, there was

a flat slab, about 14 × 10 in. and about one in. thick. It was not smoothed on the upper side. Several of these stones have been found in the corner of the digging. They remind me of the flat stones the Zunis cook tortillas on, except they are not smoothed or polished.

If these were not "piki" stones, as Guthe suggests, they may have been similar to the "flagstones" field school crews excavated in 1980 that constituted a floor excavated south of the south quadrangle. Finally, Guthe's notes indicate a three-component building scheme for Rowe that is considered in detail below as part of the architectural reconstruction.

Guthe extended his trench south of the southern roomblock of the south quadrangle. In an area about 3.5 ft (1.067 m) south of the south quadrangle wall, extending over an area that was 50 inches (1.27 m) north-south by 45 inches (1.14 m) east-west and 26 inches (66 cm) thick was a "zone" consisting of "lumps of earth, ashes, charcoal and much pottery" (Guthe's notes for October 5, 1917). The zone was apparently not associated with architectural features.

In 1980, the field school crew extended a trench south of the area of Guthe's trench to explore this area for extramural activity surfaces. Students working in T303

(Figure 6), a 2 by 2 m test, encountered a "flagstone" floor enclosed by a low adobe wall set on a masonry footing on the south and east sides in the northern two-thirds of the test unit at a depth of 60–63 cm below the ground surface. Immediately below the flagstone level a hard adobe floor was located, and the masonry footings ended just below this floor. The adobe floor rested on a midden deposit that was about 50 cm thick. Beneath the midden, sterile clay was encountered. A test outside the south wall was begun and an adobe floor was again encountered, indicating that the room partially defined in T303 was at one time part of a roomblock and not an isolated extramural structure.

Rooms south of the southern wall of the south quadrangle had not been encountered by Guthe, nor had he recorded adobe walls on masonry footings. In order to explore this structure further, extramural excavations south of the south quadrangle were again pursued in 1983 and 1984. In addition, in 1984 a series of backhoe trenches was excavated in extramural areas around the perimeter of the main quadrangles. The backhoe testing program is discussed in detail below. Test units, including the backhoe trenches, are shown on Figure 6. Three hand-excavated 2 by 2 m test units (T305, T306, and T307) confirm the 1980 evidence of an early adobe structure; an outside work area or surface, possibly covered by a ramada; burning of these features; remodeling; and trash deposition. Of particular interest is the sequence of features in T307. These include a trash pit below an adobe-walled room. The room itself appears to have been remodeled once and eventually to have burned. The room area was then again filled with trash, probably at the time that the masonry south roomblock of the south quadrangle was built. A single radiocarbon date of 1170 ± 70 (Beta-18799) was obtained from a sample of wood charcoal from the trash pit that had been sealed below the adobe-walled room. The date is undoubtedly older than the event of trash deposition; at the least it reflects some unknown number of years that the tree lived before it became the charcoal deposited in the pit. Nevertheless, the date is, appropriately, one of the earlier dates from Rowe.

The south quadrangle at Rowe has been more extensively excavated and examined than either of the other two quadrangles. The exposed stratigraphy is also more complicated than that in other parts of the site. Compared with the other quadrangles at Rowe, the south quadrangle covers the smallest amount of ground and

has the smallest plaza area. The height of the rubble mound, however, is slightly greater (20 cm higher) than that of the middle quadrangle and more than a meter higher than that of the north quadrangle. Again, although there is evidence of second-story rooms in this quadrangle, the height of the rubble mound seems to reflect architectural modifications and rebuilding.

On the basis of his excavations, Guthe discerned three building phases in the south quadrangle at Rowe Ruin, defined in the north block of rooms. Guthe very clearly states that in the area of his rooms X, XI and XII, in the south roomblock of the south quadrangle, however, there was evidence of only two building phases. All three of Guthe's construction phases were of masonry. They could be delineated stratigraphically and by changes in the adobe mortar used in walls. Evidence from the 1980–1984 excavations does not contradict Guthe's observations. The work in the 1980s demonstrates the existence of an additional, probably earlier, construction at Rowe that consisted of at least two or more rooms with adobe walls, resting on stone foundations, outside and south of the southern roomblock of the south quadrangle.

The full extent of the underlying adobe structure could not be determined in excavations contiguous to the excavated floors and adobe walls. To do so would have required excavating and removing a substantial portion of the south roomblock of the southern quadrangle. A broad horizontal exposure of the "contact" zone between the southernmost masonry roomblock and any underlying structures would apparently be necessary to determine the extent of the adobe structure and provide more information on the temporal relationships between the adobe and masonry buildings. In the absence of that kind of massive excavation and earth-moving program, a testing program involving placing backhoe trenches in extramural areas was carried out in 1984. The results of the backhoe testing are described below.

Magnetometer Survey and Backhoe Tests

In 1983, Fred Plog, assisted by university field school students, conducted a proton magnetometer survey of Rowe Ruin (in Cordell et al. 1983). The rationale for the survey was twofold. First, with respect to Rowe specifically, we wished to outline the spatial extent of the underlying adobe pueblo. The second consideration was that most excavations conducted at pueblo sites in the Southwest focus on roomblocks, plazas, and midden deposits rather than exploring extramural areas for additional, possibly isolated structures, work areas, and other features. This bias in data recovery has affected our understanding of large, late pre-contact aggregated sites. As an excavation strategy, it could prevent us from understanding overall community patterns, the histories of specific aggregated communities, and the use of space including locations of tool manufacture and other activities in aggregated settlements. Especially when questions are directed toward understanding the aggregation of previously dispersed households into communities of contiguous dwellings, important data on the configuration of settlements preceding the compact pueblo may be neglected. Plog wanted to evaluate the usefulness of the proton magnetometer in locating subsurface features in areas not usually excavated at large sites.

Proton magnetometers measure the strength of the earth's magnetic field. Certain kinds of anomalous measurements suggest subsurface features, such as hearths, pits, or buried rooms. The magnetometer survey, then, provides a nondestructive method of detecting subsurface features (Weymouth 1981).

Plog's 1983 survey covered approximately 6,000 m² of land at Rowe that was not covered by roomblocks. The magnetometer survey revealed more than 24 dipole anomalies that typically suggest underlying cultural features (Weymouth 1981; Cordell et al. 1983:7). The recognized dipole anomalies were simply hypotheses about underlying features. The 1984 backhoe testing program was designed to explore most of the anomalies mapped the previous year. Careful use of a backhoe (rather than hand excavation) was considered appropriate because features in the extramural areas surveyed were expected to be one to two meters below postoccupational deposition (Cordell et al. 1983:7).

At the beginning of the 1984 season, Plog with student assistants re-surveyed portions of the site with the magnetometer to confirm the locations of dipole anomalies mapped the preceding year. Initially, locations for 25 trenches were selected. Not all of them were excavated. Backhoe trenches were not excavated in plaza areas in deference to the landowner's request not to move heavy equipment over known roomblocks. A particularly strong anomaly in the middle of the south quadrangle plaza was explored by excavating the equivalent of a backhoe trench by hand. This unit is labeled backhoe trench 15 (Figure 6). Eventually, 17 backhoe trenches were excavated.

The dipole anomalies do not provide information about their position with respect to the cardinal directions. Therefore eight of the backhoe trenches were positioned running north-south and nine were positioned east-west. Trenches were either 10 m or 20 m long. University staff operated the backhoe, stopping the equipment when resistance was encountered. During trenching, two students served as spotters, alerting the machine operator if cultural features were observed either in the cut being made or in the dirt being removed. The walls of all backhoe trenches were cleaned by hand and profiles were mapped and drawn. Features observed in the backhoe trench walls were excavated by hand. Whether or not features were observed, 150 shovels full of backdirt from each backhoe trench was screened. All backhoe trenches and associated excavation units are shown on Figure 6.

Some anomalies apparently reflect the presence of small storage, trash, or borrow pits. They may also reflect various natural contact layers, such as between clay and sandy soil, sandy soil and bedrock, or between cultural midden and clay or sandy substrate. Table 4 lists each backhoe trench and associated features, and Table 5 provides numbers and percentages of decorated ceramics recovered in the screened backdirt.

The two strongest dipole anomalies were associated with backhoe trenches 2 and 15. Backhoe trench 2 encountered a masonry wall, a compact clay floor, two hearths and ash areas, a possible sipapu, and two loom holes at a depth of 1.70 m below ground surface. In addition, several burials and miscellaneous human bones were exposed in backhoe trench 2.

A tree-ring date of 1305vv was acquired from pinyon in the masonry wall located in backhoe trench 2. One archaeomagnetic date was obtained from each hearth. Hearth 1 yielded dates of AD 1000 to 1015 or 1325 to post-1425 (Archaeomagnetic Laboratory, Colorado State University, LA 108-1; Eighmy 1984). Hearth 2 produced an archaeomagnetic date of AD 1000–1020 or 1225–1425 (Archaeomagnetic Laboratory, Colorado State University, LA 108-2, Eighmy 1984).

Unfortunately, nowhere in the trench did the clay floor articulate with the masonry wall. Given that the burials were considerably above the level of the floor features and were also obviously intentional burials,

Table 4. Backhoe Trench Data

Trench No.	Orientation	Coordinates	Length (m)	Profile layers	Subsurface features	Depth of sterile contact (cm)
1	east-west	W9.20 N50.55 W29.55 N48.28	20	A: topsoil B: dark brown-hard C: hard clay	trash pit, 2 rock alignments, 1(?) adobe surface	76–140
2	north-south	W19.44 N18.90 W19.42 N42.12	20	A: topsoil B: ashy fill C: tan clay/caliche D: sterile clay	2 trash pits, 6 burial pits (7 individuals), pitstructure/kiva, rock alignment, ash lens, 2 hearths, ash dump, ash pit	130–180
3	east-west	W9.19 N9.71 W29.98 N8.00	20	A: topsoil B: brown-crumbly C: brown-compact D: clay/white inclusions E: hard clay	2 ash lenses, 2 ash fill depressions, trash-filled area	45–165
4	north-south	W19.55 S21.29 W19.22 N1.85	20	A: topsoil B: brown-compact C: Ash fill D: orange clay	2 ash lenses, burial pit, 2 trash pits	50–125
5	east-west	W14.37 S30.20 W32.68 S31.26	20	A: topsoil B: sandy clay C: ashy fill D: hard clay	ash lens	50–120
6	north-south	W19.67 S58.73 W20.00 S37.29	20	A: dark-soft-dry B: orange-hard		?
7	east-west	W10.51 S51.01	20	A: topsoil B: brown fill C: ashy fill D: sandy clay E: clay/caliche F: hard-buff clay	5 ash lenses, 5 daub fragments, trash pit, burial	62–130
12	north-south	W19.70 N50.59 W20.04 N57.63	10	A: topsoil B: sterile	2 ash lenses, ash-filled pit, charcoal deposit	48–90
13	east-west	W11.26 S57.65 W19.36 S56.81	10	A: topsoil B: brown-crumbly C: hard clay		120–140

Table 4. (Continued)

Trench No.	Orientation	Coordinates	Length (m)	Profile layers	Subsurface features	Depth of sterile contact (cm)
15	north-south	E8.29 S10.17 E7.90 S17.16	10	A: topsoil B: caliche C: red clay D: charcoal and daub fill E: sterile	trash pit, 2 ash lenses, rock wall; 2 compact surfaces (floor?), burial pit, rooffall, 2 rock alignments	175–210
19	north-south	E2.44 N94.39 E3.13 N114.35	20	A: dark brown topsoil B: soft, brown, crumbly C: clay/caliche		40–80
20	east-west	E13.02 N105.26 E30.64 N104.44	20	A: brown, loose topsoil B: compact brown C: sterile red clay		50–70
23	north-south	W18.36 N59.01 W18.14 N79.21	20	A: topsoil B: red-brown C: hard orange clay D: loose gravel	2 ash lenses, 1(?) pit (ash fill)	50–80
24	east-west	W15.50 N103.11 W5.43 N102.85	10			?
X	north-south	E57.27 N62.90 E51.21 N44.80	20	A: sandy B: dark fill C: orange hard pack	3 charcoal pockets; charcoal lens, 4 ash lenses	20–130
Y	east-west	E58.67 N75.15 E71.87 N74.20	10	A: brown-crumbly B: clay/caliche C: orange clay		54–80
Z	north-south	E60.87 N100.19 E58.82 N80.86	20	A: brown-crumbly B: brown clay C: red-orange clay		45–100

Table 5. Decorated Ceramics Recovered from Backhoe Tenches

Trench No.	Total Ceramics Analyzed	Rowe	Wiyo	Galisteo	Abiquiu	St. Johns Black-on red	Santa Fe	Chupadero	Glaze	Hesho-tauthla	Other White Mountain Redware	Pindi	Unidentified
1	29	6	6	5	4	1	-	-	-	-	-	-	7
2	17	-	4	6	1	-	2	-	1	-	-	-	3
3	35	6	4	9	-	2	4	-	-	1	-	-	9
4	95	16	21	13	6	-	18	-	-	-	1	-	20
5	27	2	11	8	-	-	2	-	-	-	-	-	4
6	34	1	11	10	1	-	1	-	1	-	1	-	8
7	25	2	8	7	1	2	1	1	-	-	-	-	5
12	7	-	-	-	-	-	1	-	-	-	-	-	4
13	8	-	2	1	1	-	1	-	-	-	-	-	3
15	310	42	71	66	18	5	24	7	6	1	5	2	63
19	8	-	2	1	-	1	-	-	-	1	-	-	3
20	17	3	3	2	-	-	1	-	-	-	-	-	8
23	6	1	2	3	-	-	-	-	-	-	-	-	-
X	127	30	33	23	5	2	12	1	4	-	6	-	11
Y	12	-	-	1	-	-	1	-	-	-	-	2	8
Z	12	-	-	1	-	-	1	-	-	-	-	2	8

Table 5. (percentages)

Trench No.	Total Ceramics Analyzed	Rowe	Wiyo	Galisteo	Abiquiu	St. Johns Black-on red	Santa Fe	Chupadero	Glaze	Hesho-tauthla	Other White Mountain Redware	Pindi	Unidentified
1	29	20.7	20.7	17.2	13.8	3.4	0	0	0	0	0	0	24.1
2	17	0	23.6	35.3	5.9	0	11.8	0	5.9	0	0	0	17.6
3	35	17.1	11.4	25.7	0	5.7	11.4	0	0	2.9	1.1	0	25.7
4	95	16.8	22.1	13.7	6.3	0	18.9	0	0	0	0	0	21.0
5	27	7.4	40.7	29.6	0	0	7.4	0	0	0	0	0	14.8
6	34	2.9	32.4	29.4	2.9	0	2.9	0	2.9	0	2.9	0	23.5
7	25	8.0	32.0	28.0	4.0	0	4.0	4.0	0	0	0	0	25.0
12	7	0	0	0	0	28.6	14.3	0	0	0	0	0	57.1
13	8	0	25	12.5	12.5	0	12.5	0	0	0	0	0	37.5
15	310	13.5	22.9	21.3	5.8	1.6	7.7	2.3	1.9	0.3	1.1	0.7	20.3
19	8	0	25.0	12.5	0	12.5	0	0	0	12.5	0	0	37.5
20	17	17.6	17.6	11.8	0	0	5.9	0	0	0	0	0	47.1
23	6	16.7	33.3	50.0	0	0	0	0	0	0	0	0	0
X	127	23.6	26.0	18.1	3.9	1.6	9.4	0.8	3.2	0	4.7	0	8.6
Y	12	0	0	8.3	0	0	8.3	0	0	0	0	16.7	66.7
Z	12	0	0	8.3	0	0	8.3	0	0	0	0	16.7	66.7

43

rather than the skeletons of individuals who might have died while the pitstructure was in use or upon its abandonment, it is reasonable to suggest that the earlier dates can be used to date the architectural features. I don't feel comfortable interpreting the dates any more precisely. Although I was skeptical at the time of the excavation, I now think the structure located in backhoe trench 2 was a kiva. In part, my current interpretation depends on the unusual shape of the hearth (see Figure 9) and the possible sipapu and loom holes. Loom holes were encountered in kiva floors at Forked Lightning and Pecos (Kidder 1958). Alternatively, the postholes that are viewed as having been part of the deflectors in some kivas at Arroyo Hondo (Creamer 1993:92–93) are similar to the floor features in trench 2 at Rowe Ruin. In either case the structures serving as models are clearly kivas rather than pithouses. Although the location of the kivalike features in backhoe trench 2 bothered me because they suggest that the kiva would have been spatially peripheral to the visible portion of Rowe Ruin, I recall that the large, circular kiva at Tijeras Pueblo (Cordell 1980) was also early (dating to AD 1313), had been completely obscured by later deposition, and although it was likely a focus of the early dispersed series of roomblocks at Tijeras Pueblo, was outside and unrelated to the later (AD 1370–1390) structures at that site.

The second major dipole anomaly was in the northwest corner of the south plaza, where "backhoe trench" 15, a 1 by 7 m trench, was excavated by hand. Slightly less than 4 m from the northern end of the trench, a curved masonry wall was encountered. The wall appeared to curve north. It extended from 1.5 m below the surface to at least 2.5 m from the surface. A clay floor layer was reached, but the wall continued below this level. The burial of a child (BH15-12.1) was found adjacent to the inner (north) side of the wall. The end of the wall had not been reached when excavation ceased at the end of the season. Because the wall was both curved and deeply buried, the teaching assistant's notes refer to it as the south wall of a kiva. However, because no kiva floor features (firepit, ash pit, deflector, sipapu, loom holes, etc.) were discovered, I do not use this designation. The south plaza is highly disturbed and has complicated stratigraphy. It is the area where Guthe excavated his trench and found evidence of two periods of building and some burning. How the wall we uncovered relates to any of these is not clear.

The magnetometer survey and backhoe tests did yield information about Rowe Ruin that was unexpected. Features were encountered in areas well away from the visible mounds of the site in places where there were no surface indications of buried structures. As Plog described it in 1983, the magnetometer mapping resulted in a series of anomalies that were considered possible locations of cultural remains. In this sense, the magnetometer survey was successful in locating otherwise unsuspected subsurface features. However, the testing program in 1984 was not designed to test the utility of the magnetometer survey. To have done so would have required excavation of an equal number of trenches in locations without dipole anomalies and then comparing the number and types of features located in each set of locations.

The use of the backhoe in this limited "test" was unfortunate. It is true that the subsurface features were located far enough underground that a program of shallow tests would not have revealed many of them. Yet when important features were exposed in the trench walls, there was not enough time to explore their relationships with each other or with other known parts of the site. If we had used the backhoe trenches simply as "locating devices" and then planned and executed several more seasons of large-scale excavation, I think we might have had great success in understanding how Rowe was established, grew, was abandoned, and fell into ruin. One message for other archaeologists is that excavating only in the "usual spaces" of big sites may be very misleading. Another message is that backhoe testing without a great deal of follow-up investment in excavation is terribly destructive and may not help in interpreting a site.

Summary and Conclusions

Rowe Ruin gives the appearance of having been a single, planned community that was occupied for only a short period of time. The appearance is false. Depending on one's perspective, a minimum of three and a maximum of six construction episodes can be defined. I deliberately do not use the terms "occupations" or "phases" in referring to the different building events. It seems to me, based on the skeletal remains and the material culture, that there was essentially only one group of people at Rowe. There is also no evidence that Rowe was occupied for hundreds of years or that it was intermittently occupied and abandoned over long periods of time. Rather, it seems that its configuration changed during the time it was occupied.

Guthe was able to distinguish three building episodes in the northern roomblocks of the south quadrangle. In all three episodes, walls were constructed of masonry. The three building events were differentiated by offset walls and adobe mortar of different colors. Guthe's notes indicate that none of the rooms he excavated had been constructed on culturally sterile ground. He did reach the sterile clay substrate in four locations, at varying depths, under rooms in the northern roomblock. As he worked out to the southern roomblock of the south quadrangle, he noted only two different construction periods. In 1931, long after Guthe's work at Rowe Ruin was complete, Stallings collected tree-ring samples for the Laboratory of Anthropology from "Guthe's trench." A single noncutting date of 1306vv was obtained. In 1980, we obtained one tree-ring date from room 30 in the south quadrangle. The date is 1344r. No other tree-ring and no archaeomagnetic dates came from the south quadrangle. Purely on architectural grounds, it can be argued that the south quadrangle is the oldest at Rowe Ruin, and that the earliest of the three building phases noted by Guthe is the oldest occupation at Rowe.

In the 1980s we discovered the remains of adobe wall stubs underneath and south of the south quadrangle. The stratigraphic sequence south of the southern tier of rooms in the south quadrangle is red clay substrate followed by 10 to 15 cm of trash deposits above the sterile ground; an outside work area of hard-packed clay, perhaps on the same level as a burned ramada; remains of coursed adobe walls on masonry footings and either dark, adobe floors or one adobe floor with a micaceous schist "flagstone" floor just above it; more trash; and finally the walls of the south roomblock itself. Without removing the south roomblock of the masonry pueblo, we could not follow the extent of the underlying adobe structure. I am convinced that we did encounter enough of the adobe structure to add an adobe component, of unknown size and configuration, to Guthe's sequence. Hence, I think there is evidence of four building events in the vicinity of the south quadrangle. On the other hand, it is possible to argue that modification of the adobe structure was accomplished during the occupation history of the two masonry building episodes recognized in the southern roomblock of the south quadrangle and remain with Guthe's estimate of only three building phases.

In the middle and south quadrangles at Rowe, two or three episodes of remodeling can be identified. Two-story rooms in the middle and south quadrangles were built at the same time and are tied together by walls that are alternately bonded and abutted over their height (rooms 20 and 30). Tree-ring dates indicate that the interconnected rooms of these quadrangles were built in the mid-1300s. The tree-ring date of 1344r obtained from room 30 provides a date for both constructions. More accurately, if less precisely, it dates both quadrangles to the middle of the fourteenth century. Both room 20 and room 30 were built on fill—in the case of room 20, more than 40 cm of fill. Although middle quadrangle rooms 21, 22, 23, and 24 clearly represent two periods of building modifications, these episodes cannot be tied to either room 20 or to rooms 112 and 113 by architectural links. Tree-ring dates from room 21 (1319vv; 1323vv, 1326vv, 1344vv, 1346vv, and 1351vv), room 22 (1349vv), and room 23 (1343vv) are quite consistent in placing the construction in the middle of the fourteenth century.

The kiva features identified in backhoe trench 2 cannot be tied architecturally to any of the plaza quadrangles. There seems to be equal merit in placing the kiva within the same construction episodes as the visible structures at Rowe Ruin or in suggesting that it was built somewhat earlier. I have chosen the latter because of the peripheral position of the kiva, to the west of most of the masonry buildings. The formal floor features of the Rowe kiva, including loom holes, are similar to those of early kivas at Pecos (Kidder 1958), and the peripheral location is similar to that of the early component kiva J at Arroyo Hondo Pueblo (Creamer 1993:88–95). As noted, either interpretation is consistent with the two archaeomagnetic dates obtained from hearths in that trench.

The absence of a plaza kiva at Rowe was a puzzle for Guthe and initially was for us. At both pre-contact Paako (Lambert 1954:16) and Pindi (Stubbs and Stallings 1953:31), kivas were rectangular "room kivas," incorporated into roomblocks but distinguished by wall and floor features. Those portions of Tijeras Pueblo (Cordell 1980) that dated to the mid- and the late 1300s also had only square kivas constructed within roomblocks. (The earliest kiva at Tijeras was a very large, circular kiva built in AD 1313.) At Forked Lightning Ruin, two kivas were subsurface circular structures, two were square surface rooms, and three were surface rooms with one curved wall that Kidder (1958:29) called corner kivas. Kidder considered one of the round kivas among the oldest constructions at Forked Lightning Ruin. Both the corner kivas and square kivas were in use during the later occupation of the site. The small glimpse of kivalike floor features in the backhoe trench does not provide enough information to be able to describe the kivas at Rowe Ruin, nor does the relatively small amount of excavation at Rowe Ruin allow us to resolve the building sequence of kiva and roomblock at the site. Nevertheless, I suggest that the kiva in the backhoe trench may have been the earliest kiva at Rowe and that room 30 ended its ceremonial function before Rowe was abandoned. It is entirely possible that additional rooms with kiva features are located among the unexcavated rooms at the site.

The north quadrangle continues to be a puzzle we cannot resolve. It seems to have been constructed as a detached unit. The masonry is qualitatively different than that of the other quadrangles, and the rooms, I believe, are slightly larger. On the basis of material culture it is like the rest of the site, and if the three human skeletons studied by London (1980) were associated with the north quadrangle, as I was led to believe, then the people were physically like the rest of the Rowe population. The archaeomagnetic date obtained from a burned area of clay floor in room 11 (about AD 1395) is consistent with our suspicion that the north quadrangle was contemporary with or slightly later than the rest of Rowe Ruin. The two principal difficulties with having much confidence in this interpretation are that the modern

pipeline and road through this part of the site created a magnetic anomaly that would have had an undefined impact on the magnetic readings, and second, the road through this part of the site did far more damage than is readily apparent. The damage, along with the limited extent of our excavations, does not permit interpretation of the way in which the north quadrangle was constructed in relation to other architectural components of the site.

With regard to the number of building episodes at Rowe, there would seem to be two general interpretations, and any number of possibilities between them. At one extreme, it is possible to agree with Guthe's observation of three periods of building, folding all the other architectural evidence into one or all of them. At the other end of the spectrum, the underlying adobe structure, the kiva exposed in backhoe trench 2, and the entire north quadrangle can be viewed as additional separate constructions. This would bring the total number of building episodes to six. Our excavations do not preclude any of these possibilities. Far more work at Rowe would certainly clarify the picture. Nevertheless, it seems to me that two useful and enduring observations can be made. First, as all have noted, it seems that no matter how complicated the sequence, it is likely that Rowe was occupied for about a century—perhaps 150 years—rather than 300 or 400 years. Second, the surface configuration of the site—with its three organized plaza areas—hides a great deal of architectural building, rebuilding, and remodeling, which suggests a more complicated and longer-term development of the final community plan. I suggest that all of this redoing of the basic structure was an in situ occurrence and not suggested by or an accommodation to immigrant groups.

MORTUARY DATA
AND HUMAN REMAINS FROM ROWE

Although the number of human burials excavated at Rowe Ruin is fairly small (34 individuals and fragments of an additional 19 skeletons) relative to the 1,938 Pecos Pueblo burials (Kidder 1958:281), the burials do show continuity between the two sites. Both cases exhibit little sexual dimorphism. Skulls and postcranial skeletal elements, except for pelvic girdles, are masculine in appearance, making sexual determination difficult. In both cases, long bones have robust muscle attachment sites, indicating that individuals of both sexes performed strenuous labor (Hooten 1930; London 1980). Although there is more variability among the Pecos burials than among those of Rowe, the grave types and mortuary treatments encountered at Rowe are also found among the Pecos burials (Kidder 1958:280–304).

Hooten (1930:74) noted that for the whole Pecos series, the cranial measurements in the earlier burials, those from Black-on-white and Glaze I times, show larger deviations from the mean. By Glaze V and Biscuit times, there is more homogeneity. Unfortunately, Hooten never studied the burials from Forked Lightning (Kidder 1958:283) or Rowe Ruin. Since these sites are predominantly earlier than Pecos Pueblo, it would be interesting to know whether or not the physical characteristics of these potential Pecos ancestors were very different from each other.

In 1980 we attempted to locate the 17 burials Guthe had excavated at Rowe to pursue the question of similarities among ancestral groups and to study a suggested Towa link between Jemez and Rowe based on Mackey's (1977:477–482) research at Jemez. According to London (1980), neither the Peabody Museum, the Museum of New Mexico, nor the University of New Mexico had the 17 Rowe skeletons, and they were considered lost. In March 1918, Guthe traveled to Pecos to pack, crate, and ship (to Boston) the skeletons stored in the expedition house because he had received word that the fieldhouse had been broken into. The house had indeed been vandalized, but most of the skeletal remains had not been disturbed. Guthe lists 17 specimens from Rowe, six from Loma Lothrop, and one from "Bandelier Bend" [Forked Lightning] among the 626 skeletons and groups of bones that were packed in thirteen crates. Eventually, on May 8, 1918, the skeleton boxes were uncrated and transferred to the Metropolitan Storage Warehouse in Cambridge, Massachusetts. Guthe (1918) concludes his report: "The skeletons are now all safely stored in a fireproof room, number 472 in the Metropolitan Warehouse in Dr. Peabody's name." It seems reasonable to believe they were at some time transferred to Harvard or the Peabody Foundation in Andover. In any case, we were unable to locate the remains in 1980.

In the following discussion, I summarize the minimal information I could put together from Guthe's notes, his brief paper (Guthe 1917) and photographs, Kidder's (1958) monograph, and more detailed osteological study by London (1980) and Curran (1985), supplemented by notes from field school teaching assistants and students. Guthe's notes, normally meticulous and detailed, contain very little information about the burials. This leads me to think that he kept a separate file of information on the human remains, as did Kidder (1958) at Pecos.

Guthe's skeleton 1 consisted of bone fragments, probably of an adult found in the northwest corner of room I. The fragments were found 6 ft 6 inches (1.98 m) from the surface, near the floor, but did not represent a complete individual, nor were they found in a grave.

Skeleton 2 was located in room II or III. All bones found in these rooms were so badly decayed that it was not possible to determine their position or age. In only one case (skeleton 2) could any data be obtained. The skull indicated a child, aged 6 to 8 years. [Photograph

502 in the archives at the Laboratory of Anthropology, Museum of New Mexico, is labeled skeleton 2, room IX. This is clearly an adult and not the skeleton indicated here.]

Skeletons 3, 4, and 5 were found in room VII and date to that occupation, which is more recent than that of rooms V and VI. Skeleton 3 is listed as a child aged 2 to 3. Skeleton 4 is listed as of indeterminate sex but aged 14 to 18 and buried with a black [culinary ware] bowl. Skeleton 5, also associated with a black [culinary ware] bowl, is listed as an adult male.

Skeleton 6 is listed as a 4- to 6-year-old child, and this burial was accompanied by a black-on-white pot sherd. There is no additional information.

Skeleton 7 was located in room VIII and according to Guthe's notes was well-preserved, dating to the later period. This individual was male, aged 25 years, associated with black-on-white pottery fragments and found with an arrow point lodged in the body of a cervical vertebra. The point and vertebra are illustrated in Kidder (1932:21, Fig. 5). A scattering of small stones was observed, but not at a single level. Skeletons 8 and 9 are described simply as two children's skeletons, aged 4 to 6 years, removed from the excavation trench.

The skull of Guthe's skeleton 10 was found "almost under the feet" of skeleton 7 (Guthe's notes). This is the "skeleton 2" of the notes with Guthe's photographs in the Laboratory of Anthropology archive. It was the second skeleton found in room VIII. The age is given as 16 to 20 years; sex is not indicated. Skeleton 10 was in an irregular layer of decayed wood, more small stones, two bone awls, one "stray" arrow point, and many pottery fragments. A large, broken, black-on-white bowl had been inverted over the shoulder blades of skeleton 10, and another bowl, intact, had been laid over the man's left arm. A third black-on-white bowl was found in sherds scattered over the skeleton. The decayed wood is described in two forms: as "sawdust" [quotation marks in original] and in its natural form. In the "sawdust" were thin slabs of stones, including a broken mano. A human calcaneus was found under the lowest slab. Although I do not know what the "sawdust" was, Kidder (1958) mentions bark, rushes, matting, cedar branches, and wood found with burials at Pecos. He also noted a few cases of burials found with slabs, which were apparently used to maintain the cadaver in unusual positions (Kidder 1958:286). At Pecos there is only one case of

small stones lining the sides of a grave (Kidder 1958:291), but we found small stones above two burials at Rowe (see below). We also recovered matting from an infant burial in the south plaza (backhoe trench 15, below), and burials beneath stone slabs in backhoe trench 2 (see below).

Additional information on the two skeletons in room VIII was included in Guthe's (1917:5) report:

> Two were at length on their faces. These two were both found in the same room, close against the north wall, which extended six feet above them to the surface. One was directly above the other; the head of the upper one being towards the west, and that of the lower to the east. In the east wall of this room was a door which had been sealed from the outside. This seems to indicate that the individuals were buried in the room, and the door sealed.

Skeleton 11 is listed as a female aged 40 to 50 years, buried with two black-on-white bowls. Guthe notes that the imprint of a blanket was found under the skeleton, but since none of the fabric remained it was impossible to determine the weave. Hair was preserved on the skull.

Skeleton 12, a woman 35 to 40 years of age, was found only a few inches below the surface, along the north side of the north wall of room VIII. Guthe notes that it was flexed, "indicating it was an old burial," but that no pottery was with it. Kidder (1958:285) wrote that "practically all pre-Spanish interments were flexed [at Pecos], the exceptions being a few at length, mostly small infants, also four adults." Since Pecos was also inhabited during the Mission period and "at length" burials were the European norm, Kidder was careful in his conclusion that the few pre-European extended burials were correctly placed in the Pecos chronology. The two extended burials at Rowe support Kidder's conclusion.

Skeleton 13 is listed as a child, aged 4 to 6 years. It was discovered in the trench, and nothing more is said about it.

Skeletons 14 and 15 were also located in the trench, west of room IX, and were photographed in situ. Skeleton 14 is listed as an adult of 25 to 30 years; sex was not determined. Skeleton 15 is listed as a child of 4 to 6 years. Skeleton 14 was found on top of the middle period wall, below the ash layer at the west wall of room IX. The remains of a blanket were noted underneath the burial. Skeleton 15 was in excellent condition, having (according to Guthe's notes) the first unbroken skull found.

Skeleton 16 is of a child, aged 3 to 4 years. No additional information is provided. Skeleton 17 is listed as 40 to 50 years of age. No determination of sex is given. A black-on-white bowl is listed as mortuary furniture for this burial.

In his summary, Guthe (1917) noted that all the skeletons had been found either in rooms or at the foot of walls, and that they were in uniformly poor condition. Only one person's head was oriented to the south. The rest were oriented north, east, or west. At Pecos and at Forked Lightning, Kidder (1958:285–288) found no consistent orientation. According to Guthe (1917), eight of the 17 Rowe skeletons were flexed. This was also the most common position at Pecos. As at Pecos, there was no pattern with respect to which side, left or right, the flexed skeleton rested on. Four skeletons at Rowe had their legs flexed, although the torsos and heads were on their back. Finally, there were two extended burials from room VIII.

In 1980, I brought three skeletons from Rowe Ruin to the Osteology Laboratory at the University of New Mexico. They had been excavated some time before by persons unknown and had been held by Walter Wait. No information was available on them except that they had been recovered from the site. The skeletons were accepted by Marilyn London, cleaned, inventoried, and analyzed by Lee Benshoof, and further examined by Ms. London, who then prepared a brief report. The information in that report is summarized here. In order to provide unique numbers, I assign a year date as a prefix to the burial numbers. The skeletons were not accessioned into the University collection but were returned to the Sandovals for reburial.

Skeleton 1980-1 is incomplete. Long-bone maturation and tooth eruption indicated an age at death of 13 to 15 years. Despite the absence of pelvic bones, certain characteristics of the skull indicate that the skeleton is female. Perforation of the frontal sinus of the cranium appear to be the result of an infection, as does enlargement of the shaft of the right tibia by extra bone laid down on the anterior side.

Skeleton 1980-2 consists of an adult female of advanced age (> 50 years) based on analysis of the pubic symphysis. Based on measurement of the left femur, the individual was 147 cm in stature. The cranium shows a number of masculine features with some female traits.

Sex determination was made on the basis of the pelvis. Pathologies noted include a healed depression in the occiput, healed fractures of the nasal bones, evidence of trauma on the right side of the fourth and fifth cervical vertebrae, and exostosis on the head of the right fibula. Osteoarthritis of the thumb and the vertebral column, especially in the thoracic region, is marked but probably not unusual given the advanced age of the individual. As expected, tooth loss and apical abscesses on the maxillae were noted. A defect in fusion of the corpus sterni resulted in a perforation of the bone. Abnormal thickening of the occipital, parietals, and frontal bones suggest a nutritional deficiency or anemia. Along with this skeleton were a number of animal bones and the left innominate of an adult male.

Skeleton 1980-3 consists of a nearly complete female skeleton with several miscellaneous animal bones and a distal right femur of a human male. Sex determination was based on the pelvic bones because features of the skull again appear quite masculine. Cranial suture closure and the pubic symphysis indicate an age at death of 40 to 45 years. Osteoarthritis is present on the vertebral column, in the pelvic girdle, and on the long bone extremities. A bony growth anterior to the left occipital condyle articulates with the first cervical vertebra, creating a pseudorthosis that severely limited movement of the individual's neck. Cradleboard flattening occurs in the lambda area on the occipital and both parietals. The long bones exhibit "greater than usual rugosity," but since they can be articulated with the axial skeleton, they are from the same individual. Measurement of the right femur provided an estimated stature of 160 cm.

As London noted in her report, the two older female skeletons raise questions about the division of labor in the society. The rugosity of muscle attachments on the long bones indicates unusually strenuous labor relative to some other ancient Puebloan skeletons, but not necessarily those of Pecos Pueblo.

In 1984, human skeletal remains were encountered in two contexts, regular excavation units and backhoe trenches. The complete inventory of 31 individuals consists of 12 burials and 19 additional individuals represented by miscellaneous bone fragments. All human remains were brought to the Osteological Laboratory at the University of New Mexico. They were cleaned and analyzed by Brian Curran, whose report was completed in April 1985, at which time remains that had not al-

Table 6. Fragmentary and Unassociated Human Remains Recovered from the Backhoe Trenches

Provenience	Number of bones	Elements
T305-I1-4A	1	metacarpal
T305-I2-4A	1	rib fragment
T117-2A		75 unknown, 1 cranial, 1 vertebral
BH2-W1-NA	6	left tibia, left metatarsal, 4 molar tooth buds
BH2-W1-NA	1	proximal tibia
BH2-W2-NA	>2	mandible, maxilla and teeth
BH2-W2-NA	>3	cranial fragments, teeth, rib
BH2-W2-NA	>1	cranial fragments
BH2-W2-NA	2	innominate, femur
BH2-W2-NA	1	humerus
BH2-W2-H1-NA	18	ribs, cervical vertebrae, maxilla

ready been returned were sent to the Sandovals for reburial. The burials are described here. Miscellaneous bones are listed in Table 6. As previously discussed, the highly fragmentary nature of the burials recorded was, in part, the result of an administrative decision rather than a reflection of the condition of the burials themselves. However, in general, as at Pecos, human bone was not particularly well preserved. In 1984, we conducted backhoe trenching in various parts of the site.

Two burials were excavated in T305, south of the southern roomblock of the south quadrangle. Both were located under a loose alignment of small stones that was in turn under a layer of adobe melt. The first burial was the torso of an child, aged 3 to 6 years. No skull or limb bones were found. The innominates were found southwest of the ribs and vertebrae. Sex was not determined. Incomplete fusion of the halves of the sacral neural arches of the vertebrae are consistent with spina bifida occulta (Curran 1985). The second burial, an adult female, 30 to 35 years of age, had been placed in an oval pit along with a bone awl, a piece of turtle carapace, and a mano fragment. The skeleton was tightly flexed, lying on the right side, with the head to the south and facing east. Estimated stature is 152–153 cm. In addition to degenerative pathologies associated with age, the individual had two fractured and healed ribs. A severe neck injury had resulted in fusion of the third to fifth cervical vertebrae. The cranium displayed several destructive lesions consistent with treponemal infection (Curran 1985).

Three of the burials were found in a single pit in the east wall of trench 2. One of these skeletons is a youth of 10 to 15 years and indeterminate sex; one is an infant of 9 to 18 months; and one is an adult, probably female (Curran 1985). Kidder (1958:290) notes "one certain and one probable" instance of double burials. Because the single instance of three burials in a single pit at Rowe was found in the backhoe trench wall, I am not confident that all three were actually from the same pit. Stratigraphically below the three skeletons and under several large stone slabs was a burial of a 6- to 8-year-old girl.

Also located in backhoe trench 2 was a woman older than 50 years at the time of death and a child of indeterminate sex aged 5 to 7 years. The adult was flexed, lying on her back with her head oriented north. In addition to signs of age, such as arthritic development in the right patella, phalanges of hands and feet, and the vertebra, she also had an unusually thick cranial vault, measuring up to 11 mm in thickness. Curran (1985) suggests that it represents the upper range of normal variation rather than a pathology.

An adult male and an infant were also removed from immediately in front of the west wall of backhoe trench 2. The adult male is represented only by cranial elements. The estimated age at death is over 40, based on tooth wear and arthritic development. As with other Rowe skeletons, the cranial elements were unusually thick, 10.5 mm in some locations. The infant's age at death appears to have been 2 to 3 years. The infant's bones showed no pathologies.

Finally, in backhoe trench 2, two burials, one a boy aged 9 to 10 years and one a possible girl aged 5 to 7 years, were located within a layer of rock and rubble that may have been wall fall associated with the structure found in trench 2. The structure was most likely a kiva (see discussion of architecture in the previous section), but since the burials were within the wall fall they may have been interred after the kiva was no longer used.

Backhoe trench 15 was a hand-excavated trench in the south plaza. The skeleton of an infant, possibly female, aged 0.5 to 1.0 years (Curran 1985), was found beyond an area of rock fall in the northern quarter of the trench. The right and left temporal bones, the occipital, and to a lesser degree the parietals and frontal bone show lesions characteristic of porotic hyperotosis. This condition is often interpreted as a result of severe anemia (Curran 1985). The burial was on its left side with its head facing south. It had a shell necklace around the head and what appeared to be disintegrated mat wrapped around the body. This burial was 22 cm above the floor of the structure that was located in backhoe trench 15.

A fragmentary though fairly well preserved burial was removed from a 1 by 1 m extension of trench 3, excavated into an apparent large pit. The skeleton appears to be a male of 17 to 19 years at time of death (Curran 1985). Fragmentary cranial remains of a man who was more than 30 years of age (Curran 1985) were excavated from trench 4. Male characteristics include large mastoid processes, well-developed brow ridges, rugged nuchal area, and general rugosity.

Although we were unable to date any of the human remains, there appears to have been no consistent orientation of graves or skeletons during different time periods. The same was true at both Pecos and Forked Lightning. Most burials were flexed and buried in simple oval pits, as at Pecos. Guthe's excavations also uncovered burials in rooms or next to walls, and a few extended burials. As at Forked Lightning and Pecos, mortuary furniture was extremely sparse, and as at Pecos, the small amount of shell "jewelry" was associated with infants. Matting, a turtle carapace, and utilitarian objects such as a mano were interred with burials. Unlike at Pecos, where arrow points were second only to pottery as burial furniture, the single point found in a burial context at Rowe is the one recovered by Guthe in the cervical vertebra of his skeleton 7 from room VIII. Finally, the skeletons from Rowe and Pecos are similar to one another (and unusual in terms of some other populations) with respect to the rugosity of muscle attachments and the masculine characteristics of skulls of both sexes. In comparison to those southwestern Puebloan burial populations that are geographically proximal, such as Tijeras Pueblo (Ferguson 1979) and Arroyo Hondo (Palkovitch 1980), the Upper Pecos Valley people seem to represent a very robust, possibly genetically distinct group.

DATING ROWE RUIN

THE CENTRAL FOCUS OF OUR FIELD WORK IN 1983 AND 1984 was to begin to evaluate a model of relationships among population aggregation into large settlements in the Southwest, increased regional variation in rainfall, and the development of regional systems of exchange. This interest has very specific historical components as well as general, processual aspects. For example, while there may be general patterning among horticulturists on a worldwide basis that allows specification of conditions under which aggregated populations are advantageous (e.g., defense, centrality with respect to diverse field systems), the argument with respect to ancient Pueblo archaeology entails climatic uncertainties during certain specific calendrical time periods, documented by dendroclimatology, and equally specific times when human population density was such that increased mobility was precluded.

In order to evaluate the model's historical components, it was necessary to obtain precise calendrical dates for Rowe Ruin. Because Rowe appeared to be a dual component site, it was especially important to know when the aggregated component of the site was built and occupied. I hoped that we might be able to date construction of the three plazas as well as the underlying adobe structure(s). I was overly optimistic because of my experience at Tijeras Pueblo (LA 581), which yielded nearly 500 tree-ring dates. In fact, it was very difficult to get any tree-ring dates from Rowe Ruin, and our other sources of dates were also problematic. Although I discuss the various problems we encountered here, I think we can date the occupation of Rowe, as a whole, quite confidently between about AD 1250 and 1400 or 1425.

As I have indicated, we submitted 40 obsidian samples from Rowe Ruin, but since no year-round subsoil temperature record for Rowe was taken and calibrations for the specific obsidian source areas are not yet available, those samples are not useful for dating. The samples have been chemically analyzed so their sources are known, which is useful for documenting exchange or mobility patterns.

We also submitted samples from three locations for archaeomagnetic dating. I do not question the reliability of the process of archaeomagnetic dating in general, nor do I lack confidence in the way the samples were taken or processed. Nevertheless, I have little confidence in the archaeomagnetic dates we obtained for two reasons. First, there are considerable discrepancies between the archaeomagnetic curves used by the Archaeomagnetic Laboratory at Fort Collins and those used by the Museum of New Mexico (Wolfman 1992). We obtained our dates from the Fort Collins Laboratory long before the difference was recognized and resolution sought. Second, the old road bed through the north plaza, and the buried and broken pipeline associated with the road, caused a magnetic anomaly strong enough to distort compass readings made in the process of extracting samples as well as at other times. My concern was such that I discussed these problems with the late Daniel Wolfman about a year before his untimely death in 1994. He was optimistic about the possibility of developing a correction factor for the Rowe Ruin dates if we could get back to the site and re-open the areas from which the samples had been taken. This has not been done, but it is a possibility for the future. The archaeomagnetic dates are listed here but could not become the basis of intrasite dating (Table 7).

In an effort to obtain more accurate dates for the spatially distinct architectural units at Rowe Ruin, we submitted botanical and wood charcoal specimens to Beta Analytic, Inc., for radiocarbon analysis. We had not anticipated using radiocarbon dating, so the samples had been collected as botanical samples or wood charcoal.

Table 7. Archaeomagnetic Dates for Rowe Ruin

Provenience	Year	Feature	Dates (AD)
Room 11	1980	burn on floor	1395 ± 17 (processed for Walter Wait at the University of Kansas laboratory)
BHT2	1984	hearth W2H1	1000–1015 or 1325–1425+
BHT2	1984	hearth W2H2	1000–1020 or 1225–1425

Most had been stored in plastic vials, although others were packaged in aluminum foil. Nine of 12 samples selected for dating were carbonized corncob fragments. We deliberately chose corn because it is an annual plant. The dates obtained should be closer to the time of human occupation than might be the case with wood charcoal subject to the "old wood problem" (Schiffer 1982). Beta Analytic adjusted C13/C12 for the corn samples. The laboratory made a particular effort to clean samples and to run for a longer period of time those samples that contained less than one gram of carbon.

One sample of noncarbonized wood (Beta-18801) from backhoe trench 2 proved to be modern and is not included in the table. Table 8 lists identification numbers, proveniences, and dates of the other 11 samples. Subsequently, calibrated dates were obtained for the nine samples that contained correction data (Table 9). While the range of the mean dates (from AD 898 to 1952) is disappointingly large, the dates are consistent within provenience units, and they provide accurate temporal placement for the site as a whole. The ages of the two samples from T305 are appropriate for their stratigraphic placement (level 2A was above, and therefore likely younger than, 4B). The 2A level was a hard-packed, undulating layer of adobe wash with considerable charcoal above and on it. Below it, a whole ceramic vessel of Rowe Black-on-white was found overturned, on its rim, on a hard-packed clay surface labeled 4B. The corncob fragment yielding the date of AD 1286 was underneath the overturned pot. The clay layer labeled 4B became sterile and excavation was terminated in this unit. In my opinion, the 1286 date should be very close to the earliest occupation at Rowe Ruin.

T306 consisted of two distinct midden deposits separated by a layer of adobe slump. The upper midden most likely is associated with occupation of the south masonry quadrangle. The second midden layer seems to have been related to the underlying adobe structure.

The two radiocarbon dates, AD 1403 and 1041/1150, are again ordered consistently with respect to stratigraphic position. The date of 1041 does seem early to me. The sample from T307 is of wood charcoal from a trash pit excavated into culturally sterile ground. The pit itself had been sealed by adobe melt and masonry footings of adobe walls below an adobe floor that was, in turn, under a layer of ashy fill under a flagstone floor similar to that excavated in 1980. The date of AD 1170 may be early because it is from a wood sample. Nevertheless, it seems relatively close to dates for occupation of the adobe pueblo under the south quadrangle.

T118 was a one by one meter test into midden north of the south end of backhoe trench X. The midden was slightly more than half a meter deep and was excavated in natural levels. Ashy midden materials alternated with thin layers of clay that seem to have been deposited at times when the arroyo flooded. The dates from levels 2G and 2M again are in appropriate stratigraphic order and are reasonably within the early occupation of the site.

The two dates from room 112 are also in their appropriate stratigraphic sequence. Level 3A extended from 3.70 to 4.10 m below datum (bd) and level 2G from 4.94 to 5.14 m bd. As noted above, excavation of rooms 112 and 113 demonstrated that they were part of the central quadrangle. The dates are consistent with this interpretation. The date of AD 898 is surely too early with respect to any known architecture at Rowe Ruin. The date of AD 1286 from wood charcoal, however, is a reasonable date for wood from any but the latest building events.

Beta-18790 was from a 1 by 1 m test above a pit located in the north wall of east-west backhoe trench 3. The trench is situated to the west approximately between the central and southern quadrangles. The date of AD 1286 from a corncob from the pit is consistent with the early use of the site.

Table 8. Radiocarbon Dates from Rowe Ruin

Lab number	Sample type	Provenience	C14 years (BP)	SD	Mean AD Ref to 1950
Beta-18788	corncob	T305-2A	420 ±	70	1530
Beta-18798	corncob	T305-01-4B	730 ±	110	1250
Beta-18789	corncob	T306-2B	570 ±	70	1370
Beta-18791	corncob	T306-2C	950 ±	100	1010
Beta-18799	wood charcoal	T307-F2-5B	860 ±	70	1170
Beta-18793	corncob	T118-2G	660 ±	90	1290
Beta-18795	corncob	T118-2M	790 ±	80	1170
Beta-18796	wood charcoal	R112-T2-3A	710 ±	70	1250
Beta-18792	corncob	R112T2-2G	1129±	150	850
Beta-18790	corncob	BH3-W1-2C	730 ±	70	1210
Beta-18800	corncob	BH15-n.a.	210 ±	100	1730

Table 9. Radiocarbon Dates and Calibrated Ages†

Lab number	Mean AD (uncalibrated)	Calibrated age(s) (AD)	Calibrated age(s) (AD) 1σ	2σ
Beta-18788	1530	1454	1433–1516 1591–1621	1405–1647
Beta-18798	1250	1286	1221–1316 1346–1391	1041–1427
Beta-18789	1370	1403	1307–1361 1378–1431	1290–1449
Beta-18791	1010	1041, 1150	1004–1218	890–1282
Beta-18799	1170	—		
Beta-18793	1290	1302	1281–1403	1221–1436
Beta-18795	1170	1263	1192–1290	1041–1310 1353–1386
Beta-18796	1250	—		
Beta-18792	850	898, 906, 961	727–732 772–1032	646–1229
Beta-18790	1210	1286	1251–1303	1190–1398
Beta-18800	1730	1669, 1786, 1793, 1949, 1952	1638–1710 1710–1822 1833–1882 1912–1954	1460–1955

† Calibrations derived from CALIB 3.0.3 (Stuiver and Reimer 1993) using the bidecadal tree-ring calibration curve INTCAL93.

Backhoe trench 15 was the hand-excavated trench in the south plaza. The date of AD 1669 on corn from this trench 15 does not seem reasonable for the site. On the other hand, the "n.a." designation in the provenience indicates that the sample was not vertically provenienced. Given that locations in the south plaza had been exca- vated by Guthe's crew, the volunteer crew working with Wait and Nordby, and the university excavations in 1980 and 1984, the possibility of highly mixed deposits in this part of the site seems reasonable. The calibrated date ranges for this sample suggest that it may be a modern, twentieth-century specimen.

In sum, the 11 radiocarbon dates from Rowe Ruin are internally consistent and are consistent with what we know of the stratigraphy of the site. The range expressed by the mean of each date is larger than expected but would certainly bracket the ancient occupation.

In order to use these dates for additional analyses, it was desirable to apply a method of averaging them and at the same time checking to see if there was evidence of discontinuous occupation at Rowe. Both of these matters were explored using *C14,* a module of graphical programs developed by Keith Kintigh of Arizona State University (Kintigh 1995).

C14 treats each radiocarbon date not as a single point in time but as a normally distributed probability with a mean and standard deviation given by the laboratory. Calibrated dates cannot be used in the C14 module because they are not normally distributed. Several dates are examined as a sum of their associated probabilities.

> In a sense, then, this total probability represents the number of 'complete' dates for that time period . . . . The total associated with the complete set of dates is equal to the number of dates in the sample. C14 calculates and graphs these numbers and expresses them as percentages and cumulative percentages. Given some reasonable assumptions, a unimodal graph may be indicative of a single continuous occupation, while distinctly multimodal distributions may indicate gaps in the occupation, or at least gaps in the production of dated material (Kintigh 1995).

I ran the Rowe radiocarbon dates three different ways. First, I ran all 11 dates from Rowe as one set. This produces a unimodal graph with a peak (mean date) of AD 1210 and a range from AD 650 to 1850. Eighty-eight percent of the dates fall between 650 and 1530. Nearly half of the dates (48.49%) fall within the period from 1010 to 1450. The final graph is presented in Figure 11. Since several samples had been designed to date the adobe structure underlying the major component of Rowe Ruin, the dates between 1240 and 1425 for the aggregated occupation seems entirely appropriate.

In the second run, I divided the Rowe radiocarbon dates into two proveniences to separate those dates stratigraphically related to the adobe occupation from those dates from masonry structures and related features. The following break-down of "Early" vs. "Late" proveniences was made:

		Dates BP
"Early"	T305 - 4B	730 ± 110
	T306 - 2C	950 ± 100
	T307 - 5B	860 ± 70
	T118 - 2G	660 ± 90
	T118 - 2M	790 ± 80
	BH3-W1	730 ± 70
"Late"	T305 - 2A	420 ± 70
	T306 - 2B	570 ± 79
	R112 - T2-3A	710 ± 70
	R112 - T2-2G	1129 ± 150
	BH15 - n.a.	210 ± 100

This run produces a peak (mean date) of AD 1170 for the "Early" occupation. Eighty-eight percent of the dates fall between AD 850 and 1450, and 48.49% of the dates fall between 1010 and 1330 (Figure 12). For the "Late" proveniences, the mean date from this run is AD 1370 with 88% of the dates between AD 1340 and 1930 and 48.49% of the dates between AD 1060 and 1690 (Figure 13). It seems clear that the "Late" end of this run is being heavily influenced by the radiocarbon date of AD 1730 on the corncob from backhoe trench 15. As indicated above, I cannot really explain that date but since it did come from the part of Rowe most heavily distrubed by previous archaeological work from Guthe's excavations on, it probably does not reflect either adobe or masonry structures at the site. Consequently, I conducted a third run using ten dates and deleting the suspect date from backhoe trench 15.

The final run of ten dates produces a mean of AD 1210 (Figure 14). Eighty-eight percent of the dates fall between AD 650 and 1650 while 48.49% of the dates fall between AD 970 and 1450. Dividing this into "Early" and "Late" produces the same graph as the previous run for the six "Early" proveniences. For the "Late" proveniences, the mean date is 1290, with 88% of the dates falling between AD 570 and 1650. Dates for 48.49% fall between AD 850 and 1530. This graph is the only one that approaches bimodality (Figure 15), but with only four dates, I do not think the pattern is reliable.

The information from all three runs is useful. Since all but the run involving only four dates produce unimodal curves, the occupation of Rowe appears to have been continuous. The stratigraphic evidence and the radiocarbon dates concur in supporting the idea that both the adobe and masonry structures were most likely built by the same group of people or at least without

```
Date
(relative to
AD 1950)

 450    |
 490    |
 530    |
 570    |
 610    |
 650    |
 690    |  *
 730    |  *
 770    |  *
 810    |  *
 850    |  *
 890    |  **
 930    |  **
 970  > |  ***
1010    |  ****
1050    |  *****
1090    |  ******
1130    |  *******
1170    |  ********
1210  - |  *********
1250    |  ********
1290    |  *******
1330    |  ******
1370    |  ****
1410    |  ****
1450    |  ***
1490    |  ***
1530  > |  ***
1570    |  **
1610    |  **
1650    |  *
1690    |  *
1730    |  *
1770    |  *
1810    |  *
1850    |  *
1890    |
1930    |
1970    |
```

Figure 11. Results of *C-14* analysis (Kintigh 1995): all radiocarbon dates combined

```
Date
(relative to
AD 1950)

 450    |
 490    |
 530    |
 570    |
 610    |
 650    |
 690    |
 730    |
 770    |
 810    |
 850    |  *
 890    |  **
 930    |  **
 970    |  ****
1010  > |  ******
1050    |  ********
1090    |  **********
1130    |  ***********
1170  - |  ************
1210    |  *************
1250    |  ***********
1290    |  ********
1330  > |  ******
1370    |  ***
1410    |  **
1450    |  *
1490    |
1530    |
1570    |
1610    |
1650    |
1690    |
1730    |
1770    |
1810    |
1850    |
1890    |
1930    |
1970    |
```

Figure 12. Results of *C-14* analysis of dates from "early" proveniences only

```
Date
(relative to
AD 1950)

 450    |
 490    |
 530    |
 570    |
 610    |  *
 650    |  *
 690    |  *
 730    |  **
 770    |  **
 810    |  **
 850    |  **
 890  > |  **
 930    |  **
 970    |  *
1010    |  *
1050    |  *
1090    |  *
1130    |  **
1170    |  ***
1210    |  ****
1250    |  *****
1290    |  ******
1330    |  ******
1370  - |  ******
1410    |  *****
1450    |  *****
1490    |  *****
1530    |  *****
1570    |  *****
1610    |  ****
1650    |  ***
1690  > |  ***
1730    |  ***
1770    |  ***
1810    |  **
1850    |  **
1890    |  *
1930    |  *
1970    |
```

Figure 13. Results of *C-14* analysis of dates from "late" proveniences only

56

Date (relative to AD 1950)		
450		
490		
530		
570		
610		
650		
690		*
730		*
770		*
810		*
850		*
890		**
930		**
970	>	***
1010		****
1050		*****
1090		******
1130		*******
1170		********
1210	−	*********
1250		********
1290		*******
1330		******
1370		****
1410		****
1450		***
1490		***
1530	>	***
1570		**
1610		**
1650		*
1690		*
1730		*
1770		*
1810		*
1850		*
1890		
1930		
1970		

Date (relative to AD 1950)		
450		
490		
530		
570		*
610		*
650		*
690		**
730		**
770		**
810		***
850	>	***
890		**
930		**
970		**
1010		*
1050		*
1090		*
1130		**
1170		****
1210		******
1250		*******
1290	−	*******
1330		*******
1370		*******
1410		*******
1450		******
1490		******
1530	>	******
1570		*****
1610		***
1650		*
1690		
1730		
1770		
1810		
1850		
1890		
1930		
1970		

Figure 14. Results of *C-14* analysis of all dates except the outlier from the backhoe trench 15 corncob

Figure 15. Results of *C-14* analysis of "late" dates only, including date from corncob in backhoe trench 15

Table 10. Tree-Ring Dates from Rowe Ruin

Provenience	TRL number	Field number	Species	Dates (AD) Inside	Dates (AD) Outside
Backhoe trench 2	Row 28	W1-NA-7.1	PNN	1205	1305vv
Room 21	Row 1	T1-6A-7.2	PNN	1244p	1319vv
Room 21	Row 2	T1-3B-7.2	PNN	1205p	1323vv
Room 21	Row 6	T1-3C-7.4	PNN	1271	1326vv
Room 21	Row 3	T1-6A-7.1	PNN	1243p	1344vv
Room 21	Row 5	T1-5B-7.2	PNN	1281	1340vv
Room 21	Row 7	R21-3D-7.3	PNN	1243p	1346vv
Room 21	Row 4	R21-3D-7.4	PNN	1264p	1351vv
Room 22	Row 11	T1-5C-7.4	PNN	1286+p	1349vv
Room 23	Row 10	T1-3A-7.2	PNN	1262p	1343vv
Room 30	Row 16	R30-2C-7.1	PNN	1310p	1344r
"Guthe's Trench"			PNN	1306vv	

+   one or more rings may be missing near the end of the ring series
p   the innermost ring is the pith ring, the initial growth layer
vv   there is no way of estimating how far the last ring is from a true outside ring
r   true outside ring is present though not continuous

evidence of a hiatus in occupation between them. Although the dates are spread out farther than one might hope, dating the period of aggregation to between AD 1240 and 1425 is supported.

When a single tree-ring specimen from Guthe's test trench in the south plaza, collected by Stallings in the 1950s, is included, there are 12 tree-ring dates from Rowe. They range from 1305vv to 1349vv. The dates and their proveniences are given in Table 10. All but two dates, one from Stallings's specimen and the other from wood from backhoe trench 2, are from the center masonry quadrangle and also relate to the northern roomblock of the south quadrangle. A single cutting date of 1343r was obtained from room 23. This date also applies to room 30 in the south quadrangle. We certainly do not have many dates, but those we have do show a marked clustering in the 1340s. The single date from backhoe trench 2 relates to the large pitstructure encountered in that trench. This date, 1305vv, lends credence to the inference that it is a kiva rather than a pithouse associated with the earlier occupation.

Although we were not able to obtain enough chronometric dates to establish the occupation of Rowe Ruin as precisely as we would have liked, we can place episodes of occupation and building in a temporal framework. The extent of the adobe structure underlying the main construction at Rowe is not known, but this part of the site seems to have been established in the 1240s or 1250s. I suspect that some of the earlier dates reflect long use of the site before then, at a time for which we presently have no architectural signature. Construction of the visible masonry structures seems to have occurred in the 1340s and 1350s, with episodes of remodeling and rebuilding, at least on the eastern side of the site, that may have extended into the 1360s or 1370s, although we cannot be sure. The archaeomagnetic date of 1395 from the burned area in Room 11 represents a use or abandonment date rather than a construction date for the north quadrangle. Nevertheless, the absence of trashy fill suggests that the north quadrangle of rooms was added late in the occupation of the site.

FLORA, FAUNA, AND DIET
AT ROWE

BOTANICAL AND FAUNAL REMAINS PROVIDE THE basis for understanding the diet of the inhabitants of Rowe Ruin. During the university work at Rowe, macrobotanical remains were collected and saved whenever they were encountered during excavating or screening. In 1980, pinch samples of pollen were taken from across room floors and flotation samples were taken from a variety of proveniences, including room floors. The pollen and flotation samples were analyzed by Anne Cully, Karen Clary, and Mollie S. Toll, at that time of the Castetter Laboratory of Ethnobotany in the Biology Department at the University of New Mexico. In addition, both Clary and Toll visited Rowe Ruin in 1980 and conducted an informal survey of plants in the vicinity of the site before presenting a guest lecture for the students and staff.

In 1984, macrobotanical material and pollen samples were collected, as before, but the pollen samples were not submitted for analysis. I was concerned with questions of representativeness regarding pollen that had been raised by the cautionary tale in Cully's (1979) paper. Cully reported vastly different pollen spectra from samples taken from different locations of the same house floor in an excavated structure in Chaco Canyon. The differences probably resulted from different activities, proximity to doorways, and hearths. Cully suggested that taking small "pinch" samples for pollen across an entire floor might mitigate the problems of differential deposition in rooms. Largely for this reason, we submitted pinch samples collected from the floors of rooms 10, 20, 21, and 30. Cully and Clary (1981) found corn, cheno-am, grass, high- and low-spine composites, cattail, globemallow, and pine but did not provide actual counts. The sample from room 21 contained abundant spores, suggesting fungal activity that could have affected pollen preservation negatively. Cully and Clary indicated that corn and cattail pollen from room 20 suggested these

plants may have been stored in the room. Nevertheless, in general, they found that pollen preservation in these floor sample contexts was poor. The decision not to continue analyzing pollen samples (although they were taken in the field) was influenced by not knowing how we could interpret pollen in behavioral terms when it came from contexts such as fill levels or even hearths and storage pits, and believing that pollen preservation on the room floors was poor. We did submit the 1984 macrobotanical material to Toll for analysis.

During the university excavations, the faunal remains were collected routinely during the course of excavation, usually in screens. These were cleaned, numbered, and field sorted. After the 1984 season, Linda Mick-O'Hara, who had been a graduate teaching assistant at the site and had developed the sorting method used in the nightly fauna lab, identified and analyzed the animal bone. She also prepared the report that is appended here (see also Mick-O'Hara 1987, 1988, 1989; Cordell and Mick-O'Hara 1993).

This section first addresses the botanical remains from Rowe, with the fauna considered thereafter. Except for a few brief remarks regarding botanical preservation and sampling, this section focuses on substantive results. The appended papers by Toll and Mick-O'Hara fully discuss field processing and methods of analysis. These two contributions also consider various sources of bias that are inherent in using macrobotanical and faunal remains as archaeological evidence of prehistoric diet. Finally, summary tables in both reports support the results detailed here.

Flora

Initially, macrobotanical preservation seemed to be a problem at Rowe. Wait had taken standard one-liter

Table 11. Attributes of Corn Remains at Rowe (after Toll 1981)

| | Range | | Mean | SD |
	Min.	Max.		
Cobs				
mid-cob diameter	8.0	18.6	11.8	2.42
cupule width	4.2	8.5	6.0	1.44
Kernels				
length	6.1	7.7	7.2	0.51
thickness	4.8	6.1	5.3	0.41
length/thickness ratio	1.0	1.5	1.4	0.17
	8-rowed	10-rowed	12-rowed	14-rowed
Number of cobs	5	4	7	1
Percent of cobs	29%	24%?	41%	6%

samples from the rooms he excavated, with volunteer assistance, in the north rectangle. He learned through preliminary assessment of the samples that very little macrobotanical material had preserved. In 1980, we too submitted samples from north rectangle rooms 10 and 11, in addition to samples from other contexts. In the nineteen samples analyzed for the 1980 season, Toll found very little macrobotanical material from rooms 10 and 11, and she suggested that preservation was poor in other settings as well. More than half (55%) of the identified seeds were modern contaminants. "Charred specimens, that could be clearly related to site use, were essentially restricted to corn. . . . A concentration of unburned *Physalis* (groundcherry) seeds in level 5A of Room 20 seems to represent a rodent cache" (Toll 1981:16).

In view of these difficulties, and in consultation with Toll, we changed our sampling strategy during the 1983 and 1984 seasons. We increased the standard sample size to two liters and took samples from clear cultural contexts such as room floors, hearths, and storage pits. As a result, the 1984 samples included a wider range of taxa and more abundant plant material. Here, I summarize results from Toll's reports (1981 and this volume).

Remains of corn (*Zea mays*) were ubiquitous and abundant at Rowe. Charred corncobs and cob fragments were found in virtually all cultural contexts (floors, roof fall, hearths, pits, and fill). Despite its prominence in archaeological contexts, all of the corn was small-eared, even taking into account the considerable shrinkage that results from charring.

Scholars interested in the evolution of maize suggest that a decrease in row number from 12 to 10 to 8 resulted from the introduction of Maiz de Ocho (Doebley and Bohrer 1980; Toll 1981) and its subsequent hybridization with Chapalote varieties. Although the time of this introduction is debated, scholars normally credit it to sometime before AD 1150. Given the post-AD 1200 date of Rowe, it is expected that the corn reflects the hybridization of Maiz de Ocho and Chapalote types. Most of the corn from Rowe is 12-rowed, with significant amounts of 10-rowed cobs (Table 11). The single 14-rowed cob is similar to the 12- and 10-rowed corn in size and cupule width. Toll considers this consistent with the hybrid pattern. In her final report (this volume), Toll concludes that the corn from Rowe was grown under marginal conditions for farming, reflected by small, variable cob sizes with irregular row-filling. In this respect, Rowe maize is similar to maize from other relatively high elevation sites (Toll 1984).

In addition to corn, which given its ubiquity must have been a dietary mainstay, there is macrobotanical evidence of squash (*Cucurbita*) in the form of charred seeds from one of the earliest, if not the earliest, provenience units excavated at Rowe, the hearth at the base of the midden excavated in T118. Beans were not recovered from flotation samples, but this is neither unusual nor does it constitute evidence that beans were not grown and consumed at the site.

At an elevation of 2,072 m, Rowe Ruin is in the Upper Sonoran life zone but has access to abundant perennial vegetation, chiefly pinyon and juniper on nearby mesas, and to riparian plants along the Pecos less than 2 km distant. The remains of wild plants from Rowe Ruin reflect a concentration on annual weedy plants that commonly occur at ancient Pueblo sites at similar and somewhat lower elevations (Toll 1983). The three most common are pigweed (*Amaranthus* sp.), goosefoot (*Chenopodium* sp.), and purslane (*Portulaca* sp.). Uses of these three plants are well-documented in the ethnographic literature of the Rio Grande Pueblos, Zuni, Hopi, and Athapaskan peoples of the Colorado Plateaus. Archaeologically, they are common constituents of sites dating from the Archaic through all Puebloan periods. These taxa are well represented in sites in the Upper Pecos region, including Rowe (Toll, this volume).

Additional weedy taxa with secondary or occasionally equivalent prominence include tansy mustard (*Descurainia* sp.) and groundcherry (*Physalis* sp.). Of these, only tansy mustard was found in charred form in the Rowe plant assemblage, indicating human use. Other taxa that regularly occur, although not necessarily abundantly, at ancient sites on the Colorado Plateaus also occur in low frequency at Rowe. These are prickly pear cactus (*Opuntia*), hedgehog cactus (*Echinocereus*), sunflower (*Helianthus*), dropseed (*Sporobolus* sp.), ricegrass (*Oryzopsis hymenoides*), juniper seed (*Juniperus*), and pinyon nut (*Pinus edulis*). American plum (cf. *Prunus americana*) was identified at Rowe (Toll 1981), although it is not often encountered in archaeological sites. Toll (1981), citing other sources, indicates that American plum has been an important famine food among the Pueblos of the Northern Rio Grande, because it is more reliably productive than many other higher-yielding or more nutritious plants.

The assemblage of plant remains from Rowe includes charcoal and other plant parts of woody species and some others that were not used primarily or at all for food. Seeds of *Nicotiana rustica* (wild tobacco), for example, were recovered from rooms 20, 30, and 112. The leaves of wild tobacco contain nicotine and are smoked

ceremonially by Pueblo peoples. Wood charcoal identified in flotation samples includes juniper, pinyon, oak, and willow (*Salix*). As noted above, all wood used in building and subsequently submitted to the Laboratory of Tree-ring Research was identified as pinyon. Toll (this volume) notes that willow (*Salix*) and sedge (*Scirpus*) would have been available along the Pecos. These plants may have been used for fuel and/or in the manufacture of matting, and they may have been eaten as tender shoots or roots.

In general, the plant material recovered from Rowe reflects a pattern that is also documented at many other Pueblo sites in the Upper Pecos Valley and the Northern Rio Grande region, as well as other locations on the Colorado Plateaus. In the tables accompanying her report, Toll (this volume) makes specific comparison with Pecos Pueblo, the pithouse occupation located at Pecos Monument, and Early and Late Archaic sites on the Cimarron. In an earlier report, Toll (1981) reported comparable assemblages of macrobotanical remains from Howiri Pueblo, in the Chama district, and Angus North, a high-elevation site from southeastern New Mexico. To this list, one should add Arroyo Hondo Pueblo, as reported by Wetterstrom (1986).

Toll (1983, and this volume) points out that the small and variable corn from Rowe was being cultivated under marginal conditions that are also documented for other sites at similar elevations. The wild weedy, annual species that were the common supplementary foods at Rowe and other ancient Pueblo sites do not provide optimal amounts of carbohydrates or oils. These weedy annuals thrive in disturbed soils, however, where they increase their usefulness to humans by proliferating in precisely those settings created and sustained by human activity. Such settings include settlements, middens, and agricultural fields. The presence of weedy plants in agricultural fields may be tolerated, even encouraged, but their abundance in field settings must be limited so they do not out-compete domestic crops (Wetterstrom 1986:23–24). Nevertheless, as Toll suggests:

> Weedy species offer an advantageous symbiotic relation to human subsistence in the form of adaptability, and their tendency to increase in the face of disturbance. Yet we may find that this plant group is of prime importance only when more dependable and profitable resources are in low supply (Toll 1983:4).

Fauna

Rowe Ruin occupies a setting that is potentially rich in game. The inhabitants of the site would have had immediate access to common constituents of the Upper Sonoran life zone, fauna attracted to planted fields, denizens of more mountainous elevations, and species inhabiting riparian settings or the Pecos River itself. In addition, Rowe Ruin, like Pecos Pueblo, is next to the Southern Great Plains, which historically were home to vast herds of bison. Pecos Pueblo was an important locus of trade between Pueblo and Plains peoples.

The time-depth associated with the interaction of Pueblo and Plains groups and the kinds of sociopolitical structures that might have facilitated or encouraged the exchange are the focus of recent research (Spielmann, Schoeninger, and Moore 1990). Evidence of the use and importance of bison at pre-contact Pueblo sites is meager. For example, Kidder (1932:196) found that bison bones were present at Forked Lightning and occurred at all levels at Pecos as well but "were most numerous in the upper deposits." They presumably date to post-contact times, as Kidder commented that use of the horse facilitated trips to the Plains and the transport of meat and hides (Kidder 1932:197).

Bison bones occur in very low frequency at Arroyo Hondo Pueblo, which was occupied between AD 1315 and 1425. At that site it is estimated that bison may have accounted for 5.3% of usable meat, reflecting hunting of "occasional wanderers from the great herds of the plains to the east" (Lang and Harris 1984:49–50). At Tijeras Pueblo, a pre-contact site located west of the Sandia Mountains near the edge of the grassland plains, bison bones occurred in very small numbers. Bison foot bones were the most common element recovered at Tijeras Pueblo, suggesting that they may have been brought to the site with the hides (Young 1979).

At Rowe, which of course had also been abandoned prior to contact, 31 bison bones were recorded out of 3,185 elements identified to the level of species. This number constitutes less than one percent of the identified sample. Identified elements include vertebral fragments, ulna and tibia fragments, rib fragments, tarsal fragments, and phalanges. The presence of bison rib fragments suggests the acquisition of meat rather than, or in addition to, hides. Nevertheless, the relative paucity of bison bone would seem to be similar to the small

numbers found in the early levels at Pecos. Arroyo Hondo, Tijeras, early Pecos Pueblo, and Rowe are all large sites, close enough to the Plains to have been loci of exchange if such a pattern had existed in the fourteenth century. The data we have at present show only small amounts of bison at these sites.

While the botanical remains from Rowe exemplify a pattern that is widespread among Pueblo sites in the Rio Grande region and the Colorado Plateaus generally, the record of its fauna is not typical. The list of identified fauna from Rowe Ruin, Tijeras Pueblo, and Arroyo Hondo Pueblo, a much larger settlement, is quite similar, as would be expected given their elevation and overlapping dates of occupation. A list of the most common species from all three sites is also very similar. The differences, which are striking, are in the percentages represented by each of the most common species.

According to Lang and Harris (1984:46),

> The most common animals—those on which the people of Arroyo Hondo focused their hunting, trapping and husbandry efforts—were, in numerical order: hares and rabbits (28% of the economic fauna), squirrels (17%), hoofed mammals, primarily mule deer (9%); turkeys (approximately 8%). . . . Cottontail rabbits made up 57% of the lagomorphs, and the squirrel sample was dominated by prairie dog (45%).

To my mind, this is a fairly typical Pueblo pattern. It does not indicate that hares and rabbits provided most of the meat. Mule deer, which are of course much larger than rabbits, would have been more important components of the meat supply. Nevertheless, the assemblage of archaeological bone is, as expected, weighted toward small mammals. The same is true of the assemblage from Tijeras Pueblo.

The most frequently identified species at Tijeras Pueblo and Rowe Ruin are the same, as would be expected given the similar environments of the two sites. The species are deer (*Odocoileus sp.*), pronghorn antelope (*Antilocapra americana*), jackrabbit (*Lepus* sp.), cottontail (*Sylvilagus* sp.), pocket gopher (*Thomomys* sp.), prairie dog (*Cynomys* sp.), and turkey (*Meleagris gallipavo*) (Figure 16).

Large mammals (Figure 17) make up 39.3% of the fauna from Rowe but only 18.5% of the fauna from Tijeras. These differences are not considered artifacts of excavation as long as the occupants of both sites fol-

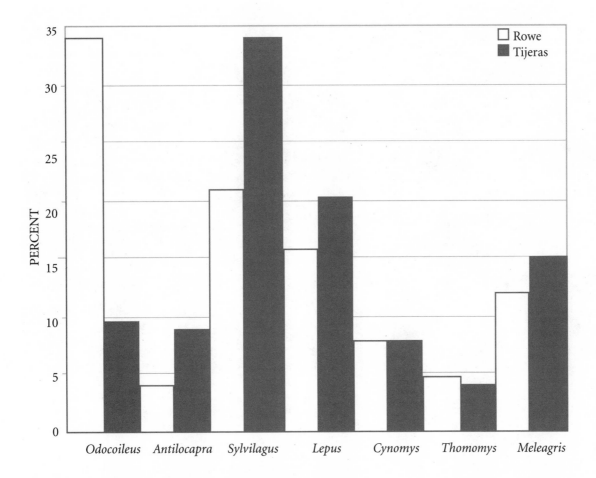

Figure 16. Faunal representation (% NISP) at Rowe and Tijeras

lowed the common southwestern pattern of disposing of large and small animal bones differently. Among most southwestern agricultural groups, the meat of larger animals is shared and the bones themselves are buried (sometimes quite elaborately) in a communal, sacred space (the ash mound). Small game is consumed within the households with no public burials of the bones. This difference does not explain the disparity between Rowe and Tijeras faunal assemblages because midden and plazas as well as rooms were excavated at both sites, even though far less of Rowe than of Tijeras Pueblo has been excavated.

At Rowe, the percentage of deer is much greater than that of pronghorn (34.5% deer to 3.8% antelope). At Tijeras, the percentages of deer and antelope are virtually the same (9.5% deer and 9.0% antelope). The ranges of these two animals overlap, but antelope prefer open,

unwooded terrain while deer browse in woodlands and forest. The amount of habitat for both species is about the same at both sites (with today perhaps slightly more open antelope habitat at Rowe); therefore the inhabitants of Tijeras were acquiring relatively more antelope than expected.

This difference may be explained either as a reflection of change in the amount of deer vs. antelope habitat at Rowe or as a difference in game procurement strategies. It is entirely possible that when Rowe was inhabited much more of the land in the vicinity was wooded, with little land having been cleared for agriculture or trees sacrificed for firewood. If such were the case, the relative abundance of deer would simply be the result of available deer habitat. Another possibility also deserves consideration. Antelope are normally taken in drives by large groups of hunters acting cooperatively,

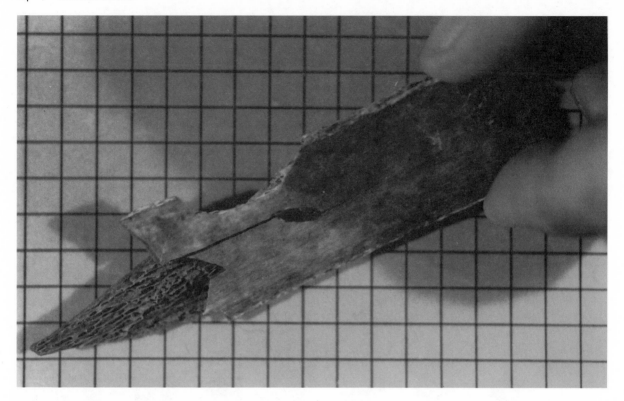

Figure 17. Artiodactyl rib fragment with obsidian projectile point tip imbedded in interior surface; excavated from T303 (level 6B), outside the south quadrangle. Grid is centimeter scale; length is 10 cm.

in quite the same way that rabbits are hunted. Deer are normally hunted by only one or a few hunters. Game drives, specifically rabbit drives, also occur more frequently among relatively intensive agricultural groups in the Southwest than among those with a more marginally agricultural strategy. It is possible that the social structures of extra-household organization at Tijeras Pueblo may have been more important than they were at Rowe. The Tijeras hunters may have used a model based on rabbit drives for the procurement of pronghorn.

There is another difference between the faunal assemblages from Rowe and Tijeras that is not obvious from the comparison of frequencies of species and may in fact be a result of less intensive excavation at Rowe. The frequencies of turkey bones are about the same (10.9% at Rowe vs. 15% at Tijeras) at both sites, but eggshell and dung were found only at Tijeras, suggesting that these animals were kept there. Since far fewer

rooms have been excavated at Rowe, we may simply have missed the pen areas. However, the remains identified are all of mature birds, which lends support to the inference that they were not raised or kept at the site.

In the conclusions to her descriptive report, Mick-O'Hara (this volume) makes the following points. First, Rowe Ruin is similar to other Pueblo IV sites in terms of the range and frequencies of animals taken for food except for the greater number of large mammal remains at Rowe. Second, although bison bone is present at Rowe, Forked Lightning, and Early Pecos, the low frequency of bison bone supports Kidder's (1932) inference that they were taken by Pueblo peoples venturing onto the Plains or hunting occasional bison closer to home. She notes that the large number of unidentifiable bones suggests that even though no protein stress seems to have existed at Rowe, all animals taken were used as completely as possible. She concludes that animal protein contributed significantly to the diet of the population at Rowe.

Summary

Considering the botanical and faunal data together, the inhabitants of Rowe, like those of other contemporary communities, may have depended on maize but were required to supplement this source of food. Either because growing conditions for corn are marginal in the cool, dry environment of Rowe or because crops were not adequately tended, or for both reasons, yields of maize seem to have been quite variable. Maize was supplemented with annual weedy species that thrived in disturbed ground and were probably tolerated or encouraged in fields and with grasses and perennials such as cactus fruits and pinyon nuts. In this strategy of gathering, the occupants of Rowe were like other ancient Pueblo peoples across northern New Mexico and central Arizona. They were also like those who had carried out the same strategy before abandoning their communities in the northern San Juan drainage and the Colorado Plateaus.

The people of Rowe also hunted the diverse species available in their vicinity, as did their ancestors and their neighbors. In contrast to most others, however, the occupants of Rowe successfully hunted large mammals, primarily mule deer, whose remains at the site suggest that animal protein made up a greater percentage of the Rowe diet than is anticipated for Pueblo farming peoples.

POTTERY AT ROWE RUIN

ALL POTTERY SHERDS WERE ROUTINELY COLLECTED during university excavations. In addition to the sherds, one whole vessel (a Rowe Black-on-white bowl) was excavated. Field school students washed, numbered, sorted, and identified these ceramics under staff supervision. Conjoinable pottery sherds were given a single laboratory number and counted only once in relevant tallies. In a few instances more than one-quarter of a single vessel appeared to be present. These sherds were counted, sacked, and stored together. No effort was made to restore them.

In 1980, Carol Raish, then a graduate teaching assistant, continued ceramic analysis during the 1980–1981 academic year. Her report, summarizing her observations on 10,225 sherds, is appended in Part II of this volume. In addition, the late Elizabeth Garrett examined 37 sherds to identify tempering material. The petrographic information is included here in the main section of this report.

A description of preliminary analyses of the additional 11,918 sherds recovered in 1984 was prepared by Kathleen Morrison, who had been the teaching assistant responsible for the on-site ceramics laboratory during that summer season. Garrett continued her investigations of the clays and tempers of 133 ceramic fragments that had been excavated from Rowe Ruin in 1983. Her results and Morrison's findings are included here in summary form.

Finally, two additional, unfunded ceramic studies were conducted. In 1984–1985 Amy Douglass, who was then also a graduate teaching assistant, did a detailed stylistic study of painted designs on 1,281 black-on-white sherds recovered from controlled proveniences during 1980, 1983, and 1984. Her results were reported at the Society for American Archaeology annual meeting in Denver in 1985. Between 1989 and 1991, I pre-

pared and examined a set of sherds from Rowe with a scanning electron microscope as part of a larger project on Pajarito White Ware (Habicht-Mauche 1993). The SEM equipment was made available to me at the California Academy of Sciences in San Francisco. During that period, I also looked at some of the Santa Fe Black-on-white sherds from Rowe with Judith Habicht-Mauche at the University of California, Santa Cruz. The results of these studies are also summarized here.

The different pottery studies performed by the university archaeologists reflect changes in the research foci of our investigations at Rowe Ruin. During the 1980 season, we were guided and constrained by the research issues that had been raised by Wait and Nordby in their proposal to the National Endowment for the Humanities. Their questions that related to ceramic studies were delineating the period during which Rowe was occupied, discerning the temporal relationship among plaza roomblocks, and discovering the "ethnic" origins of the Rowe Ruin population in general, and specifically the relationships between the inhabitants of Rowe and Jemez Pueblo, if any. Finally, they were interested in ceramic evidence of interaction between Rowe and Plains peoples similar to those later recorded between Pecos Pueblo and Apache groups.

By 1984, we were still interested in intrasite chronology but our emphasis had shifted toward attempting to identify which types of pottery and how much of that pottery had probably been imported into Rowe, and the likely source of those vessels. We were also interested in whether or not some types were differentially distributed at sites in the area covered by our site survey. These questions were pursued primarily through technological analyses. Douglass's study concerned matters of social affiliation reflected in changes through time in decorative treatment of the Rowe pottery.

I am mindful of the central place ceramic analysis holds in Southwest archaeology. I am also aware that in terms of sheer numbers, the more than 22,000 sherds are a large part of the material record of the past inhabitants of Rowe Ruin. Nevertheless, I hope to characterize the ceramic assemblage from Rowe Ruin and summarize my perspectives on both the research questions, as related to ceramics, and our results, in what I intend to be a fairly brief section of this report.

Wares and Types

As discussed, the major occupation of Rowe Ruin occurred between AD 1240 and 1425. The ceramics most frequently recovered from sites in the general Santa Fe and Upper Pecos valleys during this time period are textured cooking pots and painted types belonging to the Pajarito White Ware tradition. The categories we used for sorting the unpainted vessels relate to the surface treatment (corrugated, indented corrugated, blind corrugated, smeared indented corrugated, and plain), following Kidder and Shepard (1936), rather than types defined subsequently and named using standard binomial nomenclature. Commentary on this decision is provided in what follows.

The Pajarito White Ware types we recovered at Rowe are gray-, tan-, or white-slipped vessels decorated with black carbon-painted designs. In sorting the Rowe pottery we followed the type descriptions from Kidder and Shepard (1936), Kidder and Amsden (1931), Mera (1935), Stubbs and Stallings (1953) and Wetherington (1968). The type names we used during this portion of analysis are those derived from this literature and follow binomial nomenclature. They are Santa Fe Black-on-white, Rowe Black-on-white, Galisteo Black-on-white, Wiyo Black-on-white, and Abiquiu Black-on-gray.

Types that were present in very low frequencies and that we considered evidence of interaction outside the general Upper Pecos and Santa Fe areas are White Mountain Red Ware (particularly St. Johns Polychrome), Rio Grande glaze ware, Heshotauthla Black-on-red from the Zuni area, Chupadero Black-on-white, and Los Lunas Smudged from the area south of Albuquerque (from Los Lunas to Sorcorro and east to the Sacramento Mountains). Sources for descriptions of these types are Hawley (1936); Hayes and others (1981); Kidder and Shepard

(1936); Smith, Woodbury, and Woodbury (1966); and Carlson (1970). Although we were alert to the possibility that sherds of the earlier mineral-painted Kwahe'e Black-on-white and of Jemez, Taos, and Talpa Black-on-white might be present at Rowe, we did not record any examples of them. A few sherds of these types may have been overlooked in the "unidentified" category. In the discussion that follows, I attempt to be inclusive in my terminology in order to reflect the literature at the time the analyses of the Rowe pottery were done as well as some of the suggested revisions proposed by Habicht-Mauche (1993).

Utility Ware

Unpainted, unslipped, utility ware makes up 65.3% of the pottery from Rowe. The utility ware ranges in color from gray to black and contains abundant, coarse-grained (average 1.08 mm, range 1.00 mm to 2.00 mm) mica schist and crushed sandstone temper. Vessel form is difficult to determine in all cases because the ware is very friable. Nevertheless, a significant proportion of vessels are jars. Surface treatment in the unpainted sherds included clapboard corrugated (2.7%), blind indented corrugated (27.1%), smeared indented corrugated (6.8%), and plain or smooth (61.8%) styles. Since both "blind" and "smeared" indented corrugated surface treatments partially smooth corrugations, roughly a third of the unpainted pottery is characteristic of this overall Rio Grande pattern after about AD 1300. The micaceous residual clay fabric of these vessels, derived from the metamorphic rock of the Sangre de Cristo Mountains, occurs locally at Rowe. Rowe utility pottery does not contain clay with large fragments of pink to pinkish orange granite, gneiss, and mica that is local to Arroyo Hondo (Habicht-Mauche 1993:12–13).

I agree with Habicht-Mauche that the typological study of Rio Grande utility ware has yet to be done. Nevertheless Shepard (1936:558–560) was able to seriate test trenches at Pecos and Forked Lightning using the ratio of plain to corrugated sherds. In these tests, the corrugated style decreases over time. In a preliminary exercise, Morrison and I found that the ratio of corrugated to plain at Rowe as a whole falls precisely in between those of Forked Lightning and Pecos. That result is an accurate placement for Rowe.

Rowe Black-on-white

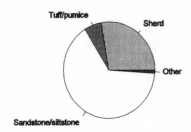

Figure 18. Temper in Rowe Black-on-white sherds recovered during 1980

Pajarito White Ware

Four ceramic types make up nearly all of the painted pottery recovered at Rowe: Rowe Black-on-white, which numerically dominates the assemblage, and Santa Fe, Galisteo, and Wiyo Black-on-white. In what follows, I derived percentages from the data presented in Raish's report (appended here), rather than using data from Morrison's preliminary report or a combination of the two. The reason for this choice is that during the 1984 season, more emphasis was given to temper categories that would reflect source locations, and there is an unknown amount of bias in the autocorrelation this produced in the tallies (see Morrison 1987).

PECOS SERIES

Rowe Black-on-white makes up 43.5% of the painted pottery from Rowe. This type is the Late Crackle type as described by Kidder and Amsden (1931) and the Rowe Black-on-white of Kidder and Shepard (1936). The name "Rowe Black-on-white" is used here to conform to standard binomial nomenclature and because the type is not later than "Crackle" (Galisteo Black-on-white). The two are contemporary (see also Habicht-Mauche 1993:30). The only whole vessel excavated by university groups at Rowe Ruin is a Rowe Black-on-white bowl.

The type at Rowe (var. Rowe) is made of coarse micaceous residual clays and is most often tempered with medium-sized siltstone and sandstone, or medium-sized siltstone and sherd particles (Figure 18). Paste is gener-

ally gray, although color often varies throughout the cross-section. The paste is friable and feels sandy with visibly heterogeneous temper. Rowe Black-on-white is slipped on both the interior and exterior. The slip may be thin, but if it is not, it is generally slightly crackled. Painted designs are in black or dark gray carbon paint (Figure 19). Designs follow the general San Juan (McElmo/Mesa Verde) style. These consist of stepped figures, triangles, zigzag lines, rim ticks, secondary dots and ticks, a predominance of solid rather than hatched banded elements, and frequent parallel lines (Douglass 1985).

PAJARITO SERIES

Santa Fe Black-on-white is the next most frequently occurring painted type at Rowe, at 16.1% of the painted pottery. This type is the Blue Gray of early descriptions (Kidder and Amsden 1931; Kidder and Shepard 1936).

Santa Fe Black-on-white has a thin, hard paste that is usually very homogeneous. The temper is generally very fine siltstone and/or very fine sandstone (Figure 20), often visible only with a hand lens or microscope. Nearly 30% of the Santa Fe Black-on-white from Rowe is tempered with pumiceous tuff. Some sherds include round brown "lumps" that appear to be mudstone or bits of clay. The interiors of bowls are slipped with a thin, flaky white slip that sloughs off. The exteriors of bowls are nearly always left slightly rough and unslipped. A few exteriors seem to have been lightly scored or wiped with grass. Designs are painted with black carbon paint in the San Juan style described above for Rowe Black-on-white (Figure 21).

Wiyo Black-on-white makes up 14.2% of the painted types from Rowe Ruin. The paste color of Wiyo sherds is usually a tan/gray to a dull green/gray and generally appears homogeneous.

At Rowe, 87% of the Wiyo is tempered with pumiceous tuff (Figure 22), which is sometimes visible to the naked eye. The interior slip of Wiyo sherds, when present, is the same color as the paste. Exteriors of bowls lack slip but are smoothed or sometimes slightly polished. Rims are occasionally flared. Paint is carbon black to gray, and design style is the McElmo/Mesa Verde described above.

Abiquiu Black-on-gray is the Biscuit A of some designations. Less than 1% of the sherds from Rowe were

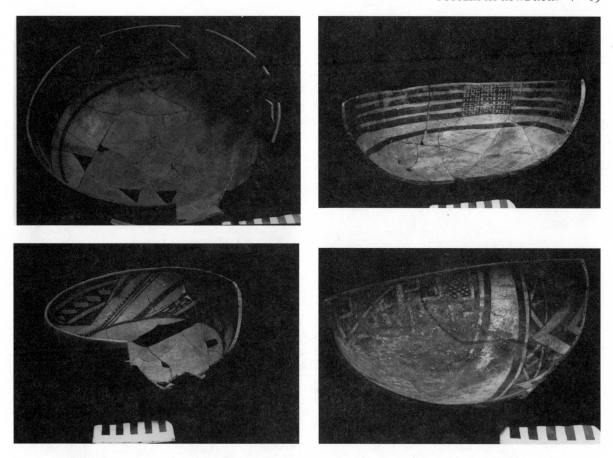

Figure 19. Rowe Black-on-white var. Rowe bowls excavated before UNM's work at the site. Bowls are slipped on both sides, often with polished interior, and decorated with black carbon paint. Description follows Habicht-Mauche (1993).

classified in this type. In all 24 cases, the paste is soft and light in both weight and color. Temper is visible only with a hand lens and is uniformly fine tuff. All sherds are from bowls. The interiors are slipped with an off-white slip, and exteriors are unslipped. The paint is a dark gray.

GALISTEO SERIES

Galisteo Black-on-white, the classic "Crackle" of Kidder and Amsden (1931), makes up 14% of the painted pottery from Rowe. The paste of this type is generally blue-gray, sometimes with a dark streak or core. The visible temper is generally coarsely ground sherd (Figure 23). Crushed siltstone or crushed sandstone temper occurs in about half of the sherds but is finer and not as prominent. Some sherds contain fragments of biotite schist in addition to sherd temper. The distinctive Galisteo slip is a thick, hard, white slip that is crackled or crazed. Slip occurs on both the interiors and exteriors of bowls. Paint is carbon gray to black and not uniform in color. Design is the San Juan McElmo/Mesa Verde style.

Santa Fe Black-on-white

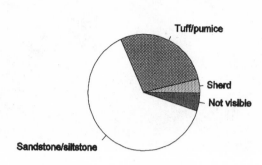

Figure 20. Temper in Santa Fe Black-on-white sherds recovered during 1980

Socorro White Ware

SOCORRO SERIES

Only five Chupadero Black-on-white sherds were recovered from Rowe. These were identified by their black mineral paint and striations on the unslipped (exterior) surface.

White Mountain Red Ware

ZUNI SERIES

White Mountain Red Ware is represented by less than 1% of the ceramics from Rowe (23 sherds). Although tabulated as 18 St. Johns Black-on-red and five St. Johns Polychrome, this count was "conservative." If white paint was not observed on the exterior, they were classified as St. Johns Black-on-red even though it is likely that white exterior lines were missing from the vessel part or, as is common in the type, had sloughed off. The paste of the 18 black-on-red sherds is buff with visible, sparse sherd temper and fine sand temper. The exterior surface slip color is a very dark red, and the paint a dark brown to black mineral paint rather than a glaze.

Heshotauthla Black-on-red makes up 3% of the painted pottery from Rowe. The paste color is generally light red/light orange. In addition to sherd temper, some biotite, augite, and zoned feldspar temper was identi-

Figure 21. Sherds of Santa Fe Black-on-white from Rowe excavations

fied petrographically. Slip color is a clear red to orange red. The paint type is a coppery glaze that appears rough or brownish.

Rio Grande Glaze Ware

Sherds of Rio Grande glaze vessels make up 7.5% of the painted pottery from Rowe; about half are rim sherds, all of which are self-rims of the Glaze A or Glaze I type. Since only the rims are diagnostic in the Rio Grande glazes, body sherds were classified simply as "glaze red" or "glaze yellow." In fact, all of the Rio Grande glaze at Rowe is probably Glaze A. In order of abundance within this class, and not counting the body sherds, the types represented are Agua Fria Glaze-on-red, San Clemente Glaze Polychrome, Los Padillas Glaze Polychrome, and Cieneguilla Glaze-on-yellow. My own experience with the Rio Grande glazes at Tijeras Pueblo (LA 581), LA 282 (Teypama or Las Huertas, near Socorro), and Pottery Mound (LA 416, near Los Lunas) has influenced the confidence with which glaze sherds were classified. In general, the Rio Grande Glaze A sherds often have an uneven paste color and frequently a dark carbon streak. The red slips tend to be deep orange red, and the paint a good vitrified glaze or a coppery glaze which appears rough. Mineral constituents identified in the temper are brown biotite and zoned feldspars characteristic of igneous rock, most likely andesite.

Pottery and Intrasite Chronology

As discussed previously, the architecture at Rowe Ruin is very complicated. There is, however, no evidence that occupation of the site was interrupted for any length of time. Rather, the inhabitants of the site seem to have modified their built space several times while still in residence. Stratigraphically, the adobe structure underneath the south plaza roomblocks and extending further south is the earliest part of the site. The north plaza area and parts of the central plaza seem to have been constructed somewhat later than other excavated rooms. The pottery chronology at Rowe fully supports the stratigraphic chronology and does not add appreciable information. As noted, the black-on-white pottery types recovered from Rowe were produced at about the same time and

Wiyo Black-on-white

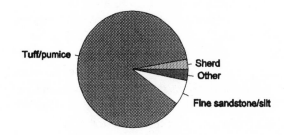

Figure 22. Temper in Wiyo Black-on-white sherds recovered during 1980

Galisteo Black-on-white

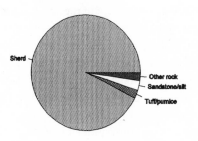

Figure 23. Temper in Galisteo Black-on-white sherds recovered during 1980

do not really help refine the chronological picture. The ratio of corrugated to plain ware is useful for overall placement of the site, but not for placement of areas within the site. The intrasite chronology is confirmed by the distribution of Rio Grande glaze wares.

The dates published by Habicht-Mauche (1993:10) for various types present at Rowe are appropriate, as are dates traditionally assigned. Thus, the earliest types produced are Santa Fe Black-on-white *var. Santa Fe* (AD 1175–1425) and Wiyo Black-on-white (AD 1250–1425). These types were produced from 50 to 125 years before the earliest Rio Grande Glaze A type (Los Padillas polychrome) was made. Stratigraphically, the lower midden of T303 at Rowe Ruin (which Raish, this volume, identifies as Units 22 and 23) was below the flagstone floor and most clearly relates to the early portion of the occupation of Rowe. Raish (this volume) states: "Of the 299 sherds in the units there are no glaze types and no red polychrome types."

Of the 115 black-on-white sherds recovered from the unit, Rowe and Wiyo occur in the greatest frequencies. As indicated elsewhere, Rowe Black-on-white *var. Rowe* is the most common pottery at the site. The excavation units of the south plaza area consistently contain fewer Glaze A sherds, and Los Padillas polychrome is the only glaze type that occurs in the oldest stratigraphic levels. The excavated areas associated with the middle quadrangle generally have more Glaze A.

For the site as a whole, Rio Grande Glaze A is not common, accounting for only 7.5% of the total. The excavation units that contained relatively more Rio Grande Glaze A are rooms 112 and 113, three levels of T212, and room 20. Rooms 112 and 113 are both located in the north roomblock of the middle quadrangle. They may well have served as areas in which trash was deposited while the north quadrangle was being built or occupied. Room 112, at least, has been described as a later addition to the roomblock. T212 was excavated in disturbed midden outside the north and middle plaza wall. The levels containing higher percentages of glaze (3.9%) were all disturbed midden (see Raish, this volume).

As Raish indicates in her report, the distribution of the black-on-white types does not allow chronological refinement. Rowe Black-on-white is the most abundant painted type throughout the site, and the other three types pattern differently in different excavation units. It is likely that differences among these types are functional as well as temporal and that the differences among the excavation units are also functional as well as temporal.

Ceramics and Cultural Affiliation

Our initial questions concerning the Rowe ceramics and cultural affiliation were Wait and Nordby's (1979) concerns about Pueblo-Plains interaction and the place of origin of the Rowe population. In her report (this volume), Raish explains how she developed attribute analyses that would help her identify ceramics of Plains cultural origin, particularly Ocate Micaceous (Gunnerson and Gunnerson 1970). She notes potential problems in differentiating Ocate Micaceous from the local Pueblo utility ware because both contain micaceous clays and temper. In addition, correctly identifying Ocate Micaceous vessels by shape was not possible because the excavated micaceous sherds were too small to manifest specific shape characteristics of the Apache ware. She concludes that on the basis of her study, no Ocate Micaceous sherds could be identified. The same conclusion was reached by Morrison (1987) in her report. The question of Pueblo-Plains interaction in the fourteenth century remains moot based on the data from Rowe. The kinds of Plains-type objects Kidder (1932, and see Spielmann 1991:8) identified at Pecos did not occur at Rowe.

The question of origin of the original inhabitants of Rowe is more difficult to phrase and less easy to resolve. Wait (personal communication, 1980) had suggested that if the Rowe population originated from the vicinity of Jemez Pueblo, then the earliest ceramic type and most consistent trade ware at the site should be Wiyo Black-on-white, which is tempered with pumiceous tuff presumably from the Jemez volcanics. As Raish (this volume) comments, Wiyo Black-on-white is among the earliest ceramic types at the site, but it shares that position with Santa Fe Black-on-white, Galisteo Black-on-white, and Rowe Black-on-white. Further, she notes that Wiyo is not the most common trade ware at the site. Rather, Wiyo and Galisteo occur in approximately the same abundance, and both are second to Santa Fe in that respect.

If one looks only at temper, 7% of the Wiyo sherds are tempered with fine sandstone or siltstone that need not have originated in the Jemez. Further, the pumiceous tuff of the Wiyo sherds is identical to the ash tempering in some of the Santa Fe Black-on-white sherds and may have originated in the vicinity of Arroyo Hondo or the Española Basin. Some of the tuff temper in Wiyo from Rowe is very coarse, clearly visible, and most likely from the vicinity of Jemez Pueblo. What percentage of the Wiyo sherds from Rowe contains this coarse tuff temper is not known. Further, the university excavations at Rowe and subsequent analyses did not conduct the clay studies that would be needed to resolve this question. At some time in the future, it should be possible to characterize the variability in temper found in the Wiyo

Black-on-white from Rowe as well as perform the necessary petrological and chemical studies of the clays. At present, the data do not strongly support the idea that the initial occupants of Rowe Ruin came from Jemez Pueblo, nor were ties between Rowe and the Jemez area marked by persistent or abundant ceramic trade.

During the 1984 season, the university work was concerned with identifying alliance systems at Rowe and perhaps beginning to integrate them into larger networks. Plog was particularly interested in learning whether or not distributions of ceramics would suggest hierarchical organizational structures. Plog reasoned that if Rowe Ruin had been occupied at the same time as the older parts of Pecos Pueblo but yielded little Rio Grande glaze while Pecos had a great deal, it could be suggested that Pecos controlled the distribution of glaze ware in the Upper Pecos Valley. This was not the case. Rowe and the earliest parts of Pecos Pueblo that have been excavated are roughly contemporary. This determination is based on tree-ring dates and the percentages of the various types of Pajarito White Ware from both sites. The amount of Rio Grande glaze in these contexts is also just about the same (Kidder and Shepard 1936; Kidder 1958). We discovered no instances at Rowe Ruin in which chronology alone could not account for the amount of Rio Grande glaze. Yet another possibility is that Rowe Ruin itself might have been the center of distribution of ceramic types to smaller settlements occupied at the same time. The results of our surveys did not reveal the presence of such a settlement system. It follows that however Rowe functioned within its larger community, social hierarchies restricting access either to ceramics or to the goods that might have been transported in ceramic containers were not present.

Interactions among settlements may well constitute social alliances of some kind without being hierarchical. Rowe Ruin did exist within a larger framework of settlements and villages with which it shared both "stylistic" as well as technological attributes. Since, in recent years, southwestern archaeologists have become far more explicit about what they mean by "style," as well as what they mean by "alliances" and "ethnicity," I present a slightly expanded treatment of my views of these issues in the context of the pottery of Rowe. These statements, in turn, are relevant to the concluding chapter of this report.

Design Style vs. Composition as Markers of Ethnicity in Rio Grande and Upper Pecos Ceramics

In my opinion, most of the steps a potter takes in making a pot are cultural and involve choice. Selecting one clay source rather than another, using one or another variety of tempering material and one or another pigment for slip and for paint, choosing one or another shape for the vessel, adopting one of several methods of building the vessel, for example, all involve choices that are made on the basis of learning. They are therefore cultural markers whether or not the choices are made consciously. An example of a cultural choice that is not necessarily conscious would be the potter who knows how to prepare black pigment only from bee plant and not from manganese. Her use of plant dye is cultural, but if it is all she knows, the selection itself is not conscious. The resulting pot will reflect her cultural repertory of appropriate actions. This to me, however, is not a reflection of "ethnicity." I have discussed this matter at length elsewhere (Cordell and Yannie 1991). It is worth reiterating some of the salient points here.

In his classic statement, Frederick Barth (1969) defined an ethnic group as a population that is largely self-perpetuating biologically, shares fundamental cultural values realized in overt cultural forms that make up a field of communication and interaction, and *most important,* one whose members identify themselves and are identified by others as constituting a category distinguishable from other categories of the same order. In Barth's view, self-ascription is the crucial element of the definition, so the sum of objectively different features is not necessarily important. Rather, the key features are limited to those that are seen by the actors themselves as significant. Clearly in most cases, including the ancient Upper Pecos Valley, archaeologists are not in a position to know how the "actors" or individual potters whose work we study identified themselves. We, as archaeologists, are limited to objectively discernible and durable contrastive features.

Americanist normative archaeology emphasizes the total shared aspects of material culture in order to delimit presumed ethnic groups. For example, in the Southwest, "branch" status is generally conferred on groups sharing visible aspects of material culture. The Mesa

Verde branch is defined with respect to generally homogeneous architecture, pottery, village layout, range of artifact types, etc. Yet, there are both ethnographic and historical archaeological examples of cases in which more than one "ethnic" group shares relatively homogeneous attributes of this sort (Naroll 1970). In historical archaeology, studies have revealed cases in which assemblage similarities in faunal remains and pottery ware and form are more indicative of general conditions of poverty than of ethnicity (Baker 1980:34–35; Otto 1977:92).

In order to avoid the confusion of looking at the totality of remains, archaeologists may emphasize those aspects of material culture that are expected to relate to communication and interaction. In this case the attempt is to delineate the attributes of what may be termed the emblematic style of materials carrying information content relevant to ethnic unity and identity. In the Southwest, features of ceramic assemblages are used in this way more than any other class of material culture. Ceramic design elements, layout, color combinations, surface treatment, and design symmetry have all been viewed as ethnic markers (see Ford et al. 1972; Lang 1982; Washburn 1977). Precisely the same attributes have been seen to mark tribal boundaries, language groups, lineage segments, and the larger categories of Western Pueblo and Eastern Pueblo. I believe that it is unlikely that a single class of artifacts would consistently carry that much information. But even if it did, there is no agreement among archaeologists about which aspect of ceramics is indicative of which kind of social group or how one measures stylistic homogeneity in ceramics, or what such homogeneity might mean if it could be measured. I am again mindful of Carol Kramer's (1985:88) insightful statement that "if ceramic vessels do not leave the household context and when they do, do not travel very far, one may ask to whom pots are signaling, what the content of the message is, and why some household vessels are more elaborately decorated than others." Ceramic attributes undoubtedly do communicate messages about ethnicity, as about other cultural choices, but far too many assumptions have been made by archaeologists about what is being communicated and to whom.

Martin Wobst (1974, 1981) has suggested that those objects that are likely to be exchanged or displayed in intergroup interactions are more likely than other objects to convey social information. Among populations of hunters and gatherers, weapons are one such class of objects. Studies of hunter-gatherers by Wiessner (1982), Larrick (1985), and Sinopoli (1985) show that among ethnographically and ethnohistorically known groups, nearly any attribute may be socially meaningful but specific meaning varies from one context to another. Further, the range of group expression may refer to everything from age cohorts to language groups. There are obviously no invariant rules that define which attributes function as emblematic style (see Wiessner 1983, 1984).

Despite this, I have suggested that two methods of determining whether or not attributes are signaling ethnic affiliation seem appropriate. One way, which has met with some success, is to use ethnographic cases or cases for which we have historical documents. Studies by Wiessner (1983, 1984) and Sinopoli (1985) are appropriate examples, as I hope is a look at the Genizaro populations of New Mexico (Cordell and Yannie 1991). Clearly, this approach is not appropriate in the case of Rowe Ruin. Second, the distributions of assemblages of potential stylistic attributes may suggest that they carried information about group identity if the distribution conforms to territory of a size appropriate to maintaining a viable breeding population, given an estimate of population density and considerations of local geography (Plog 1979). In the Southwest, the term "province" is sometimes used to refer to areas having relatively homogenous assemblages of some classes of artifacts (Ruppé 1953). Plog (1979) suggests that among the Western Anasazi, territory size appeared to be consistently about 10,000 km². Among the Eastern Anasazi, with a wetter and more lush environment, size of provinces determined on the basis of stylistic homogeneity of ceramic decoration ranges from 2,000 to 5,000 km² (Cordell 1989; Cordell and Yannie 1991). These figures should not, of course, be taken at face value. Nevertheless, they suggest the scale of potential areas of ethnic interaction. Even in these cases, however, we know that ethnic groups sometimes exist as enclaves within the territorial borders of complex societies (essentially ancient or modern states).

There are clues in the above discussion regarding what one might look for in pottery style as potentially informative in terms of bounded interactions. First, given that the focus is on *signaling* interaction, normally invisible attributes, such as paste and temper characteristics or the mineral or plant constituents of paint, while certainly cultural, are not likely to be used as a signal. If they were used as a signal, they would serve only to provide information to a very small group that would see pottery being made. Presumably, such a group would not require a signal of ethnic identification from the potter, since in all likelihood they would be known to each other. Second, we need to look at distributions over a large geographic area, one that might be expected to contain one or more boundaries. The approach Douglass (1985) took does both of these.

Douglass compared the pottery from Rowe with two defined styles of black-on-white pottery, one from the Cibola region and one from the northern San Juan. She contrasted the two styles in terms of the types of design elements, design element composition, and interaction between primary lines. She found that with regard to these characteristics as well as temporal trends in design, Rowe and the Upper Pecos Valley were tied to the northern San Juan interaction sphere by AD 1200. Although the similarity of Galisteo Black-on-white and McElmo/Mesa Verde Black-on-white is so well documented they are considered "cognate types," the stylistic similarity is not as well marked for Santa Fe Black-on-white and types such as Mancos and McElmo. Douglass's conclusions become more relevant to a consideration of aggregation in the Upper Pecos when they are combined with recent observations made by Roney (1995), which are deferred to the concluding chapter. In this case, however, I suggest that at Rowe Ruin the ceramic design style as defined in Douglass's characterization of the painted decoration is what we would consider a likely candidate for emblematic style, whereas all non-visible technological attributes are essentially cultural but without emblematic significance. I would also conclude that the style we can thus define is not what we would consider characteristic of any ethnic group by Barth's definition. Rather, the style seems to show a loose, perhaps informal, open, nonhierarchical network of interaction across an area considerably larger than the distribution of any Pueblo language or modern tribal units.

In sum, the ceramic assemblage from Rowe is dominated by locally produced, textured utility ware and Upper Pecos varieties of Pajarito Series Black-on-white. Santa Fe, Wiyo, and Galisteo Black-on-white also make up significant portions of the assemblage of painted pottery. In addition to being from the immediate vicinity of Rowe Ruin itself and the Upper Pecos in general, pottery, or temper, was derived from areas with access to pumiceous tuff. These more distant locations include the Jemez Pueblo area, the Española Basin, and possibly Arroyo Hondo. Although the spatial distributions of these types at the site are not useful for refining the intrasite chronology of Rowe Ruin, together they confirm the tree-ring and radiocarbon dates for the site as a whole. Within the site, the distribution of Rio Grande glaze was useful in separating areas of earlier and later occupation. These findings confirm that the parts of the site associated with the underlying adobe structure and the lower portions of the central and south plaza roomblocks are generally earlier than the upper rooms of the central quadrangle and probably the north quadrangle as well.

No direct ceramic evidence of interaction with Plains peoples was manifest in the pottery from Rowe Ruin. Trade wares occurring at Rowe Ruin were ultimately derived from the Zuni and central and southern Rio Grande regions, although they may have been passed to Rowe through intermediary settlements. Throughout its occupation, Rowe Ruin's inhabitants were affiliated with the Santa Fe–Pajarito province which, in turn, shared pottery decorative motifs and design organization with the northern San Juan region. Throughout this very large region and for about 250 years (from AD 1200 to 1450), ceramic design suggests at least loose levels of interaction among settlements. Within this area, there are no sharply delineated boundaries of style that would suggest marked ethnic enclaves, borders, or polities. Finally, there is as yet no evidence that trade ware was differentially distributed among sites on the Upper Pecos.

PALEOCLIMATE AND THE TIMING
OF AGGREGATION AT ROWE

Being able to assign calendar dates to the occupations of Pueblo sites in parts of the Southwest enables us to examine the climatic environment of that occupation as reconstructed from dendrochronology. Within the context of the research at Rowe Ruin, the immediate objective in making these comparisons relates to hypotheses about population aggregation and climatic variability that were discussed in the research design (Cordell et al. 1983). The focus of the 1983–1984 work was to begin to evaluate proposed relationships among population aggregation into large villages in the Southwest, increased regional variation in rainfall, and the development of regional systems of exchange.

In a number of presentations and publications, Fred Plog linked population aggregation and what he termed *stable societies* to spatial variation in rainfall across the Southwest (e.g., Green and Plog 1983; Plog 1983, 1984). Stable societies, according to his definition, are those that practice increasingly intensive agriculture, use or produce ceramics that are strongly normative in style and are therefore "diagnostic types" for the archaeologist, show at least some minimal patterns of social hierarchy, and occupy relatively large pueblos for long periods of time (relative to the length of time smaller sites were inhabited). He suggested that the formation of large habitation sites, along with the other characteristics of stable societies, was limited almost entirely to times when "rainfall conditions from area to area and region to region in the northern Southwest were far more varied than at present" (in Cordell et al. 1983).

The link between spatial variability and big sites, Plog stated, was the potential of the large sites to be centers of exchange. "It appears that exchange was one means elected to counter the increasingly high spatial variability. Exchange of some magnitude may have led to mana-gerial roles, large central settlements from which the exchange was coordinated" (in Cordell et al. 1983).

Plog needed a measure of spatial diversity in precipitation. There are 25 stations across the Southwest for which the Laboratory of Tree-Ring Research has retrodicted precipitation patterns going back to the seventh century AD. For each station, decadal tree-ring widths are plotted as standard deviations from a mean precipitation value. Plog used the standard deviations of the station values for each decadal map as his indicator of spatial diversity. His index is a simple measure of the variation among all the stations for the decade in question. It reflects the general spatial variability throughout the region as a whole rather than revealing the range of variability within the region (Jeffrey S. Dean, University of Arizona Tree-Ring Laboratory, letter to the author dated March 22, 1991).

Plog (in Cordell et al. 1983) noted that a peak in spatial variation in rainfall occurred between about AD 1260 and 1400 when "the majority of very large (100 plus rooms) pueblos known in the northern Southwest were built," Rowe among them. The supporting environmental data (Dean et al. 1985) show rainfall variability across the Southwest as a whole (Figure 24). Having worked largely in central Arizona, Plog was most familiar with the Western Pueblo data. Even more of these large, late sites occur in the Middle and Northern Rio Grande regions than in the Western Pueblo area, and they seem to have been occupied for longer periods of time in the east as well. The work at Rowe, as stated previously, was designed to provide baseline data that would eventually allow us to replace this relatively mechanical, environmentally based model with one that specified interactions between environmental and cultural patterns in detail. In addition, the work was to have been the start

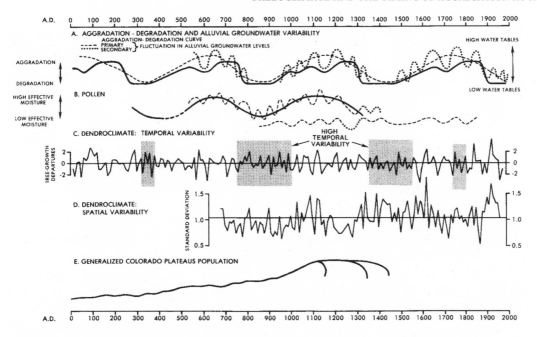

Figure 24. Environmental and demographic variability on the southern Colorado Plateaus, AD 1–1970 (Dean et al. 1985:Fig. 1) (courtesy of the authors and *American Antiquity*)
  A. hydrologic fluctuations and floodplain aggradation-degradation
  B. primary (solid) and secondary (dashed) fluctuations in effective moisture as indicated by pollen data
  C. decadal tree growth departures in standard deviation units
  D. spatial variability in dendroclimate
  E. relative population trends, AD 1–1450

of generating a data base that could be used for comparison with those being developed for the Western Pueblo (e.g., Grasshopper, Chavez Pass, the Homolovi ruins).

Before examining the relationship between regional variation in rainfall and population aggregation at Rowe, I was concerned that the pattern from the Upper Pecos, at the far eastern edge of the Pueblo world, might not be the same as or completely congruent with that in central Arizona. The issue of whether or not spatial patterning in the western portion of the Southwest was the same as in the eastern side of the region is important for at least two reasons. First, precipitation across the Southwest as a whole follows two or three different regimes. Second, a preliminary examination of the materials from Rowe indicates that what trade items there were did not

originate very far to the west. It was hard to see how exchange might even out the effects of spatial variability in rainfall without knowing how much of the variation was occurring in the vicinity of Rowe and among its probable exchange partners.

Dean's map, published in 1988 and reproduced here (Figure 25), shows a sinuous line starting north of Santa Fe, swinging northwest and west to Farmington and Holbrook, and then moving east and south to the Arizona–New Mexico border before turning west between Safford and Globe. On the west side of the line, annual precipitation follows a bimodal pattern, about half falling in summer and half in winter. East of the line a unimodal distribution occurs, with most precipitation falling in summer. The "line" is in fact a swath that may be more than fifty miles wide. Its position also varies

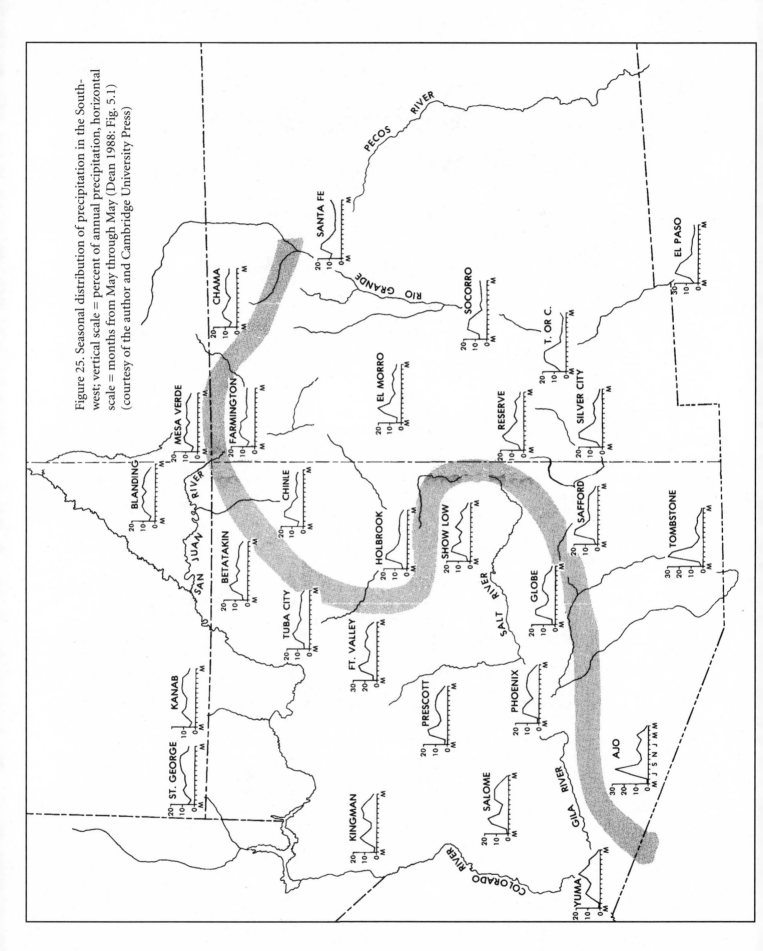

Figure 25. Seasonal distribution of precipitation in the Southwest; vertical scale = percent of annual precipitation, horizontal scale = months from May through May (Dean 1988: Fig. 5.1) (courtesy of the author and Cambridge University Press)

slightly over time. Pecos, and Rowe, are east of the line. Plog's measure of spatial variability considered deviations from the mean across the region as a whole. There is no a priori reason to believe that spatial variation east and west of the line will be the same.

Different spatial patterns in precipitation may be appreciated visually by comparing maps produced by the Laboratory of Tree-Ring Research for each decade from AD 680 on and generously provided by Jeffrey S. Dean. The map of the 1860s, for example, illustrates regional uniformity when variation across the entire Southwest is low (Figure 26). The map of 880 to 889 (Figure 27) might be considered one of moderate variation. The maps also show periods (e.g., the 680s and 890s) when variation is higher on one side of the line than on the other (Figures 28 and 29). At other times, for example in the 1080s and 1330s (Figures 30 and 31), variation is uniformly high.

As a check on these visual inferences, I used the set of decade maps showing departures from mean rainfall at each station to record the highest and lowest readings on either side of the unimodal-bimodal precipitation line. Comparisons of the high numbers and of the sum of high and low numbers for the east and for the west for each decade from 680–689 to 1960–1969 were not significantly correlated ($R^2 = 0.58$). In essence, this exercise suggests that during decades when spatial variation was high in either the west or in the east, there was only about a 50% chance that spatial variation was also high on the other side of the unimodal-bimodal line.

Following Dean's advice, I revised the inclusion of station data for one side or the other to more accurately reflect the complicated patterns of modality recognized by the Laboratory of Tree-Ring Research. The revised distribution of stations is given in Table 12. My calculations agreed with Plog's only some of the time. Obviously, low values of Plog's measure must specify uniformity across the entire Southwest because any variation in the departures would increase the standard deviation. The obverse, however, is not necessarily true. High spatial variability may occur within one rainfall regime and not others.

In order to see whether or not spatial variability in rainfall on the west side of the line was similar to that east of the line, I plotted the single decade measure (the lowest subtracted from the highest) for each group, one on either side of the east-west bimodal line. Figure 32 shows this for the years 1000 to 1550. The figure shows that at times, for example from 1300 to 1340, the east and west stations were moving in the same general pattern—first of increasing, then of decreasing, and finally of increasing variability. The same figure shows that the east vs. west patterns at 1340 begin to diverge, and they do not move in tandem again until briefly at 1390 and 1400. Immediately thereafter, divergence again becomes the rule. Figure 32 shows two periods of marked increase in spatial variability, one in the early 1100s and the other in the early to mid 1300s. I did not go beyond the visual presentation of these data and thus did not determine whether or not the differences between the east and west stations are statistically significant between 1000 and 1500.

As part of a major research project, Dean (1995) conducted a principal components analysis of data from the 25 Southwest climate stations. With the exception of minor variations, he found that the east vs. west patterns remained consistent for very long periods of time. The variations consisted of one or a very few stations near the edge of one of the patterns being classified with the other pattern for a few decades. The stability of the difference between bimodal and unimodal rainfall distributions was significant. Between abut 1250 and 1450, however, the pattern breaks down and becomes nearly chaotic, with no predictable association of stations for more than two hundred years, except in the east-southeast. Dean is continuing his investigations of this unprecedented change in conditions (Dean 1995) and its implications for the region.

For Rowe Ruin specifically, and for our research design, there are two periods of aggregation to consider. Our chronometric data suggest that an initial aggregation, represented by the adobe structure and early radiocarbon dates, occurred in the 1240s and 1250s. At this time, the graphs show only moderate spatial variation in precipitation in the east and a decline in variation between 1240 and 1250. For the principal period of aggregation, reflected by construction of the masonry quadrangles, dates between 1340 and 1360 are suggested based on tree-ring samples. The graph shows a marked increase in spatial variability in rainfall in both east and west at 1330; however, it drops in 1340 and remains low in 1350. At that date, the east and west begin to diverge again, with spatial variability in the east dropping again in 1360 and 1380. These observations at best provide

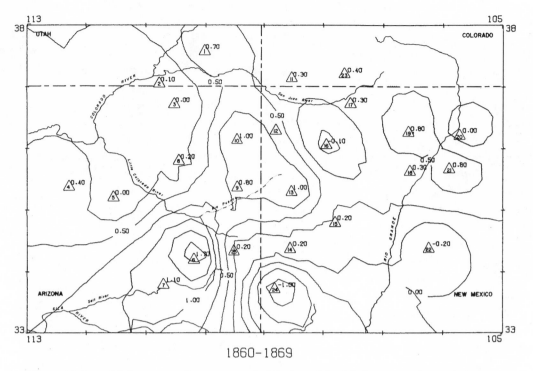

1860-1869

Figure 26. Decadal departures from mean rainfall plotted for 25 climate stations. 1860s: spatial variability is low (uniform) across the Southwest

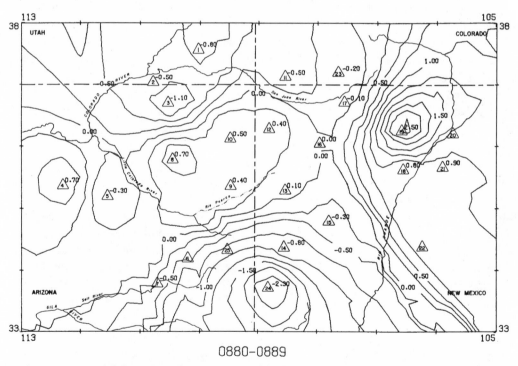

0880-0889

Figure 27. Decadal departures from mean rainfall plotted for 25 climate stations. 880s: variation is moderate

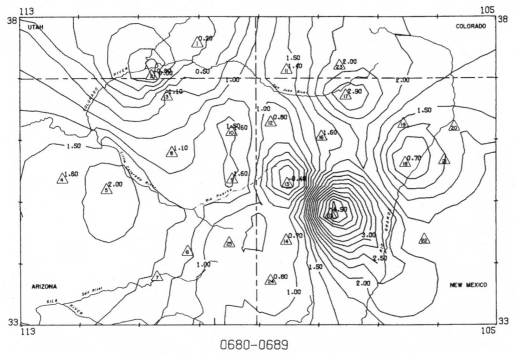

0680-0689

Figure 28. Decadal departures from mean rainfall plotted for 25 climate stations. 680s: variation in the east is higher than in the west

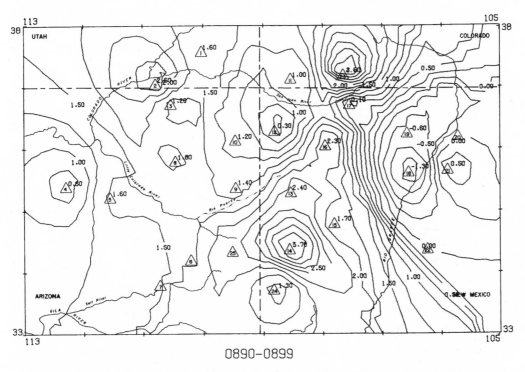

0890-0899

Figure 29. Decadal departures from mean rainfall plotted for 25 climate stations. 890s: variation in the east is higher than in the west

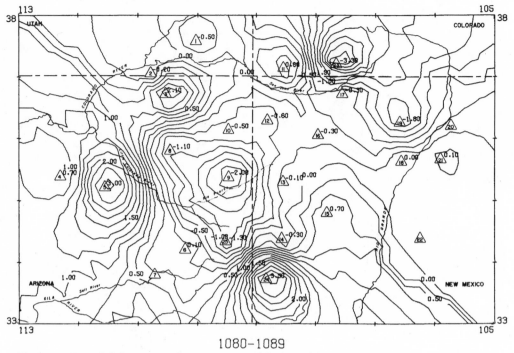

1080-1089

Figure 30. Decadal departures from mean rainfall plotted for 25 climate stations. 1080s: One of two patterns in which variation is high in both east and west

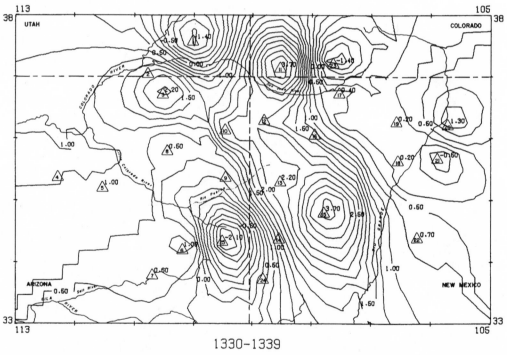

1330-1339

Figure 31. Decadal departures from mean rainfall plotted for 25 climate stations. 1330s: The second pattern in which variation is high in both east and west

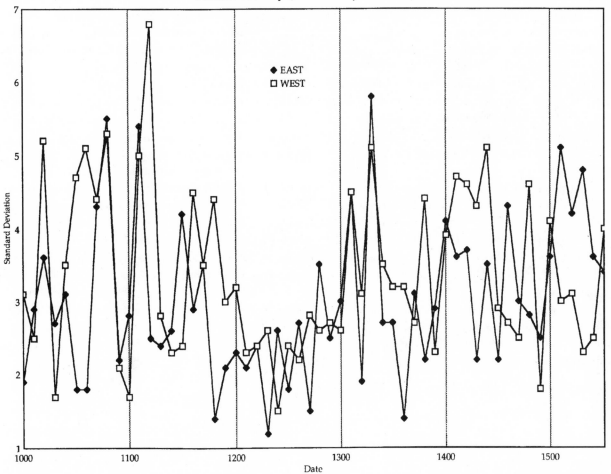

Figure 32. Decadal dendroclimatic spatial variability west of the bimodal-unimodal rainfall line and east of that line, for the years 1000–1550. The number potted for each decade is the lowest deviation subtracted from the highest deviation west and east of the line.

Table 12. Key to Groupings in Figure 32: Climate Stations and Rainfall Modality

East-Unimodal	West-Bimodal
9	1
10	2
12	3
13	4
14	5
15	6
16	7
18	8
19	11
20	17
21	23
22	25
24	

only moderate support for the original hypothesis predicting that aggregation into large sites is a response to spatial variability in rainfall or that spatial variability in rainfall favored an established aggregated settlement pattern on the eastern edge of the Southwest. Based on the increase in spatial variability in precipitation in the early 1100s, one might expect an increase in the number of large sites in the late 1100s. In the eastern part of the Southwest, however, so few sites are dated to this time period that it is likely that groups could adjust to spatial variability by moving. Mobility must still have been an option. The increase in spatial variability in precipitation in the early 1300s may have conferred some advantage on the community at Rowe, particularly if the presence of other villages in the Upper Pecos Valley, such as Forked Lightning, Dick's Ruin, and early Pecos Pueblo, were also inhabited at that time, making mobility an unlikely option.

In our discussions of the research design for Rowe Ruin and of aggregation in general, we did not propose one or more causal mechanisms, nor did we specify an expected "lag time" for aggregation to occur as a response to perceived patterns. Although we did not say so, I suspect we thought that given aggregation as one strategy, perhaps one adopted sporadically, conditions of high spatial variability in precipitation would confer advantages on those living in aggregated settlements. Such an inference is not supported on the basis of dates from Rowe Ruin and rainfall variability in the Eastern Pueblo world. This information by itself is useful in terms of pursuing our research goal of moving away from modeling cultural change as a simplistic response to environmental factors. Further, data that had not been pulled together in the 1980s provide reasons to question a view of aggregation, expressed as large sites, as having occurred sporadically or gradually, growing to encompass more areas over time. The patterns of aggregation and abandonment continue to be fertile research topics in southwestern archaeology (see Adler 1996; Cordell, Doyel, and Kintigh 1994; Kohler and Van West 1995; Tainter 1995). Some of the implications for this research of the work at Rowe and in the Upper Pecos are discussed in the concluding chapter of this section.

CONCLUDING DISCUSSION

THIS REPORT HAS FOCUSED ON RESEARCH IN THE Upper Pecos Valley of New Mexico and specifically on Rowe Ruin, a relatively large fourteenth-century community. The Upper Pecos Valley is an important locale in the history of Southwest archaeology largely because of the lengthy commitment A. V. Kidder made to the study of Pecos Pueblo and to one of its antecedents, Forked Lightning Ruin (Kidder 1926, 1958; Kidder and Shepard 1936). The first archaeological excavations at Rowe Ruin (Guthe 1917) were performed in conjunction with this work. Kidder's work set an example and a standard for future excavations throughout the Southwest, assured in part by the annual field conferences begun at his field camp and named for the site (Kidder 1927; Woodbury 1993).

Yet, as has been pointed out in a number of contexts (Wait and Nordby 1979), following Kidder's work archaeologists ignored the Upper Pecos for years. The work reported here was undertaken partly to reexamine and reevaluate some of the conclusions reached as a result of the earlier investigations. Most important, this research has altered our understanding of the details but not the overall picture obtained by Kidder and his colleagues nearly fifty years ago. We were able to answer some of the questions raised by Kidder's research, but not others.

Over the course of the university work described here, our research program underwent considerable change. The research questions that were posed in 1980 were not those addressed in 1984. Surely an entirely different set of questions would be phrased were work to begin today. In this summary, I hope to emphasize what we have learned that expands our view of culture history in the Upper Pecos Valley.

The Upper Pecos Valley is, most obviously, at the very eastern margin of the Pueblo world, nearly on the edge of the vast grassland plains to the east. The physical setting, though spectacularly beautiful, is not one that is particularly appropriate for maize horticulture. At an elevation of 2,072 m and with average annual precipitation of 38.6 cm, short growing seasons and aridity together were problems for all those needing reliable yields of corn. Agricultural, village-dwelling Pueblo people expanded into this landscape only very late in their culture history.

In 1926, Kidder expressed surprise and disappointment that despite the depth of the trash mound at Pecos Pueblo, the time represented by the accumulation was not very great (Kidder 1962:138–139). At Pecos Pueblo, the origins of Pueblo society were missing from the record. Work over the years has filled in the pre-Pecos background. As described here and elsewhere, there is now evidence of Paleoindian use of the Upper Pecos area (Anschuetz 1980; Nordby 1981; Stanford and Patten 1984; Wendorf and Miller 1958). Because both the Folsom site near Johnson Mesa and Stanford's sites near Sapello are relatively close to Rowe, the absence of known Paleoindian sites in the Upper Pecos Valley itself may seem surprising. I suspect that the primary reason for the lack of such sites is that landforms in the Upper Pecos generally are not nearly as dissected and worn down as are the "highly eroded" sites to the north and east (Stanford and Patten 1984). Surfaces of sufficient antiquity to reveal more abundant, and perhaps substantial, Paleoindian remains have not been uncovered. Also, the Upper Pecos Valley, at the base of the Sangre de Cristo Mountains, is a high-elevation setting that Paleoindian peoples may have used only sporadically and therefore one in which only sparse, surface remains are characteristic.

No Early Archaic sites are recorded in the Upper Pecos, but university surveys did locate evidence of Middle and Late Archaic occupations that can be assigned to the

Oshara tradition on the basis of projectile point types. Four Late Archaic components, at four different sites, yielded points that can be assigned to the San Jose and En Medio phases. All four sites were located in 1980 in the area southeast and east of Rowe Ruin, near the Pecos River. Although only one of the sites reflects quarrying activities, all four are located where there is easy access to the high-quality local gray chert and Tecolote chert outcrops along the Pecos. The presence of hearths and abundant lithic debris suggests that Late Archaic use of this part of the Pecos Valley may have been more intensive than previously suspected and warrants further survey and excavation. It would be useful to compare the Middle and Late Archaic of the Upper Pecos with Late Archaic sites and assemblages of the Cimarron District (Glassow 1980, 1984; Kershner 1984; Kirkpatrick and Lumbach 1984) and with the numerous Middle and Late Archaic sites of the Chama and Pajarito Plateau areas (see Lang 1980; Shaafsma 1979).

The six hundred years of the Developmental period of Wendorf and Reed's (1955) scheme is still poorly documented in the Upper Pecos. Nevertheless, the two ninth-century pithouses excavated by the Park Service at Pecos National Historic Park Headquarters (Nordby 1981) are evidence that the Upper Pecos was not entirely empty. The pithouses were discovered in the process of excavating a sewer line. There were no surface indications of their presence. Additional, similarly obscured sites may well exist. Although not published in detail, the Pecos pithouses' ceramic assemblage is not like any described for the northern San Juan drainage. There is no Lino Gray or "Lino-like" pottery, and no painted types such as Kwahe'e Black-on-white. The ceramics are described as thick-walled, undecorated, and as resembling those from Pedragosa phase sites of the Cimarron District (Nordby 1981; Glassow 1972, 1980). It is possible that initial settlement of the Upper Pecos and the Cimarron by horticultural people did not occur as a direct result of population expansion, understood either as migration or range expansion, out of the San Juan or Four Corners area. Rather, the most likely donor area may have been a local tradition on the eastern flanks of the Sangre de Cristos and the western Great Plains. A detailed comparison of the Pecos pithouse assemblage with that of the well-documented Pedragosa phase of the Cimarron District (Glassow 1972, 1980) would be in order.

Even if they were occupied simultaneously, the two Pecos pithouses would still constitute a very small settlement, not evidence of established village life. The unpainted ceramics and buried features suggest that archaeological visibility of this settlement episode is very low. Further testing of pithouse sites at the park (as revealed for example by Korsmo's 1983 magnetometer survey) could be highly productive, as might testing of ceramic and lithic scatters with essentially nondiagnostic ceramics.

Throughout the Middle and Northern Rio Grande region, the later portion of the Rio Grande Developmental of ca. AD 900 to 1150 is characterized by a variety of mineral-painted black-on-white ceramic types in the absence of carbon-painted Santa Fe Black-on-white (see Cordell 1979; Habicht-Mauche 1993; Lang 1982; Mera 1935; Peckham and Reed 1963; Sundt 1987; Wetherington 1964). The architecture and non-ceramic portions of the assemblages from these sites are highly variable. Since no sites dating to this period were located by the university surveys reported here, I cannot add information to this meagre record. Four sites in the ARMS records as of 1992 *may* date between AD 900 and 1150. These sites were neither excavated nor tested, so what information they might add to our knowledge of this period is not known. (The site numbers are LA 14100, LA 14121, LA 14130, and LA 14143.) At present, no sites that securely date between 950 and 1150 have been located in the Upper Pecos Valley. I suggest that the hiatus is apparent rather than real because of the size and possible antiquity of ruined adobe structures that continued to be occupied during the subsequent period. Nevertheless, once the information from the Upper Pecos, Taos, Cimarron, Chama, Santa Fe, and Albuquerque districts is combined, it should be possible to refine and subdivide the overly long Rio Grande Developmental period.

Wendorf and Reed's (1955) Coalition period, which they date to between AD 1200 and 1325, is divided into sequential Pindi and Galisteo phases. Although marked by changes in ceramic types, the distinctions between the phases refer to cultural change that occurred within local populations reacting to events of regional scale, on the one hand, versus change initiated at least in part by immigration. At the beginning of the Pindi phase there was a shift from mineral pigments and Chaco II–inspired ceramic styles to carbon-paint Santa Fe Black-on-white.

This change is seen as a local reflection of a broad, panregional trend, the ultimate source of which was the Northern San Juan, including Mesa Verde. In the Rio Grande the change is associated with local architectural characteristics. The most important of these, according to Wendorf and Reed (1955), are circular, subterranean kivas that lack distinctive, diagnostic Mesa Verde/San Juan features such as pilasters and benches, and rectangular domestic structures made of coursed adobe.

On the regional level, the change to styles affiliated with the Northern San Juan/Mesa Verde reflects the end of the centrality of Chaco Canyon in about AD 1130 along with the continued influence of the still densely inhabited Northern San Juan/Mesa Verde region. The change in affiliation is noted by Roney (1995) in his discussion of provinces, by Douglass (1985) regarding alliances, and by Habicht-Mauche (1993) with respect to tribalization. Virtually all studies agree that this change did not initially involve a great influx of people to the Rio Grande from Chaco Canyon or the San Juan Basin. Had that been the case, the stylistic affiliation of Santa Fe Black-on-white should have been with the Tularosa and Socorro styles rather than the Northern San Juan/Mesa Verde styles that it in fact resembles.

The data from the Upper Pecos do not contradict the inference of a lack of immigration from Chaco Canyon and the San Juan Basin. Nevertheless, the density of occupation in the Upper Pecos Valley in the thirteenth century is not at all well known, and I suspect it has been underestimated. My concern derives from the lack of visibility of sites such as Forked Lightning, which was known to be a site but not recognized as a pueblo of more than 100 rooms until it was excavated, and from the potential size of the adobe structures underlying Rowe Ruin. Further, if continued survey, testing, and excavation do not reveal Late Developmental period components in the Upper Pecos, then the population represented by the builders of Forked Lightning Ruin, Dick's Ruin, and the lower levels of Rowe must have derived from outside the immediate area. These "immigrants" may have come from just a few miles north in the Santa Fe District, perhaps from Taos, or from the Upper Cimarron. They likely did not come from the San Juan Basin. The pattern of bonding and abutting of adobe walls at Forked Lightning Ruin suggests that accretional growth was characteristic. Nevertheless, the numbers of people who occupied Forked Lightning, Dick's Ruin, and Rowe are not likely to have derived from in situ population growth unless a great many more sites dating to the AD 900 to 1150 period are documented. At this writing, the National Park Service is again involved in archaeological survey at Pecos. When these new data as well as data from their previous work are reported, our understanding of the sources of the Early Coalition period population in the Upper Pecos Valley should be much enhanced.

Rowe Ruin itself, with its complex stratigraphy spanning Pindi (Early) and Galisteo (Late) Coalition phases, does seem to represent local population growth rather than a migration into the area of people from either the Northern San Juan/Mesa Verde region or the Jemez Pueblo area, although the latter cannot and should not be completely dismissed. Rowe Ruin's organized appearance, with three contiguous plazas surrounded by masonry roomblocks, and the masonry construction itself suggest the possibility of a site unit intrusion of Mesa Verde affiliation. The architectural complexity and depth of Rowe Ruin argue otherwise.

Additional support for an indigenous population model comes from the burial population. Despite the fact that the number of skeletons excavated at Rowe is small, especially compared with the Pecos remains, there are enough to show that the two populations resemble one another physically and differ from those of other Pueblo sites. The Rowe burials manifest unusually large muscle development, rugosity, and generally masculine characteristics of the skull as well as of the infraskeleton. These characteristics set the overall population apart from those of Mesa Verde or the more immediate Tijeras Canyon and Santa Fe districts (cf. Kidder 1958:281–283; Hooten 1930; Palkovitch 1980). A comparison with Plains skeletal series might be rewarding.

The burial patterns from Rowe, Pecos, and Forked Lightning are also similar to one another but differ slightly from other Pueblo patterns. For example, as at other sites in the Rio Grande, the Upper Pecos Valley burials are generally flexed with few, if any, grave goods, but they fail to show consistent orientation of the head. In several instances, the grave pits were covered with small stones. The remains of matting and turtle carapace were found with a few burials at all three Upper Pecos sites (Ferguson 1979; Kidder 1958; Palkovitch 1980).

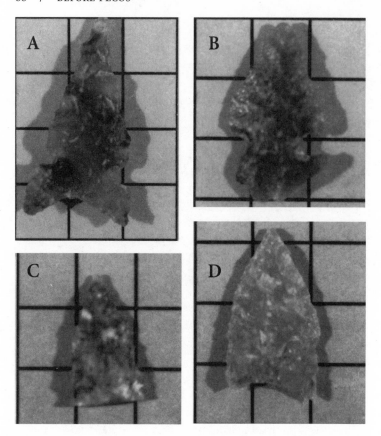

Figure 33. Projectile points of local gray chalcedonic chert, from excavated contexts. (A) Room 30, level 2c, length 2.5 cm; (B) Unit T303, level 1a, length 2.9 cm; (C) Unit T303, level 1a, length 2.75 cm; (D) Unit T303, level 2b, length 2.5 cm

Finally, I am persuaded of a generally local derivation of population by a few other considerations. The masonry style at Rowe Ruin, particularly in the later rooms around the central plaza, is virtually identical to that at Pecos and does not resemble the Cibola or Mesa Verde traditions in terms of time or labor investment. The unpainted pottery at Rowe Ruin was certainly manufactured locally. The quite high-quality lithic material at Rowe Ruin was available locally, was known, and was used throughout the occupation of the site (Figure 33). The painted pottery of Rowe Ruin, while stylistically affiliated with the general Santa Fe/Mesa Verde tradition, reflects the minor technological diversity expected if people are relying on a relatively informal, widely dispersed, in-place network of social relations. This is seen, for example, in the distribution of sandstone/siltstone, pumiceous tuff, and sherd tempers in all of the painted types. At a larger and probably more important level for those involved, the Rowe population seems to have been able to acquire medium to large body-size game in much greater frequencies than is documented at contemporary Pueblo sites. The inhabitants of Rowe hunted more, and probably more successfully, than other Pueblo peoples to the north near Santa Fe or to the south in the Galisteo Basin or in Tijeras Canyon. Nevertheless, they were like these contemporary peoples in apparently not obtaining significant amounts of bison. In this last aspect of their culture, the people of Rowe were different from their descendants at Pecos.

In sum, the visible roomblocks at Rowe seem to represent community planning in that plaza space was set aside and single rooms could not easily be added to the quadrangles. Additional plazas or quadrangles, however, could have been built. The community members making up the final occupation of Rowe were likely from the older adobe structure and perhaps other similar sites at Dick's Ruin, Forked Lightning, or possibly from other Late Coalition and Early Classic sites in the vicinity. Archaeologists frequently view seemingly planned site layouts as indicating an initial occupation. The complex underlying structures and modifications at Rowe indicate that a planned appearance can also come late in a community's existence.

Excavations at Rowe allow some comparison with the conditions of aggregation that may have obtained at Pecos Pueblo as well. A few of these were part of our mutable research design and are examined below. The first, however, is not something we addressed but relates to the role of warfare in population aggregation in the Upper Pecos Valley. In my view in addition to that of others, aggregation can certainly be a response to warfare or the threat of warfare. I agree with Bandelier's (1892:125) early observation that whereas the triple closed-plaza organization of the Rowe site may have been appropriate for defense, the location of the site, at the foot of a wooded mesa, is not. I do not believe that Rowe was situated with an eye to defense at all but was founded near a reliable supply of water from the spring.

There is also no evidence for Rowe having been abandoned because of warfare. We encountered no burned roomblocks or unburied bodies. The single instance of apparently military violence is the stone arrow point in a cervical vertebrae of a burial unearthed by Guthe and illustrated by Kidder (1932:21). Nevertheless, I am impressed here by Kidder's observation that the second most common burial artifacts at Pecos Pueblo were arrowheads. This suggests to me that there was a change of social conditions between the occupation of Rowe and of Pecos. Pecos may have been both founded and eventually abandoned largely because of warfare, as Kidder (1958) finally suggested.

A side issue here relates to the role of warfare specifically with more nomadic, buffalo-hunting, Plains tribes, as suggested by Riley (1987). Plains Indian artifacts are abundant at Pecos, apparently in all levels, although remains of bison were located primarily in the later, likely post-contact levels (Kidder 1958; Riley 1987; Spielmann et al. 1990). Pecos Pueblo seems to have had a long relationship, perhaps alternately friendly and hostile, with denizens of the buffalo plains. The inhabitants of Rowe Ruin apparently were unlike Pecos in this respect.

The research reported here was concerned with eventually understanding the context of, and perhaps the mechanisms underlying, population aggregation in the Upper Pecos Valley. In this regard, I offer conclusions based on the questions addressed in our research designs and the work reported here. These comments cannot be taken as a definitive statement for the Upper Pecos Valley. As stated, our work was aimed at beginning to understand and providing baseline information for an understanding. Our research was neither intensive nor extensive enough to be more than a start.

The principal episode of aggregation at Rowe Ruin may have begun as early as the 1240s or 1250s for the adobe ruin but certainly in the 1340s and 1350s for the masonry structures. The first dates are after the AD 1130 demise of an integrated system based at Chaco Canyon but before the abandonment of either the San Juan Basin or the Northern San Juan/Mesa Verde regions. The second construction dates shortly after the abandonment of the Northern San Juan/Mesa Verde. As argued above, in neither case does an immigrant population from either of these areas appear to be involved in settling the Upper Pecos Valley. Yet the entire period was one of considerable population movement, change, and local distress in the northern Southwest as a whole.

One of our research goals was to see if population aggregation emerged out of periods of high spatial variability in precipitation that might have been mitigated by broad, regionally based networks of exchange. The analysis of paleoclimatic data described in this report ruled out this simple solution. Occupation at Rowe closely followed a period of increased spatial varability in rainfall in the eastern portion of the Southwest. The aggregation at Rowe in the 1340s and 1350s, reflected in the masonry construction, also follows a period of increased spatial variability in the Eastern Pueblo area. However, the Rowe materials dating to the mid-fourteenth century are notably local in derivation. The conditions that favored aggregation in the Upper Pecos Valley in the thirteenth and fourteenth centuries do not seem to be related to very broad regional exchange. On the other hand, Rowe and its neighboring sites were clearly aligned with the Santa Fe and ultimately Northern San Juan districts in terms of broad ceramic styles. It is very possible that *local* exchange in foodstuffs, labor, or even residents was considerable among communities within this zone.

With Dean's (1995) recent work, we know that between AD 1250 and 1450, the previous, very long-term regional patterns of precipitation broke down. Old alliances, had they been based on exchange, would have provided no relief. Such alliances may have suggested routes of migration, but new mechanisms of integrating communities or of sharing resource landscapes among more people must also have been developed based on other kinds of interactions.

In our research proposal, we suggested that data from the Upper Pecos might indicate the existence of settlement hierarchies, with higher-order centers controlling access to certain kinds of goods. None of our data support this notion. Our findings do support the simultaneous existence of several relatively large, socially "equal" communities in the Upper Pecos Valley. For example, Rowe Ruin, Forked Lightning, Dick's Ruin, and the lowest levels of Pecos Pueblo were most likely inhabited during some of the same years. The sites may have served slightly different social roles, such as guard village or ceremonial center, without being at different status levels.

Wait and Nordby (1979) suggested that the inhabitants of Rowe moved to Pecos Pueblo during the major period of aggregation at that site. They date this aggregation to about AD 1325. However, if their date is correct, then aggregation at Pecos Pueblo occurred slightly before the major period of aggregation at Rowe Ruin and was not the result of Rowe having been abandoned. Finally, it does not appear that Rowe Ruin was the last of the Upper Pecos Valley sites, except for Pecos Pueblo itself, to have been inhabited, as is attributed to traditional accounts. Rather, as Kidder (1958) suggested, Arrowhead Ruin seems to have been the last of these sites to have been abandoned before the desertion of Pecos Pueblo itself.

The Upper Pecos Valley sites seem to represent a settlement cluster of permanent villages with evidence of contemporary agricultural settlements. If a hierarchy developed among the permanent settlements, it did so after Rowe was abandoned. There is no differential distribution of ceramic or lithic materials to indicate that one or more of these settlements had access to them. Rowe Ruin was abandoned long before this fate occurred at Pecos Pueblo and probably Arrowhead Ruin as well. It is of some interest that the postoccupation debris Guthe noted above his room 3 suggests that hunters camped at Rowe after people ceased to reside there.

As discussed, we were unable to document interaction of the inhabitants of Rowe Ruin and seminomadic groups from the Plains. Neither thin-walled, micaceous pottery in general nor the type Ocate Micaceous was identified at Rowe. Rowe also lacked specific raw materials of Southern Plains origin or tool types referable to the Plains. We did identify likely Alibates chert from sites located on the surveys, so the lack of this material at Rowe is not a function of our inability to recognize it. The few buffalo bones excavated at Rowe did include rib fragments, which points to use of the meat rather than simply the hide of this species. Nevertheless, Mick-O'Hara's conclusion (reported in Part III, this volume) is similar to Kidder's (1958): although it is not possible to determine whether or not bison were taken by Pueblo hunters or obtained by trade, the volume of bison bone at Rowe does not indicate any dependence on the species. There is just far less bison bone at Rowe than in the uppermost, post-contact period levels at Pecos.

There are many as yet unresolved questions relating to both Rowe Ruin and the Upper Pecos Valley. Among the queries raised throughout this report, the nature of the north plaza roomblock remains particularly puzzling to me. The compact soils and lack of midden debris in that part of the site may be, in part, a result of the disturbance from modern road bed and pipeline construction. The almost total lack of artifacts or darkly stained soil as well as the very late, although not reliable, archaeomagnetic date of 1395 suggest that the roomblocks were occupied only briefly, if at all. Who were the inhabitants of the north plaza rooms? Why did they not become part of a longer-lived community?

In some ways, the mystery of the north plaza rooms is a parable for the settlement of the Upper Pecos Valley in general. While Rowe Ruin, and the land upon which it is located, was occupied for longer than perhaps anyone but Guthe would credit, the settlement in its various stages and transformations reflects a kind of social instability unknown in the history of large pueblo communities until sometime after AD 1150. The thirteenth, fourteenth, and early fifteenth century villages of the Upper Pecos Valley and the Northern Rio Grande seem not to have been organized in quite the same ways that are characteristic of the villages in which their descendants live today. Aggregated settlements did not last for centuries. Their inhabitants seemed to come and go, the settlements themselves changing both size and configuration in response to social forces we barely understand. In my mind, the shifting locations of population and the modifications of community layout that suggest incorporation and dispersal of groups of people are signs of a social landscape with far fewer constraints than any we know in the region today. They are mirrored in the fluidity and lack of formality that seem to characterize the patterns of exchange in ceramics. They seem to be part of a larger but much more open social world in which the notion of abandoning a dwelling or a site may have been of minimal importance, perhaps something to have been embraced rather than resisted. Certainly, it was a world about which a great deal more needs to be learned.

Part II

CARL GUTHE'S 1917 NOTEBOOK, ROWE, N.M.

Figure 34. Guthe's 1917 photograph of the site (Neg. 534, Kidder/Pecos Collection, Archives of the Laboratory of Anthropology, Museum of Indian Arts & Culture, Santa Fe) (trees on top of site on right match with trees on left in Figure 35)

Figure 35. Guthe's 1917 photograph of the site (Neg. 535, Kidder/Pecos Collection, Archives of the Laboratory of Anthropology, Museum of Indian Arts & Culture, Santa Fe)

CARL GUTHE'S 1917 NOTEBOOK, ROWE, N.M.†

Front cover:

Excavations at Rowe, N.M., Aug. 27 – Oct. 6

Inside front cover:

<u>If found</u> return to C. E. Guthe, Dept. of Archeology, Andover, Mass. and receive reward

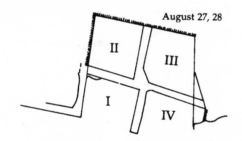

August 27, 28

Aug. 27

This morning I started work at 7:30. Hours 7:30–12 and 1–4:30. Four men are working for me, Martin and Lamberto Varela of Pecos and Lamberto Santilla[nes] and Pablo Ortiz of Rowe.

The ruin consists of three principle *[sic]* quadrangles. The creek (Arroyo del Pueblito) has cut the eastern edge

† Transcribed by Jean Bagalah with drawings by Eden A. Welker. Some punctuation and abbreviations were changed for consistency and ease of reading. Publication courtesy of Laboratory of Anthropology, Museum of New Mexico, Santa Fe.

of the southern and part of the middle quadrangles, exposing walls (Figure 34).

Work was begun at the edge of the cliff formed by the arroyo, near the northeastern corner of the southernmost quadrangle (Figure 35).

A grey ash layer 2 ft. long and 3 in. thick appeared 34 inches below the surface, 58 inches from the beginning of the trench, and 18" from north edge of trench.

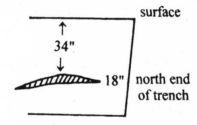

At eleven o'clock the first wall was uncovered, being the west wall of room III. [Note: room descriptions are appended to the journal and transcribed below.]

During the afternoon, an area of ash layers was uncovered.

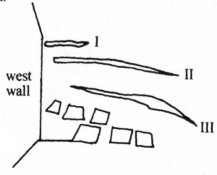

In room III — along the west wall, 8 feet from the SW corner of the room, a grey ash lense *[sic]* (I) was 30

in. below surface, and 12 in. long; 5 in. below that was a longer thinner grey ash layer about 24" long; 4 in. below II, was III, a white ash layer, 4.4" long. All three sloped with the present slope of the land. The western end of III was 38 in. below the surface; the eastern end, 34 in. below surface. Below these three layers was a heavy layer of rock, thickest near the west wall. It seemed to be a more or less horizontal layer, but too uneven for flags, or stone floor. Within this layer directly below the ash layers was some charcoal and one rock was blackened over about 4 sq. in.

Two sets of toe bones were uncovered in NW corner of room I (Skel. 1). The surface had been removed for a few inches, but an estimate made the toes 6 ft. 6 in. below surface.

Aug. 28

This morning Pablo and Martin started on the shack. I set Bert on a skeleton in Room I, which turned out to be another fragment. Ramon found the east wall of room III, which was buried below the level worked on yesterday.

I have grouped all the bones in room I, and called them Skel. 1, they were all found near the floor of the room, about 6 ft. below the surface.

In room II, three feet from NE corner and 1.6 ft. below surface, along the east wall was large piece of burnt earth, resembling an adobe, .8 ft. long, .7 ft. wide, .4 ft. thick.

In room IV, a horizontal hole was found, opening at the cliff; it was about 4 in. in diameter, and was plugged with what appeared to be an adobe hammer (No. ***). The sides of the hole are harder than the surrounding earth, but are not the characteristic red of burnt earth. All around this hole, in fact the entire north end of the room for a depth of [12] ft. just above the floor contained large pieces of burnt earth, and charcoal, with a few ash layers. There did not however seem to be any order to this deposit, unless it was the remains of an old bonfire which was built by Indians before the room was filled, against the north wall. No evidence of a fireplace could be found. The floor was found in this room.

Aug. 29

This morning Martin finished working on the shack, and started cataloguing.

Bert uncovered, in room II, a stone floor. On this floor

in the NW corner of the room, the major portion of a black bowl was found, and near it a large B. on W. sherd, — the latter in seven pieces. The stones forming the floor of this room were covered with charcoal, in an almost continuous layer.

A little below the level of the top of the west wall of Room III, was a layer, fairly thick, of rocks, as if the rocks had been thrown in, perhaps, to fill the hollow of the disused and fallen-down room. In the northwest corner of this room an ash layer covers the rock layer. This ash layer extends six inches above the top of the west wall, and across the corner of the room, and is 36 in. below surface at west wall.

Ash layer appears along the edge of digging. Must have been laid down <u>after</u> the rock deposit, and <u>on top of</u> the wall, after room had been in disuse. The layer dips at a slightly less abrupt angle than the surface and is never over 2 in. thick.

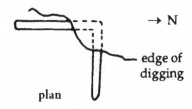

35 in. below this ash layer, 8½ feet north of S wall and 12 in. E of W wall were found the two lower leg bones of a large animal and 4 ankle bones, all in natural position. They showed no signs of being broken, and were not charred, nor were they in an ash layer.

Mixed in with the above mentioned rock layer are occasional pockets of grey ash, mixed with earth. They vary in size, one being 1 ft. wide and 1 ft. deep.

During the day, in rooms II and III, and previously in room I, traces of skeletons were found, but the bones were so badly decayed that it was impossible to ascertain anything in regard to their position, age, etc. In only one case (Skel. 2) could any data be obtained.

Aug. 30

The ash layer, above mentioned, which cuts across the NW corner of Room III, increases in thickness over the corner of the room, and contains many animal bones.

Bert finished cleaning floor of room II, after notes

were taken the stone floor was removed. Undisturbed earth was found 10 in. below floor. Between floor and bottom were several ash & charcoal layers.

Near the floor of room III, (exact floor could not be located), right against west wall was a large black, corrugated olla, right side up, but shattered. Within the bowl were bones of at least four small rodents, about the size of mice.

The centre of the bottom of the bowl (No. 30) was 39 in. from the NW corner of the room and 7 ft. 9 in. from the surface.

The floor of room III was indefinite. At the base of the walls, extending over the entire floor of the room, and lying upon undisturbed red clay was a composite ash layer 2 in. thick, composed of many very thin layers of white ash, grey ash, & charcoal. I could not however flake off any layer, as can be done so easily on some floors, due to the packed condition of the floor.

Aug. 31

This morning Martin and I started using plane table. The digging in rooms I–IV, was completed yesterday and work started to westward.

This morning, on about level of top of west wall of room III, 6½ feet west of wall, 52 inches below surface, and 3 feet south of NW corner, were found fragments of a child's skull.

Walls were found west of rooms III & II, which did not conform with these rooms. In digging on the west side of the west wall of room II, an ash layer was uncovered which is about on the same level as the top of the west wall of Room II. It is a well-defined layer of white ash and charcoal, varying from a line to 4 in. thick.

Sept. 1

It is impractical to excavate rooms V and VI, to clay bottom, for another tier of rooms are superimposed upon them. The tops of the walls of V and VI are about the same level as those of I–IV. In room VI, three skeletons have been uncovered. (3, 4, & 5). They undoubtedly belong to the same period as Room VII, which is placed on top of V and VI.

The north wall of V, passes below the east wall of VII. The southeast corner of VII was torn out, because a wall was not expected there. The walls of VII extend to the surface.

The south wall of V stops abruptly about 2 feet west of the east wall.

Just below the south wall of VII, and extending south to the edge of the digging, is a heavy ash and charcoal layer, which extends also along the east wall of VII, as far as the N wall of V. In this layer many bone implements were found. This layer is nearly horizontal, dipping slightly to the east.

The south edge of the trench passes thru a depression in the east mound of the southern quadrangle. It was probably a passageway or gate, and room VII, was the northern side of the gate.

In excavating over Room VII, a small pocket of [illegible: Quelite?] seeds were found. The pocket was about 2 in. in diameter.

Sept. 2 — Sunday

Sept. 3 — Labor Day

No work, and besides, I spent entire day repairing differential on car, which I injured Saturday.

Sept. 4

Pablo did not appear this morning. Miller brought us down & back, because car was not done.

Excavations proceeded in room VII. The general digging pottery was worked over and packed.

That found in rooms I–IV (Aug. 27–29) was fairly crude. B. on W. and black ware were in nearly equal proportions. No red pieces were seen.

In the later digging (Aug. 29–Sept. 1), the B. on W. seems to predominate. One piece of redware was found. There do not appear to be any noticeable changes in the type of work done.

In room VII, a layer was found composed of a light, yellow layer on top, which resembled decayed wood. Below that was a small-stone layer, 2–4 in. thick, mixed in with and below which was a thick white substance, like very pure white ash or lime. This was just about on the floor level. In the NE corner was a small area of hard earth, surrounded by two flat stones, which showed effects of fire. This was probably the fireplace. (See notes on room VII for measurements.)

About 1:15 it started to rain hard enough to lay off work until it stopped. Started work again 1:45.

In the NW corner room VII, lying on small-stone floor, was a large flat stone, not smoothed on upper side (Figure 36). Similar to stones taken out of other rooms.

Figure 36. Stone floor in room VII, northwest corner (Neg. 508, Kidder/Pecos Collection, Archives of the Laboratory of Anthropology, Museum of Indian Arts & Culture, Santa Fe)

Reminds me of flat stones used by Zunis to cook Tortillas on.

Sept. 5

The repairs on the car made it impossible to go to the ruins this morning. After lunch, I went down, starting work at 1:15. All four men on job, with four hours work, half day's pay.

Just west of the SW corner, room VII, a great many rocks were taken out yesterday; they looked much as if they had been piled there.

Under the stone layer in VII was a layer of white ash and charcoal which varied in thickness from a line to two or three inches. In the SE corner of the room below the stone layer was quite a heavy deposit of charcoal and white ash.

Sept. 6

All 4 men on job at 7:30. Walls were outlined in room VIII.

Under the stone floor of room VII was a peculiar formation. It was so hard that at first it was believed to be the clay bottom (See notes on room VII). A later and more careful examination of this earth disclosed charcoal 24 in. below the "stone floor," the bottom of the digging. Large areas on the cleaned face of this earth were of undisturbed clay (A red clay with fine white particles in it) — but in each case the areas was surrounded by softer earth containing charcoal. It was probably a fill from some hole dug, into which large hunks of red clay were dumped.

To find this earth disturbed is logical, for just east of room VII are rooms on a lower level apparently of an older period. The north wall of room V, which ran below the east wall of VII was found on the other side, within the room. It entered the room for about 18 in. and then very abruptly stopped, — just as the south wall of V stopped. The abrupt ending of these walls is a difficult problem. There is one piece of evidence which may point to a solution: In the eastern part of VII, below the "stone floor" was a distinct ash and charcoal layer which dipped abruptly to the east (See drawing in notes on [room] VII). This layer was formed by dumping refuse into the depression of the abandoned room V. The very hard earth in the western part of the room may have been a very old fill, which the builders of room V, built their walls against, using the earth-bank as the west wall. Even on the face of it, however, this solution sounds a bit far-fetched. The absence of a west wall to room V, may be accounted for by thinking that it fell to pieces more than the N & S walls, and since only the top 2 feet of these walls were uncovered the W wall may still be in the ground. It is however impractical to excavate for it, for two reasons, 1st the walls of room VII, which cut across room V, would have no support, and 2nd, cutting away in this room would tie up the work in such a manner that all the men could not be kept busy.

The SE & SW corners of room VII and the SW corner of room VIII are all outside corners, with no walls to the west or south in the latter two cases, and none to the E or S in the former case. At this point in the east mound of the southern quadrangle was a depression, signifying a gateway, or at least, less rooms than elsewhere in the mound. When this is considered, it seems probable that rooms VII, and VIII, are the outlying rooms of the NE corner of the northern mound of the quadrangle.

About lunch-time, skel. 7 was discovered in room VIII. This skeleton is in very much better condition than all the previous skeletons, is in a different position, and altogether upholds the supposition that these rooms are of a later period. Neither VII nor VIII had a door in the sides of the rooms.

In the entire section dug so far, the ground is full of broken building stone for 2 feet below the surface, and occasionally 3 feet.

In room VIII there was a good deal of rotten wood, in streaks, about a foot above Skel. 7, probably the remains of the ceiling.

Sept. 7 — All 4 men at work — at 7:30.
Martin & I spent morning on making profiles. The digging progressed — and the N wall of VIII was found to continue.

A definite ash layer, medium thickness, covered the entire corner, dipping slightly to the south. It was 48 in. below surface.

Sept. 8. — Sat.
The continuation of the north wall of VIII westward seems to be the main south wall of the north house of the southern quadrangle. It reaches the surface and is about 8 feet high.

In room VIII, the same sawdust-like layer is found near the bottom of the room. Small rocks also occur, but apparently in no definite layer.

In the NE corner a few pieces of burnt earth were found near the bottom. In the SE corner was a few inches of clay floor.

Two children's skeletons were taken out of the main digging. A second skeleton was discovered in room VIII.

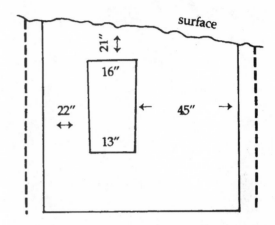

Upon cleaning the walls of VIII, a small door was found in the east wall (Figure 37). The opening had been filled. The masonry of the fill was not quite as good, and a lighter colored clay was used between the stones. The room VIII side of the fill was rough & uneven, showing that it had been filled from the east. The fill was so well done on the east side that the door would have been entirely overlooked had it not been seen in VIII. In room VII the door comes exactly in the corner. In fact it looks as if the north wall of VII had been built after the door was closed.

It rained hard from 1:15–3:00. Trenches flooded, so I dismissed the men.

Sept. 10 — Mon.
It rained during the night. Everything wet. Bert left the job and his place was taken by Federico Martinez, of Pecos town.

Martin started in, but before 8:00 his back stiffened on him so that he was unable to work. I took him home at noon.

I worked over the sherds from the general digging for the past week. There were several pieces of red ware, — I saved all of them. The B. on W. was more varied, having designs occasionally both on the outside and the

Figure 37. Filled-in door in east wall of room VIII (Neg. 510, Kidder/Pecos Collection, Archives of the Laboratory of Anthropology, Museum of Indian Arts & Culture, Santa Fe)

inside. The rim shapes varied. The great majority of rim shapes are flaring, a type very seldom seen in the early work, two weeks ago.

Appearances seem to show that the men are digging along the northen edge of the southern court with the south wall of the north building as the north edge of trench. This wall extends to the surface. The layer of fallen building stone, which occurs just below the surface is thickest near the wall, and thins out to the south. At the wall it is 47 in. thick. At the southern side, 8'8" to the south, it is 22 in. thick. Just below this layer is a zone about a foot thick, in which are ash layers, and charcoal. Below this is a zone of sand layer intermixed with charcoal and ashes.

1:30 P.M. Room VIII is a problem.

The trouble started Friday by finding Skel. 7, with the arrow in the vertebra. The closed door was disclosed late that afternoon.

Saturday A.M. while looking for a floor small stones were found scattered in the earth, but at no apparent single level. An irregular layer of the sawdust-like decayed wood was disclosed, and finally a skull was found, almost under the feet of Skel. 7.

Bert was sent in to clean the skeleton. By noon he had unearthed the major portion of a very interesting large bowl, two bone awls, one stray arrowhead, and finally an unbroken B. on W. bowl.

This noon I started in working over the earth with a trowel, preparing to clean the skeleton. More "sawdust" was found, one or two small pieces of decayed wood, still holding together; many fragments of pottery, more small stones, apparently in no order, another stray arrowhead (No. ***), stray human ribs and vertebrae, and part of a human coccyx. The latter things may have come from Skel. 7, but care was taken, when 7 was removed to get all the pieces. These stray pieces will be put with Skel. 10 which is yet to be cleaned. In the NW corner of the room, was found a large flat stone, in two pieces, tilted with the highest corner in the corner of the room, as if the floor had sunk in the centre. In the corner this stone was 72 in. below the surface. From this level down the contents of the room will be worked over by hand.

The upper side of one piece of the stone had a charcoal layer. The same was true of the lower side of the other. The reverse sides of both pieces had no charcoal. Both sides were very smooth. The stone varied in thickness from ⅝ in. in one corner to 1¼ in. in another.

The two pieces cannot be made to fit. The edges have clearly been shaped, and one surface shows scratches.

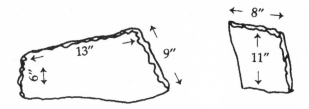

There was "sawdust" under these stones. The unbroken bowl found Sat. was 7 ft. below the surface & 28 in. west of the NE corner of the room, right along the north wall.

Just below the two stones just mentioned was another, 80 in. from surface, showing no signs of use, but resembling another large flat stone taken out by Bert Sat. They were both red and not absolutely flat, but fairly thin, like a slab.

Decayed wood, both in its natural form, and as "sawdust" was under this last stone. A few inches below this last stone, a human heelbone was found.

Near the end of the afternoon a piece of a very much-worn mano was found, and also most of the missing parts of the large B. on White bowl (No. 89). This bowl, from the disposition of the parts seems to have been inverted over the shoulderblades of Skel. 10. The unbroken bowl was over the left arm of the Skeleton.

Sept. 11 — Tues. Martin absent.
Work continued along south side of main wall.

About eleven the west corner of this wall was found.— Another outside corner.

A short time after lunch a baby's skull was unearthed with the shovel. It was in very poor condition, — other bones could not be found. It was 6 ft below surface & 3 feet south of west corner of long wall. Very much disturbed by the shovel.

At this western end of the long wall, the stratification is as follows. From the surface down, for 42" is a zone of fallen building stone. Below that is a zone of typical rubbish, with occasional streaks of charcoal & ashes. At the bottom of this zone is a prominent white ash layer, from ½ to 1 in. thick, which is composed of many very thin layers of ash & charcoal. This is 52" below the surface. Below this last layer is a wide zone, extending to the bottom of the digging, 7'6" below the surface, composed of many sand layers, of varying quality, giving the zone a banded appearance. These sand layers seem to be level, and seem to be fluvial deposits. The white ash band is also nearly level, sloping a little south and east.

On the opposite side of trench, south of the corner the bottom of the stone zone is 32" below the surface; the white ash band 37"; and the bottom of the trench 57".

Sept. 12 — Wed. Martin again absent.
Skeleton 10 was cleaned this morning. A broken black olla was found in N120 E40. It was 90 in. below the ground and 54 in. due west of the west corner of the "main wall."

While working westward, another wall was disclosed,

[***] west of the "main west corner." It was not as high as the "main" wall, and seems, therefore, to belong to the earlier period. The top of this wall was 63 in. below the surface. Sand layers (before mentioned) pass over the wall. The heavy ash layer (see previous page) is ? in. above the top of the wall. The wall runs north & south, and stops abruptly at the southern end.

While cleaning Skel. 10, another broken bowl was found, scattered over the whole body. Stones were found over the bones, flat ones, but did not cover the grave. For that reason I believe it was accidental placing of the stones.

The decayed branches and "sawdust" were found at many different levels.

In digging to bottom in N120 E40, a wall was found of the lower tier of rooms, — which quite messes things up.

Sept. 13. — Thursday
Martin returned to work this A.M. Continued digging in N130 E40 disclosed the fact that the bottom wall found late yesterday afternoon is a single room with an outside corner.

The result of this find was that I had the men work eastward in the trench, lowering the floor about two feet, so that if any other walls occurred, at the low level, they would be unearthed. Therefore no progress on the map. So far as it is possible to tell now, this lower room seems to have been an outside room jutting out from the north building into the former plaza. That is taking for granted that the plaza of the earlier house is just where that of the later house is.

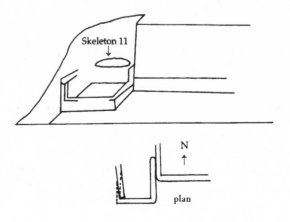

Skeleton 11

N

plan

The tops of the walls which were under the trench, are just even with the former floor. This leads to the supposition that the tops were cut thru. But care was taken while digging the trench, watching for walls.

The northern end of the east wall of the lower room is higher than the southern end by 2½ feet. It is right beside the wall running at rt. angles to the "main wall." A good metate is embedded in this east wall.

At the west end of this lower room is another peculiar feature. 8 in. above the level of the south wall the southern end of the west wall juts out to the east, over the lower part, as if the upper part had been shifted slightly to east, like one book or board on top of the other [see plan, above]. This out of line amounts to 6 in. at the southern end of the wall. At the most northern point exposed, there is no shift, it being a straight line from top to bottom. This condition may, of course, be due to the fact that the upper part of the wall, is actually, another wall of a later period.

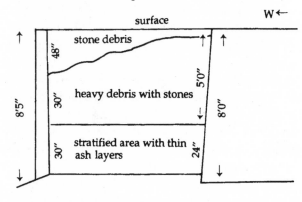

In the SE corner of this lower room the west wall is 5.2 ft. below the surface and the south wall is 7.8 ft. below the surface. Where the east wall meets the "main wall," the southern part of the east wall is 8.9 ft. below the surface, the northern part 6.6 ft. below the surface, and the bottom of the main wall 6.9 ft. below the surface.

Sept. 14

The west wall of trench, when cleaned is as follows.

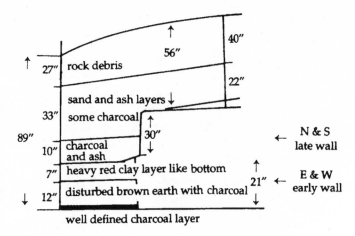

In excavating Skel. 11, the imprint of the blanket was found under the body. None of the material remained, and it was impossible to determine the weave, altho the creases in the blanket were visible. Hair was found on the skull, and along the upper cervicles. (No. ***).

Sept. 15

It was possible to work only four hours today because I had to take my wife to Santa Fe in the afternoon.

Martin & I spent the time in plane table work.

The north surface wall, north of the west corner of the "long wall" was found and excavated for four feet.

Sept. 17

A heavy rain Sunday, caused the west end of the "long wall" to fall, exposing a section of the filled room behind it.

It is to be noticed that the eastern half of this "long wall" is deeper than the western half, the place of demarkation [sic] being the partition. There are two partitions in this long wall, a fact which can be told by the less careful construction of the wall at the corners.

The outside of the western wall of room VIII is as shown. The "long wall" meets the northwest corner of this wall, and extends westward.

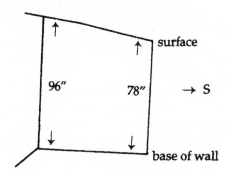

A section was taken near the location of Skel. 11. The ground plan at this point is:

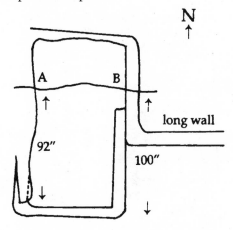

Just south of B, a little below the level of hh' [see next sketch] a rotten timber 2½ ft. long and 4 in. in diam. was found.

The cross-section is:

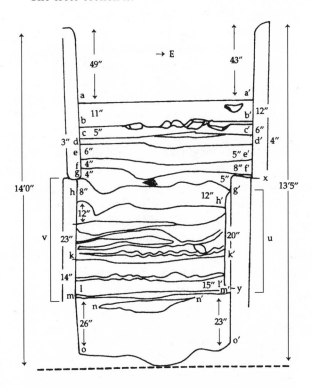

aa' = is top of section, above it has been excavated

bb' = large stone layer, mixed with heavy layer of white ash

cc' = heavy band of white ash & some charcoal

dd' = thin layer — charcoal in east side, white ash in west

ee' = a dark line resembling former surface line

ff' = a similar dark line with some white ash

gg' = top of section of hard earth, flaking in chunks, which extends to hh'

hh' = a heavy stone layer mixed with white ash

kk' = a black strip ½" to 1" thick, resembling a former surface line

ll' = a black line, with some sand on upper part. — Floor of IX

mm' = layer of charcoal & white ash averaging 2 in. below ll'

nn' = lense [sic] of gravelly, sandy brown earth

oo' = edge of undisturbed red clay

u = east wall of IX — height 59 in.

v = west wall of IX — height 55 in.

xy = western edge of "adobe"

width of section at ee' = 78"

width of section at oo' = 68"

width of section at gg' = 80"

Between hh' and kk' the earth is blotchy with streaks of brown & red earth. The same is true of the area between kk' & ll'.

Under nn' the earth is very heavy, solid, and brown. Between 2 and 6 in. above oo' red spots begin to appear in the earth. The brown color changes slowly to a red, — there is no definite division. The line oo' was made at the point where the red begins to exceed the brown earth in amount.

At mm', of course, charcoal is profuse. It diminished in amount downward, until just above oo' only a very occasional fleck of black is seen. As already brought out, the earth below nn' is barren of objects and pottery.

The lower part of the brown earth may simply have been the original loam on the surface, before the 1st pueblo was built. Therefore the base of the disturbed earth is doubtful. It must however be below nn'.

There was a heavy charcoal layer just below the base of the lowest walls, which does not appear well in the "section."

A rain which sprinkled nearly the entire afternoon upset plans somewhat, altho the men were not called out of the trench.

Martin has been working all day in room VIII cleaning it out with a trowel.

The set of walls in the 20-ft square N130 E30, which have been delt [sic] with already in the preceding pages, consitute [sic] a puzzle, which is difficult to solve.

There seem to be three sets of superimposed walls.

The lowest are the foundations of the southern end of a room with the south wall complete and part of the east and west walls, at least. Along side of the east wall is the western corner of the "long wall" which is also a high wall, and may be composed of two walls, one exactly on top of the other.

On top of the west wall of the lower room is another wall, not quite on a line with it. This extends upward for a few feet. On top of this is another wall, which at this point is a corner, apparently the outside SE corner of a room. This wall extends to the surface. At the northern end of this wall is a wall running E & W which I think connects up with the N–S wall running N of the west corner of the "long wall."

At the point at which the section was taken the east wall of the lower room assumes a most peculiar appearance. The stone masonry sort of peters out and is replaced by a very hard earth, without stratification, which

contains many small pebbles & pieces of stone. This may be adobe, — if it is, it is a very peculiar place for it.

The foundations of the lower walls appear way above the bottom of the disturbed earth. In these lower walls, on all three, are flat upright slabs on the inside, flush, apparently, with the plastered surface of the walls. What they stand for is questionable.

Martin in Room VIII, unearthed the largest & most perfect metate yet found and a much worn mano to go with it.

"The adobe" in the lowest east wall is homogeneous in texture, and shows three divisions. Two horizontal lines and one vertical line, dividing the area into three parts of different shades of brown. On the "section," along the eastern side is a vertical division line, showing the western limit of this peculiar formation.

A diagram of this follows.

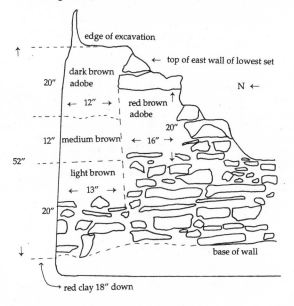

Sept. 18 — Tues.

Today I started turning the trench to the south. A new work map will be needed. Room IX, is the "lowest room," mentioned on the preceeding [sic] page.

This morning while cleaning the lower part of the "section," a layer was found from which the earth split off as if from a floor. It was covered with sand, but was hard beneath that. It was nearly level, and a few inches above the base of the walls of IX. Therefore I call it the floor of IX. It was just below this layer that the charcoal bed occurred, which was thick in some places and a line in others. It did not extend below the walls of the room.

Figure 38. Section, room IX, looking north (Neg. 520, Kidder/Pecos Collection, Archives of the Laboratory of Anthropology, Museum of Indian Arts & Culture, Santa Fe)

Figure 39. Room IX, west wall segment? (Neg. 511, Kidder/Pecos Collection, Archives of the Laboratory of Anthropology, Museum of Indian Arts & Culture, Santa Fe)

Ramon has been digging down in IX looking for the undisturbed earth. The earth below the walls is very hard, a dark brown, and resembles undisturbed earth. Small pieces of charcoal are found in it, however. It is barren, as regards objects or pottery.

Towards noon Martin finished cleaning room VIII, which was at once written up. — Thank heaven that's done.

About 1:30 bottom was found in room IX, and the notes on the "section" were completed (Figure 38).

The west wall of room IX has been a puzzle (Figure 39). I felt sure there were three super-imposed walls there but could not seperate [sic] the first and second clearly. A close examination of the wall yielded the following:

Beginning at the bottom, it was found that the lowest stones were set in red clay, and were not set in the hypothetical trench and the filling put around them. This is proved because the ground earth (that is, the earth for two feet below & under the wall) is brown. The top edge of this brown earth below the trench is well-defined,

and a straight line, nearly horizontal. Above this is a red-clay earth, which acts as a filling between the stones of the west wall of IX. Under every stone of the bottom series is at least one inch of red earth. There is only one exception to this rule. That is the large flat stone which is upright in the west wall, near the southern end (16" from end). The bottom of this stone is, however, four inches below the line between the red and brown earth.

This same condition is found in the south & east walls, with, again, the exception of the two flat upright stones, one in each wall. In the south wall this stone, the largest of the three, is at the western end, and its base is 3 in. below the line between red & brown. In the east wall the upright is 16 in. from the south end, and the base is 6 in. below the line mentioned.

To return now to the western wall. As already mentioned, red earth was used between the stones in the lowest wall. These stones were flat and thin, laid fairly carefully.

In the southwest corner of the room, 22 in. above the base of the wall, at the top of the flat stone in the south wall, the west wall juts eastward over the lower part. A section at this point would be:

This fact led me to the conclusion that this was a second wall, when the corner was first disclosed.

This afternoon has brought to light some more points. The lowest stone in the upper wall is set in <u>brown</u> earth, with one inch of brown earth <u>below</u> it.

The line between the brown earth used in the upper wall and the red of the lower is very distinct. It slopes towards the north, so that at the point at which the section was taken, the top of the lower wall is 7 in. above the base. The upper wall has all the stones set in brown earth, and all of the lower layers of stones of this wall have one in. of brown earth below them.

Another point, easily seen, when the red-brown line between the two walls is pointed out, is that the upper wall is built of thicker, heavier flat stones than the lower. This should be very evident in the photograph taken this morning.

This explanation explains other points also. At first it was difficult to see why the tops of the southern [wall] and the southern half of the eastern wall should be so much lower than the top of the western [wall]. But now it is clear that the western wall of room IX is only a few inches (4–6 in.) higher than the southern wall.

It also explains away the "adobe" theory advanced several pages back in regard to the northern end of the eastern wall. It will be noticed in the diagram, that the stones in the lower half are thin, long stones, and that the top of the group slopes northward. At the "section" face this wall remnant is 14 in. high, while 2½ feet to the south it is 21 in. high — precisely the same condition as brought out in the western wall. The stones above these thin ones (seven are pictured in drawing) may be accidents, as regards placement. The two uppermost stones are on the same level as the zone hh' in the "section." This explanation does not, however, account for the peculiar horizontal and vertical divisions in the earth noticed in the previous discussion.

Another point in regard to this west wall. The upper, or second wall is the straighter. At the northern end it is exactly above the lower wall. This question of red & brown earth is not conclusive proof, since they may have run out of red mud and simply mixed some brown. The style of masonry is harder to account for.

Sept. 19 — Wed.

This second wall is 30 in. high at the southern end. There is no wall above it here. 67 in. from the southern end, at the top of this wall is the corner of another wall (apparently a SE outside corner of a room). At the "section" face this second wall is 47 in. high.

The third and top wall, which extends to the surface, juts out to the east over the second wall, just as the 2nd juts out to the east, over the first at the southern end. It is interesting to notice that the earth between the stones near the top of the second wall, is nearly the same color as that of the first wall. There is <u>not</u>, however, any distinct line of demarkation [sic] anywhere within the second wall.

There is no appreciable difference between the earth of the second and that of the third wall. There can, however, be no question but that there is a third wall, for there is a corner in the 3rd and not in the 2nd. Moreover the stones of the third wall are chunkier — more nearly cubes — than those of the second. There is also an unusually thick layer of earth between the lower stones of the third and the top stones of the 2nd wall.

Another point aids in differentiating the three walls. That is, that in all three cases the lowest stones of the wall are invariably heavier and larger than the stones above them.

Several pages back a diagram was made of the then west end of the trench, which takes in the first & second walls. Another diagram now follows:

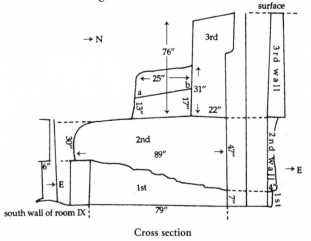

Cross section

The clear [unshaded] area is debris with a clear ash layer (ab) 1½" thick in it.

The top of the "section" does not reach the surface. This accounts for the very much foreshortened bench near the top of the 3rd wall. On each side of the opposite diagram [reproduced above] are cross sections at the respective end of the diagram.

Yesterday afternoon I set Martin to work running a small trench, about 12 in. wide and 12 in. deep along the unexcavated tops of all exposed walls, in order that the cross walls could be found. This morning he uncovered Skel. 12, a few inches below the surface, along the north side of the north wall of room VIII. The body was flexed, showing it was an old burial, but unfortunately no pottery was found with it.

The other men continued along to the south, finding much pottery and bones, but little else. A new work-map was begun today.

At 11:00 A.M. I let the men go to the station to say goodby [sic] to the drafted men from Pecos & Rowe (18 in all). They did not return until noon.

Sept. 20 — Thurs.

This morning Martin finished exposing the available walls. We spent most of morning taking level notes. This afternoon I set him to work on the "section." I have made a test out of it. (Test I)

A — from top of section to cc'
B — cc' – hh'
C — hh' – kk'
D — kk' – [***]

He has finished A and B and finds results very meagre. There is some doubt in my mind in regard to finishing it.

The rest of the men have been digging across the the courtyard towards the southern mound. The earth here is very abundant in potsherds & bones, but few cositas.

The afternoon was spent by myself straightening up the notes taken with the plane table.

Sept. 21 — Fri.

This morning Martin finished B of Test I. The material found was a mere handfull and of no apparent value. I spent the morning in working over Gen. Dig. sherds.

The trench work across the "court" has turned out to be very rich indeed. A heavy ash zone supplies an amazing number of bones and sherds. Cositas are also plen-

tiful. Another clay hammer (fragment) like that found in Room IV, was dug up at 1:30 P.M.

A very large B. on W. bowl was discovered about 11:30 by myself in C, test I. It is broken into many pieces. It is 11 feet below the surface, close against the north end of the room. It would be close against the north wall which connects the west and east walls of the third set in room IX, if that wall continued downward. It extends however only 7'9" down from the surface. The bowl was 29 in. east of the west wall (2nd wall). The bowl was inverted, resting on kk' (see "section"). Some rocks had fallen on it and smashed it into about 120 pieces. Right beside the bowl, on the same level, was a worked sherd with 4 holes.

Most of the rest of the "long wall" caved about 4:00 P.M.

Sept. 22 — Sat.

22 cositas were found yesterday. This is high record.

In the trench, I am having the men slope the trench downward to the south, so that we will be nearer bottom when the southern mound is reached.

I have decided to take all the sherds found in the trench between 3 P.M. Thurs. & 3 P.M. Friday (a boxful) and have them washed, packed, and labelled "Gen. Dig. Sept. 21." Up to this time I have been picking out the worthwhile pieces, and having them only packed. This gives no idea of the relation of the different forms of pottery to one another, as regards amount & percentage. Therefore, this collection.

B. on W. is most abundant, either with a straight rim or a bent one. Black ware is next, and redware is always comparatively rare.

In excavating the "section" down to kk' several interesting things were found. First the bowl and the sherd with 4 holes.

It has been explained that the north wall of the top room did not extend way down, but only to the base of what was before shown to be the top or "3rd" wall.

The northern limit of the excavation was this north wall, and therefore the limit below the base of the stone wall was a dirt (artificial) wall, of course. The interesting point is that about two feet above the plane kk' the earth could be chipped off, or away from this northern face, just as it can from a plastered wall or a floor. Still there are no stories behind this face.

The curious condition found in the NE corner of this room has been refered [sic] to several times — namely the section of earth with <u>vertical</u> and horizontal lines of demarkation *[sic]*.

In excavating behind the "section" care was taken to notice the effect of the western edge of this formation. This edge was a vertical stratum — line about two inches from the eastern edge of the "section." It was found that here also the earth chipped away as from a floor or wall.

The north "wall" of this material met the east "wall," at a corner six inches due west, along the north stone wall from the NE corner of the uppermost room. Seperated *[sic]* from this north "wall," and only two inches south of it, was a layer of decayed sticks, which from their imprints in the earth averaged about ¼ in. in diameter. A branch of this vertical layer extended southward, but sloped to the north, <u>towards</u> the north "wall" and <u>not</u> away from it.

Another point is that the heavy stone layer (apparently building stones) hh' extended northward <u>to</u> this clay "wall," and then <u>stopped abruptly</u>, and was not found to the northward. The obvious off-hand conclusion is that the stones were in some way connected with the uppermost room, if not with the middle room.

The stratum kk', which was first taken to be the floor of the middle room, extends westward to the stone wall and north and east to the two clay "walls." It chipped like a floor, was covered with charcoal and was hard. The rim of the broken bowl found yesterday rested on it, and the worked sherd was flat, directly on the top of the layer. This surface of the layer was, however, none too flat, and was occasionally hard to find. While cleaning it, I was tempted once or twice to doubt whether it was a floor, but can give no real reason for this opinion.

The earth found between hh' and kk' contained quite a bit of rock, some sand, and was almost barren of archeological objects (5 black sherds, and one large B. on W. sherd found, — in addition to the bowl & worked sherd).

In cleaning the east wall of the uppermost room, it was found that the part near the surface had broken down and that the remaining part was put together very slovenly, and composed of small stones. In the NE corner of the room the stones and adobe between them were covered with a deposit of soot. The heat had been great enough to cause the phenomenon of exfoliation on some of the stones. The sooty portion was in the form of a triangle on the east & north wall.

On the east wall it extended southward at the bottom 17 in., and the point was 38 in. above the base of the triangle. On the north wall the base of the triangle was 10 in., and the height 38 in. The base of the triangle was 3 in. above the base of the wall.

My conclusions are, from this, (1) That this room was in use without having plaster on the stones to smooth the walls. At least a fire was built in it. (2) The floor of the room was 3 in. above the base of the walls in the NE corner. — otherwise the lower stones would have had soot.

Just below the wall was found again the vertical stratum mentioned before. It shows here that it extended beyond the clay "wall," running east and west for it is found to the north of it at this point.

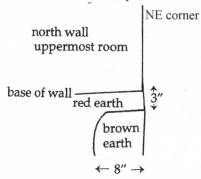

This fact further complicates the question of the purpose of this formation.

In the N.W. corner of the uppermost room are also signs of soot. The triangles here are 43 in. high, and have bases of 12 in. and 9 in. The bases are 6 in. above the base of the wall.

This condition explains why it has been so hard to find plaster on the walls, — a fact which at first I laid up to my carelessness.

Correlated with this soot phenomenon is the occurrence of flat rocks laid against the wall, literally plastered up against the face of the wall. These are comparatively small stones, and thin, and are of no structural value. Their purpose puzzled me because I was taking for granted plaster on the walls. It is clear from their location that they are used to cover irregularities in the actual wall itself. The most striking examples of this are the three large stones, one in each of the W, S, and E walls of the lowest room IX.

The base of the W wall of the highest room IX juts out farther over the west wall of the middle room IX at the northern end than at the southern, namely 4 in. (at S.W. corner only 2½ in.).

The highest room IX is, of course, really not a room, but a jag in the court or southern wall of the northern house. This is shown by the lack of a south wall, the S.E. corner & the S.W. corner being both outside corners, and the west wall being 44 in. long, and the east one 68 in.

Sept. 24 — Mon.

<u>All</u> the sherds of Sept. 22 were again cleaned and washed.

In the trench red clay bottom has been found. It seems to slope upward to the south.

Test II is near the center of the court. It is a column 3 feet square.

aa' is a half inch layer of charcoal & ash. Above it is brown earth unstratified but with pottery & charcoal.

bb' is a white ash layer. Below it is a charcoal layer. Between aa' and bb' is ash and charcoal, very rich, but not very clearly stratified. At x, below bb' the ribs and back bone of an animal were found in natural order (66 in. below surface).

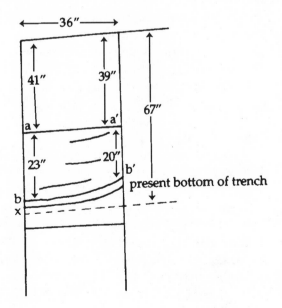

Sept. 25 — Tues.

This morning Martin finished Section A of Test II. The floor of Sec. A I had made horizontal, since there was no stratification to go by. Due to the unevenness of the surface, the four corners vary some in depth.

N.E. corner – 12 in.   S.E. corner – 12 in.
S.W. corner – 8 in.   N.W. corner – 11½ in.

Test I was abandoned because of the great scarcity of material, making the careful working of the column useless. The material of the first section has been packed. It speaks for itself.

Yesterday I noted that red clay had been found. Above the red clay is a very hard brownish clay which did not contain carbon, much less anything else. For that reason I have shifted the floor of this trench upward, so that only a few inches of the brown clay will be exposed on the sides of the trench.

The absence of kivas has puzzled me greatly. There is no sign of one anywhere near the ruin. Yesterday, I dug below the surface a few inches around a <u>very shallow</u> depression in the court, just south and a bit west of Test II. No walls could be found. This small depression had thicker grass than the rest of the court, which was the cause for my idea in regard to a kiva at this point.

The situation in room IX continues to puzzle me. Excavations yesterday and today have exposed several more facts.

Digging below the "floor" kk', it was found that the eastern & northern clay "walls" extended downwards below the floor — down to the base of the lowest room IX. The clay "walls" are hard to locate at times. There seem to be several layers of clay, with none too even surfaces. If, by accident, the knife goes thru the first layer, this will split away from the second. The result is a very uneven looking surface to the "wall."

It was found that the stone east wall of lowest IX extended northward behind this clay "wall." It did not, however, reach the north clay "wall" but stopped abruptly 14 in. south of it. At this point the wall is 17 in. high, the top being only slightly below the level of the top of the wall at the S.E. corner of the lowest room.

On the west wall, the wall of lowest IX peters out, until at the northern edge of the digging it is 3 in. high, the thickness of one stone. The west wall of middle IX swings a little east again, so that its base is 5 in. east of the top of the W wall of lowest IX.

The west wall of middle IX stops abruptly 2–3 in. north of where it meets the north clay "wall." The southern end of this wall showed no corner. There was no southern wall to middle IX, and the only evidences of the eastern and northern walls are the two clay "walls." It is perfectly possible that in digging this part of the trench the southern and part of the eastern walls were destroyed, for a clay or adobe "wall" at this point was the last thing expected. Oh for more time and money to solve these problems! The sudden ending of the west wall of middle IX rather lends more proof to the use of clay "walls."

Looking at the north end of the room as it is now cleared, the following measurements were taken:

	N.W. corner	N.E. corner
base of highest wall	7.7 ft	7.9 ft
[base of] middle wall	11.9 ft.	
top of lowest wall		11.5 ft
[base of] lowest wall	12.2 ft.	12.8 ft

Highest wall extends to surface

width of north end: at top = [missing]
   base of highest = 72 in.
middle IX — stone to clay wall = 69 in.
   lowest wall = 74 in.
length of west wall middle IX = 9'6".

I think I have exhausted everything on room IX. I can neither think of nor see any point which remains unnoted. 12 film pictures and 7 plates were taken of this room (or set of rooms) and contents. The room was first uncovered on Sept. 12. — and work has been going on with it more or less continuously ever since then.

In lowest IX

South wall - height

1 ft. from S.W. corner   14 in.

[1 ft. from] S.E. corner   17 in.

My intention is to make a series of drawings showing the west side of the trench across the plaza, with notes in regard to the east side when feasible.

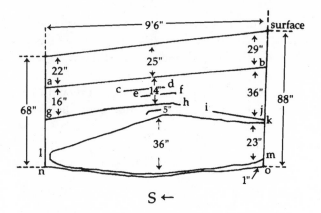

ab marks the lower limit of the fallen rock (wall debris). At the northern end there is much rock. At the southern just a few pieces, with much earth. In fact from this point south the rock is so scarce that it can no longer be called wall debris. This same condition exists on the east wall of trench.

klm is a large zone of red clay, with some bands of brown in with it. Between this zone and the debris zone is a zone of brown earth, with much charcoal, and a few strata.

gh is the best of these strata, and is charcoal. cd is a short white ash stratum. ef is a short charcoal stratum. ij is an indefinite charcoal stratum.

no is a sand layer averaging half an inch thickness. Below this is brown earth, with charcoal extending below the floor of the trench.

66 in. below the surface, and near the end of the digging marked today is a heavy ash layer, charcoal & burnt earth. Several potsherds were found in close proximity. They are catalogued as one pot (only one today) and may be parts of one bowl with extra sherds. A piece of the burnt earth, with impressions, was saved.

Sept. 26 — Wed.
Work in the trench continued. The first wall (N–S) of the south building was uncovered.

Martin spent morning on Test II, finishing section B.

Afternoon spent in leveling. My spare time in drawing cross-section from leveling notes.

In the morning a piece of burnt clay was uncovered and kept, which had impressions of branches (?) in it. It is 6 in. long and 4 in. wide.

Test II, section B is 12 in. thick. The corners at floor of B read NW — 24", NE — 24", SE — 24", and SW — 20".

Sept. 27 — Thurs.

This morning early the crosswall (E–W) was found at the southern end of the wall mentioned above. Martin started Section C, Test II. I worked on contour work, making cross sections.

About noon Section C, Test II was finished. Depth in corners: NW corner — 32", SW corner — 28", SE corner — 32", NE corner — 32".

During the day a door was found in the E–W wall. Also a very good clay pipe was discovered.

The afternoon was spent by Martin and myself in plane table work.

Fri. — Sept. 28.

I worked out contours on the cross sections. Martin on Section D, Test II. Trench continues along north side of E–W wall, which seems to be the main north (or courtyard) wall of the southern house.

Test II, Section D, finished about noon. Corner depth, SW — 39", SE — 41", NW — 42", NE — 40". This was down to the ash layer aa' in the drawing of this section. [reproduced above]

Martin & I spent afternoon in plane table work.

Sat. — Sept. 29.

Morning spent in running levels. In trench, N–S wall was found, and progress towards east was halted for time being.

Martin began Test II, Sec. E about 11:00 A.M.

The wall with the door has a wall less than a foot south of it. In this "door wall," at the SE corner, the top is 38 in. below surface. At the door also 38 in. below surface; at eastern end, 48 in.

In the afternoon, the walls in the trench were uncovered, and cleaned. The men, after cleaning out the loose dirt, were shifted to just west of room IX, to clean up a wall there.

Martin finished Sec. E of Test II, just at quitting time. Depth at corners, NE — 50", NW — 52", SE — 52", SW — 50".

A child's skeleton was uncovered in trench — (in N60 E30) — and left until Monday. (after recovering)

Mon. — Oct. 1

Men still working west of room IX. Martin sorting and packing material from test II, sec. E.

Saturday P.M. I started sorting the pottery for the week. This morning decided to save the whole thing, (one box full). The little sorting done Saturday will not change the percentage to any great extent.

In N130 E30 (west of room IX) the men discovered 2 skeletons (14 & 15), which it took all day to work up.

At noon I shifted the diggers to N20 E20, to start a trench northward to the southernmost mound.

Martin spent afternoon on Test II, sec. F.

Skel. 14 had the remains of a blanket visible, consisting of discolored earth (a green-grey) and imprint of body in places.

In N130 E30 two walls were found, corresponding to late and middle IX.

Skel. 15 had the first unbroken skull found, and was in remarkable condition.

Tues. — Oct. 2.

Martin finished Test II, Sec. F this morning. Depths at corners, NE — 59", NW — 61", SW — 59", SE — 60".

The digging continued south of the southern building, without many results. (only a few cositas)

Skel. 14 (yesterday) was on top of the middle period wall. The skull was directly on one of the top stones of the wall. It was below the ash layer pictured previously in the sketch of the west wall of IX.

Late in the afternoon, I shifted the diggers to N130 E30, where they removed the rest of the dirt against the walls.

At quitting time Martin finished Test II. Sec. G. Depth at corners, SE — 68", SW — 64", NW — 66", & NE — 68".

I worked on maps during day.

Wed. Oct. 3rd

After cleaning loose dirt out of old trench the men went back and continued work in N40 E20. During the morning the south wall of the southern building was exposed.

Martin, after cleaning and packing the material from Test II, Sec. G, was set to work cleaning the exposed portions of the north wall of the southern building.

I spent morning working on the map of the northern quadrangle, finishing just at noon.

The map is a contour map with an interval of 2½ ft. The contour lines were drawn in with the aid of the following data:

1. N–S cross section
2. E–W cross section
3. Heights of 38 points on the mounds.

Of course, the actual lines were drawn in with the eye. For this reason they are not absolutely accurate at <u>all</u> points, and must be considered in that light. They are the best that can be done with the available time and instruments.

The section of the northern wall of the southern building which has been exposed consists of a long E–W wall with a N–S wall at each end.

Altho the top of the long wall curves some, the base is a straight line. The exposed walls are of two periods: 1) The latest (top at the surface) — and, apparently 2) the middle period. The diagram of the base of the walls is:

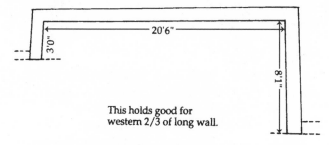

This holds good for western 2/3 of long wall.

These walls apparently had plaster on them, for the earth broke away from them, leaving a smooth surface of hard earth against the stones. This surface was whitened by the lime from plant roots, probably. Near the surface of the ground, this "plaster" surface of the wall was not found, due, probably, to the effects of water.

The west wall was:

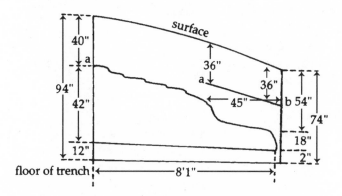

The ground slopes to the north. ab is an ash and charcoal layer. The top of the wall slopes abruptly to the north. The base slopes more gradually. Judging by the eye the northern end of the base of the wall is about a foot lower than the southern.

This wall is 10 in. thick.

ab is only distinguishable for 45 in. South of "a" it mingles with the rubbish & looses [sic] its identity.

Late in the afternoon a bowl was found in the trench (N40 E20). It was 27 in. below the surface and close against the E–W wall.

Oct. 4th — Thurs.

The long wall in the north walls of the south buildings may be described in two sections, the western and the eastern.

In the <u>western</u> part the late and middle period walls are very clearly separated, the middle period being somewhat to the north of the late period wall.

A diagram of the middle period wall is:

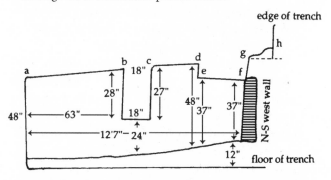

This wall contains a door. The base of the wall slopes upward to the west. At the western end (g) is a crosswall (N–S) which runs southward under the late period wall. At a is a "joint," clearly marked, which is the sign of another wall running southward from this point. The wall is not vertical, the top being somewhat north of the base, as if it (the wall) had been bent outward. This wall had a very hard coat of clay covering the stones, which I believe was plaster.

The top of the wall was below the surface the following distances at these points:

a — 48"; b — 44"; c — 43"; d — 39"; e — 48"; f — 47"; g — 34"; h — 29"

The surface slopes to the north and for that reason the top of the wall, according to the above measurements, seems to be quite a bit above the base of the main wall. Actually, at the door, the top of this wall was 5 in. above the base of the late wall. The top of this middle wall was covered with a hard layer of earth, containing much lime, and grass roots, in spite of its depth from the surface. I am inclined to consider this an indication of the former surface level, at the time the later period house was inhabited.

The wall is 12 in. thick.

The late wall, just south of this wall, is a straight vertical wall, reaching to the surface, with little to notice. It, as well as all the walls of this group, are well put together, with comparatively little clay between the stones. It gives the impression of having been very carefully, and well put together. At the western end, just at the edge of the trench, as shown on the work map is a "joint," signifying another crosswall. West of this the base of the wall is heigher [*sic*].

At the eastern end of this wall, slightly west of the "joint" in the middle period wall is a jog in the late wall, signifying another crosswall.

A diagram of this wall follows:

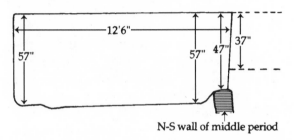

N-S wall of middle period

Looking directly down upon this section of the long wall just described we have:

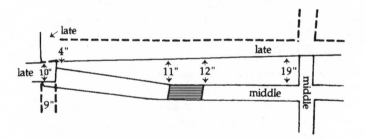

Martin just finished Test II, Sec. H; Depth at corners: SE — 73"; SW — 70"; NW — 67"; NE — 73"

The base of this section was a heavy charcoal layer with burnt twigs and corncobs, 1 in. thick.

The eastern end of the long wall, is, superficially, one wall. Is is, however, composed of a middle & late period wall. This is shown by the fact that the base of the late wall juts out to the north over the top of the middle wall, on the average of three inches. Both walls are straight and without any peculiar feature.

The diagram is:

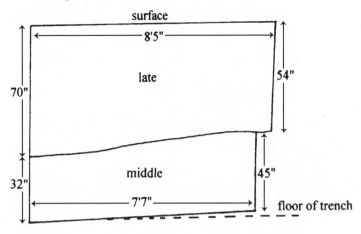

At the eastern end of this wall is a N–S wall, with an outside corner at the northern end. This wall extends to the surface. It seems to be only a later period wall, for near the bottom the wall formation of the stones breaks down, and below that are many stones in no definite order, as if a hollow had been filled with loose rock. This rubble does not extend to the base of the middle period wall. Diagram is:

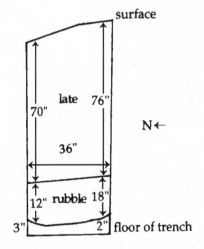

In this corner (SE) between the two walls Skel. 13 was found. On the stones in the corner is soot, as found in room IX. Its location shows it was formed during the late period. It is in the shape of a double triangle.

On the long wall this triangle is 24 in. high, with a base of 9 in., which is 58 in. below the surface. On the N–S wall, the base is 8 in., its depth & the height of the triangle being the same as on the long wall.

In the trench (N40 E20) I had the men dig down for bottom. It was much below the floor of the trench. Down near the bottom, three bowls were found. One ([no.] ***), a black one was almost directly below the bowl found yesterday, at a depth of (***) in. The other two (no. 200, no. ***) were along the south edge of the trench, (***) in. below the surface, and very close together. Their depth, as well as their designs, show a very early stage in the development of this pueblo.

Martin started on Test II Sec. I, but found only a half inch or so between the heavy charcoal layer, and hard red earth. In this there were no objects. Therefore there is no Sec. I in Test II. He spent the rest of the morning cleaning walls in N130 E30. In the afternoon he took out the bowls above mentioned. The black bowl was rather scattered.

I spent nearly the entire day upon the car, replacing a damaged spindle & hub in the left front wheel.

In the afternoon the diggers were put to work in the rooms of the southern building, between the two trenches.

Oct. 5 — Fri.

In getting out the rest of the black bowl in N40 E20, it was found that a large zone existed there, running about 3½ ft. south of the wall and taking up the entire eastern end of the trench. This zone was a mass of lumps of earth, ashes, charcoal and much pottery. Counting the three bowls mentioned yesterday, major fragments of <u>at least</u> seven bowls have been found. Three black bowls, one black olla, three B. on W. bowls, and possibly more. <u>All</u> the pottery from this zone, 1½ ft. thick on the average, has been saved, and marked N40E20 Oct. 4, and Oct. 5. The potsherds collected in the box by the diggers from this area have been labelled "Gen. Dig Oct. 1–4." The dumpheap has been combed, and the loose dirt in the trench also, for potsherds.

My statement in regard to the depth showing the age of the bowl yesterday, has been disproved by the large fragment of a very nicely worked & decorated B. on W. bowl right beside the other.

It is impossible to designate the position of any particular bowl within this zone just described, because different parts of the same bowl are scattered thruout the zone. The base of the zone is 116 in. below surface.

The greatest dimensions of this zone are length (N–S) 50 in.; width 45 in; height 26 in.

The edge of digging in room XI was

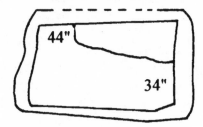

Oct. 6 — Sat.

A low middle period wall was disclosed in the south trench N40 E10.

Another bowl and more sherds were found in N40 E20. Why so many bowl fragments are here I cannot explain. A section of hard earth was found, from which the earth chipped as if from a floor.

This was also in N40 E20 — at a depth of 106". No walls were near it at all. — I cannot explain it. The men were put to work on rooms XII and XIII, and dug there only a short distance down. (see room notes). It seemed really unnecessary to dig farther because the base of the walls was known both on the north and south sides of the southern house.

Most of the day was spent in cleaning the last skeletons in room X. Some delay was caused by two groups of rather talkative visitors.

This day was the last day of regular work. I dismissed the three diggers at 4:30. Martin and I will spend a few days surveying, packing and taking notes next week.

Oct. 8 — Mon. — Cloudy & cold.

The south wall of the southern building consists, in the part exposed, only of the later period. In the western end, is a short fragment of a middle period wall. This lower wall does not extend above the base of the late period wall, because at this point no break occurs in the late wall. The late wall at this point has a peculiar feature not seen elsewhere in the ruin, namely, the entire lower tier of stones, from one end to the other, consists of comparatively flat stones, which project from the base of the wall from 4–9 in. This gives the effect, in the trench, of an irregular shelf running along the base of the wall. The base of the wall is not horizontal, but slopes noticeably to the east. The top of the wall, which reaches the surface, is nearly horizontal. The wall is a little crudely constructed, compated with the others of this building.

Otherwise, the wall exposed here differs in no way from the rest.

A diagram would be:

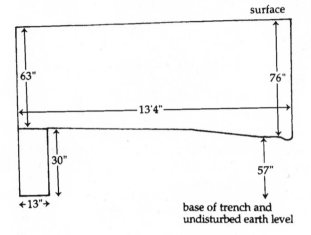

A diagram of the upper wall is:

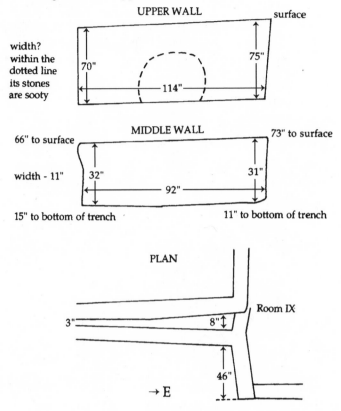

The undisturbed earth at this point is a reddish sand without charcoal. The floor mentioned on the other page is on the south side of the trench. It is just above the undisturbed earth. The many bowls found in this vicinity were found in a zone extending upward from this "floor" level, about 20 in. on the average. This excavation will be reburied, so that, in case work continues here next year, the place will not have been rifled in the meantime.

In N40 E10, just south of the middle period wall 24 in. and 80 in. below the surface another bowl was found.

At present I believe we have removed all the sherds from N40 E20.

The bowl just mentioned turned out to be a large rim sherd of a corrugated olla, — like many already packed, — and was not saved for that reason.

In N130 E30, the walls just west of room IX have been uncovered. There is a late period and a middle period wall. As usual the late period extends to the surface, and the middle period to about the base of the late period. No early period wall exists west of room IX, as far as the excavations are concerned. The position of these two walls uphold my theory in regard to the division into three parts of the composite west wall of room IX. Both walls are straight, and examples of the better type of masonry.

The surface, at this point slopes to the south, making the base of the late wall appear lower than the top of middle wall. Actually they are on a level.

Below the base of the middle wall is very hard clay, with very little charcoal in it. Were it not for the charcoal, I would not hesitate to call it undisturbed earth.

The piles of animal bones and pottery not taken East were reburied, cashed [sic] in between the middle and late period walls, at the western end of the trench in N60 E10. — Marked on work map with "X".

Oct. 9

I started awhile back to make a diagram of the west wall of the trench (connecting trench) thru the court. Now the end of the work has come and time was not available. Very little of value, I believe, is lost by this omission. The west wall consists of nummerous irregular ash and charcoal layers, with no definite former surface indication. Test II, is typical of this series of layer. The heaviest ash deposits are near this test. To the south, the main earth is hard red clay, with a little ash and charcoal.

There is one very pronounced band 3 in. thick, running parallel to the surface, and seems to be a former surface line (See Photo 20 [not included]).

A diagram of this:

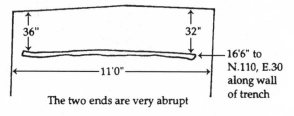

The two ends are very abrupt

This morning I finished the contour map of the middle quadrangle.

The large stone objects were reburied in N40 E20. (Marked on work map III with Y).

Martin finished packing.

Late in afternoon I took last plane table work of contour maps.

Oct. 10

This morning we tore down the shack.

The freight was taken to the station & shipped to Moorehead at Andover. (526 pounds).

The lumber, and incidentals (dishpans, boxes, paper, string, etc.) were left at the shack at the big ruins.

The big ruins were carefully examined. All exposed human bones were buried in the refuse piles of their own trench. All walls were inspected but all seemed to be in same condition as when seen in spring, and none, in my judgment, needed strengthening.

The remaining shovel, wheelbarrow, and box of small tools (the rest had been transferred on Oct. 8) were taken to Harrison's shack, in which they were kept last year, and packed away for the winter.

Oct. 11

Was spent visiting nearby ruins. (See other notes).

Oct. 12

The plane table and alidade and a box of office materials, etc. were taken to Santa Fe and left in the care of the Museum of Archeology.

Most of the day was spent in developing my plates, with Mr. Bradfield's aid.

Oct. 12 [sic]

Today the car was put away for winter. Tires removed, oil, gas, and water drained, wheels blocked up, and carbon removed from engine. The tubes, casings, and tools were left with Mr. Miller in the store (also 4 spark plugs [extra], two blow-out patches, one tire shoe, tire patches, & two extra tubes). The pump, and two oil cans and one gasoline can were left in car. Top and side curtains were put up.

The camping outfit, used in the early part of summer was packed in a box, and a crate, the latter containing only 1 camp stove, 1 grub box with funnel and camp cooking outfit, and 1 dutch oven. Both of these were left in the store, in Mr. Miller's care.

Left for K.C. on No. 2.

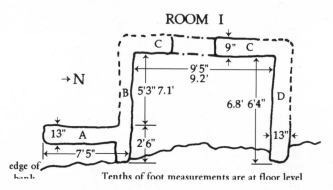

ROOM I

Tenths of foot measurements are at floor level

Room I   Excavated Aug 27 & 28

This room has been exposed by the rain and the wash of the Arroyo. The east wall has fallen out, but the other three walls are still in position.

A section of the west wall seems to have fallen out, by erosion. The N.W. corner of wall is just 12" below the surface. The wall (C) is exposed here for a height of 42". The wall A is exposed for 38 in. The wall D for 46", the top being about a foot below the surface. The interior of the room was, on the average three feet below the original surface. It may have been dug out by a pot hunter. The walls are the same masonry as rooms II and III. Wall B extends beyond A for a distance and forms the north end of a shelf at the foot of wall A. The tops of walls D & B slope toward the arroyo. The breach in W. wall is 1:6 from S.W. corner is 2:3 wide & goes down from surface for 3 ft. [Note: Guthe uses three notation styles for measurements—0"0', 0:0, and 0.0'— and all three probably indicate feet and inches.]

In the S.W. corner of the room, the undisturbed earth is 5 ft. 3 in. below the surface. The base of the wall in this corner is 4 in. above the bottom. Below the wall are several horizontal ash beds.

The base of wall B (south) is set back from the main wall 2–3 in. for a height of about six inches. This lower six inches of wall was embedded in ash layers. The actual floor of the room was not found, but it seems probable that the ash layers were deposited on the floor. In the middle of the west wall the floor layers were 5'4" below the surface; in the N.W. corner, which showed the thickest ash deposit, the layers were 6 ft. below surface, and the base of the wall 6'2". The undisturbed earth began at 6'2" below the surface.

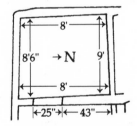

setback in
Base of Wall B, RM I

The men say that boys partially dug this room. On the west wall just below where I found it exposed, the stone cracks were filled with sand, blown or washed in lately. Skel. 1 was found scattered all over the room, near the floor. The walls consist of flat rocks laid with little earth, very careful masonry.

ROOM II

Room II Excavated Aug 27–30

This room is directly west of Room I. At the eastern end the walls reach the surface. In the N.E. corner a large cactus fell into room I, tearing part of the upper wall away. In the S.W. corner the top of the wall is 21 in. below the surface. In the N.W. corner, 33 in.

There is a stone floor in this room. It consists of the same kind of stones as the walls, laid flat over the whole floor. (See photo) The resulting surface is rather uneven. A careful search was made for a clay floor covering the stones. No well-defined layer was found. For an inch or so above the stones, more charcoal was found in the

earth, than elsewhere. Some ashes too. The floor is below the top of the wall in the four corners as follows: N.E. 47 in.; S.E. 44 in.; S.W. 47 in.; N.W. 54 in.

In the northwest corner of the room, fragments of a black, and a B. on W. bowl were found, on a level with the floor. Some burnt earth also. This corner was probably the fireplace. In the eastern part of the room, two rather crude metates were found, and some manos. The pottery from this room was corrugated and B. on W.

There was much charcoal & ash between the stone floor and the red clay bottom.

The east wall, between this room and room I, was broken. At first I believed it to be a natural cave-in of the wall. The north side of the aperture is, however, almost a vertical wall. Unfortunately the south side fell to pieces. The bottom of the opening is 7 in. above the stone floor. This was probably a door.

The stone floor is 16 in. above the base of the west wall in room I. Too short a distance for a second story. This building was probably built on a hillside.

The E. W. & S. walls consist of medium large stones, laid flat, in irregular lines. The north wall, however, is partly like the others, and partly consists of small stones set in, with much clay. As if a door had been carelessly sealed. (See Photo.) If it was a door, the east side of the door is cleaer, being 19 in. from the N.E. corner. The west side is, however, too indefinite to determine.

The red clay at bottom of walls is the following distance from top of wall. N.E. corner 60 in.; S.E. corn. 62 in; S.W. corner 58 in; N.W. corner 62 in.

ROOM III

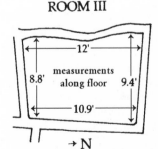

Room III Excavated Aug. 27–30

This room is the largest of first four. It is north of II, and west of IV. The masonry is the same as in rooms I, II and IV, flat slabs laid with little clay. The west wall bulges a bit, which I think was done in the construction and not by pressure in the earth.

The south wall of this room is laid better than the north wall of II. In room II, I spoke of the possibility of a walled up doorway. In the south wall of this room this doorway appears more plainly. Imaginations plays a large part in this conclusion; other people see it, however, the same as I do. On the S. wall of III this walled up door is thus:

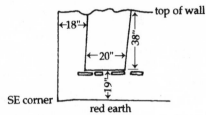

There was no stone doorstep, but four flat stones, on a level, might have formed a sill.

The earth from the top of the wall down, showed no distinct stratification until within six inches of the bottom. In those last six inches there are several layers of charcoal & white ash.

Along the east wall, from the S.E. corner to 6 ft. north of there, is a heavy charcoal layer, slightly below level of red clay bottom about two feet long and 4–6 in. deep.

It was, however, impossible to locate any definite floor level, altho it surely is within those six inches. The top of the undisturbed red clay is not level, being slightly undulating. In the S.E. corner a charcoal pocket was found, 10 in. in diameter and about six inches deep. The fireplace was probably there.

A black corrugated olla was found along the west wall, right side up, with skeletons of small rodents in it. The bottom rested on an ash layer within six inches of bottom. Along the east wall a skeleton of a child (Skel. 2) was found, in very poor condition.

N.W. corner; top of wall, 4.5 ft. from surface
    red clay bottom, 8.7 ft. from surface.
N.E. corner, top of wall, 1.7 ft. from surface
    red clay bottom, 6.8 ft. from surface
S.E. corner, top of wall, 0.4 ft. from surface
    red clay bottom, 6.2 ft. from surface
S.W. corner, top of wall, 2.3 ft. from surface
    red clay bottom, 7.5 ft. from surface

The base of the walls rest on the undisturbed red clay.

Across the N.W. corner of the room, passing over both the west & the north walls was a distinct ash layer, from 6–12 in. above wall top. Directly over the corner the layer becomes a pocket 6–8 in. deep, with many animal bones.

ROOM IV

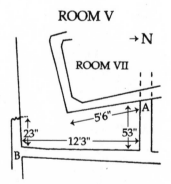

measurements are at floor

Room IV   Excavated Aug. 28

This room is directly north of room I. Like room I, the east side has fallen away, since the arroyo has washed into the room. The west wall is a bit lower than the others, but this can be accounted for by the fact that the men may have cut thru it the previous day.

A floor was found in this room. In the N.W. corner it was 6.1 ft. below the surface. The top of the west wall is 2.4 ft. below the surface, and the wall is 3.7 ft. high. The south wall is six inches higher than west one, in S.W. corner, but slopes with the original surface level, towards the arroyo. The north wall did not extend to the surface. The top was 1.6 ft. below the surface.

As in room I, several ash layers were found near the base of the walls, above and below the floor. The floor is .6 above the undisturbed red clay. In the northern end of the room, burnt earth and charcoal was found, but in no definite order. No fireplace was seen. Masonry same as in room I.

ROOM V

Room V   Excavated Aug. 30, 31

This room belongs to the same tier of rooms [as] at I–IV. The top of its walls are about on the same level, as the tops of the previous rooms.

At A the top of the wall is 48 in. below the surface; at B, 12 in.

The south wall of the room stops abruptly about 2 ft. west of the east wall.— The rest may have been disturbed by the Indians of the later pueblo.

It was impractical to excavate this room to the bottom, for room VII of a later period was built on top of it, and the latter's walls would have had to been sacrificed.

The south wall of V may extend farther west below the level excavated.

Room VI   Excavated Aug. 31 & Sept. 1

ROOM VI

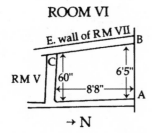

This room belongs to the lower tier of rooms (I–V). The room is just west of III, and north of V.

It was impractical to excavated this room to the bottom (which is probably the same as that of III), for the east wall of VII (of later period) cuts across the western part. The south wall of this room is 6–8 in. higher than the east wall.

The north wall is not a continuation of the north wall of III.— The north wall was not found, because of the edge of the trench.

The ash layer noted in room III as passing over the N.W. corner of the room, continues across the northern part of room VI, and passes under the east wall of VII. At A, this layer was 1 ft. above the east wall. At B, it was 65 in. below the surface. All of the skeletons found in this room (4, 5, & 6) were below this ash layer.

At C the E. wall of VII rests on the S. wall of VI, which is here 52 in. below surface. At B, the bottom of the E. wall of VII is 60 in. below surface. At A the top of east wall of VI is 60 in. below surface.

ROOM VII

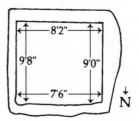

Room VII   Excavated Sept. 1-7

This room is on top of V and VI.

The east wall extends to the surface. This wall is placed on, and passes over the north wall of room V. At this point the east wall of VII is 48 in. high, from the surface, down to the top of the N. wall of V.

The S.E. corner of this room was torn out, because a corner was not expected there.

The south wall of the room is fallen out near the surface.

Two feet west of S.E. corner,
   top of south wall, 12 in. below surface
   base of south wall, 42 in. below surface
At S.W. corner,
   top of south wall, 29 in. below surface
   base of south wall, 59 in. below surface

The walls of this room (E. & S. walls) are built like the walls of the lower tier of rooms, but with a little less care. The north and west walls are comparatively well put together. The north, west, and east walls extend to the surface.

About where one would expect the floor, an ellaborate [sic] formation was found, about a foot above the base of the walls.

There was a very distinct layer of small stones, laid closely together, but rather uneven. (See photos). These stones were surrounded by a substance, which greatly resembled lime. It looked as if the stones had been laid in this lime. Over the stones was a layer of fine yellow earth, which seemed to be decayed wood. Between this layer (which may have been the remains of the roof) and the stones, may have been a floor, but it could not be definitely cleaned. In the N.E. corner of the room, was a slight depression, with a clay surface much resembling a floor. It was bordered by two comparatively large stones, which showed effects of fire. This may have been the fireplace. In the N.W. corner was a flat slab, about 14 × 10 in. and about one in. thick. It was not smoothed on the upper side. Several of these stones have been found in the corner of the digging. They remind me of the flat stones the Zunis cooked Tortillas on, except that they are not smoothed or polished. This stone layer could not have been refuse, for the stones were too evenly distributed, and are too small for wall stones. Under this stone layer was an ash and charcoal layer, which seemed to cover nearly the whole floor. The top of this stone layer was the following inches below the surface at the three corners.— N.E. 49 in; N.W. 76 in; S.W. 57 in. In the S.E. corner the surface had been destroyed before the floor was found. Here the floor was 10 in. above the base of the wall.

[Room VII (p.3.) The corners of the room were not tied, and the resulting vertical cracks were plugged with small stones.]

Along the east side of the rooms one band of ashes & charcoal bent downward towards the east. In the rest of the room the hard clay bottom occurred surprisingly early, for the location of rooms I–VI lead me to believe that VII was built on top of an earlier set of rooms.

The measurements from surface are as follows in the following corners:

N.E. cor.,— base of wall 54 in;
N.W. cor. [scratched out]
S.W. cor.,— base of wall] 60 in;
S.E. [scratched out]

section taken about 55" from S. wall.

stone floor
ash and —50"—
east wall
31"
undisturbed earth —25"—
charcoal
The long layer is a line in west and 2 inches in east.
no bottom 5'0" below floor.

The "undisturbed earth" just mentioned, upon careful examination, proved to be rubbish, packed fairly hard, with large lumps of the undisturbed red clay in it, as if the refuse of digging a hole in the hardpan had been dumped here, and the refuse (charcoal, ashes, pottery)

had washed in around it. Two feet below the base of the walls, charcoal was found.

The north wall of room V, which disappeared below the east wall of VII, was found to continue on the other side, under the stone wall. The median line of this wall was 69 in. from the inside S.E. corner of the room. The top of the wall was 12 in. below the base of the east wall of VII, and 18 in. below the stone layer. It extends westward into the room 21 in., and then stops abruptly (See note on south wall of room V). The top of this wall is 59 in. below the surface.

The lime and small-stone layer extends across the room about on a level with the base of the walls. The N.W. corner of the stone-layer was left — for visitors.

ROOM VIII

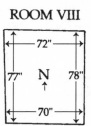

Room VIII   Written up 9/18/17

This is the smallest room so far found and also the richest. Skeletons 7 and 10 were taken out on the northern side. A fine metate, two manos, several bones, one comal, three bowls, and sherds, many small objects were found here (See Catalogue).

All four walls of the room reached the surface. The depth of the foot of the wall below the surface, in the corners were:

N.E., 93"; S.E. 82"; S.W. 82"; N.W. 92"

No floor, as such, was found, but varying from 4–10 inches above the base of the walls, was a horizontal streak of white, like whitewash, which may have been the floor.

In the east wall was a filled-in door, which had been filled from the outside,— that is, room VII.—

In the N.W. corner, just under the foot of the wall was an ash deposit. Under the walls was disturbed earth. Depth of undisturbed earth?

For details of excavation, see "running" notebook.

Room IX   Excavated 9/12 – 9/25

This room contains the most complicated series of walls yet found.

There are three sets of walls here, superimposed; They are designated — Lowest IX, middle IX, and heighest [sic] IX.

Highest IX reaches the surface and is really only an indentation in the south wall of the north building of the southern quadrangle. The S.E. and S.W. corners are outside corners.

Middle IX has a west wall, no southern wall, and probably clay or adobe north & east walls.

Lowest IX consists of the foundations of the southern, eastern and western walls of a room.

Skel. 11, some bowls, a metate, and cositas were found in this room. On the whole, however, the area was relatively barren.

For measurements and details see Diary of diggings.

ROOM X

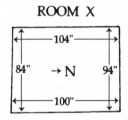

Room X

This room is in the south building. It was dug deeper than any of the other rooms. The depths at the corners are given on Work Map III.

Time was running out and therefore it seemed unadvisable to dig to the bottom of the walls, especially since on the south and north sides of the building the base of the walls were found.

The walls of this room extend to the surface. There is some evidence of the walls having been plastered. Of course, there is also the white, lime-like deposit which I atribute [sic] to plant roots. Otherwise the walls resemble all the others.

Skel. 16 & 17 were found in this room.

Measurements were taken at base of digging.

ROOM XI

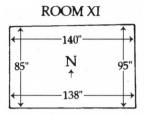

Room XI

This room is just west of room X.

The depth to which this room was excavated is shown on Work Map III, by the measurements at the corners.

There is nothing to note about this room except the door in the south wall — The walls of this room also reach the surface.

The door in the south wall is:

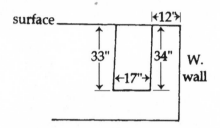

The measurement[s] of [the] room were taken at base of digging.

In the S.E. corner is the soot triangle found several times elsewhere, here also directly on the stones, altho in places the walls look plastered.

ROOM XII

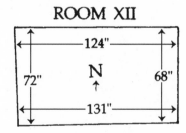

Room XII

This room is just south of X. Here also the depths on the Work Map III, show the amount of excavation.

There is nothing to note in this room, except that the walls are like all the rest.

Measurements taken at base of diggings.

Part III
TECHNICAL REPORTS

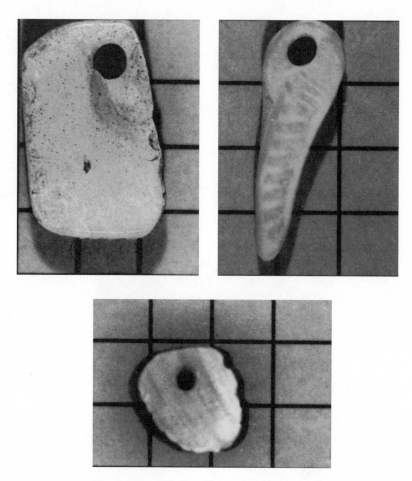

Figure 40. Pendants of bone (above) and shell (below)

FAUNAL REMAINS
FROM THE 1984 EXCAVATIONS

Linda Mick-O'Hara

ALL OF THE FAUNAL REMAINS ISOLATED DURING the 1984 excavations at Rowe Pueblo were identified as specifically as possible using the criteria listed below. All mammalian identifications were done during the field season or during a student lab offered for the fall semester of 1984 and the spring semester of 1985 and supervised by the author. All other remains (including problematic mammalian remains) were identified by the author.

The faunal materials were brushed clean of excavation matrix and a preliminary sorting and size-grading was done by unit and level. Each class of remains was then sorted by unit and level for further analysis, with provenience information being maintained. This procedure enabled the identification of one class of remains at a time and their reintegration during the later analysis phases.

All faunal remains were identified using comparative collections provided by the Physical Anthropology Lab of the Department of Anthropology, and by the Museum of Southwestern Biology. References dealing with the identification of archaeological faunal remains were also used (Olsen 1964, 1968; Gilbert 1980; Gilbert et al. 1981). Bone fragments that could be reconstructed into a more complete element were considered as one unit. Remains were identified to the most specific level possible, depending on the degree of fragmentation, burning, and erosion of each piece. Element, portion of each element present, side, and relative maturity reflected by bone fragments were noted where possible. In addition, degree of fragmentation and presence of any working or burning were noted (Figure 40). Data recorded for each fragment are tabulated in the appendices of the original field school report (on file, Clark Field Archive, University of New Mexico).

Of the 9,866 bone fragments identified from the 1984 excavation at Rowe Pueblo, 6,681 fragments (67.7%) could be identified only to the general categories of small mammal, medium mammal, large mammal, or bird. The remaining 3,185 elements (32.3%) were identified as representing 36 different species or, less specifically, 10 genera, 14 families, and 3 orders (Table 13). The possible associations of these species with the early, middle, or late portion of the rather lengthy occupation of the site will be made whenever possible.

The Faunal Assemblage

The faunal assemblage can be split into two separate segments, those bone fragments that could not be identified beyond the level of class and those elements that were identifiable to more specific levels. Table 13 presents the percentages assignable to the sample as a whole as well as to the portion that could be identified. This highly fragmented bone assemblage gives us some indication of the intensity of processing or the effect of taphonomic processes at the site on bone from various mammal groups. Elimination of the unidentifiable part of the sample clarifies the representation of different species (Table 13, column 4).

Although differential processing and preservation have certainly influenced the analyst's ability to identify certain species, the percentages of bone assigned to species in the identifiable sample can be used to evaluate trends in the use of certain body-size categories of mammals and specific species. Preservation would tend to favor the recovery of larger species and specifically those bones with greater amounts of compact tissue (Binford and Bertram 1977). Differential preservation and recovery may also be affected by processing activities such as butchering and boiling. During what might be called

Table 13. Frequencies of Specimens from 1984 Excavations Identified
to the Most Specific Taxonomic Level Possible

Species	n	% of total	% of identified sample
MAMMALS			
Mammal	64	0.65	
Small mammal (mouse to prairie dog size)	1143	11.58	
Medium mammal (rabbit to wolf size)	3498	35.45	
Large mammal (antelope to bison size)	1774	17.98	
Order Rodentia	18	0.18	0.56
Family Sciuridae	17	0.17	0.53
Ammospermophilus spp. (antelope ground squirrels)	6	0.06	0.19
Spermophilus spp. (ground squirrels)	8	0.08	0.25
Spermophilus variegatus (rock squirrel)	33	0.33	1.04
Cynomys spp. (prairie dog)	4	0.04	0.12
Cynomys gunnisoni (Gunnison's prairie dog)	70	0.71	2.23
Sciurus spp. (squirrels)	4	0.04	0.12
Family Geomydiae (pocket gophers)	53	0.54	1.66
Thomomys bottae (Botta's pocket gopher)	179	1.81	5.62
Thomomys talpoides (northern pocket gopher)	3	0.03	0.09
Pappogeomys castanops (yellow-faced pocket gopher)	6	0.06	0.19
Family Heteromyidae	2	0.02	0.06
Dipodomys ordii (Ord's kangaroo rat)	3	0.03	0.09
Castor canadensis (beaver)	2	0.02	0.06
Family Cricetidae	6	0.06	0.19
Peromyscus spp. (mouse)	23	0.23	0.72
Peromyscus maniculatus (deer mouse)	5	0.05	0.16
Neotoma albigula (white-throated woodrat)	27	0.27	0.85
Neotoma mexicana (Mexican woodrat)	37	0.38	1.16
Microtus spp. (voles)	3	0.03	0.09
Ondatra zibethicus (muskrat)	13	0.13	0.41
Erethizon dorsatum (porcupine)	1	0.01	0.03
Family Leporidae	11	0.11	0.34
Sylvilagus spp. (cottontails)	89	0.90	2.79
Lepus spp. (jackrabbits)	57	0.58	1.79
Sylvilagus auduboni (desert cottontail)	583	5.91	18.30
Lepus californicus (black-tailed jackrabbit)	139	1.41	4.36
Family Canidae	33	0.33	1.04
Canis spp. (dog, coyote, wolf)	50	0.51	1.57
Canis latrans (coyote)	4	0.04	0.12
Canis familiaris (Puebloan dog)	3	0.03	0.09
Canis lupus (gray wolf)	14	0.14	0.44
Urocyon cinereoargenteus (gray fox)	15	0.15	0.47

Table 13. (Continued)

Species	n	% of total	% of identified sample
Procyon lotor (raccoon)	3	0.03	0.09
Felis concolor (mountain lion)	1	0.01	0.03
Lynx rufus (bobcat)	1	0.01	0.03
Order Artiodactyla	128	1.30	4.02
Family Cervidae	5	0.05	0.16
Cervus canadensis (wapiti/elk)	3	0.03	0.09
Odocoileus spp. (deer)	889	9.01	27.91
Odocoileus hemionus (mule deer)	101	1.02	3.17
Family Antilocapridae	18	0.18	0.56
Antilocapra americana (pronghorn)	73	0.74	2.29
Ovis canadensis (big-horned sheep)	4	0.04	0.12
Bison bison (bison)	31	0.31	0.97
AVES			
Bird	202	2.05	
Buteo jamaicensis (red-tailed hawk)	20	0.20	0.63
Falco sparverius (sparrow hawk)	1	0.01	0.03
Colinus virginianus (bobwhite)	4	0.04	0.12
Meleagris gallopavo (turkey)	347	3.52	10.89
Family Columbidae (pigeons and doves)	2	0.02	0.06
Geococcyx californianus (roadrunner)	1	0.01	0.03
Family Picidae (woodpeckers)	6	0.06	0.19
Melanerpes erythrocephalus (red-headed woodpecker)	1	0.01	0.03
Family Tyrannidae (flycatchers)	1	0.01	0.03
Family Corvidae (jays, magpies, crows)	1	0.01	0.03
Aphelocoma coerulescens (scrub jay)	7	0.07	0.22
Corvus brachyrynchos (common crow)	3	0.03	0.09
REPTILES			
Pseudomys scripta (pond slider)	1	0.01	0.03
Terrapene ornata (ornate box turtle)	7	0.07	0.22
Family Colubridae (nonvenomous snakes)	2	0.02	0.06
FISH			
Family Percidae (perch, pike, darters)	1	0.01	0.03
INVERTEBRATE			
Shell	2	0.02	0.06
TOTAL	9866	99.95	99.92

Note: Of the total faunal sample, 3185 fragments (32.28% of the sample) were identifiable beyond general categorization to mammal or bird.

"staged butchering," elements are discarded in different locales at one site or at different sites. This activity would decrease the number of some elements that could (with perfect preservation) be recovered from any one locale or site (Binford and Bertram 1977; Binford 1978).

Boiling reduces preservation by removing soluble materials from the compact and cancellous tissue of an element. This process produces a surface that is more easily eroded. Carnivore scavenging (e.g., by dogs) during the occupation of the site as well as after the site was abandoned would also affect our sample. Dogs are given portions of carcasses as well as scavenge through midden areas. Carnivores and raptors could alter the assemblage by introducing predominantly small species to the upper levels of the site postoccupationally. Interpretations of the identified species from the 1984 sample take these processes into account.

Six species dominated the identifiable sample from the 1984 excavations at Rowe: *Odocoileus hemionus* (mule deer), *Sylvilagus auduboni* (desert cottontail), *Meleagris gallopavo* (turkey), *Lepus californicus* (black-tailed jackrabbit), *Thomomys bottae* (Botta's pocket gopher), and *Cynomys gunnisoni* (Gunnison's prairie dog). For analytical purposes genus-level identifications (see Table 13) are used for all frequencies.

The faunal assemblage at Rowe Pueblo is dominated by large mammal remains; some 1,252 elements could be placed in this category. This combined category represents 39.3% of the identifiable sample and consists of *Antilocapra americana* (pronghorn antelope), *Ovis canadensis* (bighorn sheep), and *Bison bison* (bison) as well as *Odocoileus hemionus* (mule deer) remains. Mule deer is clearly predominant in the large mammal sample (990 elements or 31.1% of the identified sample) and in the sample as a whole. The identification of large mammal species other than mule deer indicates the extent to which this size range of mammals was utilized by the Rowe population. All of these species were available within a short distance of the pueblo. The use of these large species of mammal indicates a subsistence strategy with a greater emphasis on hunting than is indicated by faunal samples from other large Pueblo IV pueblos, as discussed below.

The elements identifiable as *Odocoileus hemionus* include at least 12 individuals when a standard MNI count is used but may actually consist of segments of many more individuals that were butchered elsewhere and shared along family lines (Beaglehole 1936; Bradfield 1971). The lack of bias in element recovery in this sample indicates that all portions of this species were introduced to the site at least intermittently over the period of occupation. Mule deer would have been available in the immediate area, and the use of both mature and immature individuals suggests that they were hunted during the spring and fall and sporadically throughout the year.

A large number of elements assignable to *Sylvilagus auduboni* were also identified in this sample. Desert cottontail represents 21.1% of the identified sample and comprises 672 identifiable elements. The large number of bone fragments only identifiable as medium mammal (rabbit to wolf size) would suggest that processing has lowered the number of remains assignable to this species and that utilization of this species roughly compares with that of mule deer in the sample. Though the usable meat from a single desert cottontail (1.75 lbs) is only 1.8% of the usable meat from a single mule deer, as protein added to the stew pot it could still make a significant contribution to the diet.

Desert cottontail was also available in the general site area and may have been attracted to and hunted in the agricultural fields tended by the Puebloan population. Certainly, the entire individual was introduced into the site in the case of both desert cottontail and all the rest of the predominant species in the sample, but processing strategies such as boiling would tend to erode bones and thus affect preservation. The small size of some elements, in addition to the type of processing, would decrease the likelihood of their preservation.

Meleagris gallopavo (turkey) is the next most frequently identified species in the 1984 Rowe sample. The 347 elements assigned to this species represent 10.9% of identifiable sample. The maturity of most of the bone and the fact that no eggshell was recovered in the sample suggests that this species was not kept at the site.

The other frequently identified species are medium and small mammals that would have been taken when encountered in the fields or while pueblo residents were hunting and would have been included in the stew pot. Their occurrence in this sample could have been the result of field hunting (Bradfield 1971). *Lepus californicus* (black-tailed jackrabbit) and *Cynomys gunnisoni* (Gunnison's prairie dog) may also have been taken during hunting trips at lower elevations and in open country when larger mammals were not encountered.

The other species identified in the faunal sample from Rowe are, again, species that according to ethnographic observations were included in the stew pot as they were encountered. Some of the small mammals identified may have been intrusive either as burrowers or through later visits to the site by carnivores or raptors. The bird species identified include a number that were used primarily for their feathers. The provenience of these species may help to identify specific features, such as kivas. This question as well as others will be approached by looking at the faunal remains recovered from various excavation units.

Differential Recovery from Excavation Units and Trenches

Three different types of excavation strategies were undertaken during the 1984 season at Rowe Ruin. Units measuring 2 by 2 m were excavated south of the pueblo, two rooms were excavated in the northern roomblock of the central plaza, and a number of backhoe trenches were excavated around the perimeter of the ruin and in the south plaza to look for features that were not visible on the surface (see Figure 6). The faunal remains from these various units differed because of varying recovery techniques and preservation; frequencies of bone in each excavation unit are presented in Table 14.

The majority of the fauna recovered during the 1984 excavations came from the excavation units south of the southern roomblock and from the room excavations. The excavations were both more intensive and more extensive in these areas, and quarter-inch mesh screening was used on all of the matrix. Units T305, T306, and T307 produced 48.5% of the total sample of bone recovered, and the room excavations R112T2, R113, and T113 produced 23.1% of the sample (Table 14).

Excavation of the backhoe trenches removed large quantities of matrix that was not screened, but even in these units the differential recovery of faunal remains was an indicator of buried cultural features. The backhoe trenches exposed cultural remains in a number of areas, but the most significant cultural features were excavated in trenches X, 2, 3, 4, and 15. The increased

Table 14. Summary of Faunal Recovery from the 1984 Excavations at Rowe Pueblo

Excavation Unit	n	%
Backhoe Trenches		
BHX	150	1.52
BH1T1	86	0.87
BH1	19	0.19
BH2	320	3.24
BH3	117	1.19
BH4T1	11	0.11
BH4	180	1.82
BH5	1	0.01
BH6	24	0.24
BH7	49	0.50
BH12	20	0.20
BH13	4	0.04
BH15	440	4.46
BH19	1	0.01
Room or Grid Unit		
R112T2	1316	13.34
R113	864	8.76
T113	102	1.03
T114	7	0.07
T115	10	0.10
T116	41	0.42
T117	14	0.14
T118	1230	12.47
T119	49	0.50
T304	23	0.23
T305	1376	13.95
T306	2329	23.61
T307	1083	10.98
Total	9866	100.00

recovery of faunal remains noted in backhoe trenches 2 and 15 was the result of hand excavation in both of these units and the exposure of cultural features containing some trash.

Tables 15 and 16 tabulate the faunal assemblage by taxonomic identification and by type of recovery unit. Only the units that contained more than 100 fragments are discussed in any detail. Additional data on element, portion, side, and age are on file at the University of New Mexico in the Maxwell Museum's Clark Field Archive.

Backhoe Trench X and T118

Trench X exposed a midden area on the east side of Rowe Ruin. T118 was a 1 by 1 m test pit excavated off the side of the main trench to investigate strata noted in the trench walls. Since both of these units were dug to investigate one feature, the data are combined here for a total of 1,380 elements or 14.0% of the site assemblage. Of this total, 981 bone fragments or 71.1% of the unit sample were only identifiable to the level of class. The identifiable elements from these units parallel the identifiable species frequencies for the whole sample, with large mammal species, especially *Odocoileus,* predominating, followed by *Sylvilagus* and the other smaller mammals and turkey. In the unidentifiable fraction of the remains from these units, the number of medium mammal fragments is considerably greater than that of fragments assigned to large mammals. This suggests that preservation and fragmentation have decreased the identifiable portion of the sample and that the amount of large mammal and medium mammal remains, especially *Odocoileus* vs. *Sylvilagus,* is more equally distributed than is suggested by the identifiable sample. The small mammal species identified from this midden area appear to represent refuse from processing of animals for the stew pot, if element frequencies are considered (Thomas 1971).

Backhoe Trench 2

Backhoe trench 2 encountered two pits containing burials and a pitstructure/kiva with an antechamber and two hearth areas. Several additional burials were excavated from an area of rockfall in the northern part of this trench. Since human bone and architectural materials were present, excavation proceeded by hand and all of the matrix was screened. This technique increased the faunal recovery for this unit. Large mammal remains clearly predominate in this sample. Archaeomagnetic samples taken from an adobe-collared hearth in this area place the structural occupation at AD 1350 or contemporaneous with the major occupation at the site. The differences in faunal assemblage composition between this unit and the site as a whole may be due to greater use and disposal of large mammal remains in this area or the use of this structure as a locale for the distribu-

tion of large mammal kills. If the structure is more recent than the main occupation at Rowe, as suggested by Cordell in this report, the large mammals may have been processed sometime following the primary occupation.

Backhoe Trench 3

Trench 3 exposed a hearth associated with a possible pitstructure. The majority of the remains recovered (92 bone fragments or 78.6% of the unit sample) were only identifiable to the level of body size or class. The paucity of identifiable elements renders species frequencies for this unit meaningless. A look at the unidentified fragments, however, suggests that all of the dominant mammalian species at Rowe were used and disposed of about equally in this area.

Backhoe Trench 4

Trench 4 and BH4T1, an associated test unit, exposed a possible structure that was never clearly interpreted. The combined unit excavations resulted in the recovery of 191 bone fragments. The two major groups of faunal remains from this unit are the 114 bone fragments (60.0% of the unit sample) that could only be identified to the level of class or body size and the 57 elements (30.0% of the unit sample) that could be assigned at various levels to large mammal species.

Large mammal remains dominate among both the identified species and the less specifically identifiable categories for these units. In this respect this area is very similar to that investigated by backhoe trench 2. The relative abundance of large mammal bone in this area may exist for the same reasons that it dominates the trench 2 sample.

Backhoe Trench 15

Trench 15 was hand-excavated in the south plaza of Rowe Pueblo but the matrix was only partially screened. Excavation exposed a complex set of strata indicating possible plaza surfaces and encountered a small section of a wall located in the northwest corner of the plaza. This unit contained the only felid remains isolated at

Table 15. Specimens Identified from the Trench Excavations at Rowe Pueblo, 1984

Species	Backhoe Trench													
	X	1T1	10	2	30	4T1	4	5	6	7	12	13	15	9
MAMMALS														
Mammal														
Small mammal (mouse to prairie dog)	3	5		61	27	2	9				4		27	
Medium mammal (rabbit to wolf)	30	25	9	87	26	8	37		17	15		2	112	
Large mammal (antelope to bison)	39	21	5	105	39		58	1	6	20	1	1	75	
Order Rodentia				2										
Family Sciuride														
Ammospermophilus spp. (antelope ground squirrels)														
Spermophilus spp. (ground squirrels)														
Spermophilus variegatus (rock squirrel)					1									
Cynomys spp. (prairie dog)														
Cynomys gunnisoni (Gunnison's prairie dog)	1			1			1						2	
Sciurus spp. (squirrels)														
Family Geomydiae (pocket gophers)					1									
Thomomys bottae (Botta's pocket gopher)				2										
Thomomys talpoides (northern pocket gopher)														
Pappogeomys castanops (yellow-faced pocket gopher)													2	

131

Table 15. (Continued)

Species		Backhoe Trench												
	X	1T1	10	2	30	4T1	4	5	6	7	12	13	15	9
Family Heteromyidae														
Dipodomys ordii (Ord's kangaroo rat)														
Castor canadensis (beaver)														
Family Cricetidae														
Peromyscus spp. (mouse)													2	
Peromyscus maniculatus (deer mouse)														
Neotoma albigula (white-throated woodrat)		1		1										
Neotoma mexicana (Mexican woodrat)				2									1	
Microtus spp. (voles)														
Ondatra zibethicus (muskrat)														
Erethizon dorsatum (porcupine)														
Family Leporidae														
Sylvilagus spp. (cottontails)										1				
Lepus spp. (jackrabbits)														
Sylvilagus audoboni (desert cottontail)	5	3	1	4	1		2			3			23	
Lepus californicus (black-tailed jackrabbit)	4	2		1			2						16	
Family Canidae														
Canis spp. (dog, coyote, wolf)				1			2						2	
Canis latrans (coyote)		1		1	2		2							
Canis familiaris (Puebloan dog)				1										
Canis lupus (gray wolf)	2			1			6							
Urocyon cinereoargenteus (gray fox)	2	1											3	

Table 15. (Continued)

Species						Backhoe Trench									
	X	1T1	10	2	30	4T1	4	5	6	7	12	13	15	9
Procyon lotor (raccoon)				2									1	
Felis concolor (mountain lion)													1	
Lynx rufus (bobcat)														
Order Artiodactyla	4	6		2	6		12						21	
Family Cervidae														
Cervus canadensis (wapiti/elk)														
Odocoileus spp. (deer)	32	11	1	26	3	1	30		1	8		1	61	
Odocoileus hemionus (mule deer)				3	4		10						8	
Family Antilocapridae	11													
Antilocapra americana (pronghorn)		4		5	2		4					1	5	
Ovis canadensis (big-horned sheep)													1	
Bison bison (bison)					1								4	
AVES														
Bird		1		1							10		5	
Buteo jamaicensis (red-tailed hawk)													18	
Falco sparverius (sparrow hawk)														
Colinus virginianus (bobwhite)														
Meleagris gallopavo (turkey)	17	5	3	8	4		5			2	4		49	1
Family Columbidae (pigeons and doves)														
Geococcyx californianus (roadrunner)														

Table 15. (Continued)

Species	Backhoe Trench													
	X	1T1	10	2	30	4T1	4	5	6	7	12	13	15	9
Family Picidae (woodpeckers)														
Melanerpes erythrocephalus (red-headed woodpecker)														
Family Tyrannidae (flycatchers)														
Family Corvidae (jays, magpies, crows)														
Aphelocoma coerulescens (scrub jay)														
Corvus brachyrynchos (common crow)													1	
Total	150	86	19	320	117	11	180	1	24	49	20	4	440	1

the site, a partial pelvis of *Felis concolor* (mountain lion) with fleshing cutmarks and an ulna awl assignable to *Lynx rufus* (bobcat). Parts of at least three *Buteo jamaicensis* (red-tailed hawk) individuals were excavated from this unit, and the elements present suggest that the individuals were not processed for consumption but were buried as articulated specimens and may have been kept as live birds for a time. The complete right and left humeri of one *Urocyon cinereoargenteus* (gray fox) individual were also recovered from this area.

In addition to these more unusual specimens, this unit contained 96 elements assigned to various large mammal species (21.8% of the unit sample, *Odocoileus* being dominant), 49 elements (11.1% of the unit sample) identified as *Meleagris gallopavo* (turkey), and 23 elements assigned to *Sylvilagus auduboni* (desert cottontail) (see Table 14 for details). The large number of bone fragments assigned only to the medium mammal category suggests that more species in this size range were present than is apparent in the identified specimens. In terms of faunal remains, this unit was clearly the most productive of all the trenches.

R112T2

Test unit 2 in room 112 continued the investigation of a room that was partially excavated in 1983. More than half of the sample recovered from this excavation (58.8%) was identifiable only to a general level. The remaining sample paralleled the overall site species pattern: *Odocoileus* dominated the identifiable species, followed by *Sylvilagus*. The numerous species of small mammal that were identified from this unit suggest dumping from stew pots into this abandoned room late in the occupation at Rowe. Some of the smaller mammals clearly could have been intrusive, but the spectrum of elements present supports the interpretation provided above.

Room 113

T113 was the test excavation that led to the identification of room 113 and is included in this analysis of the unit. More than half of the sample recovered from this unit (58.5%) could be identified only to general cat-

egories, and these categories are dominated by remains assigned to the medium mammal category. The identified sample is dominated by *Sylvilagus*, and this finding is supported by the large number of generally identified specimens in this size range (see Table 15). The evidence of large mammal species, especially *Odocoileus*, equals the evidence of cottontails in this unit sample. In addition to these genera, a large number of small mammals were identified and are probably, again, the result of the dumping of stew pot refuse into the abandoned room.

T305, T306, and T307

Three 2 by 2 m units were excavated in a checkerboard configuration to the south of the southern roomblock at Rowe. They confirmed the presence of an early adobe component at the site. Their proximity to one another makes their combined consideration relevant.

The assemblage from these units is dominated by bone fragments that could only be identified to very general categories (80.0%, 70.0%, and 64.3% from the three units, respectively). The dominant identified species tend to parallel those for the site as a whole, and many of the same species of small mammals that were recovered from the two excavated rooms were identified from these units as well. Though numbers and species vary from unit to unit, the remains recovered from these units suggest that the same species were emphasized in the subsistence strategy at Rowe throughout most of its occupation. The continuous use of large mammal species also suggests that a hunting strategy was far more productive at this pueblo than at other Pueblo IV sites west of the Pecos area.

Contact and Exchange at Rowe Pueblo

The faunal materials recovered during the 1984 excavations at Rowe present a view of subsistence that is quite different from that observed at other Pueblo IV pueblos. The consistent use and predominance of large mammals in addition to the presence of a large amount of bone assignable to *Sylvilagus auduboni* (desert cottontail) suggest a greater emphasis on hunting, or at least

Table 16. Specimens Identified from the Room and Grid Unit Excavations at Rowe Pueblo, 1984

Species	R112T2	R113	T113	T114	T115	T116	T117	T118	T119	T304	T305	T306	T307
MAMMALS													
Mammal	4	15									18	22	5
Small mammal (mouse to prairie dog)	154	101	8	2	4	1	2	96	6	8	240	233	150
Medium mammal (rabbit to wolf)	432	275	35	3	4	16	3	529	13		572	961	287
Large mammal (antelope to bison)	167	114	15	1	1	17	3	263	17	8	250	322	233
Order Rodentia	6	3						1			1	5	
Family Sciuridae	3	7	1								1	4	1
Ammospermophilus spp. (antelope ground squirrels)	2	1						2					1
Spermophilus spp. (ground squirrels)	2	4						1					1
Spermophilus variegatus (rock squirrel)	19	8						1				2	2
Cynomys spp. (prairie dog)												4	
Cynomys gunnisoni (Gunnison's prairie dog)	16	29						5			1	10	4
Sciurus spp. (squirrels)											2	2	
Family Geomydiae (pocket gophers)	10	9	5								8	19	1
Thomomys bottae (Botta's pocket gopher)	31	40	1			1	4	9			4	31	56
Thomomys talpoides (northern pocket gopher)		1									1		1
Pappogeomys castanops (yellow-faced pocket gopher)	1	2											1
Family Heteromyidae	1	1											
Dipodomys ordii (Ord's kangaroo rat)	1	2						1					

Table 16. (Continued)

Species	R112T2	R113	T113	T114	T115	T116	T117	T118	T119	T304	T305	T306	T307
Castor canadensis (beaver)								1				1	1
Family Cricetidae	3	3											
Peromyscus spp. (mice)	13	4									3	1	
Peromyscus maniculatus (deer mouse)		4											1
Neotoma albigula (white-throated woodrat)	3	7	1								1	6	7
Neotoma mexicana (Mexican woodrat)	2	11						1				9	11
Microtus spp. (voles)		2										1	
Ondatra zibethicus (muskrat)	7	2						1				3	
Erethizon dorsatum (porcupine)												1	
Family Leporidae	2	1						1				4	3
Sylvilagus spp. (cottontails)	14	9	1								18	39	7
Lepus spp. (jackrabbits)	9	3	10								14	30	1
Sylvilagus audoboni (desert cottontail)	90	73			1	1		50	1	2	22	146	145
Lepus californicus (black-tailed jackrabbit)	23	15						24	1		9	21	21
Family Canidae	4	7	1					6			5	4	1
Canis spp. (dog, coyote, wolf)	5	9						5			2	18	5
Canis latrans (coyote)	1							2					
Canis familiaris (Puebloan dog)												3	
Canis lupus (gray wolf)	3							7				2	
Urocyon cinereoargenteus (gray fox)		1										1	
Procyon lotor (raccoon)												1	

Table 16. (Continued)

Species	R112T2	R113	T113	T114	T115	T116	T117	T118	T119	T304	T305	T306	T307
Felis concolor (mountain lion)													
Lynx rufus (bobcat)													
Order Artiodactyla	4	5	3			5	1	14			13	24	3
Family Cervidae													
Cervus canadensis (wapiti/elk)													
Odocoileus spp. (deer)	206	64	19					73	4		135	181	32
Odocoileus hemionus (mule deer)	11	5					1	27	2		7	5	18
Family Antilocapridae	2	2						2			2	1	
Antilocapra americana (pronghorn)		3						18			5	17	7
Ovis canadensis (big-horned sheep)	1	1						1					
Bison bison (bison)	7	8		1				2			7	6	
AVES													
Bird	17	2						21	1	9	21	92	22
Buteo jamaicensis (red-tailed hawk)								1			1	1	
Falco sparverius (sparrowhawk)													
Colinus virginianus (bobwhite)	4												
Meleagris gallopavo (turkey)	20	9	2					62	4	4	9	90	49
Family Columbidae (pigeons and doves)												2	
Geococcyx californianus (roadrunner)								1					
Family Picidae (woodpeckers)													
Melanerpes erythrocephalus (red-headed woodpecker)		1											6

Table 16. (Continued)

Species	R112T2	R113	T113	T114	T115	T116	T117	T118	T119	T304	T305	T306	T307
Family Tyrannidae (flycatchers)	1												
Family Corvidae (jays, magpies, crows)													
Aphelocoma coerulescens (scrub jay)	7											1	
Corvus brachyrynchos (common crow)	1							1					
REPTILES													
Pseudomys scripta (pond slider)													1
Terrapene ornata (ornate box turtle)	6										1		
Family Colubridae (nonvenomous snakes)	2												
FISH													
Family Percidae (perch, pike, darters)												1	
NONVERTEBRATES													
Shell		1						1					
Total	1316	864	102	7	10	41	14	1230	49	23	1376	2329	1083

a better success rate. Many of the small and medium mammals that dominate other Pueblo IV faunal samples are present in this sample in the same percentages (relative to each other) as they are at other sites, but the large mammal species have been added to the subsistence strategy.

The faunal materials recovered during the first extensive excavations at Pecos Pueblo are not available for consideration, but some indications about those remains can be made by looking at the published bone tool data (Kidder 1932). The bone artifacts from Pecos suggest that the occupants of Pecos may have had access to large mammals similar in types and amounts to those found at Rowe. The number of bison bone tools from Pecos compared with the 31 bone fragments assigned to that species at Rowe suggests that use of this species was greater at Pecos than at Rowe. Pecos also had a considerable number of artifacts made from elk and mule deer bones, indicating significant use of these species as well. Kidder states that one-half to three-quarters of the bone at Pecos was mule deer and that bison was present in all levels, but remains of this species were more numerous in the upper deposits (Kidder 1932:196). He also mentioned that bison bone was present at Forked Lightning. The bison elements found at Pecos indicate that the species was taken by hunting parties venturing onto the Plains, and that the animals were dressed out elsewhere or brought back in segments.

The few bison bones recovered from Rowe indicate that the use of this species at Rowe was not as great as it was at Pecos. Since Rowe is positioned in a corridor providing access to the Plains and thus to bison, perhaps the small amounts of bison at this site relative to Pecos indicates that the occupants of Rowe may have been procurers or middlemen for the bison meat used by the population at Pecos. Spielmann (1982, 1991) suggested that from the middle to late 1400s a state of mutualism existed between the Plains bison hunters and the Puebloan farmers and that the Plains hunters procured bison for the Pueblos in exchange for agricultural products. Since Rowe was occupied before this postulated development, and with the Plains bison existing in fairly close proximity to Rowe and Pecos, Kidder's inference about Pueblo hunters taking the bison themselves seems likely.

Rowe Pueblo, Pecos, and Forked Lightning all contained numerous large mammal remains, and there was apparently an emphasis on this size range of mammals in the subsistence regimes at these sites. In contrast to the faunal evidence from Pecos and Rowe, the faunal sample from Arroyo Hondo pueblo was dominated by the use of jackrabbits, cottontails, and squirrels. Mule deer remains represent only 9% of the identifiable sample (Lang and Harris 1984:46). Though the recovery of turkey remains is approximately the same at all of these pueblos, the difference in large mammal use between Arroyo Hondo and the others is striking. Numerous other Pueblo IV ruins exhibit samples similar to those recovered from Arroyo Hondo and unlike those of Pecos and Rowe. This makes the interpretation of the samples from the Upper Pecos Valley even more intriguing. No matter how the inhabitants of Pecos and Rowe were obtaining large mammals, they do not seem to have been trading them further west.

Conclusions

The faunal materials recovered during the 1984 excavations at Rowe Pueblo provide an interesting contrast to the samples obtained from other Pueblo IV sites. Large mammal remains, especially mule deer, provided the major portion of their animal protein, and yet rabbit, turkey, and several small mammalian species remained a significant part of the diet. If the large number of large mammal bones were removed from the sample, it would appear similar to those from many other Pueblo IV settlements (e.g., Arroyo Hondo). This large mammal addition to the subsistence strategy necessarily had some effect on the overall mix of hunting, gathering, and agriculture, but the extent of this effect remains unknown.

The occupants of Pecos and Forked Lightning as well as Rowe used large numbers of deer and other large mammals, including bison. Procurement of bison by the Puebloan populations has been the source of some speculation, and an exchange system with the Plains populations has been considered (Spielmann 1987). Kidder argued that Pueblo hunting parties were traveling to the Plains to hunt bison, and the evidence of the bison elements from Pecos seems convincing. The few bison elements identified in the Rowe faunal sample would tend to support Kidder's conclusions but do not negate Spielmann's theory of "mutualism." If bison meat was being exchanged between Plains groups and the Pueblos, this trade may initially have extended only to those pueblos nearest the plains.

The rather large number of unidentifiable bone fragments suggests that even though no protein stress existed, all animals were utilized as completely as possible. This intensity of use adds another dimension to the mix of subsistence strategies at Rowe. The faunal remains indicate that animal protein contributed significantly to the diet of the population at Rowe. Rowe's placement on the landscape and access to a variety of animal species made this option possible for the inhabitants of the pueblo.

PRELIMINARY CERAMIC REPORT,
1980 FIELD SCHOOL

Carol Raish

During the summer of 1980 the Archaeo-logical Field School of the University of New Mexico conducted test excavations at Rowe Pueblo. As a part of these excavations, a ceramic analysis was also conducted in the field. The primary goal of this preliminary ceramic study was to obtain chronological information concerning the time range of occupation for the entire site and for each of the three plaza areas. This information would be used in conjunction with other dating techniques. The other major goal of the study was to determine the temper profile of pottery types present at the site in order to determine location of manufacture of presumed "trade" wares. Special interest was focused on determining locality of manufacture for Rowe, Santa Fe, and Galisteo types since nonlocal manufacture of all or parts of these types would indicate contact between Rowe and these other relatively close areas. Ancillary goals of the study were to examine contacts between the people of Rowe Pueblo and those from the Jemez area as well as Plains groups such as the Apache.

The ceramic analysis was conducted during labora-tory sessions held in the evenings during the field sea-son. Both field school students and staff participated in recording information on the pottery found during ex-cavation. Information was recorded on all sherds above thumbnail size and entered into a microcomputer in the field. Counts alone were made of all sherds below thumb-nail size. All computer programs used to produce the counts used in this study were designed and executed by Walter Wait, National Park Service, Santa Fe.

The type definitions used in this study are those of Mera (1933, 1935) and Kidder and Shepard (1936). We recorded surface finish, paint type, and temper infor-mation on sherds that could not be typed to identify possible presence of pottery like Ocate Micaceous that has been associated with later Apache sites (Gunnerson 1969; Gunnerson and Gunnerson 1970). Classification of unknown sherds as "unidentifiable" might preclude identification of these possible Plains ceramics. Other information, such as design element, presence or absence of fire smudging, and presence or absence of food re-mains, was recorded for future, more in-depth analyses.

Chronology

Of the 11,408 sherds recovered from the site 10,225 are of sufficient size and provided useful information for this study. A substantial number of sherds had to be excluded because of improperly coded data. This is an important point to bear in mind for future studies in which students are doing the coding. Constant checks must be made to minimize coding errors. The total pot-tery count for the analytic units is 7,533 sherds or 73.7% of the working total (10,225) and 66% of the total re-covered from the site (11,408). Table 17 lists the count and percentage information for each type by analytic unit.

Table 18 consists of type counts and percentages for the three plaza areas and their environs. Separate ex-aminations of room 30 (south plaza) and T303 are also included. T303 is a 2 by 2 m test located south of the south plaza roomblock. It is particularly informative since a subsurface room was uncovered in part of the test unit. Midden deposits cover this room; there are also midden deposits overlying sterile soil underneath the room. The "room" portion of the test contains a flag-stone floor with a possible hard-packed clay floor un-derneath. The stone floor effectively separates the room area into an upper and a lower component. Particularly interesting were the possible differences in ceramic types between the upper and lower components of the room

Table 17. Ceramic Counts and Percentages for Analytic Units

Analytic Unit / Ceramic Type	N	%
Unit 1, Room 10		
Galisteo B/w	2	25.0
Indented Corrugated	4	50.0
Plainware	2	25.0
	8	100.0
Unit 3, Room 11 rubble fill		
Santa Fe B/w	4	2.1
Rowe B/w	27	14.4
Wiyo B/w	6	3.2
Galisteo B/w	10	5.3
Indented Corrugated	24	12.8
Smeared Indented		
Corrugated	17	9..0
Clapboard Corrugated	3	1.6
Plainware	94	50.0
Glaze Red	1	0.5
Unidentified Type	1	0.5
Small Fragment	1	0.5
	188	99.9
Unit 5, Room 11 floor and hearth		
Plainware	1	100.0
Unit 6, trenches outside north plaza wall (T101, T102)		
Santa Fe B/w	3	2.4
Rowe B/w	6	4.8
Wiyo B/w	1	0.8
Galisteo B/w	2	1.6
St. Johns B/r	2	1.6
Heshotauthla	2	1.6
Agua Fria G/r	1	0.8
San Clemente G/p	1	0.8
Indented Corrugated	5	4.0
Smeared Indented		
Corrugated	4	3.2
Clapboard Corrugated	1	0.8
Plainware	90	72.6
Glaze Red	4	3.2
Unidentified Type	2	1.6
	124	99.8
Unit 7, midden outside north plaza wall, upper level (T103)		
Santa Fe B/w	33	6.2
Rowe B/w	56	10.6
Wiyo B/w	26	4.9
Galisteo B/w	17	3.2

Table 17. (Continued)

Analytic Unit/ Ceramic Type	N	%
St. Johns B/r	1	0.2
St. Johns Poly.	1	0.2
Heshotauthla	1	0.2
Agua Fria G/r	5	0.9
San Clemente G/p	2	0.4
Los Padillas G/p	3	0.6
Indented Corrugated	80	15.1
Smeared Indented		
Corrugated	21	4.0
Clapboard Corrugated	14	2.6
Plainware	254	47.9
Incised/Tooled/Scored	2	0.4
Glaze Red	8	1.5
Unidentified Type	6	1.1
	530	100.0
Unit 8, midden outside north plaza wall, middle level (T103)		
Santa Fe B/w	14	3.5
Rowe B/w	100	25.2
Wiyo B/w	10	2.5
Galisteo B/w	11	2.8
St. Johns B/r	2	0.5
Heshotauthla	1	0.2
Agua Fria G/r	3	0.7
Indented Corrugated	96	24.2
Smeared Indented		
Corrugated	12	3.0
Clapboard Corrugated	10	2.5
Plainware	133	33.6
Unidentified Type	4	1.0
	396	99.7
Unit 9, midden outside north plaza wall, lower level (T103)		
Santa Fe B/w	8	6.8
Rowe B/w	14	11.9
Wiyo B/w	10	8.5
Galisteo B/w	6	5.1
Agua Fria G/r	1	0.8
Indented Corrugated	26	22.1
Smeared Indented		
Corrugated	6	5.1
Clapboard Corrugated	1	0.8
Plainware	44	37.3
Small Fragment	2	1.7
	118	100.1

Table 17. (Continued)

Analytic Unit/ Ceramic Type	N	%
Unit 10, outside north plaza wall (T105)		
Santa Fe B/w	3	50.0
Rowe B/w	1	16.7
Plainware	2	33.3
	6	100.0
Unit 11, disturbed midden (T212)		
Santa Fe B/w	29	3.1
Rowe B/w	132	14.2
Wiyo B/w	34	3.7
Galisteo B/w	71	7.7
Abiquiu B/w	1	0.1
Chupadero B/w	2	0.2
St. Johns B/r	2	0.2
St. Johns Poly.	1	0.1
Heshotauthla	6	0.6
Agua Fria G/r	36	3.9
San Clemente G/p	3	0.3
Los Padillas G/p	1	0.1
Indented Corrugated	164	17.7
Smeared Indented		
Corrugated	42	4.5
Clapboard Corrugated	15	1.6
Plainware	348	37.6
Other Glaze	3	0.3
Glaze Red	20	2.2
Unidentified Type	15	1.6
Miscode	1	0.1
	926	99.8
Unit 12, Room 20 upper floor and lower room fill		
Santa Fe B/w	4	1.2
Rowe B/w	43	13.3
Wiyo B/w	12	3.7
Galisteo B/w	18	5.6
Heshotauthla	2	0.6
Agua Fria G/r	12	3.7
Indented Corrugated	59	18.3
Smeared Indented		
Corrugated	3	0.9
Clapboard Corrugated	11	3.4
Plainware	141	43.6
Glaze Red	12	3.7
Glaze Yellow	2	0.6
Unidentified Type	4	1.2
	323	99.8

Analytic Unit/ Ceramic Type	N	%
Unit 13, Room 20 ground floor		
Indented Corrugated	2	100.0
Unit 14, Room 20 subfloor		
Clapboard Corrugated	1	16.7
Plainware	5	83.3
	6	100.0
Unit 15, Room 21 rubble fill and roof fall		
Santa Fe B/w	30	5.1
Rowe B/w	50	8.5
Wiyo B/w	16	2.7
Galisteo B/w	2	0.3
Abiquiu B/w	2	0.3
Heshotauthla	14	2.4
Agua Fria G/r	5	0.8
San Clemente G/p	7	1.2
Indented Corrugated	59	10.0
Smeared Indented		
Corrugated	20	3.4
Clapboard Corrugated	10	1.7
Plainware	331	56.0
Other Glaze	5	0.8
Other White Mtn. Red	1	0.2
Glaze Red	23	3.9
Glaze Yellow	2	0.3
Unidentified Type	7	1.2
Small Fragment	4	0.7
Los Lunas Smudged	3	0.5
	591	100.0
Unit 16, Room 22 rubble fill and roof fall		
Santa Fe B/w	32	6.0
Rowe B/w	60	11.3
Wiyo B/w	19	3.6
Galisteo B/w	26	4.9
Abiquiu B/2	1	0.2
St. Johns B/r	3	0.6
Heshotauthla	25	4.7
Agua Fria G/r	12	2.2
San Clemente G/p	11	2.1
Cieneguilla G/y	2	0.4
Indented Corrugated	85	16.0
Smeared Indented		
Corrugated	11	2.1
Clapboard Corrugated	2	0.4

Table 17. (Continued)

Table 17. (Continued)

Analytic Unit/ Ceramic Type	N	%
Plainware	210	39.5
Glaze Red	18	3.4
Unidentified Type	11	2.1
Small Fragment	4	0.7
	532	100.2
Unit 18, Room 23 (below room 21)		
Santa Fe B/w	4	1.8
Rowe B/w	45	20.7
Wiyo B/w	4	1.8
Galisteo B/w	12	5.5
Agua Fria G/r	1	0.5
San Clemente G/p	1	0.5
Indented Corrugated	33	15.2
Smeared Indented		
Corrugated	7	3.2
Clapboard Corrugated	5	2.3
Plainware	102	47.0
Glaze Red	1	0.5
Unidentified Type	2	0.9
	217	99.9
Unit 19, Room 24 (below room 22)		
Santa Fe B/w	6	1.8
Rowe B/w	45	13.9
Wiyo B/w	15	4.6
Galisteo B/w	19	5.9
Abiquiu B/w	1	0.3
Heshotauthla	1	0.3
Agua Fria G/r	4	1.2
Indented Corrugated	111	34.2
Smeared Indented		
Corrugated	27	8.3
Clapboard Corrugated	2	0.6
Plainware	90	27.8
Glaze Red	1	0.3
Unidentified Type	2	0.6
	324	99.8
Unit 20, midden outside south plaza wall (T303)		
Santa Fe B/w	147	7.6
Rowe B/w	260	13.4
Wiyo B/w	109	5.6
Galisteo B/w	95	4.9
Abiquiu B/w	8	0.4
Chupadero B/w	2	0.1

Analytic Unit/ Ceramic Type	N	%
St. Johns B/r	1	0.05
Heshotauthla	3	0.1
Los Padillas G/p	1	0.05
Indented Corrugated	307	15.8
Smeared Indented		
Corrugated	153	7.9
Clapboard Corrugated	52	2.7
Plainware	771	39.7
Incised/Tooled/Scored	1	0.05
Other Glaze	2	0.1
Glaze Red	6	0.3
Unidentified Type	10	0.5
Small Fragment	10	0.5
Tsankawi B/c	1	0.05
Los Lunas Smudged	2	0.1
Polished Black	1	0.05
	1942	99.9
Unit 21, upper floor in T303 room		
Santa Fe B/w	1	0.7
Rowe B/w	2	1.4
Wiyo B/w	3	2.0
Galisteo B/w	3	2.0
Indented Corrugated	68	46.6
Smeared Indented		
Corrugated	2	1.4
Plainware	67	45.9
	146	100.0
Unit 22, lower floor in T303 room		
Rowe B/w	6	33.3
Galisteo B/w	5	27.8
Indented Corrugated	6	3.3
Plainware	1	5.5
	18	99.9
Unit 23, subfloor, T303		
Santa Fe B/w	13	4.6
Rowe B/w	46	16.4
Wiyo B/w	29	10.3
Galisteo B/w	14	5.0
Abiquiu B/w	2	0.7
Indented Corrugated	101	35.9
Smeared Indented		
Corrugated	6	2.1
Clapboard Corrugated	3	1.1

Table 17. (Continued)

Analytic Unit/ Ceramic Type	N	%
Plainware	65	23.1
Unidentified Type	2	0.7
	281	99.9
Unit 25, subfloor, T303		
Santa Fe B/w	2	2.2
Rowe B/w	5	5.5
Wiyo B/w	5	5.5
Galisteo B/w	2	2.2
Indented Corrugated	44	48.9
Smeared Indented		
Corrugated	3	3.3
Plainware	27	30.0
Unidentified Type	2	2.2
	90	99.8
Unit 26, T303, lowest level to sterile		
Santa Fe B/w	6	5.0
Rowe B/w	22	18.2
Wiyo B/w	12	9.9
Galisteo B/w	10	8.3
Indented Corrugated	22	18.2
Smeared Indented		
Corrugated	12	9.9
Clapboard Corrugated	5	4.1
Plainware	29	24.0
Unidentified Type	3	2.5
	121	100.1
Unit 27, Room 30, rubble fill		
Santa Fe B/w	5	3.2
Rowe B/w	14	9.0
Wiyo B/w	8	5.1
Galisteo B/w	11	7.0
Abiquiu B/w	1	0.6
St. Johns Poly.	1	0.6
San Clemente G/p	1	0.6
Indented Corrugated	33	21.1
Smeared Indented		
Corrugated	13	8.3
Clapboard Corrugated	2	1.3
Plainware	63	40.4
Glaze Red	2	1.3
Unidentified Type	2	1.3
	156	99.8

Table 17. (Continued)

Analytic Unit/ Ceramic Type	N	%
Unit 28, Room 30, roof fall (second story) and roof fall and fill (ground floor)		
Santa Fe B/w	21	4.5
Rowe B/w	73	15.7
Wiyo B/w	32	6.9
Galisteo B/w	40	8.6
St. Johns B/r	1	0.2
St. Johns Poly.	1	0.2
Heshotauthla	1	0.2
Indented Corrugated	81	17.4
Smeared Indented		
Corrugated	25	5.4
Clapboard Corrugated	2	0.4
Plainware	177	38.1
Glaze Red	4	0.9
Unidentified Type	7	1.5
	465	100.0
Unit 30, Room 30 subfloor		
Santa Fe B/w	2	9.1
Indented Corrugated	8	36.4
Clapboard Corrugated	1	4.5
Plainware	11	50.0
	22	100.0

Table 18. Ceramic Types by Area (Rim and Body Sherds)

Analytic Unit/ Ceramic Type	N	%
North Plaza—rooms, tests, and associated midden areas (Units 1, 3, 5, 6, 7, 8, 9, 10, 11)		
Santa Fe B/w	94	4.1
Rowe B/w	336	14.6
Wiyo B/w	87	3.8
Galisteo B/w	119	5.2
Abiquiu B/w	1	0.04
Chupadero B/w	2	0.09
St. Johns B/w	7	0.3
St. Johns Poly.	2	0.09
Heshotauthla	10	0.4
Agua Fria G/r	46	2.0
San Clemente G/p	6	0.3
Los Padillas G/p	4	0.2
Cieneguilla G/y	-	-
Indented Corrugated	399	17.4
Smeared Indented Corrugated	102	4.4
Clapboard Corrugated	44	1.9
Plainware	968	42.1
Incised/Tooled/Scored	2	0.09
Other Glaze	3	0.1
Other White Mtn. Red	-	-
Glaze Red	33	1.4
Glaze Yellow	-	-
Unidentified Type	28	1.2
Small Fragment	3	0.1
Tsankawi B/c	-	-
Los Lunas Smudged	-	-
Polished Black	-	-
Tewa Polychrome	-	-
Miscode	<u>1</u>	<u>0.04</u>
	2297	99.8
Center Plaza—rooms and tests (Units 12, 13, 14, 15, 16, 18, 19)		
Santa Fe B/w	76	3.8
Rowe B/w	243	12.2
Wiyo B/w	66	3.3
Galisteo B/w	77	3.8
Abiquiu B/w	4	0.2
Chupadero B/w	-	-
St. Johns B/w	3	0.1
St. Johns Poly.	-	-
Heshotauthla	42	2.1
Agua Fria G/r	34	1.7
San Clemente G/p	19	0.9

Table 18. (Continued)

Analytic Unit/ Ceramic Type	N	%
Los Padillas G/p	-	-
Cieneguilla G/y	2	0.1
Indented Corrugated	349	17.5
Smeared Indented Corrugated	68	3.4
Clapboard Corrugated	31	1.5
Plainware	879	44.1
Incised/Tooled/Scored	-	-
Other Glaze	5	0.2
Other White Mtn. Red	1	0.05
Glaze Red	55	2.7
Glaze Yellow	4	0.2
Unidentified Type	26	1.3
Small Fragment	8	0.4
Tsankawi B/c	-	-
Los Lunas Smudged	3	0.1
Polished Black	-	-
Tewa Polychrome	-	-
Miscode	-	-
	1995	99.6
South Plaza—room, tests, associated midden and extramural "room" (Units 20, 21, 22, 23, 25, 26, 27, 28, 30)		
Santa Fe B/w	197	6.1
Rowe B/w	428	13.2
Wiyo B/w	198	6.1
Galisteo B/w	180	5.5
Abiquiu B/w	11	0.3
Chupadero B/w	2	0.06
St. Johns B/w	2	0.06
St. Johns Poly.	2	0.06
Heshotauthla	4	0.1
Agua Fria G/r	-	-
San Clemente G/p	1	0.03
Los Padillas G/p	1	0.03
Cieneguilla G/y	-	-
Indented Corrugated	670	20.7
Smeared Indented Corugated	214	6.6
Clapboard Corrugated	65	2.0
Plainware	1211	37.4
Incised/Tooled/Scored	1	0.03
Other Glaze	2	0.06
Other White Mtn. Red	-	-
Glaze Red	12	0.4
Glaze Yellow	-	-

Table 18. (Continued)

Analytic Unit/ Ceramic Type	N	%
Unidentified Type	26	0.8
Small Fragment	10	0.3
Tsankawi B/c	1	0.03
Los Lunas Smudged	2	0.06
Polished Black	1	0.03
Tewa Polychrome	-	-
Miscode	-	-
	3241	99.9
South Plaza, Room 30 (Units 27, 28, 30)		
Santa Fe B/w	28	4.3
Rowe B/w	87	13.5
Wiyo B/w	40	6.2
Galisteo B/w	51	7.9
Abiquiu B/w	1	0.1
Chupadero B/w	-	-
St. Johns B/w	1	0.1
St. Johns Poly.	2	0.3
Heshotauthla	1	0.1
Agua Fria G/r	-	-
San Clemente G/p	1	0.1
Los Padillas G/p	-	-
Cieneguilla G/y	-	-
Indented Corrugated	122	19.0
Smeared Indented Corrugated	38	5.9
Clapboard Corrugated	5	0.7
Plainware	251	39.0
Incised/Tooled/Scored	-	-
Other Glaze	-	-
Other White Mtn. Red	-	-
Glaze Red	6	0.9
Glaze Yellow	-	-
Unidentified Type	9	1.4
Small Fragment	-	-
Tsankawi B/c	-	-
Los Lunas Smudged	-	-
Polished Black	-	-
Tewa Polychrome	-	-
Miscode	-	-
	643	99.5

T303 (outside South Plaza), midden down to stone floor of extramural "room" (Units 20, 21)

	N	%
Santa Fe B/w	148	7.1
Rowe B/w	262	12.5
Wiyo B/w	112	5.4

Table 18. (Continued)

Analytic Unit/ Ceramic Type	N	%
Galisteo B/w	98	4.7
Abiquiu B/w	8	0.4
Chupadero B/w	2	0.1
St. Johns B/w	1	0.05
St. Johns Poly.	-	-
Heshotauthla	3	0.1
Agua Fria G/r	-	-
San Clemente G/p	-	-
Los Padillas G/p	1	0.05
Cieneguilla G/y	-	-
Indented Corrugated	375	17.9
Smeared Indented Corrugated	155	7.4
Clapboard Corrugated	52	2.5
Plainware	838	40.1
Incised/Tooled/Scored	1	0.05
Other Glaze	2	0.1
Other White Mtn. Red	-	-
Glaze Red	6	0.3
Glaze Yellow	-	-
Unidentified Type	10	0.5
Small Fragment	10	0.5
Tsankawi B/c	1	0.05
Los Lunas Smudged	2	0.1
Polished Black	1	0.05
Tewa Polychrome	-	-
Miscode	-	-
	2088	99.9

area. Consequently, room areas were kept separate from the area outside the room wall during excavation of T303.

As stated previously, the primary goals of the present ceramic study are to examine site chronology in conjunction with other dating techniques and to examine contact between the Rowe site and other areas. Dendrochronological samples (mainly from the middle plaza) indicate a construction date for the masonry structures of AD 1330–1350. An archaeomagnetic sample from a burned area in the north plaza dated to 1395 ± 17 (for a full discussion of these dates, see the section on dating by Cordell). There are no independent dates for the south plaza.

In her regional overview, Cordell (1979) lists the types of ceramics present at Pueblo sites in the Middle Rio Grande Valley. Comparison of the types present at Rowe with those at other sites in the vicinity aids in establishing the amount of contact between groups and the period of occupation for Rowe. The areas that seem most similar to Rowe, and thus most applicable for this study, are the Galisteo Basin and Cochiti–White Rock Canyon areas of the Santa Fe District, the Pajarito Plateau District, and the Chama District. The common denominator at sites in these areas is the presence of Santa Fe Black-on-white pottery. Best dates for Santa Fe Black-on-white are AD 1200–1350 (Cordell 1979; cf. Breternitz 1966). Later sites in this Pueblo III–early Pueblo IV time range and later components of continuously occupied sites contain small amounts of Rio Grande glaze wares, which are generally estimated to have appeared shortly after 1300 and perhaps earlier (Cordell 1979).

Sites from the Santa Fe, Chama, and Pajarito districts also contain smaller percentages of Galisteo and Wiyo Black-on-white, with Galisteo considered to originate from the Galisteo Basin and Wiyo from the west, especially the Pajarito Plateau. The Rowe site also contains Santa Fe, Galisteo, and Wiyo Black-on-white ceramics and also falls within the dated time range for Santa Fe Black-on-white and the first appearance of the early Rio Grande glaze wares. The four most common painted wares at the site are Rowe, Santa Fe, Wiyo, and Galisteo Black-on-white. Small percentages of glaze painted, red, and polychrome wares also occur at Rowe. The most abundant painted ware at Rowe, however, is Rowe Black-on-white, which is a locally produced type.

On the basis of temper comparison, it is possible that some of the Galisteo sherds and some of the Santa Fe sherds were also locally produced as they show similar temper profiles to the Rowe sherds. (See the discussion by Cordell in the section on pottery.) Other Galisteo and Santa Fe sherds show different temper profiles and probably were not locally produced, which indicates contact between the people of Rowe and people from areas producing Santa Fe and Galisteo pottery. The Wiyo sherds show different temper profiles from the Rowe sherds and, thus, were probably not produced locally. This shows contact between Rowe and western groups producing Wiyo pottery. A more definite statement concerning these contacts cannot be made at this time.

To return to the question of intrasite chronology, which is concerned with determining whether the three plaza areas at Rowe were occupied contemporaneously, each of the plaza areas is examined in terms of the occurrence of Rowe, Santa Fe, Wiyo, and Galisteo Black-on-white as well as Rio Grande glaze wares. Discrete sections within plaza areas and the T303 test area are also examined. Areas showing the same patterns of occurrence of ceramic types are considered roughly contemporary. It is also assumed that areas lacking Rio Grande glaze wares may be earlier than areas that have these wares. When the large groupings of the three plaza areas are examined (Table 18), it is apparent that Rowe is the most predominant of the types under consideration in all plaza areas and that the percentage of occurrence remains fairly constant. The other three black-on-white types—Santa Fe, Wiyo, and Galisteo—occur in similar percentages in both the north and middle plazas. The south plaza area shows slightly higher percentages of Santa Fe and Wiyo than do the other two areas, although these percentages are all small and are separated by only a few percentage points.

The occurrence of glaze wares, especially Agua Fria and Glaze Red (in this analysis, all body sherds), shows some interesting differences for the three areas. When these two ceramic categories are combined, the north plaza has 3.4%, the middle plaza 4.4%, and the south plaza only 0.4%. The south plaza also lags behind the other two areas in the occurrence of other glaze and trade wares.

At this point it is helpful to examine particular room areas within the plazas to remove from consideration midden areas that might be distorting the percentages. Table 19 lists the rooms from the three plaza areas and the percentages of occurrence of the types of interest in each of the rooms. The intention of this examination is to determine if patterns of occurrence change not only from plaza to plaza but also from lower to higher levels within rooms. Unfortunately, many of the lower levels of rooms contain too few ceramics to make meaningful comparisons. Only in the middle plaza, where room 23 is under room 21 and room 24 is under room 22, is this possible. The table is difficult to interpret in the absence of tests to determine statistical significance. Several points can be made, however. Rooms 23 and 24, room 30, and room 11 have the lowest percentages of Agua Fria and Glaze Red wares. It would be tempting to say that the lower rooms of the middle plaza, room 30, and room 11 are earlier than the other areas. This would be unwarranted, however. Room 11 is in the north plaza, which has the latest archaeomagnetic date at the site. Also, the four rooms do not share a distinctive pattern of occurrence with respect to the other types.

Another problem area concerns rooms 20 and 30. These two rooms have similar occurrences of Rowe Black-on-white and different percentages for all the other types. The highest percentage of Agua Fria/Glaze Red occurs in room 20, while the second to lowest occurs in room 30. Room 30 also has higher percentages of Wiyo and Galisteo than the other rooms. This kind of difference would be expected if the rooms were built and occupied at different time periods. However, construction evidence indicates that at least the upper stories of the two rooms were built together.

This discussion reveals some of the difficulties of studying ceramics from room contexts. It is often difficult to tell where sherds in room fill are actually coming from. Often there are very few ceramics in behaviorally important levels. Small percentages, small differences in percentage points, and differences in sample size as well as small sample sizes in general cause considerable interpretive problems. Functional differences in rooms can lead to differential presence of types that have no chronological significance whatsoever—to name just a few difficulties.

In order to alleviate some of these problems, percentage of occurrence of the same types is also examined at an undisturbed midden area divided into three levels

(Table 16, Units 7, 8, 9). Again, no clear, potentially time-related patterning can be discerned for the four black-on-white types. The top and bottom levels of the midden are most similar to each other whereas the middle level is different from the other two. The two lower levels do contain a lower percentage of Agua Fria/Glaze Red and the lowest level contains a higher percentage of Wiyo.

The four diagnostic black-on-white types are present throughout the occupation of the three plaza areas of Rowe. Rowe Black-on-white remains the predominant type, while the three other types undergo minor variations in frequency. These variations are not related to location in either a particular plaza or midden area or an upper or lower level. Minor percentages of the Rio Grande glaze ware Agua Fria/Glaze Red also occur throughout the levels of the plaza areas and the midden area. The amounts vary from lower to upper levels, however. The fact that the black-on-white types show no consistent pattern of occurrence that can be related to upper or lower levels, combined with the fact that the glaze ware occurs throughout upper and lower levels, argue for contemporaneity of the various site areas. The somewhat lower percentages of the glaze ware in rooms 30 and 11, the two lower rooms of the center plaza, and the lower levels of the midden indicate that further research is needed in these areas, however. Independent dates for the south plaza and construction dates for the north plaza would be particularly helpful in making a firm determination of contemporeneity.

The two components of trench 303, which have been described previously, were also analyzed in terms of the percentage of occurrence of Rowe, Santa Fe, Wiyo, Galisteo and Agua Fria/Glaze Red for the same reasons and with the same assumptions as discussed above. The upper component, which includes the midden down to the stone floor (Units 20 and 21 in Tables 16 and 17), has percentages of the black-on-white types that are consistent with those from other areas of the site. There are no Agua Fria sherds, and the 0.3% Glaze Red is consistent with the room 30 percentages but not with those from other previously discussed areas of the site. This midden, which is located closest to the south plaza, repeats the low number of Agua Fria/Glaze Red pottery that is found within the excavated room of the south plaza and serves as a further indicator that more research into the period of occupation of the south plaza is needed.

Table 19. Percentage of Selected Ceramic Types in Excavated Rooms, Rowe Pueblo (LA 108)

| Room (Plaza) | Black-on-white | | | | Agua Fria / Glaze Red |
	Santa Fe	Rowe	Wiyo	Galisteo	
North Plaza					
Room 11 (Unit 3)	2.1	14.4	3.2	5.3	0.5
Middle Plaza					
Room 20 (Unit 12)	1.2	13.3	3.7	5.6	7.4
Room 21 (Unit 15)	5.1	8.5	2.7	0.3	4.7
Room 23, below room 21 (Unit 18)	1.8	20.7	1.8	5.5	1.0
Room 22 (Unit 16)	6.0	11.3	3.6	4.9	5.6
Room 24, below room 22 (Unit 19)	1.8	13.9	4.6	5.9	1.5
South Plaza					
Room 30 (Unit 28)	4.5	15.7	6.9	8.6	0.9

Note: Room 10 (North Plaza) is not included because it contained only eight sherds.

The lower midden level of T303 (Units 22 and 23, Table 16) does indeed seem to represent an earlier component of the site on the basis of its location and the kinds of ceramics present in the component. Of the 299 sherds in these units, 115 are black-on-white, and there are no glaze and no red or polychrome types. Of the black-on-white types, Rowe and Wiyo occur in slightly greater percentages than in most other areas of the site.

Intergroup Contact

The interest in Wiyo Black-on-white stems from the secondary research goal of the study, which is to explore possible connections between Rowe and Jemez. Walter Wait (personal communication, 1980) suggests that groups from the Jemez area might have founded Rowe. In this case, relatively greater percentages of Wiyo Black-on-white might be found in lower levels of the site and Wiyo might also be expected to be the predominant trade ware at the site. As outlined in the discussion of plaza areas and T303, several of the lower levels do show slightly higher percentages of Wiyo whereas others do not. On the other hand, Wiyo is not the predominant trade ware at the site. Santa Fe is second in importance to Rowe while Galisteo and Wiyo are third in importance with virtually equal percentages. Thus, the ques-

tion of Jemez influence at Rowe Pueblo or the founding of Rowe by peoples from Jemez remains unresolved. The higher incidence of Wiyo in some of the lower levels suggests that this question should be pursued in future work. A comparison of Rowe and Jemez Black-on-white would be helpful in this respect.

As discussed earlier, a special category was set up in an attempt to identify Ocate Micaceous, a type that is associated with the Apache. This identification is especially difficult as some sherds of the clearly identifiable utility wares of local origin are also mica-tempered. The temper profiles of the unidentified micaceous sherds are similar to the temper profiles of some of the known Pueblo utility wares (e.g., Indented Corrugated), indicating local or at least Pueblo manufacture of both. No sherds of definite Plains origin or Ocate Micaceous sherds were found during the 1980 excavations.

Summary

This report deals mainly with the chronology of the Rowe site itself and the contacts that people from Rowe may have had with other areas. The following conclusions are drawn from this study:

1. Contemporeneity of occupation of the three plaza areas at Rowe is not firmly determined. The

overall pattern of occurrence of ceramic types in the three areas indicates contemporeneity. However, specific examination of lower percentages of occurrence of Rio Grande glaze types in certain areas indicates the possibility of earlier occupation, especially the south plaza and lower rooms of the center plaza.

2. There is strong evidence of an earlier occupation of the site south of the south plaza area in the form of an apparent subsurface room resting on midden which contains no glaze pottery.

3. Throughout its occupation, Rowe had contact with areas producing Santa Fe, Galisteo, and Wiyo ceramics.

4. Higher percentages of Wiyo ceramics in some of the lower levels of the site indicate that further research into early influences from the Jemez area might be profitable.

5. Determination of Rowe/Plains contact on the basis of pottery is not realistic.

Acknowledgments

Walter Wait provided computer consultation and Joyce Gerber assisted in the laboratory at UNM.

PLANT USE AND SUBSISTENCE
AT ROWE PUEBLO

Mollie S. Toll

As a continuation of earlier botanical studies at Rowe Pueblo (Toll 1981), this report provides documentation of materials in areas of the site not investigated previously and evidence of exploitation of a considerably wider array of wild plant products, in line with assemblages noted at other nearby sites. This study encompasses 20 flotation samples taken from room 112 in the north plaza area, an intact midden, an adobe or jacal structure outside the south plaza rooms, and features exposed by backhoe trenching outside the pueblo. The 15 samples previously reported came from north, middle, and south plaza room contexts. Recovery of plant remains was considerably better in this second round of excavation and analysis. Sample size was increased to two liters, and this larger sample volume may be responsible for the addition of certain low-frequency taxa *(Opuntia, Echinocereus, Helianthus, Scirpus* and *Cucurbita)*. However, a tenfold increase in average seed density per liter (Table 20) can best be attributed to factors of sample location. Primary contexts with better preservation were encountered and selected with signifi-

cantly greater regularity in the second field season. Such notable differences in flotation recovery are not unusual (Toll 1984b) and point out the need for planning and attention to sampling criteria.

The botanical data gathered in this study are examined particularly with regard to understanding the full array of subsistence activities at Rowe, and these findings are compared with results from other sites in the area. Plant use in the piñon-juniper belt focused on a characteristic array of native species whose natural ranges overlap at this elevation.

Methodology

Soil samples collected during excavation were processed in the field by University of New Mexico archaeological field school students using the simplified "bucket" version of flotation (see Bohrer and Adams 1977). Sample volume was two liters, measured at time of excavation. Each sample was immersed in a bucket of wa-

Table 20. Seed Density and Diversity: 1980 vs. 1984 Field Seasons

Field season	Average number of seeds per liter	Total number of taxa observed		Average number of taxa per sample	
		All	Burned	All	Burned
1980	4.1	11	4	2.0	0.9
1984	46.3	11	14	5.7	3.5

ter and allowed to settle for 30–40 seconds. The solution was then poured through a fine screen (about 0.35 mm), catching organic materials floating or in suspension. After the recovered material had dried, each sample was reviewed microscopically at 7–45×. Taxonomy and scientific nomenclature follow Martin and Hutchins (1981), and common names are used according to the Field Guide to Native Vegetation of the Southwest Region (USDA 1974). Actual number of seeds recovered is reported, as well as the standardized seeds-per-liter. One sample (sample 5, from backhoe test 1) contained a very large number of seeds and was subsampled. For this sample the adjusted seeds-per-liter figures reflect the estimated number of seeds for the entire sample.

In each of the 13 samples with sufficient charcoal, a sample of 20 pieces was identified. Each piece was snapped to expose a fresh transverse section and examined at 45×. Low-power, incident light identification of wood specimens does not often allow species- or even genus-level precision, but it can provide reliable information useful in distinguishing broad patterns of utilization of a major resource class.

Results

Room 112

The roof fall (levels 3B, 3C) in room 112 contains a narrow array of low-frequency economic plant materials (Table 21). Carbonized juniper twigs may relate to burned roofing material or hearth debris. Corn and the few edible weed seeds (Cheno-ams, mustard) may be debris from rooftop food-processing activities, or from a hearth. Material from a fill layer below the roof fall but above the floor (level 2F) is quite different in character. Carbonized items may belong to a single taxon *(Chenopodium);* corn is absent. A sizable concentration of wild tobacco seeds is especially notable.

In comparison with empty samples from rooms 10 and 11 (Toll 1981), room 112 proveniences reveal byproducts of a variety of plant utilization activities. The general level of cultural activity observed earlier in the north plaza, as evidenced in ceramics and lithics as well as floral remains, is not borne out in room 112. *[Editor's note: In fact, it became clear that room 112 is actually a* *back tier room of the north roomblock of the central quadrangle. It is not surprising, then, that it contrasts with rooms 10 and 11.]*

Intact Midden (T118)

Several characteristics of the midden deposits on the northeast side of the site suggested that botanical preservation would be particularly good here. Deposits appeared undisturbed below caps of overburden and clay. The matrix was described as dark brown or gray, highly organic, with lenses of ash and charcoal throughout and high densities of corncob fragments as well as bones and ceramics (Linda Cordell, personal communication).

Flotation samples 9 through 15 document natural levels from top to bottom. Carbonized corn remains are abundant in all samples. The occurrence of kernels (especially dense in level 2G) is evidence of accidental loss during processing or storage, in addition to probable reuse of cobs as fuel as signified by the occurrence of shanks, cupules, and cob fragments. Also found throughout the midden are burned juniper twigs and scale leaves (likely related to juniper fuel use, highly evident in the charcoal assemblage; Table 22) and goosefoot seeds. Other economic taxa present in Rowe midden deposits include squash, piñon nut and juniper seed, ricegrass, dropseed, prickly pear and hedgehog cactus, pigweed, purslane, sunflower, and bugseed. The uppermost layer of midden (level 2C) stands out as having a particularly diverse assemblage of cultural botanical materials. Density of seeds is high only in level 2K, owing to a concentration of unburned tobacco seeds. Cucurbit seeds are unique at the site to feature 1, a small firepit at the bottom of the midden. Fill in this same firepit includes several carbonized corncobs, some with husk still present. Carbonized cucurbit seeds and corn husk indicate a low-heat, low-oxygen fire; both are delicate materials, not often preserved in charred condition.

Charcoal is significantly more preponderant in midden matrix than in other sampled locations in the site. All eight midden samples contained sufficient charcoal for species composition identification; midden locations constitute 40% of all sorted flotation samples, but 62% of the samples with substantial charcoal components (Table 22). Charcoal composition in the midden parallels that in other site locations: nearly all charcoal is coniferous (juniper, piñon, and ponderosa pine) with small segments of nonconiferous types (oak and willow).

Adobe/Jacal Structure

Test excavations outside the walls of the south plaza revealed remains of an adobe structure underlying the main (masonry) pueblo at Rowe. In T305, samples 17 and 18 document level 4A, a compacted surface (probably a ramada floor or outside work area) associated with the adobe structure. Sample contents are quite different, with carbonized juniper twigs and corn cupules plus seeds of hedgehog cactus and three economic weedy annuals in sample 17, but only charred goosefoot seeds in sample 18. Below this hard surface was a layer of fill (level 2A) with inclusions (orange-burned daub with wood and wattle impressions) suggesting a burned ramada roof. Flotation of sample 19 yielded chiefly unburned weed and grass seeds but also charred juniper twigs and corn cupules. While the juniper twigs may relate to ramada roofing materials, the corn cupules more likely derived from redeposited hearth debris. Charcoal in this level includes willow as well as the usual predominance of coniferous types.

In T306, sample 16 documents the few cultural floral remains (charred corn cupules) associated with a refuse pit cut into adobe melt. All charcoal from this provenience is coniferous, with elements of juniper, piñon, and ponderosa present.

Feature 2 in T307 (sample 20) is from a trash pit located at 4.8 m below datum in light midden below a flagstone floor associated with the adobe structure underlying the masonry pueblo. Stratigraphically, this is the earliest provenience known at Rowe, though a chronological affiliation of no earlier than AD 1270–1300 based on ceramic types places the trash pit only a few decades before the main site occupation in the early fourteenth century. [Editor's note: The radocarbon dates obtained after this report was written modify this conclusion only slightly. Dates of between 1240 and 1250 are suggested for initial construction of the adobe structures.] Floral material from this pit includes charred corn cupules in considerable quantity, consistent with expectations of trash contexts. Also present are small numbers of charred seeds from three annual weeds (pigweed, goosefoot, and purslane) that appear regularly in both the ethnobotanical literature (Castetter 1935; Ford 1968; Jones 1931) and archaeological assemblages (Gasser 1982; Minnis 1978; Toll 1985a, 1985b; etc.) as substantial components in the wild food diet. Dropseed grass and several weeds (globemallow, mustard, and members of the borage and nightshade families) occur only as eroded but uncarbonized seeds; they may be postoccupational intrusives. Charcoal is again predominantly coniferous.

Backhoe Tests

Backhoe test 1 (sample 5) yielded carbonized corn cupules, juniper twigs, and Cheno-am seeds with large numbers of unburned dropseed grass and purslane seeds. Some of the unburned seeds are eroded, dull, darkened by oxidation, or coated with matrix, indicating they've been in the soil for at least a few months if not longer. Others are pristine and clearly intrusive, deposited as a result of rodent or insect activity or simply with exposure of the matrix during excavation. A trash pit encountered in the profile of BH 1 was explored by means of a 1 by 1 m test (T114). Sample 7 produced nothing in the way of identifiable cultural floral material.

Located over a magnetic anomaly in the area west of the pueblo, backhoe test 3 revealed a pitstructure or great kiva not visible from the surface. The structure dates to about AD 1300 (Linda Cordell, personal communication). [Editor's note: The tree-ring date of 1305vv further substantiates this inference.] Carbonized corn cupules, juniper twigs, and Cheno-am seeds are again encountered. Charcoal is entirely coniferous.

Discussion

Data added by this second season of excavation and analysis help considerably to define plant utilization patterns at Rowe Pueblo. The first series of 15 flotation samples (Toll 1981), mostly from room contexts, provided an incomplete picture of late Puebloan subsistence. The ubiquity of corn remains is a clear sign of dependence on this agricultural staple, although the absence of cucurbit and bean specimens from these initial samples does not indicate the absence of these taxa from

Table 21. Flotation Results, Rowe Pueblo

Sample No. and Location	Pinus edulis	Juniperus	Sporobolus	Other Gramineae	Cactaceae	Amaranthus	Chenopodium	Cheno-ams	Cruciferae	Descurainia	Solanaceae	Nicotiana	Portulaca	Other Possible Economics	Probable Contaminants	Zea	Cucurbita	Unknown/Unidentifiable	No. of Taxa	No. of Taxa Burned	Total Seeds Actual	Total Seeds Estimated
1: Room 112, level B								1* 0.5		1* 0.5									2	2	2	1.0
2: Room 112, level 3C		T*					1 0.5	1* 0.5								C*			4	3	2	1.0
3: Room 112, level 3C							4* 2.0		1 0.5				3 1.5			1* 0.5			4	1	6	3.0
4: Room 112, level 2F		T*				2* 1.0		18* 9.0			1 0.5	172 86.0	1 0.5	2[A] 1.0		C*			6	2	197	98.5
5: Backhoe trench 1		T*	43 166.9					8* 4.8		1 5.0			506 325.0	1[B] 0.5	4[C] 2.5	C*		1* 0.5	10	4	565	505.7
6: Backhoe trench 3		T*				2* 1.0	1* 0.5				1 0.5		1 0.5			C* 1* 0.5			6	4	6	3.0
7: Test 114, feature 1																			0	0	0	0
8: Test 118, feature 1 (firepit)		T*				3* 1.5						1 0.5				C* 2* 1.0	1* 0.5	5* 2.5	6	5	12	6.0
9: Test 118, level 2C	1* 0.5	T* 1* 0.5				4* 2.0	11* 5.5						3* 1.5	2*[D] 1.0	1[E] 0.5	C*			9	8	23	11.5
10: Test 118, level 2E		T*	1 0.5				5* 2.5									C* 4* 2.0			4	3	10	5.0
11: Test 118, level 2G							2* 1.0					1 0.5	1 0.5			C* 37* 18.5			4	2	41	20.5

12: Test 118, level 2K	T*	1* / 0.5				4* / 2.0							C*	3	3	4	2.0
13: Test 118, level 2K	T*	1* / 0.5	1* / 0.5			14 / 7.0			335 / 167.5	1 / 0.5	1[F] / 0.5		C*	8	4	353	176.5
14: Test 118, level 2I	T*	1 / 0.5		1*[G] / 0.5		4* / 2.0		1 / 0.5	1 / 0.5	1 / 0.5		1[H] / 0.5	C*; 1* / 0.5	10	5	12	6.0
15: Test 118, level 2O	T*	1 / 0.5	1*[I] / 0.5			5* / 2.5			15 / 7.5				C*; 1* / 0.5	6	4	23	11.5
16: Test 306, feature 12	T*					2 / 1.0							C*	2	1	2	1.0
17: Test 305, level 4A	T*	1 / 0.5		1*[K] / 0.5	1* / 0.5	10* / 5.0				1* / 0.5			C*	8	7	15	7.5
18: Test 305, level 4A	T*				2 / 1.0	8* / 4.0				1 / 0.5				3	1	11	5.5
19: Test 305, level 2A	T*	2 / 1.0				40 / 20.0		1 / 0.5					C*	6	3	44	22.0
20: Test 307, feature 2 (trash pit)	T*	4 / 2.0			6* / 3.0	15* / 7.5	3 / 1.5	7 / 3.5		5* / 2.5		2[L] / 1.0	C*	10	5	42	21.0

* Some or all items carbonized. First number shows actual seeds counted; second number indicates estimated number of seeds per liter of soil.
T* twigs
C* cupules, cob fragments
[A] 1 (0.5) Helianthus, 1 (0.5) Scirpus
[B] Helianthus
[C] Lappula
[D] 1* (0.5) Helianthus, 1* (0.5) Corispermum
[E] Euphorbia
[F] Scirpus
[G] Opuntia
[H] Salsola
[I] Oryzopsis
[K] Echinocereus
[L] 1 (0.5) Sphaeralcea, 1 (0.5) Boraginaceae

157

Table 22. Charcoal Composition of Flotation Samples: Frequency and Weight

| FS | Prov. | Unknown | Conifers | | | | | | Nonconifers | | | | Total |
			Junipers	*Pinus edulis*	*Pinus ponderosa*	Undetermined	Subtotal		*Quercus*	*Salix*	Undetermined	Subtotal	
5	BH 1			5	2	12	19		1			1	20
				0.4	+	0.3	0.7		+			+	0.7g
6	BH3		6	3		11	20		+			+	20
			0.2	+		0.2	0.4					—	0.4g
8	T118	5	1	2	2	5	10		1	1	2	4	19
		0.4	+	0.2	0.1	0.1	0.4		+	+	+	+	0.8g
9	T118		5		1	10	16			4		4	20
			0.1		+	0.4	0.5			0.2		0.2	0.7g
10	T118		5	2	1	10	18				1	1	19
			0.3	+	+	0.1	0.4				0.1	0.1	0.5g
11	T118		5	1	1	13	20					—	20
			0.2	+	+	0.2	0.4					—	0.4g
12	T118		5	1	1	9	16				4	4	20
			0.1	+	+	0.1	0.3				0.1	0.1	0.4g
13	T118		7	1		12	20					—	20
			0.2	+		0.2	0.4					—	0.4g
14	T118		3	1	2	12	18			1	1	2	20
			0.1	+	0.1	0.2	0.4			0.1	+	0.1	0.5g
15	T118		9	1	2	7	19		1			1	20
			0.3	+	0.1	0.3	0.7		+			+	0.7g
16	T306		2	4	2	12	20					—	20
			0.1	0.3	+	0.1	0.5					—	0.5g
19	T305		1		3	13	17			2	1	3	20
			0.1		0.1	0.2	0.4			0.1	0.1	0.2	0.6g
20	T307	1	6		2	10	18			1		1	20
		+	0.2		+	0.2	0.4			+		+	0.4g
Number of pieces		6	55	21	19	136	231		3	9	9	21	258
% of pieces		2%	21%	8%	7%	53%	89%		1%	3%	3%	7%	98%
Total wt. (g)		0.4	1.9	1.0	0.4	2.6	5.9		—	0.4	0.3	0.7	7.0g
% of total wt.		6%	27%	14%	6%	37%	84%		—	6%	4%	10%	100%

158

Table 23. Presence of Economic Taxa in North-Central and Northeastern New Mexico Sites

	No. of Samples	Juniperus	Pinus edulis	Prunus	Rhus	Opuntia	Echinocereus	Yucca	Oryzopsis	Sporobolus	Amaranthus	Chenopodium	Portulaca	Helianthus	Iva	Cleome	Nicotiana	Scirpus	Zea	Cucurbita	Phaseolus
Rowe Pueblo (Late Pueblo)																					
Toll 1981	15	T*	N	†*	-	-	-	-	-	†	†*	†*	-	-	-	-	†	-	†*	-	-
this study	20	T*, N*	N*	-	-	†*	†*	-	†*	†*	†*	†*	†*	†*	-	-	†	†	†*	†*	-
Kidder 1932	0	?	†*	?	?	?	?	†*	?	?	?	?	?	†	?	?	?	?	†*	†*	†*
Pecos pithouses (Basketmaker III)																					
Minnis 1978	?	-	N*	-	-	-	-	-	-	†*	†*	†*	†*	†*	†*	-	-	-	†*	-	-
Cimarron (Basketmaker II)																					
Kirkpatrick and Ford 1977	?	N*	N*	†*	†*	†*	†	†*	-	†*	†*	†*	†*	†*	†*	†*	-	†	†*	†*	†*
Cerrososo (Archaic to early Basket-maker), Toll 1984	21	T*	T	-	-	-	†	-	†*	-	-	†*	†	†	-	-	-	-	†*	-	-
Red Bow Shelter (Late Archaic to early Ceramic), Donaldson 1983	14	N*	N	-	-	†	†*	†	-	-	-	†*	†*	†	-	-	-	-	†*	-	-

† present
* some or all items carbonized
T twigs/scale leaves/needles
N nuts/cones
? Indicates taxa that might have been recoverable using flotation or fine-screening techniques. It is not clear whether the cache of sunflower seeds (Kidder 1932:303) is charred.

the local farming complex. Squash and beans have decidedly poor preservation records, and several writers have carefully outlined logical explanations for both the low representation of these remains in original deposits and their selective deterioration (Cutler and Whitaker 1961; Gasser and Adams 1981; Kaplan 1956).

In the second round of flotation samples, charred squash seeds recovered from a firepit at the bottom of the midden show that squash was indeed used at Rowe. After the first field season, wild plant products that could be linked with thirteenth and fourteenth century subsistence at Rowe included only wild plum, piñon, pigweed, and goosefoot. To this we can now add ricegrass, dropseed, sunflower, purslane, hedgehog and prickly pear cactus, and sedge.

The array of documented plant resources now more closely parallels that known from contemporaneous or earlier sites in the Pecos Valley or at similar elevations nearby (Table 23). Taxa common to most of these sites include juniper, piñon, and a variety of economic weeds—pigweed, goosefoot, purslane, and sunflower. The natural range of these weedy annuals is sufficiently wide that, while common in the piñon-juniper plant community, these taxa also form a significant portion of the resource base at lower elevations. Other taxa found at fewer sites include grasses (ricegrass and dropseed), perennials (wild plum, squawberry, cacti, and yucca), and among weeds, beeweed. Although the number of edible weeds found or consumed at these sites is a significant proportion of total taxa documented in the floral assemblages, weeds are still overall of far less relative importance than at either Archaic or earlier Anasazi sites at lower elevations in central and northwestern New Mexico. Fruits and nuts of woody perennials and fruits of succulent species are more abundant at higher elevations and were probably preferred because of the high caloric return in relation to collecting and processing effort.

Taxa that are unique to Rowe in this selection of sites in the piñon-juniper belt include wild tobacco (found in more locations and greater density in this second phase of analysis) and sedge. *[Editor's note: Nicotiana was also recovered from Tijeras and San Antonio pueblos, and at several sites in the Galisteo Basin, further south but in the same floral zone and approximately contemporary in time.]* It is unlikely that either taxon figured principally as a food source. *Nicotiana* leaves (with flowers sometimes included) were chiefly dried and smoked, or chewed as a quid (Hough 1897; Morris and Jones 1960; Stevenson 1915). Ethnographic accounts, plus the scattered and sparse distribution of *Scirpus* achenes in archaeological sites, support an emphasis on use of sedges for manufacture of mats and similar products (Doebley 1981; Judd 1954). Incidental presence of seeds in sites may relate to manufacturing or consumption of raw roots and tender shoots (Swank 1932). Low-frequency occurrences of sedge seeds and willow charcoal at Rowe testify to utilization of riparian taxa from the nearby river corridor.

Subsistence alternatives in the Pecos Valley are governed in large part by the elevation. Precipitation, at 12–16 annual inches (30–40 cm), is less of a critical problem than in many portions of the arid Southwest; rather, the principal limiting variable may be the shortened growing season (100–120 days; Williams and McAllister 1979). A short growing season reduces overall production and duration of availability for wild food products and imperils entire agricultural crops. At this elevation, for agriculture to serve as a reliable subsistence core, farmers must have the ability to plan based on detailed knowledge with respect to climatic and topographic variables.

To date, the small and variable cob sizes and irregular row-filling of corn recovered at Rowe provide evidence of marginal conditions for farming, as has been noted at sites with similar elevations (Donaldson 1983; Kirkpatrick and Ford 1977; Toll 1984a). Recovery of corn belonging to a distinct morphometric population (larger and more regular) would be excellent support for trade with areas outside the Pecos Valley (Wait 1979).

Acknowledgments

This report was originally published as Castetter Laboratory for Ethnobotanical Studies, Technical Series 147 (June 28, 1985). Beth Crowder performed microscopic sorting of flotation samples, and Vorsila Bohrer provided useful comments on the identity of *Prunus* specimens.

Part IV

UNM FIELD SCHOOL SURVEYS

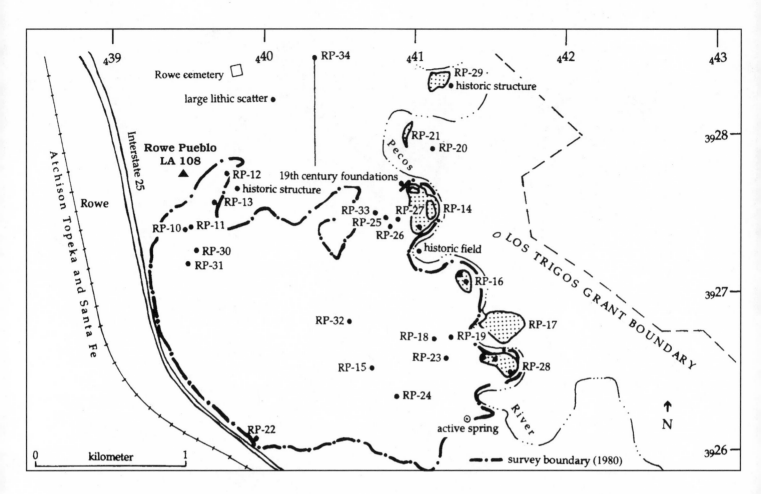

Figure 41. Map of survey area, 1980 field school

UNM FIELD SCHOOL
SITE SURVEYS

During both the 1980 and 1984 field seasons, archaeological surveys were conducted in the vicinity of Rowe Ruin. Although the organization and goals of the surveys were different, the type of information recorded was quite similar and can be used to address general research questions.

In 1980, site survey was under the direction of Kurt Anschuetz, who was then a graduate teaching assistant. The survey worked outward from Rowe Ruin with the goals of locating and identifying the kinds of sites in the immediate vicinity of the pueblo and getting an idea of the density of sites in the area. Of particular interest was identifying potential agricultural fields and sources or quarries of lithic materials that were identified during the excavations. An area of 3.20 km² (1.25 mi²) was systematically surveyed by student crews (Figure 41). Students walked parallel transects, following natural contours, at an average transect interval of 15 m. Twenty-three archaeological sites were mapped, photographed, and described in detail on site forms. Site locations were plotted on the USGS Rowe NM 7.5-minute topographic map. Systematic collections of artifacts were made. Anschuetz later added these sites to the New Mexico Archaeological Resources Management System (ARMS) files maintained by the Laboratory of Anthropology in Santa Fe. At the request of the late "Buddy" Fogelson, then owner of Forked Lightning Ranch on which all sites were located, the artifacts recovered through survey were turned over to the Superintendent of Pecos National Monument along with copies of the survey forms, notes, and maps.

The 1980 survey identified sites that dated from the late Archaic to the nineteenth century. Site dating was accomplished using projectile point types, ceramic types, glass, metal artifacts, and architecture as indicators of chronological age. Two lithic procurement areas were recorded (see descriptions of RP-21 and RP-29) as well as several sites at which stone tools were apparently refurbished and maintained. Although identifying agricultural features was an important survey objective, none were located in 1980.

In 1984, the archaeological survey was supervised by two professional archaeologists, Richard Boston and Barbara Kauffman. Like Anschuetz, they led crews of students who rotated from excavation to survey assignments. As in 1980, survey goals were to identify the different kinds of sites in the vicinity of Rowe Ruin, including agricultural features and field areas, and to obtain an idea of the density of sites in the area. The survey was also directed toward identifying residential sites that might have been occupied at the same time as Rowe Ruin and Pecos Pueblo.

In 1984, a wider area was selected for coverage by means of a two-phase sampling strategy (Figure 42). A region of 87.55 km² (27.36 mi²) was the sampling universe. The survey universe was divided into 3.2 km² (1 mi²) blocks. Transects were then randomly chosen from among four possible directions: north-south, east-west, northeast-southwest, and northwest-southeast. All transects chosen in this way were to have been 3.2 km long and approximately 50 m wide. Forty-four transects were surveyed. Of these, 40 were 3.2 km long, three were 1.92 km long, and one was 5.44 km long. The second phase of the sampling strategy was the use of "reconnaissance areas," which were completely inventoried. The reconnaissance areas were irregularly shaped locations specifically chosen from a variety of topographic settings. Eight reconnaissance areas, covering 3.42 km², were surveyed. The total area surveyed in 1984, including both randomly oriented transects and reconnaissance area transects, was 6.09 km².

As was the case during 1980, sites located in 1984 were mapped, described on site forms and in a notebook,

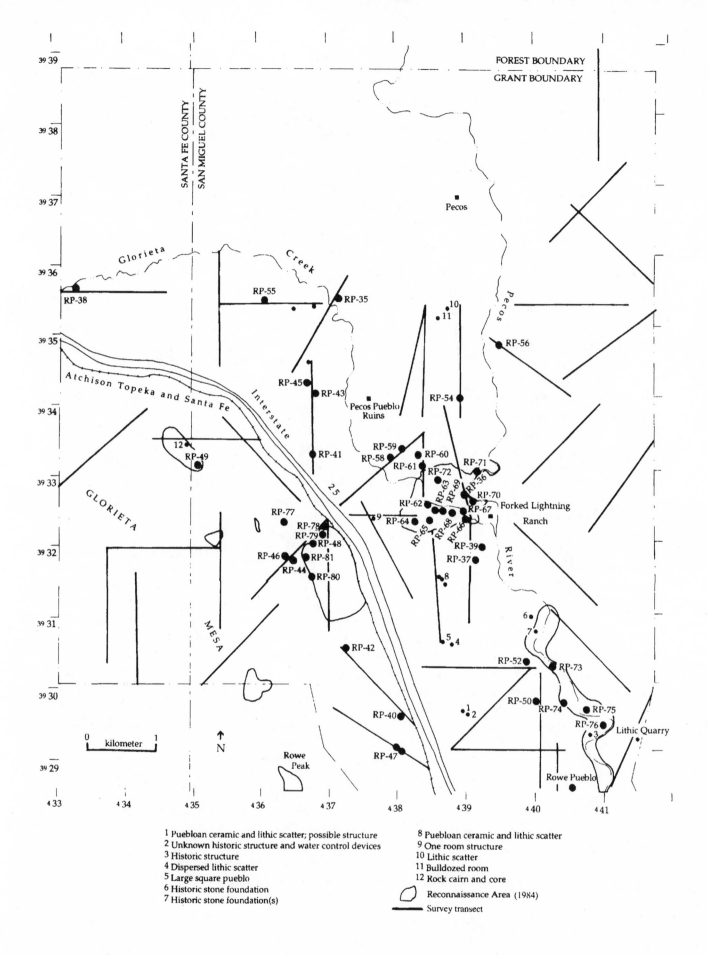

1 Puebloan ceramic and lithic scatter; possible structure
2 Unknown historic structure and water control devices
3 Historic structure
4 Dispersed lithic scatter
5 Large square pueblo
6 Historic stone foundation
7 Historic stone foundation(s)

8 Puebloan ceramic and lithic scatter
9 One room structure
10 Lithic scatter
11 Bulldozed room
12 Rock cairn and core

⬡ Reconnaissance Area (1984)

▬▬▬ Survey transect

photographed, and plotted on USGS Rowe NM and Pecos NM 7.5-minute topographic maps. Samples of artifacts were collected. In 1984, in an attempt to develop a chronology of sites independent of ceramic seriation, an extensive program of obsidian hydration analysis was carried out. When present, obsidian flakes were collected from all sites encountered. A preliminary site survey report was completed by Kathleen D. Morrison (1987) and filed with the Laboratory of Anthropology and the Superintendent of Pecos National Monument. Morrison also completed ARMS forms for the Museum of New Mexico.

In her report, Morrison (1987) compared site densities obtained by the 1980 and 1984 surveys. She found that the 48 sites located and mapped in 1984 yield a site density of 7.88 sites per square kilometer, which is comparable to the figure of 7.19 sites per square kilometer obtained from the 1980 survey. In addition, as she noted, because transect surveys tend to overestimate site density, the site densities estimated from the 1980 and 1984 surveys are even more similar.

The research design used in 1984 reflected a concern that the use of ceramic types as chronological markers might not be entirely appropriate. The concern stems from Plog and Upham's experience at Chavez Pass Ruin in the Middle Little Colorado drainage of Arizona. Upham (1982) argued that the inhabitants of Chavez Pass Pueblo and outlying, smaller communities had differential access to some red-on-black and polychrome ceramic types. In part as a result of this restricted access, Upham and Plog maintained, some black-on-white types were in use longer than is usually credited. In view of this, the 1984 survey attempted to obtain chronometric dates from the site survey that were independent of ceramic cross-dating. The method selected was to collect and submit as much obsidian as possible for hydration studies. The 64 hydration dates obtained from the sites located during the survey are listed in Table 24 by site and by chemically determined flow source.

As the table reveals, a very wide range of dates was

obtained for each site. At the time, these disappointing results were inexplicable from our perspective. Subsequent studies of the hydration process by Christopher Stevens (1992) of the Obsidian Hydration Laboratory at New Mexico State University go a long way toward clarifying the reasons for our poor results. Stevens's research indicates that the rate at which obsidian hydrates is determined by the amount of intrinsic water in the source (different for each flow) and the ambient temperature during the period over which hydration occurs. Rates for the sources of obsidian debitage recovered during our surveys had not been determined as of 1992. Further, we had not obtained or estimated soil temperatures at Rowe or the survey locations. Since the Las Cruces laboratory retained the collected samples, it should be possible to obtain relevant dates at some time in the future. Nevertheless, the obsidian hydration dates were not useful for chronological placement of the surveyed sites reported here and are therefore not included in the site descriptions that follow.

Dates were assigned to sites reported here using published dates for diagnostic ceramic types (Ahlstrom 1989; Breternitz 1966; Warren 1979, 1980), ethnohistoric information for the immediate area (Earls 1980, and David Snow, personal communication 1980), published dates for Archaic dart point types (Irwin-Williams 1973), and a chronology of projectile point types and knives developed as part of the Los Esteros Reservoir Project survey (Rogers 1987). Although not ideal, these techniques were adequate to address our research objectives, as discussed below. A further comment regarding the projectile points and knives is in order here. It is highly unusual, if not unheard of, for Anasazi sites to be ordered chronometrically on the basis of the styles of formal lithic tools. The Upper Pecos, historically, was an area of Pueblo-Plains interaction, and sites characterized as Apishapa focus and Panhandle aspect are described for the Las Vegas plateau (Rogers 1987). The dates of point types reported in the site descriptions corroborate the ceramic dates in all cases. In addition, although described in terms of Plains traditions, all the points located on our surveys are illustrated by Kidder (1932) from the excavations of Pecos and are also illustrated in reports of Pueblo sites along the Chama (Wendorf 1953) and for Paa-ko (Lambert 1954) south of Cerrillos.

In 1980, the survey area centered on the unnamed limestone mesa just east of Rowe Ruin (Figure 1). This

Figure 42. Map of survey area and transects, 1984 field school (unlabeled dots are isolated occurrences or other unrecorded cultural features)

Table 24. Obsidian Hydration Measurements for the Sites Surveyed in 1984

Site (RP-) and Artifact No.	Lab. No.	Source	Rim width (mm)	s.d.	Date
34-88	402	Obsidan Ridge	4.25	0.03	514 BC ± 303
34-126	403	Obsidian Ridge	4.46	0.02	770 BC ± 317
34-168	404	Polvadera	2.60	0.02	AD 1234 ± 151
34-370	405	Cerro del Medio	2.93	0.03	—
34-373	406	Polvadera	2.40	0.04	AD 1346 ± 140
35-415	413	Obsidian Ridge	2.60	0.04	AD 1048 ± 188
			1.69	0.04	AD 1589 ± 126
35-439	414	Obsidian Ridge	3.15	0.03	AD 611 ± 227
35-443	415	Obsidian Ridge	3.58	0.02	AD 210 ± 257
35-444	416	Obsidian Ridge	4.26	0.04	528 BC ± 304
36-14	422	Obsidian Ridge	3.06	0.03	AD 688 ± 221
36-29	423	Obsidian Ridge	1.57	0.02	AD 1643 ± 117
36-73	424	Obsidian Ridge	2.62	0.02	AD 1034 ± 190
36-78	425	Cerro del Medio	3.34	0.05	—
36-80	426	Obsidian Ridge	3.08	0.03	AD 671 ± 222
36-81	427	Obsidian Ridge	5.79	0.03	2658 BC ± 409
47-53	430	Obsidian Ridge	3.85	0.03	68 BC ± 275
47-55	431	Obsidian Ridge	3.00	0.06	AD 738 ± 216
47-57	432	Obsidian Ridge	2.27	0.04	AD 1271 ± 166
47-64	433	Obsidian Ridge	3.71	0.02	AD 79 ± 266
47-68	434	Obsidian Ridge	3.90	0.03	122 BC ± 278
47-70	435	Obsidian Ridge	3.13	0.04	AD 628 ± 225
52-3	484	Obsidian Ridge	2.40	0.02	AD 1187 ± 175
52-5	376	Cerro del Medio	2.65	0.04	—
52-8	377	Obsidian Ridge	1.87	0.03	AD 1500 ± 138
52-11	378	Obsidian Ridge	2.08	0.03	AD 1385 ± 152
			3.82	0.03	36 BC ± 273
52-13	379	Cerro del Medio	2.20	0.03	—
52-16	380	Obsidian Ridge	3.16	0.04	AD 602 ± 228
52-17	381	Obsidian Ridge	2.57	0.03	AD 1070 ± 187
55-79	407	Polvadera	3.61	0.05	AD 538 ± 207
55-82	408	Cerro del Medio	2.76	0.02	—
55-83	409	Cerro del Medio	2.52	0.03	—
56-229	369	Cerro del Medio	5.06	0.04	—
56-235	370	Obsidian Ridge	4.95	0.05	1408 BC ± 352
			3.33	0.05	AD 449 ± 239
56-240	371	Cerro del Medio	5.43	0.05	2098 BC ± 385
56-242	372	Cerro del Medio	3.67	0.04	—
61-199	346	Cerro del Medio	1.56	0.04	—
61-200	347	Obsidian Ridge	1.42	0.03	AD 1705 ± 107
61-201	348	Cerro del Medio	2.11	0.03	—
61-202	349	Cerro del Medio	2.72	0.03	—
61-203	350	Obsidian Ridge	1.83	0.04	AD 1521 ± 136
63-151	340	Obsidian Ridge	3.97	0.03	198 BC ± 283
63-168	341	?	6.57	0.03	—
63-175	342	Obsidian Ridge	4.68	0.02	1048 BC ± 333
63-176	343	Polvadera	7.91	0.03	4966 BC ± 446
64-117	351	Cerro del Medio	2.17	0.02	—
64-118	352	Obsidian Ridge	3.26	0.04	AD 513 ± 234

Table 24. (Continued)

Site (RP-) and Artifact No.	Lab. No.	Source	Rim width (mm)	s.d.	Date
64-119	353	Obsidian Ridge	2.03	0.03	AD 1414 ± 149
64-120	354	Obsidian Ridge	1.70	0.02	1584 BC ± 126
64-123	355	Obsidian Ridge	3.10	0.03	AD 654 ± 224
64-125	356	Obsidian Ridge	2.57	0.04	AD 1070 ± 187
64-126	357	Obsidian Ridge	3.07	0.04	AD 679 ± 221
64-127	358	Obsidian Ridge	3.36	0.04	AD 421 ± 241
64-129	359	Cerro del Medio	5.07	0.03	—
64-130	360	Cerro del Medio	5.76	0.03	—
64-131	361	Obsidian Ridge	3.43	0.03	AD 355 ± 246
64-132	362	Obsidian Ridge	3.34	0.03	AD 440 ± 240
64-133	363	Obsidian Ridge	5.42	0.04	2083 BC ± 384
65-117	335	Obsidian Ridge	3.67	0.03	AD 119 ± 262
65-118	336	Cerro del Medio	4.41	0.04	—
65-124	337	Cerro del Medio	4.94	0.02	—
65-136	338	Cerro del Medio	4.99	0.04	—
65-138	339	Obsidian Ridge	5.00	0.04	1477 BC ± 355
65-111	476	Obsidian Ridge	6.62	0.03	4084 BC ± 467
65-112	477	Cerro del Medio	—		—
65-113	478	Cerro del Medio	5.30	0.05	—
65-115	479	Polvadera	5.52	0.02	1399 BC ± 314
65-116	480	Cerro del Medio	—		—
72-79	483	Obsidian Ridge	3.29	0.05	AD 486 ± 237
72-62	382	Polvadera	2.36	0.04	AD 1367 ± 138
72-65	383	Cerro del Medio	4.80	0.02	—
72-74	384	Cerro del Medio	5.94	0.03	—
72-75	385	Polvadera	2.99	0.03	AD 992 ± 172

landform gradually rises to the east from 2,072 m (6,800 ft) at Rowe Ruin to a point that is 2,149 m (7,049 ft) in elevation. Both the northern and eastern edges of this mesa are relatively steep and rugged. Below the northern edge, an unnamed wash leads from the spring and side drainage at Rowe Ruin to the Pecos River about 3.2 km east. The eastern edge of the mesa terminates at the second bench above the right bank of the Pecos. The bench is composed of lag gravel that provided much of the lithic source material for the inhabitants of Rowe Ruin (see site description for RP-21, below). The survey crossed the small drainage and explored part of the next ridge to the north. Sites RP-21, 29, and 34 were found on this side of the drainage. At the southeastern edge of the limestone mesa, another small spring and unnamed drainage join the Pecos. The survey did not extend south

of this feature. A brief reconnaissance was conducted across the Pecos in the vicinity of the confluence of the northern side canyon and the river. An extensive lithic quarry (RP-29) was located above the left bank of the Pecos. Several sites recorded on the survey, including RP-16, can be related directly to the use of the Santa Fe Trail. At RP-16, the Pecos is quite shallow and easily forded. Wagon wheel ruts from the Santa Fe Trail are clearly visible on both sides of the river at this location. RP-16 is the historic site of the community of Las Ruedas (the wagon wheels), which had been established on the trail and was abandoned somewhat before completion of the Santa Fe Railroad in 1880 (Figure 43).

In addition to being immediately adjacent to Rowe Ruin, the 1980 survey contrasted with the 1984 survey in that no attempt was made to include land closer to

Figure 43. Las Ruedas (RP-16) and the Pecos Valley. The Santa Fe Trail forded the Pecos River at the mid-nineteenth-century community of Las Ruedas. The village was probably abandoned by the 1870s. Parts of the site, including ruts of the trail itself, were recorded during the UNM 1980 field school survey.

Pecos Pueblo, Forked Lightning Ruin, or any of the known large, Classic sites of the region. The sites found in 1980 reflect a range of time periods and activities, but except for the quarry locations they do not seem to have functioned as support sites used by inhabitants of the large pueblos.

The 1984 survey sampled an area bounded by 2,455 m (8,053 ft) high Rowe Peak on the southwest and Rowe Ruin on the southeast. Rowe Peak was the highest elevation surveyed. No sites were located in the area that included Rowe Peak or in the two relatively high reconnaissance areas (Figure 41) on Glorieta Mesa just north of Rowe Peak. The eastern survey boundary was the Los Trigos Land Grant boundary, between one and two kilometers east of the Pecos River. Several sites were located east of the Pecos River where side canyons with ephemeral streams join the river. The northern survey

boundary was defined by a line between Glorieta Creek and the mouth of Canyon de la Madera. To the west, the survey extended to the wide, flat top of Glorieta Mesa and the eastern boundary of Santa Fe National Forest. Several structural sites and agricultural features were located between Pecos Monument and the Forked Lightning Ranch headquarters. These sites are all on a low ridge above the Pecos River in a wide, relatively low (2,072 m; 6,800 ft) portion of the Pecos Valley, where there is a confluence of side canyon drainages and springs. This area, along with most of the locations surveyed in 1984, is easily reached from Pecos Pueblo and the other large Classic period sites in the vicinity, as well as from Rowe Ruin.

Although Morrison (1987) suggested that the 1980 and 1984 surveys produced comparable estimates of the density of sites in the Rowe area, the two surveys produced results that were quite different in regard to numbers of different kinds of sites (Figures 44 and 45). In all, 71 sites were located: 23 (32%) in 1980 and 48 (67.60%) in 1984. In 1980, 17 sites were single-component and 6 had two or more components. In 1984, 44 were single-component and only 4 had two or more components. More nineteenth-century sites were located in 1980 (10) than in 1984 (2). The difference in this case seems to reflect the fact that the 1980 survey area included a segment of the Santa Fe Trail, together with a location where the trail fords the Pecos, whereas the 1984 survey did not.

Interestingly, both surveys reported approximately the same percentage of sites that might have been contemporary with Rowe Ruin: 6 (26%) of the 1980 sites and 15 (31%) of the 1984 sites. On the other hand, 12 sites recorded in 1984 may have been contemporary with Pecos Pueblo, and none of the sites recorded in 1980 were thought to have been contemporary with Pecos Pueblo. I suspect that this difference is simply a result of the fact that the 1984 survey area was closer to Pecos Pueblo than the 1980 survey area was. About the same percentage of sites—6 (26%) in 1980 and 11 (22%) in 1984—could not be placed chronologically. This rather large number is discussed in the summary section below.

There was a major difference in the numbers of structural versus nonstructural prehistoric sites recorded in 1980 and 1984. In 1980, three sites had remains of structures whereas 20 sites did not. In 1984, 30 sites were structural and only 14 were not. I suggest that this difference reflects two considerations. First, the 1980 survey concentrated on quite rugged terrain, whereas the 1984 survey included extensive areas of the wide Pecos Valley floor, an area that is appropriate for farming. Second, the 1980 survey, centered on Rowe Ruin and covering a smaller area, located sites that would have required only a short walk by the inhabitants of Rowe Ruin. The nonstructural sites may have been the result of Rowe Ruin's inhabitants procuring lithic material, hunting, or processing plants. There was no need to build structures for staying overnight or for caching raw material or tools. None of the sites recorded in 1980 was associated with agricultural fields that might have entailed construction of fieldhouses. The sites recorded in 1984 were more distant from Rowe and Pecos Pueblo than those recorded in 1980. The agricultural features recorded in 1984 may have been used by the former inhabitants of Pecos Pueblo, Rowe Ruin, or any of the

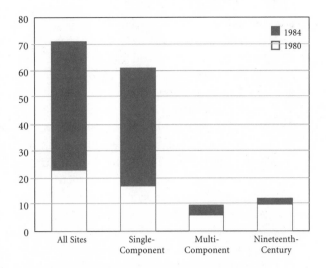

Figure 44. Single-, multicomponent, and nineteenth-century sites recorded in 1980 and 1984

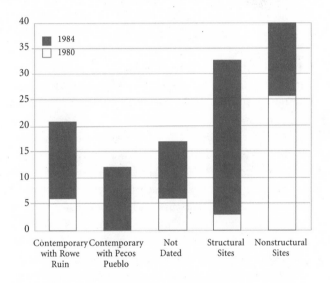

Figure 45. Dating of sites and structural/nonstructural sites recorded in 1980 and 1984

known Coalition or Classic period sites in the area (i.e., Forked Lightning Ruin [LA 672], Loma Lothrop [LA 277], Arrowhead [LA 251], and Dick's Ruin [LA 276]).

In the site descriptions below, an effort has been made to assign dates to the span of use of the sites. As noted above, we had hoped to establish a chronology independent of ceramic types in 1984, but this was not possible. In 1980, survey collections were analyzed by field school students under the supervision of Kurt Anschuetz, who had considerable experience with lithic artifacts dating to the Archaic and later time periods. The projectile point categories he used for chronological placement are those used in the Anasazi Origins Project, led by the late Cynthia Irwin-Williams, on which he had served as a crew chief. The ceramics from the 1980 survey were also analyzed by field school students with the assistance of David Snow, then of the Museum of New Mexico. Snow's experience with historical ceramics was particularly valuable.

In 1984, the survey crews and leaders had more experience with ceramic artifacts and the use of ceramics for dating than they did with lithic artifacts. Ceramics were not assigned to types unless diagnostic portions (e.g., glaze ware rims) were recovered. Broader categories (such as glaze period or Glaze Red body sherd) were used for sherds lacking diagnostic attributes. Long after the completion of the survey, I reanalyzed most of the ceramic and lithic artifacts collected in 1984. I relied heavily on projectile point descriptions published by Rogers (1987) as part of the Lower Pecos River survey in conjunction with the Los Esteros Reservoir Project (Ward 1987) and the lithic artifacts illustrated by Kidder (1932). In the discussions below, the dates provided for the lithic artifacts are those Rogers (1987) gives as "best dates" for the Lower Pecos. Most of the Pueblo period points located on survey and in the excavation of Rowe Ruin are similar to those from the Lower Pecos, from Pecos Pueblo, and from Paa-ko (Lambert 1954) as well as Leaf Water Pueblo (Wendorf 1953).

In 1980, Anschuetz developed a lithic type collection based on those available at the Laboratory of Anthropology at the Museum of New Mexico. His particular concern was attempting to differentiate lithic artifacts made with locally available materials from those that were made of imported stone. As quarries, outcrops, and lag-gravel workshops were discovered, the list of locally available materials grew (Table 25).

Long after the 1984 survey was completed, I reassigned the lithic artifacts that had been collected using the categories developed by Anschuetz. I was also able to compare the relatively few probable Alibates chert artifacts with material obtained from the Alibates quarry by Douglas Bamforth. The artifacts from Rowe visually match the material from Texas, but in the absence of chemical attribution the Rowe survey materials can only be considered "probable Alibates." The obsidian we submitted for hydration studies was, of course, analyzed chemically, and each piece was assigned to a particular obsidian source. As will be noted, the lithic materials from Rowe and the sites recorded on our surveys, as well as the material from Pecos, are diverse and of high quality for flaking (Kidder 1932). Most are available locally. The imported lithic materials consist primarily of obsidians from the Jemez area, probable Alibates chert from western Texas, and some Pedernal cherts from Pedernal Peak.

Site Descriptions

[Site numbers 1–9 were not assigned.]

RP-10 consists of a pre-contact lithic and ceramic scatter and a historical short-term camp located on the northwestern slope of the large unnamed ridge immediately east of LA 108. The site is 400 m southeast of LA 108. The sherds collected—one Wiyo Black-on-white, two Agua Fria Glaze-on-red, and two plainware—suggest a date of ca. AD 1325–1425. The 50 chipped stone items consist of primary, secondary, and tertiary reduction flakes and angular debris. No retouched lithic items were found. Lithic material types are gray chalcedonic chert, and green and gray river cobble cherts. All are locally available. The historical component, represented by about 25 objects including fragments of a cast iron stove, probably dates to the 1920s or 1930s.

RP-11 consists of an eroded sherd and lithic scatter and a historical campsite on the same northwestern slope of the unnamed ridge adjacent to LA 108. The single sherd is a plainware body sherd. The 11 chipped stone items include about equal numbers of secondary and tertiary reduction flakes and pieces of angular debris; none are retouched. Material types include gray chalcedonic chert, Tecolote chert, igneous river cobble, and petrified wood. All are probably of local origin. The historical component has rock alignments representing the remains of two structures. The artifacts, including a "Hoover for President" lapel pin, tin cans, and a meat tin imported from Uruguay, indicate a date from the late 1920s or early 1930s.

RP-12 is a ceramic and lithic scatter on the north-facing slope of the unnamed mesa on the east side of LA 108. The site is on an eroded surface and consists of two clusters of ceramic and lithic artifacts. Within the second cluster is the remains of a surficial unlined hearth. Cluster 1 contains 25 sherds and 75 lithic artifacts. The sherds are predominantly Galisteo Black-on-white, with some Rowe Black-on-white and one sherd of St. Johns Black-on-red, suggesting a date of AD 1270 to 1350. The lithic materials are gray chalcedonic chert, Tecolote chert, chalcedony, fine-grained basalt, and Jemez obsidian. All but the obsidian are available locally. The lithic artifacts include one Tecolote chert core and one Tecolote flake with retouch. The obsidian flake also exhibits good unifacial retouch. The rest of the lithic assemblage consists of secondary or tertiary flakes and a few primary reduction flakes and pieces of angular debris. The second cluster consists of 10 to 15 Galisteo Black-on-white sherds and a chipped stone assemblage of 85 items like that of cluster 1, including a small quantity of Jemez obsidian secondary and tertiary reduction flakes and some with unifacial retouch.

RP-13 is a lithic and ceramic scatter on a bench on the slope of the same unnamed ridge adjacent to the east side of LA 108. It is about 200 m from LA 108, appears to be contemporary with it, and represents a lithic manufacturing area, at least in part. The lithic artifacts consist of more than two hundred pieces of predominantly tertiary reduction flakes and angular shatter but also include three cores and some primary and secondary reduction flakes. The raw materials are gray chalcedonic chert, Tecolote chert, chalcedony, white river cobble chert, and some Jemez obsidian. The 35 to 40 ceramics include Galisteo Black-on-white, indented corrugated, smeared indented corrugated, clapboard corrugated, and plainware. The site is considered contemporary with LA 108 and on the basis of the ceramics is dated to AD 1250–1350 or 1400.

RP-14 (LA 69439) is a large, multicomponent site, no part of which dates to the precolumbian period with

Table 25. Locally Available and Imported Lithic Material Types Identified in the 1980 and 1984 Survey Collections

Code	Material Type
Local	
L01	Gray chalcedonic chert
L02	Tecolote chert
L03	Limestone
L04	Basalt
L05	Granite
L06	Igneous river gravel
L07	Schist
L08	Black river cobble chert
L09	Green river cobble chert
L10	White river cobble chert
L11	Quartzite
L12	L11 with white mottled inclusions
L13	Local sandstone
L14	Local petrified wood
L15	Local quartzite river cobble
L16	Local slate
L17	Massive quartz
L18	Conglomerate
L19	White chert (solid)
L20	Amphibrolite
L21	Hematite
Nonlocal	
001	Jemez obsidian
002	Other obsidian
003	Chert
004	Chalcedony
005	Basalt
006	Quartzite
007	Schist
008	Limestone
009	Sandstone
010	Pedernal cherts/chalcedonies
011	Alibates chert
012	Edwards Plateau chert
013	Turquoise
014	Other unknown
015	Unidentified igneous
016	Non-igneous chalcedony
017	Petrified wood

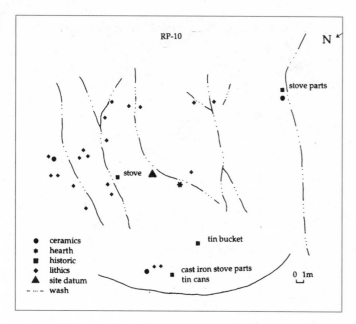

RP-10

- ● ceramics
- ✳ hearth
- ■ historic
- ◆ lithics
- ▲ site datum
- –··– wash

stove parts

stove

tin bucket

cast iron stove parts
tin cans

0 1m

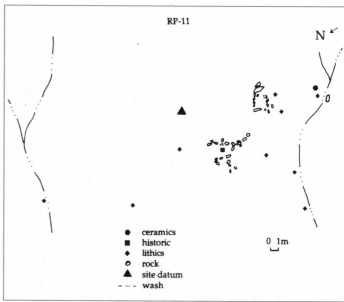

RP-11

- ● ceramics
- ■ historic
- ◆ lithics
- ○ rock
- ▲ site datum
- –··– wash

0 1m

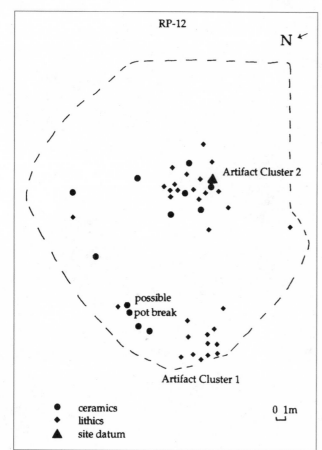

RP-12

Artifact Cluster 2

possible
pot break

Artifact Cluster 1

- ● ceramics
- ◆ lithics
- ▲ site datum

0 1m

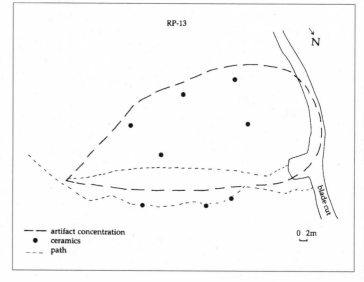

RP-13

- –– artifact concentration
- ● ceramics
- ---- path

blade cut

0 2m

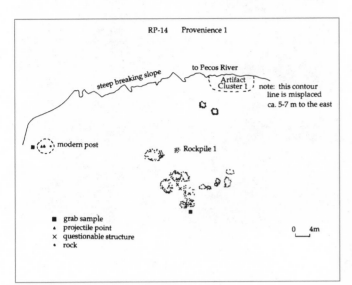

RP-14   Provenience 1

steep breaking slope

to Pecos River

Artifact Cluster 1

note: this contour line is misplaced ca. 5-7 m to the east

modern post

Rockpile 1

■ grab sample
▲ projectile point
✕ questionable structure
• rock

0   4m

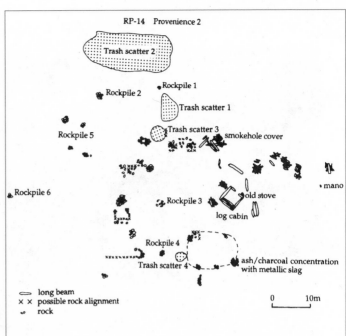

RP-14   Provenience 2

Trash scatter 2

Rockpile 2

Rockpile 1

Trash scatter 1

Rockpile 5

Trash scatter 3   smokehole cover

mano

Rockpile 6

Rockpile 3

old stove

log cabin

Rockpile 4

ash/charcoal concentration with metallic slag

Trash scatter 4

long beam
✕ ✕ possible rock alignment
• rock

0   10m

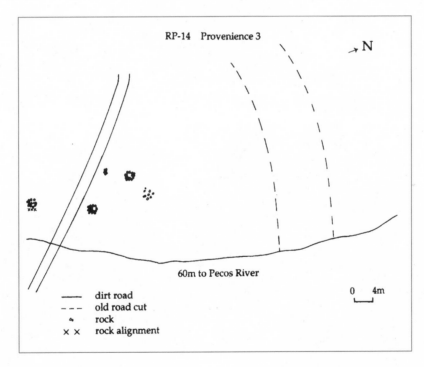

RP-14   Provenience 3

N

60m to Pecos River

0   4m

―――― dirt road
- - - old road cut
• rock
✕ ✕ rock alignment

173

Figure 46. Tipi ring at RP-14

Figure 47. Pin flags marking artifacts at tipi ring site

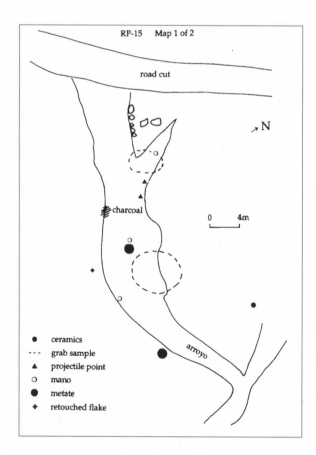

RP-15   Map 1 of 2

road cut

N

charcoal

0   4m

arroyo

● ceramics
--- grab sample
▲ projectile point
○ mano
● metate
✛ retouched flake

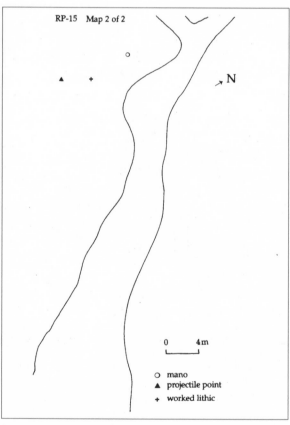

RP-15   Map 2 of 2

N

0   4m

○ mano
▲ projectile point
✛ worked lithic

any certainty. The site is on the first bench above the right bank of the Pecos River and the right bank of the small unnamed arroyo flowing into the Pecos from Rowe. The earliest component is a tipi ring site, consisting of ten ring structures and six smaller circular rock rings (Figure 46). No diagnostic artifacts were recovered from this component. However, a light scatter of chipped stone flakes of heterogeneous raw materials and one exhausted core of gray chalcedonic chert were found (Figure 47). The lithic assemblage is not distinguishable from any of the other lithic scatters recorded on the survey, in that it consists of the same range of materials and forms. The second component is probably a mid-nineteenth century Hispanic settlement that may be related to the community of Las Ruedas (see RP-16 below). Ceramics from this component include polished black ware, Tewa polychrome, one glaze-on-red body sherd, and plainwares. The third component appears to be a ranching camp dating to the turn of the century.

RP-15 is a lithic manufacturing and food processing area with ceramic evidence indicating use by Anasazi. The site is on the southeastern slope of the unnamed ridge east of LA 108 and west of the Pecos. The site is just south of a Forked Lightning Ranch service road and has been cut by a small arroyo. A spring with good flow is located immediately to the southeast. The site yielded one En Medio phase point of local gray chalcedonic chert and three additional whole or partial corner-notched projectile points, two of local gray river cobble chert with mottled inclusions and one of Jemez obsidian. Between 200 and 300 lithic items dispersed throughout the site area, including several retouched flakes and several exhausted cores, represent all phases of stone tool manufacture and maintenance. In addition, four one-hand sandstone manos and a broken slab sandstone metate were found on the site. A second broken metate, possibly of highly indurated sandstone, was found in the arroyo that bisects the site. The three Wiyo sherds on the periphery of the site are considered incidental associations. The major use of the site may date to ca. 800 BC to AD 400.

RP-16 is the mid-nineteenth century Hispanic town of Las Ruedas. Complete foundations of 16 structures were found along with five partial structures, a *capilla* (chapel) with part of one wall and corner still standing to a height of 1.5 m (Figure 48), and a *camposanto* (graveyard) (Figure 49). A large wooden cross was found next

Figure 48. Corner of adobe *capilla*, RP-16

Figure 49. *Camposanto* wall, RP-16

to the capilla. Wagon ruts marking the Santa Fe Trail cross the river at a ford at Las Ruedas and continue along the southern and western edges of the site (Figure 50). Residents of Rowe provided ethnohistoric information about the settlement (see Earls 1980). Las Ruedas was probably abandoned before the 1870s because it does not appear on the survey maps produced in 1879 in conjunction with the rights-of-way for the Southern Pacific Railroad.

RP-17 is a late nineteenth century village site across the river and downstream from Las Ruedas. It was not recorded during the survey.

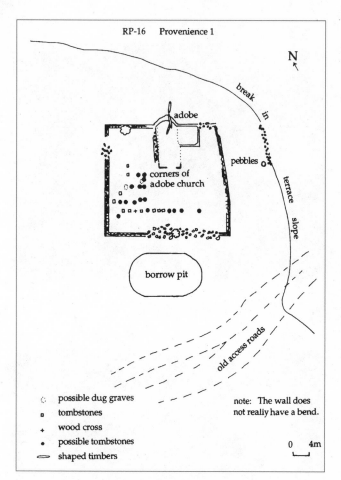

RP-16   Provenience 1

break in   terrace   slope

N

adobe

corners of
adobe church

pebbles

borrow pit

old access roads

⋮ possible dug graves
□ tombstones
+ wood cross
● possible tombstones
⬭ shaped timbers

note: The wall does
not really have a bend.

0   4m

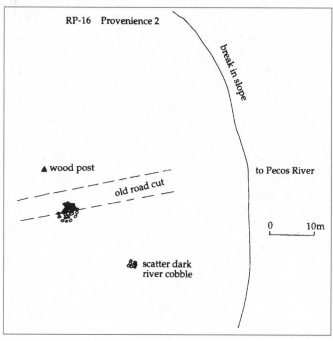

RP-16   Provenience 2

break in slope

N

▲ wood post

old road cut

to Pecos River

0   10m

scatter dark
river cobble

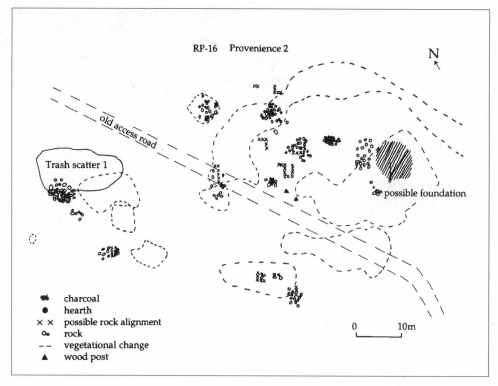

RP-16   Provenience 2

N

old access road

Trash scatter 1

possible foundation

🐾 charcoal
● hearth
× × possible rock alignment
o。 rock
- - vegetational change
▲ wood post

0   10m

Figure 50. Ruts of the Santa Fe Trail

Figure 51. Cobble-strewn surface at RP-21

RP-18 is a large lithic artifact scatter located on a badly eroded southeastern slope of a ridge 2.3 km southeast of the village of Rowe and 225 m west of the Pecos River. Although the lithic artifacts and the remains of three ash/charcoal concentrations, possibly hearths, may date to late Paleoindian or Archaic times, the site also yielded five sherds (one unidentifiable and four plainware body sherds) indicating subsequent use. The single possibly Paleoindian point is, unfortunately, a midsection that cannot be identified. It is heavily patinated and of nonlocal quartzite. The point form and quality of flaking indicate that it may date to as early as ca. 5000 BC. Additional tools consist of two one-hand manos made from river cobbles, one drill, two blades, and one unifacially retouched flake located near the two hearths. Of the 150 lithic flakes, 65–75% are of locally available raw materials (primarily gray chalcedonic chert and Tecolote chert). The remaining raw materials are nonlocal probable Alibates chert, a nonlocal quartzite, and Jemez obsidian. Cortex was exhibited only on the obsidian flakes. This and the virtual absence of angular debris suggest that the site was used for tool-maintenance and food processing.

RP-19 is a chipping station and lithic scatter extending for 3 m along the crest of an eroded remnant that forms a ridge with a good view of the Pecos Valley to the east. No diagnostic artifacts were recorded. About 100 flakes and angular debris representing all stages of reduction, except core fragments, were found. Hammerstones

were absent. A few pieces of angular debris are chalcedony; the rest are gray chalcedonic chert.

RP-20 is a lithic scatter covering an area of about 600 m² on the top of a spur of land 32 m above and 225 m east of the Pecos River and above a small side drainage 175 m to the south. Lithic debris is predominantly gray chalcedonic chert, Tecolote chert, chalcedony, and gray chert with white mottled inclusions. Except for exhausted cores, all stages of reduction are present, with small flakes predominating. The lack of cores and scarcity of primary reduction flakes suggest tool maintenance and/or manufacture from previously prepared blanks. RP-21 and RP-29 are in the immediate area and might be the lithic quarries where blanks were produced. Three small, triangular projectile points of local gray chert are similar to those excavated at Rowe Ruin. A fourth point fragment consisted only of a tip. The site is considered Anasazi because of the morphology of the three complete points.

RP-21 is a lithic "quarry" composed of waterworn river cobbles and an artifact scatter extending 150 m along the gravel terrace remnant of the second bench above the left bank of the Pecos River (Figure 51). Eleven spatially distinct chipping stations contain several thousand artifacts. The chipping stations range from 0.75 to 2.5 m in diameter. Outcropping lithic materials include local gray chert, Tecolote chert, fine-grained basalt, chalcedony, and quartzite river cobbles. All stages of core reduction were recorded, including exhausted cores and

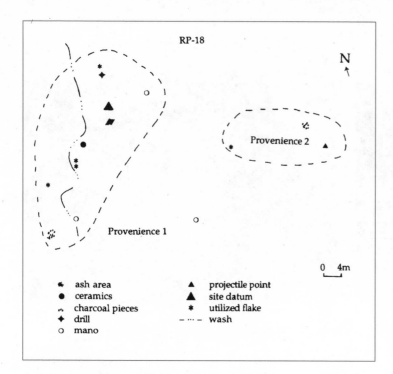

RP-18

Provenience 2

Provenience 1

0 4m

- ✦ ash area
- ● ceramics
- ⸬ charcoal pieces
- ✦ drill
- ○ mano
- ▲ projectile point
- ▲ site datum
- ✳ utilized flake
- –·–·– wash

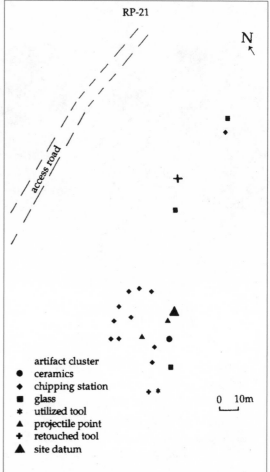

RP-21

N

access road

0 10m

- ● artifact cluster
- ● ceramics
- ◆ chipping station
- ■ glass
- ✳ utilized tool
- ▲ projectile point
- ✛ retouched tool
- ▲ site datum

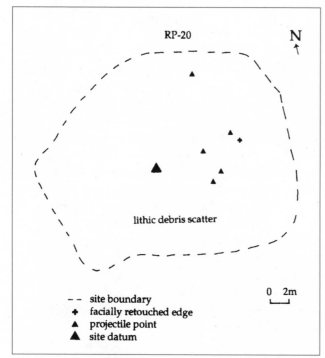

RP-20

N

lithic debris scatter

0 2m

- – – site boundary
- ✛ facially retouched edge
- ▲ projectile point
- ▲ site datum

angular debris. Hammerstones were not observed. One to five different types of raw material were noted at each chipping station. Many broken, discarded cobbles occur at each station. In one location, cobble fragments on the surface could easily be refitted. Two late Archaic points, one San Jose and the other En Medio, indicate use of the site between 3200 and 1800 BC and from 800 BC to AD 400, respectively. A small concentration of plainware sherds, suggesting a "pot break," indicates use of the site in Anasazi times. Use of the site at the turn of the century is indicated by a concentration of brown and purple glass.

RP-22 is composed of a small, light, discontinuous scatter of lithic debris on an eroded sheet-wash slope about 100 m south of a small, unnamed tributary east of the Pecos. The site lacks features or any indications of subsurface deposits. The lithic debris consists of about 150 to 200 flakes and angular debris fragments, predominantly local gray chert. Most flakes are small. One Pueblo side-notched point and one point tip of Jemez

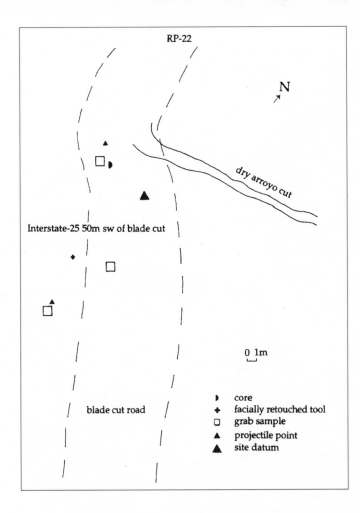

RP-22

N

dry arroyo cut

Interstate-25 50m sw of blade cut

0 1m

blade cut road

▶ core
+ facially retouched tool
□ grab sample
▲ projectile point
▲ site datum

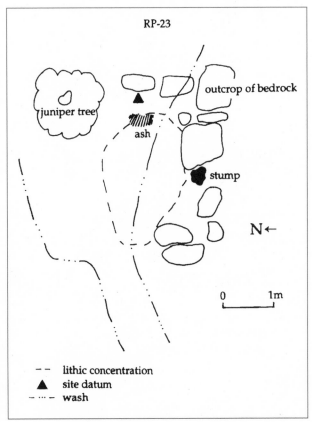

RP-23

juniper tree

outcrop of bedrock

ash

stump

N←

0 1m

-- lithic concentration
▲ site datum
-..- wash

obsidian were the only tools recorded. The point is similar to those recovered at Rowe, suggesting use of the site between about AD 1270 and 1400.

RP-23 is a surficial lithic scatter and a hearth on a wide bench 35 m northeast of an unnamed tributary canyon southwest of the Pecos. Thirty lithic artifacts of gray chalcedonic chert and Tecolote chert and one exhausted gray chert core were recorded. A few of the flakes and the core remnant appear to be heat treated. The hearth consists of a roughly circular ash lens 30 cm in diameter. A test probe showed that the hearth was not lined and contained ash and charcoal fragments to a depth of 10 to 12 cm. A small cluster of plainware sherds 15 m south-southeast of the site appears unrelated.

RP-24 is a nonstructural site composed of chipped and ground stone artifacts on the southeast slope of a large unnamed ridge 2.3 km southeast of Rowe. A spring was noted 500 m east-southeast of the site in a canyon that provides easy access to the Pecos River one-half kilometer to the east. Although no features or activity areas

could be isolated, hundreds of flakes and bits of angular debris occur on the site. All stages of reduction are represented, including two exhausted cores. Eighty percent of the debris is of Tecolote chert. The rest is gray chalcedonic chert and local gray chert, quartzite, and nonlocal chert. Three projectile points were recovered. One is an En Medio point of fine-grained chalcedony. The other two seem to be more recent, probably Basketmaker II or III. One is of Jemez obsidian and the other of local river cobble chert. The points suggest an age of about AD 400 to 600.

A sandstone slab metate measuring 22 by 33 cm was recorded but not collected. Five one-hand manos are of "river cobble quartzite." Two one-hand manos are of sandstone. A quartzite hammerstone was collected. No ceramics were found at this site.

RP-25 is 300 m west of RP-14 on the first bench above the right bank of the Pecos River and the right bank of the small unnamed arroyo flowing into the Pecos from Rowe. The site lies between two old wagon trails that originate near the town of Rowe and continue past the

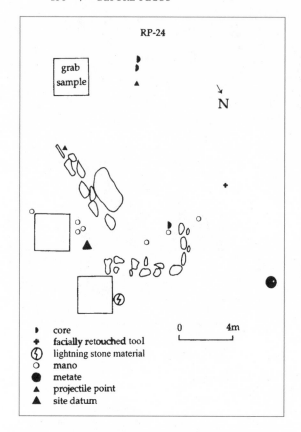

RP-24

grab sample

N

core
facially retouched tool
lightning stone material
mano
metate
projectile point
site datum

0   4m

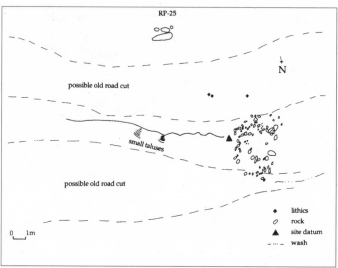

RP-25

N

possible old road cut

small taluses

possible old road cut

0   1m

lithics
rock
site datum
wash

site toward Las Ruedas (RP-16). At the time of survey, RP-25 appeared to have been looted within the previous five to ten years. The site consists of the remains of a single room, 3.5 by 2.5 m, outlined by one course of unshaped limestone blocks; within the structure a pit had been excavated. The only artifacts noted on the site were three pieces of nondiagnostic lithic debris that might have eroded out of RP-26, located a scant 26 m away. No cultural determination was made.

RP-26 is 26 m south of and slightly uphill from RP-25. The site consists of a moderately dense scatter of lithic debris covering an area of 50 by 30 m. Hundreds of chipped stone flakes and angular debris were present, as were six one-hand manos; ten unworked, waterworn cobble manuports; and one whole and three partial projectile points. The whole point is typologically a late En Medio point, dating to ca. AD 400. It is made of an exotic, orange chert. The point fragments are a tip and midsections that are not diagnostic. Several retouched flakes were collected. All stages of lithic reduction are present, including exhausted cores. The dominant material types are local gray chalcedonic chert and Tecolote

chert. A few of the flakes are Jemez obsidian. Some gray chert appears heat treated. One core is of a fossiliferous brown chert that may be exotic. The manos are of local quartzite, granite, and amphibrolite. They display one or two grinding surfaces but are otherwise not modified. The survey crews estimated a late Archaic affiliation for the site. No ceramics were found. The site appears to have been used for tool manufacturing and maintenance and food processing. No spatially patterned activity areas were observed.

RP-27 is located just 225 m west of RP-14, at the southeastern corner of an unnamed ridge 1.8 km east of the town of Rowe. The site consists of a moderately dense lithic scatter and a surficial hearth in an area measuring 120 m². No distinct activity areas were noted. The lithic artifacts represent all stages of reduction, including four exhausted cores. Two projectile points, seven facially retouched flake tools, and three flakes with utilized edges were collected. The points are typologically En Medio. One is of local gray chalcedonic chert, the other is obsidian. Three of the four exhausted cores are of the same chert, as are the vast number of flakes. The retouched flakes are carefully shaped tools with an average of two to four worked edges. Three one-hand manos of locally available river cobble quartzite and amphibrolite were recovered. Fire-cracked rock is fairly abundant and also

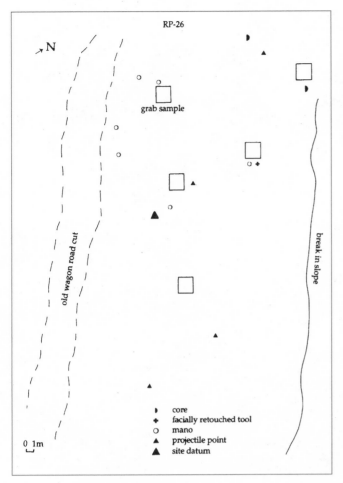

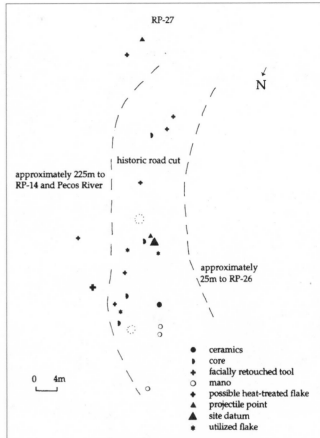

derived from river cobbles. An ash lens measuring 2 by 1.5 m, possibly 5 to 8 cm thick, was mapped. No hearth-stones were noted, but artifact density was higher near the hearth than elsewhere on the site. One nondiagnostic plainware body sherd was recovered. This site, like RP-26, appears to have been used for tool manufacture, maintenance, and food processing and dates to the late Archaic.

RP-28 is a dual-component site on a broad terrace remnant on the right bank of the Pecos River 550 m downstream from Las Ruedas (RP-16). One component is a lithic scatter of indeterminate age and cultural affiliation. The other component is a small, late nineteenth century settlement. The lithic scatter (mapped as provenience 3) consists of 150 to 200 flakes and angular debris on an eroded surface. Most of the assemblage is of local gray chert and Tecolote chert. A few pieces are of exotic blue-gray chert and orange chert. All stages of reduction are present, including one core and one biface.

A one-hand mano made on a local river cobble was also recovered. The historical component consists of a 36 m long by 3.5 m wide alignment of rock paralleling the terrace slope and two house foundations of rock and cobble with some adobe melt and associated porcelain and purple glass.

RP-29 is an extensive (150 by 100 m) lithic quarry on the uppermost bench on the crest of a large terrace remnant 27 m above the left bank Pecos River floodplain. Limestone outcrops, with nodules of chert, are on the northern, eastern, and southern edges of the site. The surface of the site is littered with tens of thousands of exhausted cores, flakes, and angular debris. The debris occurs as discrete "pockets" associated with local outcrops of limestone which contain the gray chalcedonic and Tecolote chert nodules. Most material is of poor quality, and most of the worked pieces are large angular debris. A road leading past a long-abandoned ranch house cuts through the southwest corner of the site.

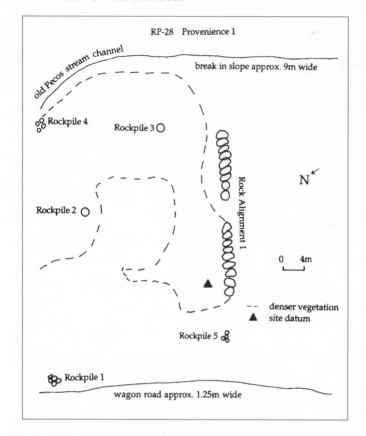

RP-28   Provenience 1

old Pecos stream channel

break in slope approx. 9m wide

Rockpile 4

Rockpile 3 ○

Rock Alignment 1

N

Rockpile 2 ○

0   4m

- - -   denser vegetation
▲   site datum

Rockpile 5

Rockpile 1

wagon road approx. 1.25m wide

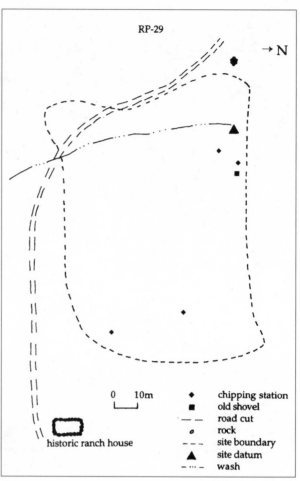

RP-29

→ N

0   10m

◆   chipping station
■   old shovel
— —   road cut
○   rock
- - -   site boundary
▲   site datum
—·—   wash

historic ranch house

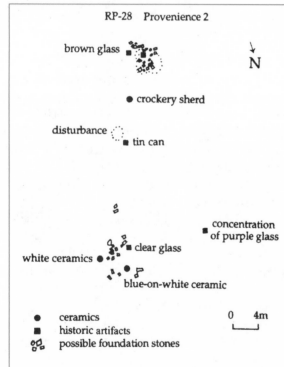

RP-28   Provenience 2

brown glass

N

● crockery sherd

disturbance   ■ tin can

concentration
of purple glass

clear glass

white ceramics ●

blue-on-white ceramic

● ceramics
■ historic artifacts
possible foundation stones

0   4m

RP-30 is a recent (twentieth century) structure composed of pinyon and juniper branches. It is probably a child's playhouse or fort.

RP-31 is a late nineteenth or early twentieth century trash dump located 600 m southeast of modern Rowe on the crest of a ridge in an area that has been chained to cut down shrubs and trees. It has been heavily grazed by cattle. The 30 to 50 artifacts visible in the surface are mostly brown, green, clear, and purple glass shards. One bottle neck with an applied lip was found, along with one fragment of an ironstone vase and one of an earthenware crock.

RP-32 appears to be an isolated, modern hearth measuring 1 m in diameter. The circular hearth is outlined by unburned limestone cobbles with some charcoal and ash in the interior. An ax-cut pinyon or juniper branch lies next to the hearth. No artifacts were located.

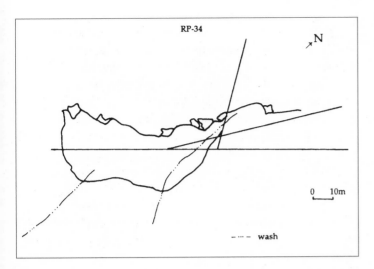

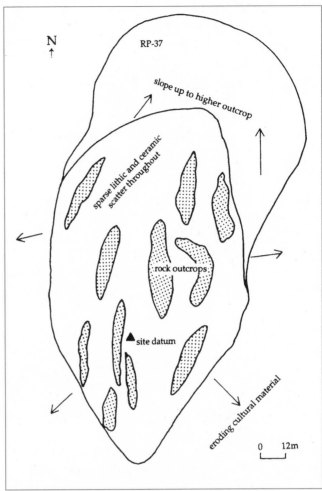

RP-33 is a lithic scatter located on a narrow bench on the north slope of the major ridge that separates the modern town of Rowe from the Pecos River. All stages of reduction were noted, including two cores. One facially retouched flake was also recorded. The debitage is of gray chalcedonic chert with the exception of one piece of quartzite angular debris. The 75 artifacts on the site were dispersed over an area measuring 33 m².

RP-34 is a structural site consisting of two small rubble mounds with an associated ceramic and lithic scatter on top of a ridge. The site is on the north side of the unnamed drainage leading from the spring at Rowe Pueblo to the Pecos River, about 0.5 km from the river. Surface artifacts include chipped stone, ground stone, and ceramics. The hundreds of pieces of chipped stone, in decreasing order of abundance, are gray chalcedonic chert, Tecolote chert, fine-grained quartzite, and obsidian. All stages of reduction were noted, including exhausted cores. One dark gray chert point base, three mano fragments, one river cobble–sized polishing stone, one battered cobble, and several unifacially retouched flakes make up the formal tools. The point base falls within the range of Bonham points that date to the period from AD 1000 to 1500 (Rogers 1987:Fig. 14c-d). The 75 sherds collected and analyzed span black-on-white and glaze types, plainware, and smeared-indented corrugated ware. Included are four Wiyo, one Galisteo, three San Clemente Glaze Polychrome, and two Glaze C-D and seven Glaze E-F rim sherds, indicating a span of AD 1320–1540.

RP-35 is due north of Pecos Pueblo near a small unnamed tributary of Glorieta Creek and only 0.2 km from Glorieta Creek. The site consists of a small (3 m diameter) rubble mound on a low rise, a single 3 by 3.5 m rectangular masonry room below the ridge, and one possible isolated hearth. Lithic and ceramic scatters are associated with the structural loci. Fewer than 100 items of lithic debris were observed. They are of gray chalcedonic chert, quartz, a dark red chert, and some obsidian. One obsidian point midsection fragment and one broken chalcedony drill comparable to drills found at Pecos Pueblo (Kidder 1932:Fig. 11j, 12b) were collected, and one metate was recorded. The pottery assemblage (one Galisteo Black-on-white, one San Clemente Glaze Polychrome, seven plainware, two other glaze, two Glaze B, and five unidentifiable) is consistent with an early glaze period date of AD 1300 to 1475.

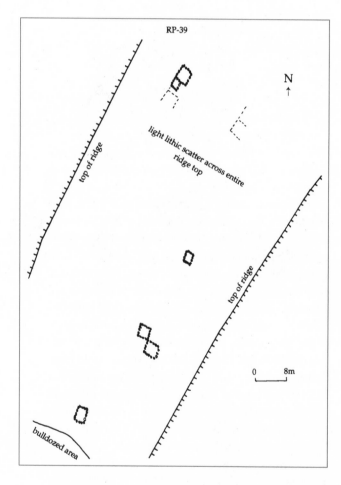

RP-36 is a lithic scatter with some ceramics located on a hilltop ridge overlooking the Pecos River, about 150 m from Glorieta Creek. The site has been eroded by grazing and disturbed by construction of a nearby road. Approximately 200 lithic artifacts were examined. They are predominantly Tecolote chert with some gray chalcedonic chert, fine-grained quartzite, and fine-grained basalt. No primary decortication flakes, no cores, and no ground stone objects were observed. Five small obsidian flakes were collected for dating. Nine bowl sherds were collected: two glaze-on-red body sherds, four Glaze C-D rim sherds, two Glaze E-F rim sherds, and one unidentifiable sherd. The ceramics suggest a late glaze occupation, ca. AD 1425–1540.

RP-37 consists of a sparse scatter of lithic, ceramic, and ground stone artifacts on a hillside one-quarter of a kilometer west of the Pecos and with a good view of the river. The site surrounds an area of rock outcrops. The lithic artifacts consist primarily of gray chalcedonic chert and fine-grained quartzite with some Tecolote chert. Six pieces of obsidian were recovered but none were dated. All stages of lithic reduction were observed, including two exhausted cores.

Five sherds were collected and analyzed: three plainware sherds, one glaze-on-red body sherd, and one Glaze E-F rim sherd, suggesting late glaze period use of the site (ca. AD 1425–1540).

RP-38 is a small rockshelter overlooking Glorieta Creek, just within the Pecos Grant near the boundary with Forest Service land. The rockshelter contains vandalized pictographs that are too badly damaged to record. No ceramics were present. Lithic artifacts consist of five small flakes of Tecolote chert and one large primary decortication flake of the same material, one gray chalcedonic chert flake, a 5 cm long bifacially flaked side scraper of probable Alibates chert, and one whole, stemmed obsidian point. The point is corner-notched, resembling Scallorn points but not as deeply notched. It measures 1.75 by 1 cm. Rogers (1987:93) provides dates of AD 1000 to 1500 for the type.

RP-39 consists of the dispersed remnants of nine rectangular structures on a ridge top above the right bank of the Pecos just north of the modern town of Rowe. A check dam is located across the small arroyo northwest of and downslope from the site. An old wooden stake suggests that the site has been visited by artifact collectors. No ceramics and only a dozen dispersed lithic artifacts were noted on the site. The masonry alignments were difficult to discern. The lack of wall fall suggested that they may have been foundations for jacal walls. The lithic items include six primary decortication flakes of Tecolote chert and one of gray chalcedonic chert, two secondary decortication flakes of gray chalcedonic chert, and one unifacially retouched jasper flake. There was no obsidian.

RP-40 is located on a slope at the extreme southwestern edge of the Pecos Valley at modern Rowe. The site consists of a 4 by 4 m rubble mound upslope from a small lithic scatter that, in turn, is upslope of five stone drainage-control features associated with two unnamed washes coming down from Glorieta Mesa to the east-southeast of the site. The water-control features appear to be prehistoric. A single Glaze B, worked bowl sherd was collected. Two river cobbles, each with one ground surface and one of which also has a battered end, and one cobble mano were also collected. A sample of lithic artifacts was collected, consisting of flakes of Tecolote and gray chalcedonic chert. No primary decortication flakes or cores were recovered. Although the data are insufficient for chronological placement, use in the 1400s is suggested.

RP-41 consists of the remains of a single, small (4 by 4 m), U-shaped masonry structure located in the Pecos Valley 0.4 km west of Glorieta Creek about 0.8 km west of the boundary of Pecos Monument. No artifacts were associated with the site.

RP-42 is located in the Pecos Valley about one-half of a kilometer north of RP-40. The site consists of two masonry roomblocks about 45 m apart. The first measures 12 by 5 m. The second measures about 9 by 4 m but is more difficult to discern. No artifacts were found on this badly deflated site.

RP-43 consists of a small structure defined by a rubble mound of about 5 by 6 m. This feature, which may have been used for storage, was built against a rock overhang above an unnamed western tributary wash of Glorieta Creek. The site is less than a kilometer due north of RP-41. A light scatter of ceramic and lithic artifacts is associated with the site. Three sherds were collected and analyzed: one plainware, one St. Johns Polychrome, and one unidentifiable polychrome sherd with black mineral paint. The lithic artifacts consist of about 25 flakes of Tecolote chert and gray chalcedonic chert, one very fine grained chert flake of unknown source material, one

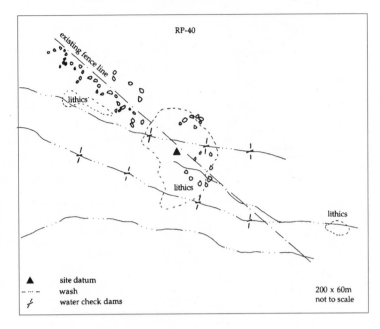

RP-40

▲ site datum
— · · · — wash
⌿ water check dams

200 x 60m
not to scale

unifacially retouched obsidian flake, and one broken, bifacially flaked obsidian tool. A date in the late 1200s is possible given the single sherd, but any accurate assignment would obviously require a larger sample of pottery.

RP-44 is a small block of two or three masonry rooms with an associated ceramic and lithic scatter and a check dam 10 m to the southwest below Glorieta Mesa in the Pecos Valley. Of the 287 ceramics from the site, 102 sherds were analyzed. They represent the full range of glaze rims (two A-B; seven C-D; nine E-F) as well as plainware sherds (2), body and other glaze sherds (30), and 51 unidentified (including polychrome) sherds. The two flakes collected were gray chalcedonic chert and Tecolote chert secondary flakes. No obsidian was collected. Based on the likelihood that most of the unidentified sherds are matte painted or polished, the site would date from perhaps the late glaze period to around 1700.

RP-45 is a lithic scatter with a few sherds on a point of land jutting into a wide, flat-bottomed wash west of Arroyo del Pueblo at Pecos Monument. The landform consists primarily of a boulder-strewn ridge. Artifacts collected from a transect cross-cutting the site included 15 flakes of gray chalcedonic chert, one of which was a primary decortication flake; one flake of Tecolote chert; and five small obsidian flakes. The five sherds analyzed

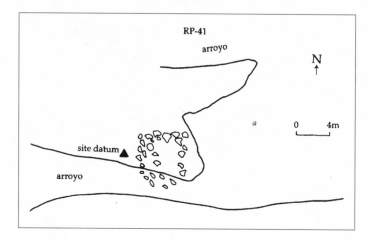

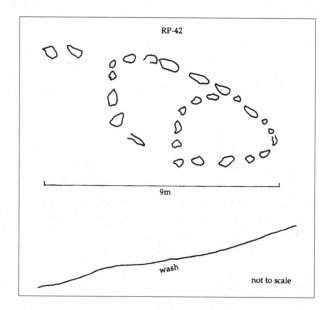

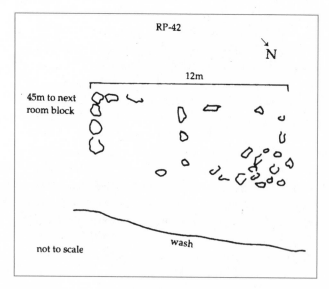

were a single Galisteo Black-on-white, two glaze-on-red body sherds, and two other glaze sherds. Although the sample of ceramics is far too small for reliable chronometric placement, the lack of later glazes suggests that the site may be contemporary with Rowe and early Pecos Pueblo.

RP-46 consists of the poorly defined, single-course rubble foundations of up to three masonry rooms. No artifacts or areas of wall fall were found. The site is located on the lower slopes of Glorieta Mesa, 2.5 km southwest of Glorieta Creek and about 0.3 km southwest of RP-48. One 3 by 3 m structure is U-shaped. To the northeast, and perhaps at one time connected to it, are two stone alignments that might represent two more rooms. None of the structures have evidence of a west wall.

RP-47 is an extensive lithic scatter with a few undecorated brownware ceramics. The site is located on a severely eroded slope on a ridge near the base of Glorieta Mesa, about 0.75 km southeast of RP-42. The artifacts are sparsely distributed over a 300 by 50 m area in two loci separated by about 50 m. Locus 1 measures 100 by 40 m. Materials collected include 50 flakes, mostly of gray chalcedonic chert with some Tecolote chert and some dark red opaque chert or jasper; two flakes of banded brown Alibates chert; two exhausted cores of Tecolote chert; two unifacially retouched flake scrapers; and seventeen small obsidian flakes. A bifacially flaked, gray chalcedonic chert knife was also recovered. The knife, pointed at both ends, measures 75 by 50 mm and closely resembles one from Te'ewi (Wendorf 1953:Pl. XXXVIII, k). Six samples of obsidian were submitted for dating. The site is clearly prehistoric, but finer chronological placement is not possible.

RP-48 is a single masonry room with a probable outside hearth associated with a scatter of ceramics and lithics. The site is located about 0.3 km southeast of RP-46, on a ridge on the lower slope of Glorieta Mesa. The site measures 7 by 7 m, with the structure occupying about 5 by 5 m. Wall fall is abundant, suggesting full-height masonry walls. The hearth consists of a ring of seven stones southwest of the southwest corner of the room. Ceramics (33 sherds) and lithic artifacts were collected. The sherds are 14 plainware, three glaze-on-red body sherds, three glaze-on-yellow body sherds, five other glaze sherds, and seven unidentifiable. The lithic artifacts are one large Tecolote chert core, one probable Alibates end scraper on a flake,

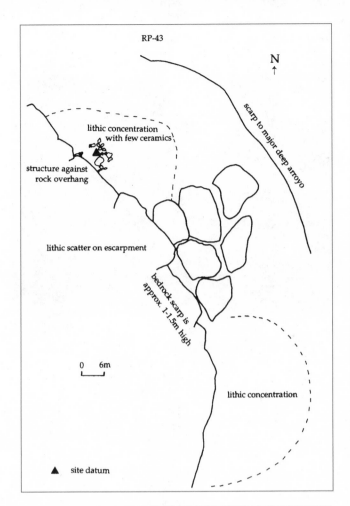

RP-43

N

scarp to major deep arroyo

lithic concentration with few ceramics

structure against rock overhang

lithic scatter on escarpment

bedrock scarp is approx. 1-1.5m high

0 6m

lithic concentration

▲ site datum

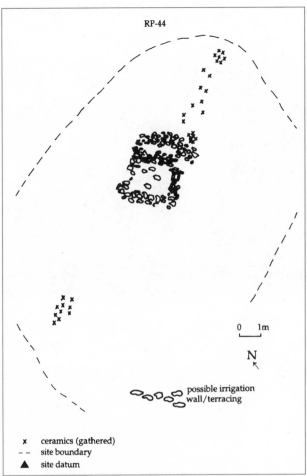

RP-44

0 1m

N

possible irrigation wall/terracing

x   ceramics (gathered)
- - -   site boundary
▲   site datum

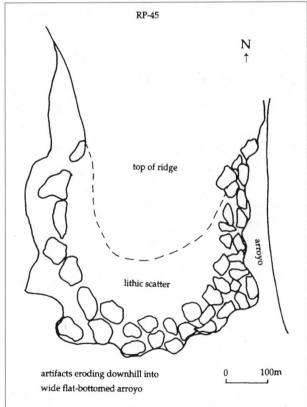

RP-45

N

top of ridge

arroyo

lithic scatter

0 100m

artifacts eroding downhill into
wide flat-bottomed arroyo

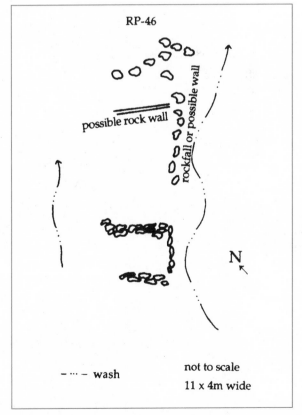

RP-46

possible rock wall

rockfall or possible wall

N

- · - · — wash

not to scale
11 x 4m wide

187

Figure 52. Pictographs at RP-49

Figure 53. Close-up of pictographs at RP-49

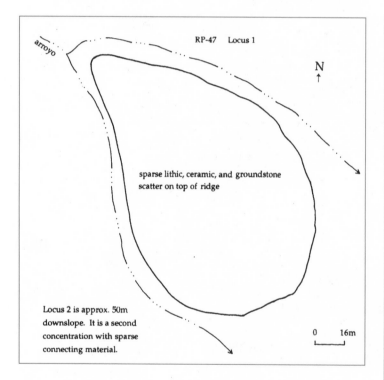

RP-47   Locus 1

N
↑

sparse lithic, ceramic, and groundstone
scatter on top of ridge

arroyo

Locus 2 is approx. 50m
downslope. It is a second
concentration with sparse
connecting material.

0   16m

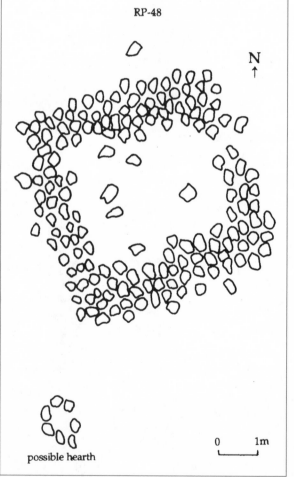

RP-48

N
↑

possible hearth

0   1m

188

three Tecolote chert secondary flakes, and one side-notched projectile point. The point is made of dark gray chert and is within the range of illustrated Harrell points (cf. Rogers 1987:Fig. 14h). The tip of the point is broken but the remainder measures 3.2 by 1.2 cm. Rogers (1987) provides dates of AD 1000 to 1500 as the best dates for Harrell points. On the basis of the ceramics, the site can be placed generally in the glaze period, ca. 1325 to 1700.

RP-49 is a rock art site with no associated features or artifacts. The site is on top of Glorieta Mesa, 3 km northwest of the origin of Padre Spring Creek. The site consists of 14 pictographs on a vertical cliff face just below the top of the mesa. They extend for about 8 m. Half-moon or semicircular shapes in orange, yellow, and brown are the most common depiction (Figures 52 and 53).

RP-50 is a dispersed lithic scatter with two sherds on a ridge slope that runs perpendicular to the Pecos River, less than 0.5 km to the east. The site was noted in the 1980 survey but not numbered or described at that time. One late glaze ware sherd and one plainware sherd were recovered. Most of the lithic artifacts are Tecolote chert flakes. Others include seven small obsidian flakes, one of which had some cortex and might have come from a river pebble; one small gray chalcedonic chert flake; and seven incomplete points, six of which are obsidian. All the points are small arrow points rather than dart points. Two of the items with sufficiently complete bases for identification are a dark gray chert point resembling Bassett points (Rogers 1987:Fig. 14a-b) and an obsidian point that resembles Fresno points (Rogers 1987:Fig. 14h-k). Rogers (1987:92) gives AD 1300 to 1500 as best dates for Bassett points, and AD 1000 to 1500 for Fresno points. A single river cobble ground on two surfaces is the only ground stone item collected.

RP-51 is a site with the foundations of at least seven very small (1.5 by 2.0 m) structures that, in the absence of wall fall, may have had jacal walls. Only three artifacts were noted. The site is on a low ridge in the Pecos Valley, near the northwestern edge of the survey area. The foundations occur in four discrete clusters, three of which are aligned north-south. In all, however, the site only encompasses 17 by 10 m. The three ceramic sherds, glaze-on-red body sherds from bowl forms, suggest use of the site after AD 1325.

RP-52 is located in an extremely disturbed (chained or bulldozed) area on a low hilltop on the right bank of

the Pecos River, less than 1 km upstream from RP-50. The site consists of a low-density scatter of chipped stone, ground stone, and ceramics dispersed over a 450 by 175 m area. Three sherds were collected but only one, a glaze ware body sherd, was analyzed. The approximately 130 lithic items collected are predominantly Tecolote chert, including two exhausted cores and several primary decortication flakes. The remainder are unretouched flakes from quartzite river cobbles, two dark red chert flakes, and 12 small obsidian flakes. Two obsidian points were recovered. One, resembling a Bassett point (Rogers 1987:Fig. 14a), is stemmed. The artifact measures 25 by 15 mm, although the tip is missing. The other point is broken at the base. Two ground stone items were noted but not collected. Rogers (1987) gives dates of AD 1300 to 1500 for Bassett points, which is comparable with the date suggested by the single glaze ware body sherd.

RP-53 consists of two small (2 by 2 m) masonry room foundations with a moderate amount of wall fall and very sparse ceramic and lithic scatter, slightly north of RP-51 on a ridge on the unnamed tributary of Glorieta

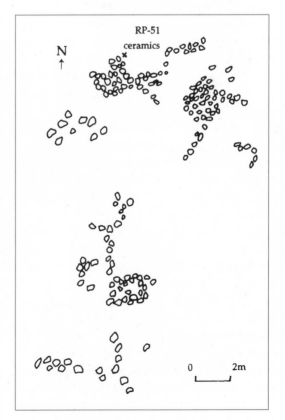

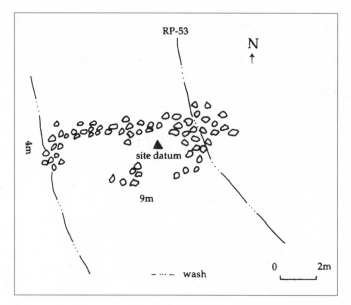

RP-53

N

4m

site datum

9m

--- wash

0   2m

Creek. Three sherds were collected: two smeared indented corrugated and one plainware. The lithic artifacts included three very small obsidian flakes, one primary decortication flake of Tecolote chert, four Tecolote chert flakes, and one opaque dark red chert flake. Although hardly an adequate sample, the single smeared indented corrugated sherd suggests a date after 1325.

RP-54 is a large (100 by 50 m) lithic scatter on the slope of a terrace due east of Pecos Monument and above the right bank of the Pecos River, approximately 550 m to the east. A hill adjacent to the site has a wooden stake with the number "76" on it. A grab sample of the first 100 lithic artifacts consists almost entirely of angular debris and flakes of Tecolote chert. All stages of reduction are present, including two exhausted cores. One small broken obsidian biface (possibly a point fragment) is the only formal stone tool.

RP-55 is a sparse ceramic and lithic scatter located below a small sandstone outcrop northeast of RP-51 and 1 km south of Glorieta Creek. The scatter measures 37 by 30 m. Eighty-seven sherds were collected: one Rowe Black-on-white, one Abiquiu Black-on-gray, 63 plainware, six smeared indented corrugated, one White Mountain redware, two glaze-on-red body sherds, two Glaze B rim

sherds, two other glaze sherds, and nine other sherds (including two carbon-paint and two mineral-paint black-on-white).

Four samples of obsidian were submitted for hydration, but only one date was obtained. The lithic assemblage included one very small point of gray chalcedonic chert, four obsidian flakes, angular debris, and some flakes of Tecolote chert and gray chalcedonic chert. A single triangular point of gray chalcedonic chert with convex edges was recovered. This artifact resembles Fresno points (cf. Rogers 1987:Fig. 14e, f; Kidder 1932: Fig. 3f). It measures 15 by 12 mm. No primary decortication flakes or exhausted cores were recovered. The ceramics suggest a date of AD 1320 to 1425. Rogers (1987:92) suggests best dates of AD 1000 to 1500 for Fresno points.

RP-56 is a lithic and ceramic scatter located on the first terrace above the left bank of the Pecos River about 2.5 km southeast of the modern settlement of East Pecos. The scatter occurred in a roughly triangular area measuring 55 by 40 m. Seventeen sherds were collected: one Rowe Black-on-white, one Los Padillas Glaze Polychrome, three glaze-on-red body sherds, one glaze-on-yellow body sherd, six Glaze C-D and six Glaze E-F rim sherds, and four unidentified sherds. Four obsidian samples were submitted for hydration. The remaining 100 lithic items were 90% Tecolote chert angular debris and secondary flakes, six gray chalcedonic chert flakes, three "tested" chert river cobbles, and one broken bifacially modified Tecolote chert flake tool. The ceramics indicate a date during the glaze period, from AD 1325 to 1700.

RP-57 is a rockshelter with the remains of a masonry structure, pictographs, and a lithic scatter. The shelter is on top of the second bench above and overlooking the Pecos River to the west. The site is almost directly opposite the Forked Lightning Ranch house and RP-39. The rockshelter is 12 by 5 m with a fire-blackened roof, two small mask pictographs, and modern graffiti (Figure 54). The masonry walls stand to a height of 2.5 m in the front part of the shelter. The site has been heavily disturbed and vandalized by modern campers. Lithic artifacts were collected from the ground in front of the shelter. These consist of fewer than 100 Tecolote chert and gray chalcedonic chert flakes, one broken obsidian point or knife, one "tested" cobble of gray chalcedonic chert, and one banded, probable Alibates chert flake. Not enough information is available to date the site with any confi-

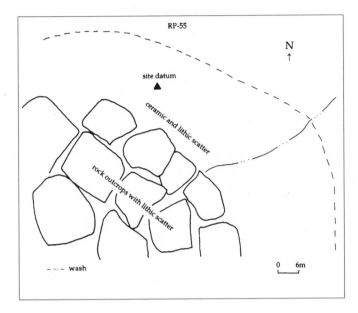

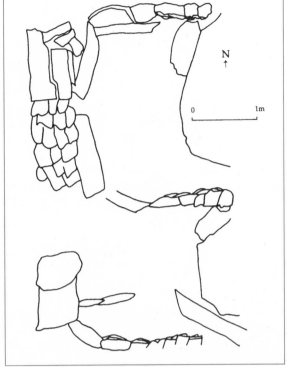

dence. The mask pictograph and masonry suggest a date after AD 1325.

RP-58 consists of the remains of a small structure (a rubble mound measuring 10 by 10 m) and an associated ceramic and lithic scatter on a low ridge above Glorieta Creek, less than 1 km southeast of Pecos Monument. The site has been disturbed by construction of a nearby road and vandalized by pot hunters. The 50 analyzed sherds consist of a single San Clemente, two Los Padillas, and seven other glaze-on-yellow sherds; one Tsankawi Black-on-cream; one Tewa Polychrome; three Glaze C-D and three Glaze E-F rims; two other glaze body sherds; and 28 unidentifiable sherds. In the analyzed sample, 21 are bowl sherds and 14 are jar sherds. The lithic artifacts are an obsidian flake, five Tecolote chert flakes, seven gray chalcedonic chert flakes, one piece of basalt angular debris, and one dark red chert angular debris. One gray chalcedonic chert flake exhibits retouch on one edge. The ceramics suggest a date contemporary with Pecos Pueblo, ca. AD 1425 to 1750–1800.

RP-59 is an oval rubble mound, 20 by 12 m, on a valley floor slope about one-quarter of a kilometer northeast of RP-58. As with RP-58, the site is disturbed and potted. The mound represents an estimated four rooms. This part of the site, designated locus 1, also had chipped stone, ceramics, and ground stone on the surface. Locus 2, a ceramic and lithic scatter, is 62 m south of

Figure 54. Pictographs at RP-57

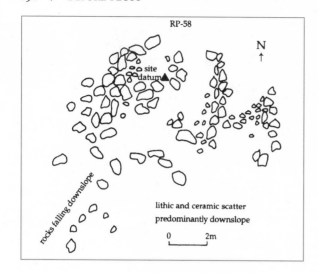

RP-58

site datum

lithic and ceramic scatter
predominantly downslope

rocks falling downslope

0   2m

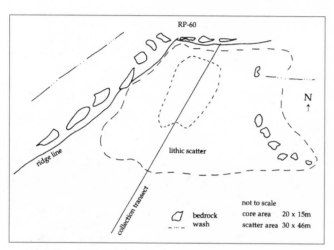

RP-60

ridge line

collection transect

lithic scatter

bedrock
wash

not to scale
core area   20 x 15m
scatter area 30 x 46m

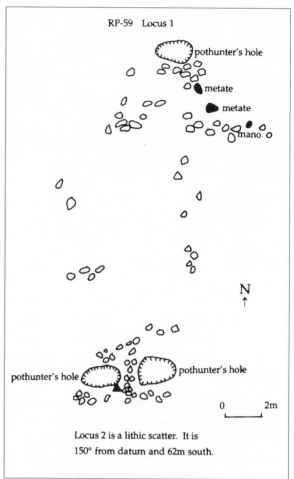

RP-59   Locus 1

pothunter's hole

metate

metate

mano

N

pothunter's hole

pothunter's hole

0   2m

Locus 2 is a lithic scatter. It is
150° from datum and 62m south.

locus 1. The two loci are separated by a modern erosion-control feature and an area of disturbed ground. Eight sherds were collected: one Galisteo Black-on-white, one Chupadero Black-on-white, four White Mountain redware, and one unidentifiable. The lithic artifacts from locus 1 are twenty small obsidian flakes, 30 Tecolote chert flakes, eight gray chalcedonic chert flakes, and one flake of fine-grained basalt. No primary decortication flakes or cores were recovered. Locus 2 lithics are primarily Tecolote chert with some gray chalcedonic chert. All stages of reduction are present, and some flakes have one utilized edge. The ceramics suggest dates of AD 1300 to 1425.

RP-60 is a lithic and ceramic scatter on low ridge in the Pecos Valley that is just across the unnamed wash east of RP-59. A randomly selected sample yielded the following sherds: one Galisteo Black-on-white; one Agua Fria Glaze A, one Los Padillas Glaze Polychrome, 30 other glaze sherds, six White Mountain redware, one Glaze B rim, twenty plainware, and six unidentifiable. The lithic artifacts consist of four small obsidian flakes; fewer than 100 pieces of Tecolote chert representing all stages of reduction, including angular debris and one exhausted core; some gray chalcedonic chert flakes; one green chert flake; and one very fine grained quartzite flake. The ceramics suggest a date of ca. AD 1300 to 1475.

RP-61 is located just 100 m south of, and on the other side of a small wash from, RP-60. The site consists of two areas of collapsed masonry and an associated ceramic and lithic scatter. The first area is a single course of masonry, apparently representing the remains of a single room. The second area is a 2 m high mound of collapsed masonry with a 1.5 m deep bulldozer cut running north-south directly through it. The 31 analyzed sherds are a single Wiyo Black-on-white, one San Clemente Glaze Polychrome, four other glaze, three glaze-on-red, and seven glaze-on-yellow body sherds; two Glaze C-D and two Glaze E-F rim sherds; and ten unidentifiable sherds. Two obsidian hydration dates were received. Sixteen additional obsidian flakes were collected. All stages of reduction of Tecolote chert are represented, including two exhausted cores. A smaller number of lithic artifacts are gray chalcedonic chert and flakes and angular debris of a reddish chert with white flecks. One petrified wood flake was also collected. The masonry and ceramics suggest an age within the span of occupation of Pecos Pueblo, ca. AD 1300 to 1700.

RP-62 lies on a steep slope above (south of) the Glorieta Creek floodplain, south of Pecos Monument and less than a kilometer from the Pecos River. The site consists of a one-room sandstone structure. The site has been disturbed and vandalized. No ceramics were recovered. Lithic items are sparse: five small pieces of obsidian; 12 Tecolote chert flakes, two of which are primary reduction flakes; a few gray chalcedonic chert flakes and angular debris; and two broken obsidian points were recovered. Both points are triangular with convex edges and resemble Fresno points (Rogers 1987:Fig. 14e-g; cf. Kidder 1932:Fig. 3f, d). One point, missing the tip, measures 20 by 15 mm. The other point consists of the base and about one-quarter of the blade. It is 7.5 mm wide. Ground stone was noted but not collected. The site may date to AD 1300 or later, based on the type of masonry. Rogers (1987:92) suggests best dates of AD 1000 to 1500 for Fresno points.

RP-63 is on the same ridge as, and about 2 km southeast of, RP-62. The site contains a small (5.5 by 5 m) masonry roomblock with very few artifacts and a second, even smaller (2 by 3 m) rubble mound 14 m away but connected to the roomblock by a thin scatter of lithics and ceramics. Ground stone was noted but not collected. Six sherds were collected: one Rowe Black-on-white, two glaze-on-red body sherds, one Glaze C-D rim sherd, and two plainware sherds. Five samples were submitted for obsidian hydration and four dates were received. The lithic items from RP-63 include 73 small obsidian flakes, 11 dense gray chert flakes that are too small to analyze (generally less than 2 mm across) but

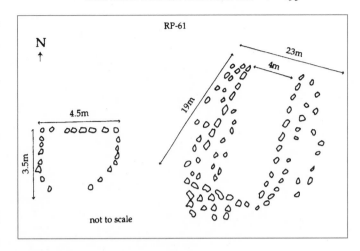

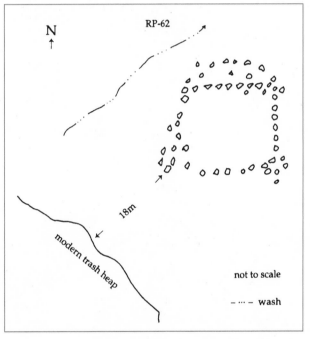

one of which has a small amount of cortex, five flakes of dense gray chert, and one exhausted core of the same material, flakes of Tecolote chert, gray chalcedonic chert, two flakes of brown-banded Alibates chert, and five partial obsidian points. Three of the obsidian points are midsection fragments that are too small to identify. They range in length from 10 to 20 mm. The other two are within the range of Fresno points (Rogers 1987:Fig. 14f; cf. Kidder 1932:Fig. 3f). Both are broken but measure 14 mm and 13 mm at the base. Rogers (1987:92) suggests best dates of AD 1000 to 1500 for Fresno points. The ceramics suggest a date from perhaps AD 1270 to 1475.

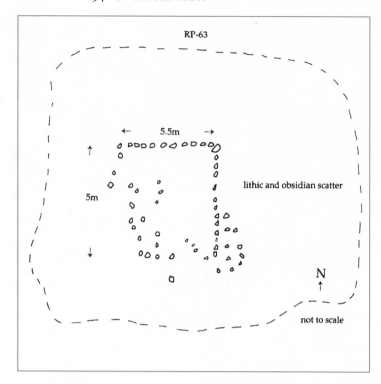

RP-63

5.5m

5m

lithic and obsidian scatter

N

not to scale

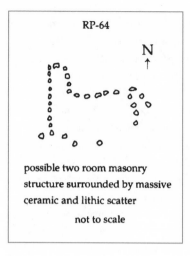

RP-64

N

possible two room masonry
structure surrounded by massive
ceramic and lithic scatter

not to scale

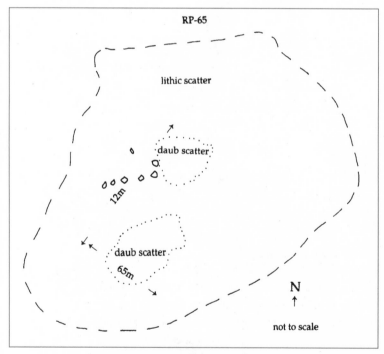

RP-65

lithic scatter

daub scatter

12m

daub scatter

65m

N

not to scale

RP-64 is a structural site on a terrace slightly above the Pecos Valley, about one-half of a kilometer southwest of RP-63. The closest sources of water are an unnamed wash and Glorieta Creek. The site contains a possible two-room masonry structure in an extensive, deflated lithic scatter. The land has been heavily grazed by cattle. Ground stone was noted as abundant but not collected. Fourteen of 33 ceramic sherds were analyzed: one Santa Fe Black-on-white; one Abiquiu Black-on-gray, two glaze-on-red body sherds, two other glaze sherds, two Glaze C-D rim sherds, two unidentifiable sherds with mineral paint, and four unidentifiable sherds. Fourteen obsidian samples were submitted and 11 dates obtained. The remainder of the collected artifacts were a grab sample of the first 100 lithic artifacts encountered. The sample consists of nine small obsidian flakes; Tecolote chert and gray chalcedonic chert flakes showing all stages of reduction, including two exhausted cores and some angular debris; and one dark red chert flake. Like at RP-63, the lithic assemblage is notable for the small size of the flakes. The ceramics suggest a date of ca. AD 1270 to 1475.

RP-65 is located on the same terrace and about 400 m southwest of RP-63 and east of RP-64. The site consists of the remains of a possible fire pit, surrounded by stones, and an oval area of daub with some lithic artifacts scattered nearby and two corrugated sherds. A second scatter of debris, rock, and daub is 22 m north of the first, and a third area of rock and daub is 40 m north of the first. No sherds were found at either locus 2 or 3.

Lithic artifacts were collected only from locus 1. Ten samples of obsidian were recovered from locus 1 and submitted for dating. An additional 29 small obsidian flakes were collected, as were 50 unretouched flakes, about two-thirds of which are of Tecolote chert and the rest of gray chalcedonic chert. None of these flakes shows evidence of primary decortication, and many are very small. No exhausted cores were recovered. There were also three dark red chert flakes, one of which has unifacial retouch on one edge and resembles a side scraper illustrated by Kidder (1932:Fig. 20d). One triangular obsidian point with convex edges, resembling Fresno points (Rogers 1987:Fig. 14d), was also recovered. The point measures 25 by 13 mm. Ground stone was observed but not recovered. The corrugated sherds suggest a date in the AD 1100s or 1200s. The "best dates" given by Rogers for Fresno points are AD 1000 to 1500.

RP-66 consists of a single erosion-control feature with no associated artifacts, located above Glorieta Creek on a 6 slope. It is east of RP-65. The feature consists of a single 12 m long alignment of stones running parallel to a small wash and creating a small terrace.

RP-67, like RP-66, is an erosion-control feature with no associated artifacts; it is only 100 m north of that site. The feature runs parallel to the Glorieta Creek drainage and is 20 m long.

RP-68 consists of a small, disturbed rubble mound of sandstone masonry (6 by 4 m and 0.2 m in height), a thin scatter of lithic artifacts, and a few sherds on the same ridge as RP-63 and 65, but north and slightly east of those sites (closer to RP-67). A possible check dam across the small, unnamed wash was mapped as part of this site. Two glaze polychrome body sherds from a redware bowl were collected, along with one obsidian flake that was not submitted for dating. Fifteen additional lithic artifacts were collected: flakes of Tecolote chert, gray chalcedonic chert, and fine-grained quartzite, and one exhausted core of a banded chert. No primary decortication flakes were recovered. Ground stone was noted but not collected. The ceramics suggest a date of AD 1425 to 1700.

RP-69 lies on the same ridge as RP-62, 63, 65, and 68, about 100 m west of RP-68 and on a steep slope above Glorieta Creek. It consists of a small (3 by 3 m inside dimensions) masonry structure, a sparse lithic scatter obscured by pine duff, and some ground stone that was recorded but not collected. No ceramics were found. The

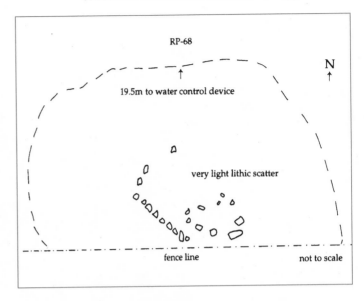

lithic artifacts include one obsidian flake with some cortex, as though it had been removed from a very small cobble, and 11 flakes of Tecolote chert and gray chalcedonic chert. Two of these chert flakes had some cortex. There is insufficient information to provide an assessment of age for this site. If all the sites on the ridge are of the same age, however, this site would also be contemporaneous with Pecos Pueblo.

RP-70 is located on a steep ridge above the right bank of the Pecos River, east of RP-36. The site is a large (70 by 50 m for the central area, 100 by 90 m maximum area) lithic scatter with chipped stone, ground stone, and hammerstones. One unidentifiable sherd was recovered, which has a white interior slip but no paint on either surface. The crushed sherd temper indicates that it may be from an early Santa Fe Black-on-white bowl, slipped on only the interior. A lithic sample includes 23 very small obsidian flakes, 50 Tecolote chert, and 15 gray chalcedonic chert flakes with all stages of reduction present, and a few flakes of dark red chert. Three formal lithic tools were also collected: one broken, gray chalcedonic chert end scraper, measuring 40 by 20 mm; one gray chalcedonic chert point; and one fine-grained basalt point. The chert point resembles one illustrated by Kidder (1932:Fig. 3f) but is broken at the base. The basalt point most resembles Kidder's (1932:Fig. 3a) triangular point with convex edges. This point does not look like any illustrated by Rogers (1987) for the Lower Pecos. The surveyors noted hammerstones of gray chalcedonic chert.

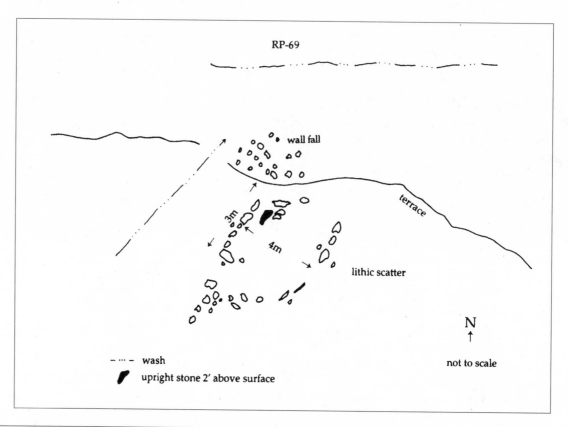

RP-69

wall fall

3m

4m

terrace

lithic scatter

N

not to scale

– ··· – wash

upright stone 2' above surface

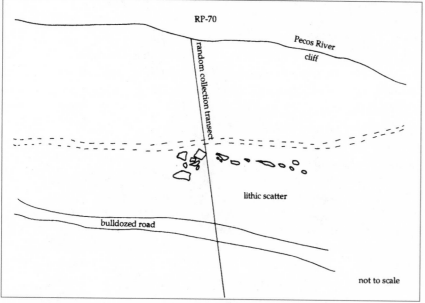

RP-70

Pecos River cliff

random collection transect

lithic scatter

bulldozed road

not to scale

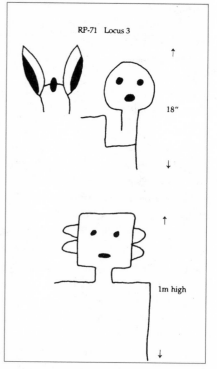

RP-71 Locus 3

18"

1m high

Figure 55. Rockshelter at RP-71

Figure 56. Pictographs at RP-71

RP-71 consists of two rockshelters, one above the other; a pictograph panel; and an artifact scatter on the right bank of the Pecos River, upstream from RP-36 and the Forked Lightning Ranch Headquarters. The lower, smaller shelter is about 4 by 3 m and one-third of a meter high. The larger shelter seems to be about 4 by 4 m and perhaps 4 m high at the mouth (Figure 55). Pictographs are associated with both shelters and are found on a panel 40 m south of the shelters. Some of the rock art has been vandalized. The motifs are largely anthropomorphic (Figure 56). Artifacts are thinly scattered throughout the area but were collected only from the lower shelter. Four sherds were collected at the lower shelter, but none could be identified. Only one sherd was slipped on both faces, but it lacked paint. The sherd is tuff-tempered and likely to be Wiyo Black-on-white. The lithic artifacts from the lower shelter consist of four fairly large obsidian flakes and 17 Tecolote chert flakes. Five of the chert flakes have ca. 10% cortex. Ground stone was observed but not collected. Use of the shelters in the AD 1300s is likely.

RP-72 is a small masonry roomblock that has been bulldozed, leaving only one room partially intact, with three walls reaching a maximum height of 1.5 m. A wooden stake at the site suggests that it was recorded during Nordby's survey. The site is on a ridge, near RP-60 and RP-61, and it is situated above Glorieta Creek, which lies about one-third of a kilometer to the south. Twenty sherds were analyzed: one Agua Fria Glaze-on-red, one Glaze C-D and one Glaze E-F rim sherds, five

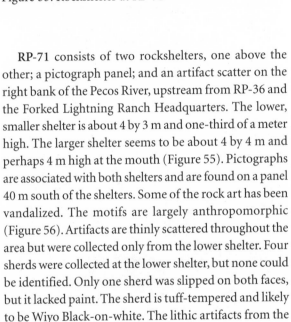
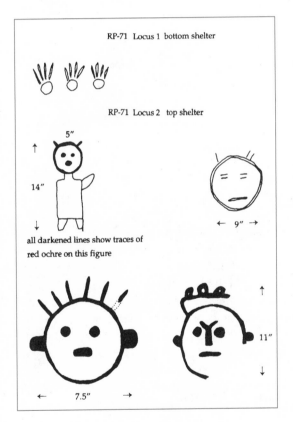

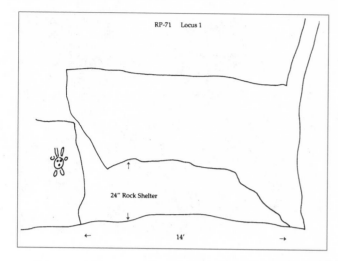

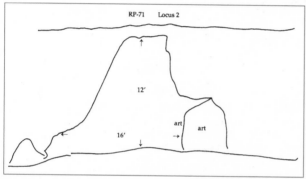

other glaze, and 12 unidentifiable, two of which are black-on-white with mineral paint.

Five samples of obsidian were submitted for dating. The remaining lithic items include 21 obsidian flakes, 35 Tecolote chert flakes, one of which has some cortex; seven dark red chert flakes, two chert cores; two unifacially retouched, red/gray banded, probable Alibates chert flakes; and six broken projectile points. Four of the points are obsidian. One of them is about one-fourth of its original size but the base is within the range of Plains side-notched points (Rogers 1987:Fig. 19q), though not as deeply notched. It also resembles Kidder's (1932:Figs. 1j and 7, 22) subtype 3-B, "Broad with wide notches." The point is 14 mm wide at the base. Rogers (1987:93) gives dates of AD 1000 to 1500 for Plains side-notched points on the Lower Pecos. Two of the obsidian points are most similar to Fresno points (Rogers 1987:Fig. 14f; cf. Kidder 1932:Fig. 3f). Both are broken and both are 10 mm wide at the base. Rogers (1987:92)

gives dates of AD 1000 to 1500 for Fresno points on the Lower Pecos. The fourth obsidian point, also consisting of the base and less than one-third of its original length, has a wide stem with a narrow basal notch. It is 27 mm wide at the base. One of the remaining points is quartz. The base is missing but it resembles the Fresno points (Rogers 1987:Fig. 14g; Kidder 1932:Fig. 3f). The final point is a fine-grained quartzite. It most resembles Bassett points (Rogers 1987:Fig. 14a; Kidder 1932:Fig. 3c). Best dates for Bassett points on the Lower Pecos are AD 1300 to 1500 (Rogers 1987:92). Finally, two sidescrapers were made on banded dolomite flakes. One measures 34 by 30 mm, the other 20 by 25 mm (both measurements are length by width). The ceramics indicate use throughout the glaze period, ca. AD 1325–1700.

RP-73 consists of a single check dam on a ridge above the Pecos River and an associated lithic scatter. The check dam runs northwest-southeast, perpendicular to three small washes which flow east-west down a terrace on the west side of the Pecos River (100 m away). The dam is one or two courses wide, about 25 cm wide on average. No ceramics were noted. Lithic artifacts recovered from the site consist of one very small obsidian flake, 25 flakes of Tecolote chert, and five flakes of gray chalcedonic chert. Two flakes had some cortex. No cores were recovered.

RP-74 is on the western edge of the Pecos River floodplain, downstream from RP-73. One structure is represented by a large (9 by 6.5 m) rectangle of limestone slab masonry that appears to have no internal divisions. A smaller (4 by 5 m) limestone slab and boulder structure may have been vandalized. The two structures are 16 m apart. A nonrandom sample of ceramics and chipped stone was collected. The analyzed pottery consists of one glaze-on-yellow, three other glaze, and one unidentifiable sherd. All are bowl forms. The lithic artifacts are two flakes and one core of Tecolote chert. On the basis of the admittedly small ceramic sample, the site may date to the middle and late glaze periods, ca. AD 1425 to 1700.

RP-75 is just above the left bank of the Pecos River, downstream from RP-74. The site consists of two rubble mounds with an extensive lithic and ceramic scatter. Recent use of the area is indicated by modern ceramics and glass. The archaeological structures are two rubble mounds measuring 4.5 by 6 m and 2.5 by 3 m,

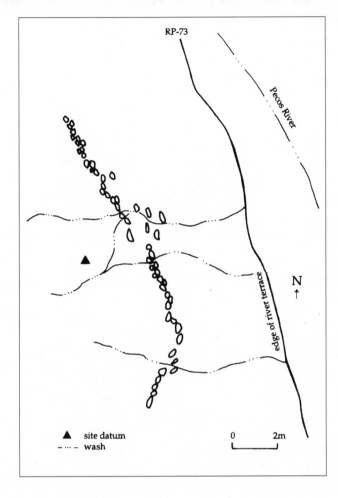

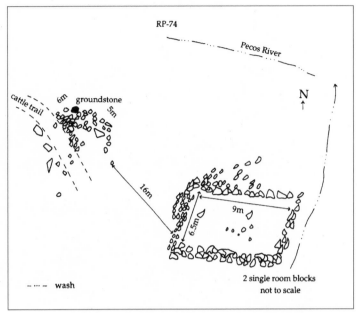

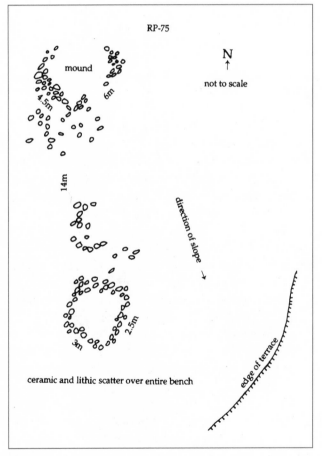

each probably representing a single room. The mounds
are 23 m apart. Some stone is scattered between the two,
but no alignment could be discerned. Of the 195 collected ceramics, 101 were analyzed. They include one
Santa Fe Black-on-white; two Abiquiu Black-on-gray;
seven Chupadero Black-on-white; five plainware; two
glaze-on-red body sherds; one San Clemente Glaze Polychrome; one glaze-on-yellow body sherd; and four other
glaze sherds. Of the 79 unidentifiable sherds, 48 are mineral-paint black-on-white, five are carbon-paint black-
on-white, four are polychrome, and four are red-slipped.
No historical ceramics were collected. Ground stone was
observed on the site but not collected. Lithic artifacts
from the site include one large, unifacially retouched
obsidian flake; 20 flakes of Tecolote chert; 25 flakes of
gray chalcedonic chert, with some cortex visible on a
few of them; and one small, stemmed obsidian projectile point. The point fragment consists of just the base
and about 25% of the point's original length. It most
resembles Fresno points (Rogers 1987:Fig. 14f). Best

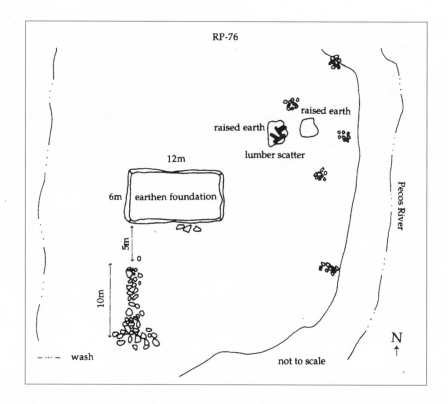

dates for Fresno points on the Lower Pecos are given as AD 1000 to 1500 (Rogers 1987:92). The ceramics suggest a date in the 1300s.

RP-76 is on the first bench above the right bank of the Pecos River where the Pecos makes a wide meander to the east, downstream and across from Manzanita Canyon. The site contains numerous structural remains, reflecting at least two components. A 10 m long, 1 m wide rock wall is located 5 m south of the southwest corner of a 12 by 6 m, 1 m high, rectangular earthen mound with a central depression. Puebloan ceramics were found in this area along with purple glass, blue transfer ware, and other historical artifacts. There are also six to eight circular to square mounds and rings of cobbles, all about 1.5 m in diameter. The entire site extends for 200 by 200 m. Of the 55 sherds collected, 13 were analyzed: one Wiyo Black-on-white, two Abiquiu Black-on-gray, one plainware, three other glaze, one glaze-on-yellow body sherd, and four unidentifiable sherds, of which three have mineral paint on a white slip. A single Glaze C-D rim sherd was also found. No historical ceramics were collected. Lithic artifacts include four obsidian flakes, one broken obsidian biface (probably a point midsection), one Tecolote chert flake with unifacial retouch on one

edge, and 15 Tecolote chert and gray chalcedonic chert flakes, a few of which have 10% cortex. The site was clearly used historically and may extend back to 1425.

RP-77 is an agricultural site consisting of a gridded garden covering at least 55 by 42 m and divided into more than 100 units, each measuring approximately 2 by 4 m. The grid dividers are aligned and stacked stones 0.2 m high. The site is on the lower slopes of a ridge extending east from Cerro de Escobas on the northeast face of Glorieta Mesa, southwest of Pecos Monument. Five sherds and a few lithic artifacts were recovered from the site. The ceramics are two Los Padillas Glaze Polychrome, two glaze-on-red body, and one unidentifiable sherd. The lithic artifacts are 17 obsidian flakes, one of which has some cortex, and about 25 flakes of Tecolote chert and gray chalcedonic chert and seven of dark red chert. Five flakes are retouched on one edge. The field system may have been in use in the fifteenth and sixteenth centuries.

RP-78 is a small, one-room, masonry structure with an associated ceramic and lithic scatter at the foot of Glorieta Mesa, about 0.25 km northeast of RP-77. Abundant masonry wall fall suggests full-height walls for the structure, which measures 5 by 4 m. Three sherds were

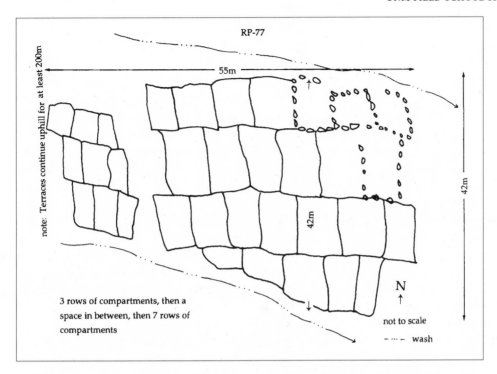

RP-77

55m

note: Terraces continue uphill for at least 200m

42m

42m

3 rows of compartments, then a
space in between, then 7 rows of
compartments

N

not to scale

- ··· - wash

analyzed: one other glaze and two unidentifiable. The single lithic artifact is a small flake of gray chalcedonic chert. The site may have been used sometime between AD 1325 and 1700.

RP-79 is located 0.1 km southwest of RP-78. It consists of the remains of a small, one-room structure, measuring 4 by 3 m. No artifacts were observed or collected.

RP-80 lies 0.1 km southwest of RP-78. The site consists of two contiguous, U-shaped structures made of large stone cobbles, open to the east, and built against and incorporating a bedrock outcrop. The structures measure 8 by 6 m and 7 by 5 m. Two bedrock mortars are also located in a detached section of the outcrop. Ceramics from the site consist of one glaze-on-red body sherd, two glaze polychrome, two glaze-on-yellow body and nine unidentifiable sherds, one polychrome, and one carbon-painted black-on-white sherd. The lithic artifacts are two small pieces of obsidian angular debris, 18 Tecolote chert secondary flakes, and one dark red chert flake. The site was in use sometime during the glaze period, ca. AD 1325 to 1700.

RP-81 consists of a single isolated masonry room adjacent to a fairly large, unnamed arroyo draining Glorieta Mesa on the north. It is 0.15 km east and downslope of RP-44. The tumbled masonry measures 4 by 4 m and 0.5 m high. Dispersed rock suggests full-height masonry walls. Three rock alignments spaced 2 m apart are adjacent to the room on its west side. They average 2 m long. A single glaze ware sherd was collected, as were one obsidian flake and one Tecolote chert flake. The site may have been in use at the same time that Pecos Pueblo was occupied.

Concluding Discussion

The 1980 and 1984 surveys were designed to evaluate the length of occupation and the diversity of site types in the vicinity of Rowe Ruin and in the Upper Pecos Valley in general. In addition, we hoped to locate quarries or other procurement areas for the lithic materials found at Rowe Ruin and at other sites in the area. Finally, we wished to document features related to ancient farming. The surveys suggest occupation of the Upper Pecos from at least the Archaic San Jose phase (ca. 3000 to 1800 BC) to the present. The surveys also recorded a variety of precolumbian structural and nonstructural site types and components (Table 26) in addition to a tipi-ring site (RP-14) and Las Ruedas (RP-16), a settlement associated with the Santa Fe Trail. The surveys located parent sources of lithic material for most of the flaked stone artifacts excavated from Rowe Ruin and found on other sites in the valley. Finally, agricultural features and likely fieldhouses, which were probably associated with Pecos Pueblo, were located and mapped. The density of sites in the Upper Pecos Valley is estimated at approximately 7.2 sites per square kilometer.

An occupational history of the Upper Pecos area cannot be derived from our survey data. A major gap in our information concerns sites located within and in the immediate vicinity of Pecos Monument. The National Park Service sites documented by Nordby (1990) and others (Fliedner 1976) are not included here, nor are they recorded on the ARMS records in Santa Fe, so those files too are deficient. Nevertheless, the survey data do reveal some patterning related to population aggregation. Together, the 1980 and 1984 surveys located 71 sites, of which 30 are structural and 41 are nonstructural. Four sites with structures that may date to the Anasazi period lacked any associated artifacts and therefore could not be assigned definite temporal affiliations. One structural site had lithic debitage but no sherds that would enable it to be assigned to a cultural or temporal position. Four sites without surface artifacts seems an unusually high number to me. Although I suspect that they might have been recently collected by National Park Service crews, according to our survey notes this was apparently not the case. The lack of surface artifacts might indicate that these sites were simply not being eroded or perhaps they were visited by unauthorized collectors. In any case, for the 30 structural sites with surface artifacts, 15 had components that were considered contemporary with Rowe Ruin and 24 had components that were considered to have been occupied at the same time as Pecos Pueblo. In some cases, these are the same sites. It is also true that for approximately 50 years or so Rowe Ruin and Pecos Pueblo were occupied at the same time (Kidder and Shepard 1936). Arrowhead, Dick's Ruin, Loma Lothrop, and Forked Lightning Pueblo also would have been occupied at the same time as Rowe Ruin and Pecos.

In 1980 and 1984, survey and excavations at Rowe Ruin were also directed toward understanding the context of aggregation in the Upper Pecos. In the second full season, we were particularly interested in whether or not aggregation occurred along with, or as a consequence of, the establishment of a local hierarchy of sites reflecting managerial control of labor, probably based on agricultural intensification and suggested by differential access to certain ceramic types. The pattern we thought we might see is described by Upham (1982; Upham and Bockley 1989) for the region around Chavez Pass, Arizona. The key observations presented with regard to Chavez Pass are that the large settlement of Chavez Pass Pueblo is thought to have depended on intensive agricultural production and been surrounded by smaller sites inhabited by people who did not have access to certain high-status ceramic goods.

According to Upham (1982:173–174), the inhabitants of Chavez Pass Pueblo controlled access to a spring that is the only permanent water source in the area. In addition, agricultural intensification at Chavez Pass is seen in a network of three, possibly four, rainfall- and runoff-fed reservoirs and a system of agricultural terraces and other water-control and diversion features. He notes that 40% of the sites with architecture within a radius of 1.6 km of Chavez Pass Pueblo are water- and soil-control features (54 of 136 sites). If likely fieldhouses are included, an additional 49 of 136 sites, or nearly 80% of all the architectural sites, are associated with agriculture (Upham 1982:175).

One question we wanted to address is whether or not aggregation at Rowe, and in the Upper Pecos Valley in general, was associated with evidence of agricultural intensification. If so, there should be a fairly high density of sites with agricultural features (terraces, check dams, fieldhouses, reservoirs) in the immediate area.

To test this hypothesis, two sets of data were examined. One set consists of the survey results reported here. The second set is the information on all Anasazi sites recorded in the ARMS site files at the Museum of New Mexico for the USGS Rowe and Pecos 7.5-minute quadrangles. Looking at the second set represents an attempt to be inclusive rather than restricting discussion to those sites described by the field school surveys. The ARMS file lists 124 sites with a total of 246 separate features and offers a larger sample than is otherwise available. Two caveats are in order. First, all of the 71 sites recorded by the field school are included in the ARMS file record. Second, the National Park Service sites from their recent survey of Pecos Monument and the surrounding area are not included in either record. Pecos Pueblo it-

Table 26. Number of Components by Type Found during the 1980 and 1984 Surveys

Type	Number
Lithic scatter	11
Ceramic scatter	1
Lithic and ceramic scatter	13
Agricultural features	4
Lithic quarry/workshop	3
Rockshelter	3
Single-room structure	14
Structure with 2–5 rooms	13
Structure with >5 rooms	2
Isolated rock art	1
Mound	1
Tipi rings	1
Other historical component	5

self and the well-known sites in the immediate vicinity are, of course, included in the ARMS data, but small sites that presumably were recorded on the Park Service surveys in the 1970s and 1980s are not. Although the Park Service survey data are not included in the ARMS file and have not been published, Welker (1997:160) cites information from the Park Service that is mentioned here.

Of the 71 sites recorded by the field school, only 7 (9.9%) had any agricultural features. Fourteen sites were single-room structures that might be interpreted as fieldhouses. This figure represents only 19.8% of the field school sites recorded, and a lower percentage than is indicated for Chavez Pass. For the ARMS file, 82 architectural features are recorded (including mounds, room-blocks, and single rooms). Of these, only eight (9.75%) are related to agricultural features: water catchment features, fieldhouses, and gardens. If isolated rooms are added to this figure, 23 features (28%) could be considered evidence of agricultural intensification. According to Welker (1997:160), 15 agricultural features have been located by Park Service surveys at Pecos to date. Both Rowe Ruin and Pecos Pueblo are immediately proximate to springs, but evidence of agricultural intensification at these sites and in the Upper Pecos in general is meager, particularly compared with the evidence from Chavez Pass. The evidence is also scant compared with well-surveyed areas in the Galisteo Basin. Welker (1997:159–160) reports a total of 378 agricultural features, including terraced fields, bordered and gridded gardens, check dams, fieldhouses, and pebble-mulch gardens in the immediate vicinity of Pueblo San Marcos, a very large Galisteo Basin site that was occupied at the same time as Pecos Pueblo.

In addition to evidence of agricultural intensification, issues related to the chronology of Chavez Pass Pueblo and sites in the vicinity are important to the argument regarding settlement hierarchy and therefore to this discussion. There is controversy surrounding the dating of Chavez Pass Pueblo, and reliance on mean ceramic dates is far from ideal. Nevertheless, as Upham and Bockley (1989) state, throughout much of the Southwest, black-on-white pottery antedates black-on-red and polychrome types. At issue is the persistence of black-on-white types and how they are maintained. At Chavez Pass Pueblo itself, preliminary examination suggested that the core of the site was occupied from at least AD 1100 to 1400 (Upham 1982:168). Using mean ceramic dates, the most intensive occupation of the pueblo (the most people) should have been at AD 1323 ± 36, which Upham interprets as an indication that population at the site increased through time until the mid-fourteenth century, when it experienced a decline. Yet within the immediate sustaining area of Chavez Pass Pueblo, chronologies based on ceramic types produced an occupational pattern in which only 2.2% (3 of 136) of the sites were occupied at the same time that Chavez Pass Pueblo was at its maximum size (Upham and Bockley 1989:485).

At Chavez Pass Pueblo the ceramic dates suggest that 70% of all artifacts date to the period after AD 1300, whereas using the same ceramic dating methods, 97.8% of the sites in the area date to between AD 800 and 1250. Upham (1982) and Upham and Bockley (1989) argue that the "later" ceramic types (some red-on-black and polychrome types) were restricted to "elite" individuals or groups resident at Chavez Pass Pueblo itself and were therefore not generally available to those living in the smaller sites in the vicinity. The observation that is key to the Upham (1982) and Upham and Bockley (1989) discussion is a marked "inhomogeneity" between dates based on ceramic cross-dating and those derived from tree-ring and radiocarbon determinations.

If one made the same arguments for the Upper Pecos, the occupants of Rowe Ruin or Pecos Pueblo might have had access to status-restricted ceramic types. If so, there should be a high percentage of "early" ceramic types on small sites in the survey area and a relatively greater proportion of "later" types at Rowe Ruin and Pecos Pueblo. Further, if a situation like that described for Chavez Pass existed in the Upper Pecos Valley, then most of the structural sites located by the survey should appear to be older than either Rowe Ruin or Pecos Pueblo.

The 1980 and 1984 surveys located 33 sites with evidence of structures. Of these, 21 (63%) were expected to be contemporaries of Rowe Ruin or Pecos Pueblo, or both, based on ceramic cross-dating. Our surveys did not suggest that either Rowe Ruin or Pecos Pueblo existed in a "vacant landscape." In addition, for the Upper Pecos, Anna Shepard's pioneering work (Kidder and Shepard 1936) demonstrates that the early glazes found in abundance at Pecos Pueblo had most likely not been made there. We felt that Glaze A (and the late Glaze F) should therefore be candidates for types that reflect restricted access. We also knew that the relatively few White Mountain redwares found in the Upper Pecos were imported from elsewhere. To restate the expectations, then, small sites in the vicinity of Rowe Ruin and Pecos Pueblo should lack Glaze A, White Mountain redwares, and Glaze F if access to these imported types was restricted. Our site surveys did not confirm this expectation. Surface collections from small sites, such as RP-55, 56, 58, 59, 61, 63, and 64, contained Rio Grande Glaze A and/or White Mountain redwares. Many small sites also contained Glaze F.

It might also be suggested that the relatively high quality lithic material noted at Pecos by Kidder (1932) and in our excavations at Rowe Ruin does not reflect the importing of exotic materials because quarries and chipping stations were located near at hand. The obsidian items recovered were among the few that would have come from any great distance. In the chemical analyses conducted as part of the obsidian hydration study, source areas were documented for most of the obsidian (Table 24, above). As the table indicates, obsidian from a variety of sources was collected from sites of different sizes, including those contemporary with Rowe Ruin and Pecos Pueblo. Again, there is no indication of restricted access to this material.

The survey data from Rowe and the Upper Pecos in general suggest that the process of population aggregation was either protracted or episodic, over a period of perhaps 200 to 300 years. It appears that population aggregation in north-central New Mexico, on the eastern edge of the ancient Pueblo world, was marked by settlement instability (Cordell 1989, 1996; Cordell, Doyel, and Kintigh 1994). Aggregation in the Upper Pecos took place in the absence of great investment in agricultural features. Elsewhere in the vicinity, such as the Santa Fe and Chama districts, agricultural intensification seems to have preceded aggregation. At Rowe, there is no evidence of restricted access to either certain ceramic wares or lithic materials. As discussed elsewhere (Cordell, Doyel, and Kintigh 1984), the processes of aggregation and the development of social hierarchies must be addressed separately.

REFERENCES

Adler, Michael, editor
  1996 *The Prehistoric Pueblo World, A.D. 1150–1350.*
        University of Arizona Press, Tucson.
Ahlstrom, Richard V. N.
  1989 Tree Ring Dating of Pindi Pueblo, New Mexico.
        The Kiva 54:361–384.
Anschuetz, Kurt
  1980 Report of the Preliminary Survey of the Vicinity
        of Rowe Pueblo, New Mexico. Ms. on file, Pecos
        Pueblo National Historic Park, Pecos, New Mexico.
Bandelier, Adolph F.
  1892 *Final Report of the Investigations among the
        Indians of the Southwestern United States, Carried
        on Mainly in the Years from 1880–1885.* Papers of
        the Archaeological Institute of America.American
        Studies IV(2). Cambridge, Massachusetts.
Baker, Vernon G.
  1980 Black Lucy's Garden. In *Archaeological Perspec-
        tives on Ethnicity in America,* edited by Robert L.
        Schulyer, pp. 29–37. Baywood, Framingdale, New
        York.
Barth, Fredrik
  1969 Introduction. In *Ethnic Groups and Boundaries:
        The Social Organization of Cultural Difference,*
        edited by Fredrick Barth, pp. 9–38. Little Brown,
        Boston.
Beaglehole, Ernest
  1936 *Hopi Hunting and Hunting Ritual.* Yale Univer-
        sity Publications in Anthropology No. 4. New
        Haven.
Binford, Lewis R.
  1978 *Nunamiut Ethnoarchaeology.* Academic Press,
        New York.
Binford, Lewis R., and J. B. Bertram
  1977 Bone Frequencies and Attritional Processes. In
        For Theory Building in Archaeology, edited by L. R.
        Binford, pp. 77-156.
Bohrer, Vorsila L., and Karen R. Adams
  1977 *Ethnobotanical Techniques and Approaches at the
        Salmon Ruin, New Mexico.* San Juan Valley Archeo-
        logical Project, Technical Series 2; Eastern New
        Mexico University Contributions in Anthropology
        8(1). Portales.
Bradfield, Maitland
  1971 *The Changing Pattern of Hopi Agriculture.* Royal
        Anthropological Institute Occasional Papers, No.
        30.
Breternitz, David A.
  1966 *An Appraisal of Tree-Ring Dated Pottery in the
        Southwest.* Anthropological Papers of the Univer-
        sity of Arizona 10. Tucson.
Carlson, Roy L.
  1970 *White Mountain Redware.* Anthropological
        Papers of the University of Arizona 19. Tucson.
Castetter, E. F.
  1935 *Uncultivated Native Plants Used as Sources of
        Food.* Ethnobiological Studies of the American
        Southwest 1, University of New Mexico Bulletin
        Biological Series (4)1. Albuquerque.
Classen, M. M., and R. H. Shaw
  1970 Water Deficit Effects on Corn, Part II. Grain
        Component. *Agronomy Journal* 62:652–655.
Cordell, Linda S.
  1977 *The 1976 Excavation of Tijeras Pueblo, Cibola
        National Forest, New Mexico.* Archeological Report
        No. 18. USDA Forest Service, Southwestern Re-
        gion, Albuquerque.
  1979 *A Cultural Resources Overview of the Middle Rio
        Grande Valley, New Mexico.* Bureau of Land Man-
        agement and USDA Forest Service. US Govern-
        ment Printing Office, Washington, D.C.
  1984 *Prehistory of the Southwest.* Academic Press,
        Orlando.
  1987 Rowe Project: Preliminary Report, 2 vols. Sub-
        mitted to the National Science Foundation. Ms. on
        file, Clark Field Archives, Maxwell Museum of
        Anthropology, University of New Mexico, Albu-
        querque.

1989 Evaluating Population Models of Ethnic Diversity. Paper presented at the First Joint Congress of the Archaeological Institute of America and the Society for American Archaeology, Baltimore.

1996 Big Sites, Big Questions: Pueblos in Transition. In *The Prehistoric Pueblo World*, AD 1150–1350, edited by Michael A. Adler, pp. 228–240. University of Arizona Press, Tucson.

Cordell, Linda S., editor

1980 *Tijeras Canyon: Analyses of the Past.* Maxwell Museum of Anthropology and University of New Mexico Press, Albuquerque.

Cordell, Linda S., and Linda Mick-O'Hara

1993 Comments on Strategies of Organization at Tijeras and Rowe Pueblo Ruins. Paper presented at the annual meeting of the American Anthropological Association, November 17–21, Washington, D.C.

Cordell, Linda S., and Vincent J. Yannie

1991 Ethnicity, Ethnogenesis and the Individual: A Processual Approach toward Dialogue. In *Processual and Postprocessual Archaeologies*, edited by Robert W. Preucel, pp. 96–108. Occasional Paper No. 10. Center for Archaeological Investigations, Southern Illinois University at Carbondale.

Cordell, Linda S., F. Plog, and S. Upham

1983 Investigations at Rowe Pueblo (LA 108). Proposal submitted to the National Science Foundation, Washington, D.C.

Cordell, Linda S., David E. Doyel, and Keith W. Kintigh

1994 Process of Aggregation in the Prehistoric Southwest. In *Themes in Southwest Prehistory*, edited by George J. Gumerman, pp. 109–135. School of American Research Press, Santa Fe.

Cordell, Linda S., Jane H. Kelley, Keith W. Kintigh, Stephen H. Lekson, and Rolf M. Sinclair

1994 Toward Increasing Our Knowledge of the Past: A Discussion. In *The Organization and Evolution of Southwest Prehistoric Societies*, edited by George Gumerman and Murray Gell-Mann, pp. 149–163. Addison Wesley Press, Reading, Massachusetts.

Creamer, Winifred

1993 *The Architecture of Arroyo Hondo Pueblo, New Mexico.* School of American Research Press, Santa Fe.

Cully, Anne C.

1979 Some Aspects of Pollen Analysis in Relation to Archaeology. *The Kiva* 44(2–3):95–100.

Cully, A., and Karen Clary

1981 Pollen Analysis at Rowe Pueblo. Ms. on file, National Park Service, Southwest Regional Office, Santa Fe, and Castetter Laboratory, Department of Biology, University of New Mexico, Albuquerque.

Curran, Brian K.

1985 Human Skeletal Analysis, UNM-NMSU 1984 Field Season, Rowe New Mexico. In Rowe Project: Preliminary Report, Vol. 1, Technical Report 11. Submitted to the National Science Foundation. On file, Clark Field Archives, Maxwell Museum of Anthropology, University of New Mexico, Albuquerque.

Cutler, Hugh C., and Thomas W. Whitaker

1961 History and Distribution of the Cultivated Cucurbits in the Americas. *American Antiquity* 26:469–485.

Dean, Jeffrey S.

1988 A Model for Anasazi Behavioral Adaptation and Dendochronology and Paleoenvironmental Reconstruction on the Colorado Plateaus. In *The Anasazi in a Changing Environment*, edited by George J. Gumerman, pp. 25–45 and 119–167. Cambridge University Press, Cambridge.

1995 Demography, Environment, and Subsistence Stress. In *Evolving Complexity and Environmental Risk in the Prehistoric Southwest*, edited by Joseph A. Tainter and Bonnie Bagley Tainter, pp. 25–56. Proceedings, Vol. XXIV, Santa Fe Institute Studies in the Sciences of Complexity. Addison-Wesley, Reading, Massachusetts.

Dean, Jeffrey S., Robert C. Euler, George J. Gumerman, Fred Plog, Richard H. Hevley, and Thor N. V. Karlstrom

1985 Human Behavior, Demography and Paleoenvironment on the Colorado Plateau. *American Antiquity* 50:537–554.

Doebley, John F.

1981 Plant Remains Recovered by Flotation from Trash at Salmon Ruin, New Mexico. *The Kiva* 46(3):169–187.

Doebley, John F., and Vorsila L. Bohrer

1980 A Report on the Maize Remains from Salmon Ruin, New Mexico. Ms. on file, Cultural Resources Management Program, Navajo Nation, Window Rock, Arizona. University of Arizona Ethnobotany Lab, Technical Series No. 32. Tucson.

Donaldson, Marcia L.

1983 Plant Remains from Red Bow Shelter, Northeastern New Mexico. Prepared for Kaiser Steel, York Canyon Mine, Raton, New Mexico. Castetter Laboratory for Ethnobotanical Studies, Technical Series 87. University of New Mexico, Albuquerque.

Douglass, Amy A.

1985 The Pottery of Rowe Ruin: A Stylistic Analysis of the Black-on-White Ceramics. Paper presented at the 50th annual meeting of the Society for American Archaeology, Denver.

Earls, Amy C.

1980 Report on the Ethnohistory of Rowe. Ms. on file, Museum of New Mexico, Santa Fe.

1987 *An Archaeological Assessment of "Las Huertas," Socorro, New Mexico.* Papers of the Maxwell Museum No. 3. Bureau of Land Management, Socorro District Office, and Maxwell Museum of Anthropology, University of New Mexico, Albuquerque.

Eighmy, G.

1984 Letter report on file, Maxwell Museum of Anthropology, University of New Mexico, Albuquerque.

Ferguson, Cheryl

1980 Analysis of Skeletal Remains. In *Tijeras Canyon: Analyses of the Past,* edited by Linda S. Cordell, pp. 121–149. Maxwell Museum of Anthropology and University of New Mexico Press, Albuquerque.

Fewkes, Jesse W.

1900 Tusayan Migration Traditions. In *Bureau of American Ethnology, Annual Report* No. 19, pt. 2 (for 1897–98), pp. 573–633. Smithsonian Institution, Washington, D.C.

Fliedner, Dietrich

1981 *Society in Space and Time. An Attempt to Provide a Theoretical Foundation for an Historical Geographic Point of View.* Arbeiten aus dem Geographischen Institut der Universität des Saarlandes, Band 31. Saarbrücken.

Ford, Richard I.

1968 *An Ecological Analysis Involving the Population of San Juan Pueblo, New Mexico.* Ph.D. dissertation, University of Michigan. University Microfilms, Ann Arbor.

1975 Re-excavation of Jemez Cave, New Mexico. *Awanyu* 3(3):13–27.

Ford, Richard I., Albert H. Schroeder, and Stewart L. Peckham

1972 Three Perspectives on Puebloan Prehistory. In *New Perspectives on the Pueblos,* edited by Alfonso A. Ortiz, pp. 22–40. School of American Research, Santa Fe, and University of New Mexico Press, Albuquerque.

Garrett, Elizabeth

1980 Preliminary Petrographic Study. In The Rowe Archaeological Research Project, Final Report to the National Endowment to the Humanities, RS-1144-79, by Walter K. Wait, Appendix 1. On file, National Park Service, Southwest Regional Office, Santa Fe.

1987 Preliminary Report, Petrographic Analysis of Rowe Ruin Ceramics. In Rowe Ruin Project: Preliminary Report, Vol. 2, Technical Report 16. Submitted to the National Science Foundation, BNS-831981. On file, Clark Field Archives, Maxwell Museum of Anthropology, University of New Mexico, Albuquerque.

1987a Geologic Assessment of Rowe Ruin. In Rowe Ruin Project: Preliminary Report, Vol. 2, Technical Report 10. Submitted to the National Science Foundation, BNS-831981. On file, Clark Field Archives, Maxwell Museum of Anthropology, University of New Mexico, Albuquerque.

Gasser, Robert E.

1982 Anasazi Diet. In *The Coronado Project Archaeological Investigations, the Specialists' Volume: Biocultural Analyses,* compiled by Robert E. Gasser. Coronado Series 4, Museum of Northern Arizona Research Paper 23. Flagstaff.

Gasser, Robert E., and E. Charles Adams

1981 The Plant Remains from Walpi: Phase II. Analysis of Plant Remains in 37 Rooms and 11 Rodent Nests from Walpi, Hopi Indian Reservation, Navajo County, Arizona. Ms. on file, Heritage Conservation and Recreation Service, Interagency Archaeological Services, San Francisco.

Gilbert, B. Miles

1980 *Mammalian Osteology.* Privately published, Flagstaff, Arizona.

Gilbert, B. Miles, L. D. Martin, and H. G. Savage

1981 *Avian Osteology.* Privately published, Flagstaff, Arizona.

Glassow, Michael A.

1972 Changes in the Adaptations of the Southwestern Basketmakers: A Systems Perspective. In *Contemporary Archaeology,* edited by Mark P. Leone, pp. 289–302. Southern Illinois University Press, Carbondale.

1980 *Prehistoric Agricultural Development in the Northern Southwest: A Study in Changing Patterns of Land Use.* Anthropological Papers 16. Ballena Press, Socorro.

1984 An Archaeological Survey of Vermejo Canyon, Colfax County, New Mexico. In *Papers of the Philmont Conference on the Archeology of Northeastern New Mexico,* edited by Carol Condie, pp. 93-115.

New Mexico Archeological Council Proceedings, Vol. 6, No. 1. Albuquerque.

Green, Dee F., and Fred Plog
1983   SARG: A Test of Locational Diversity. Paper presented at the annual meeting of the Society for American Archaeology, Pittsburgh.

Gregg, Josiah
1954   *Commerce of the Prairie,* edited by Max L. Moorhead. University of Oklahoma Press, Norman.

Gumerman, George J. (editor)
1988   *The Anasazi in a Changing Environment.* School of American Research, Santa Fe, and Cambridge University Press, Cambridge.

Gunnerson, James H.
1969   Apache Archaeology in Northeastern New Mexico. *American Antiquity* 34:23–39.

Gunnerson, James H., and Dolores A. Gunnerson
1970   Evidence of Apaches at Pecos. *El Palacio* 76:1–6.

Guthe, C. E.
1917   The Pueblo Ruin at Rowe, New Mexico. *El Palacio* IV(4).
1918   Andover Pecos Expedition. Report on the Packing and Shipping of Skeletons, Spring 1918. Ms. on file, Laboratory of Anthropology, Museum of New Mexico, Santa Fe.

Habicht-Mauche, Judith A.
1993   *The Pottery of Arroyo Hondo Pueblo, New Mexico: Tribalization and Trade in the Northern Rio Grande.* School of American Research Press, Santa Fe.

Hammond, George P., and Agapito Rey (translators, editors, and annotators)
1940   Narratives of the Coronado Expedition, 1540–1542. *Coronada Cuarto Centennial Publications, 1540–1940,* Vol. 2. University of New Mexico Press, Albuquerque.

Hawley, Florence M.
1936   Field Manual of Prehistoric Southwestern Pottery Types. University of New Mexico Bulletin 291. Albuquerque.

Hayes, Alden C.
1974   *The Four Churches of Pecos.* University of New Mexico Press, Albuquerque.

Hayes, Alden C., Jonathan Young, and A. Helene Warren
1981   *Excavation of Mound 7, Gran Quivira National Monument, New Mexico.* Publications in Archeology 16. National Park Service, Washington, D.C.

Hill, James N.
1970   *Broken K Pueblo: Prehistoric Social Organization in the American Southwest.* Anthropological Papers of the University of Arizona 18. Tucson.

Hewett, Edgar Lee
1904   Studies on the Extinct Pueblo of Pecos. *American Anthropologist,* n.s. 6(4):426–439.

Hodge, F. W.
1907   Jemez. In *Handbook of American Indians North of Mexico,* edited by Frederick W. Hodge, Vol. 1, pp. 629–631. Bureau of American Ethnology Bulletin 30. Washington, D.C.

Holden, Jane
1955   A Preliminary Report on Arrowhead Ruin. *El Palacio* 62:102–119.

Hooten, E. A.
1930   *The Indians of Pecos Pueblo: A Study of Their Skeletal Remains.* Papers of the Southwestern Expedition, No. 4. Phillips Academy, Andover, and Yale University Press, New Haven.

Hough, Walter
1897   The Hopi in Relation to Their Plant Environment. *American Anthropologist* 10:33–44.

Irwin-Williams, Cynthia
1973   Picosa: The Elementary Southwestern Culture. *American Antiquity* 32:441–456.

Jeançon, Jean A.
1923   *Excavations in the Chama Valley, New Mexico.* Bureau of American Ethnology, Bulletin 81. Washington, D.C.

Jones, Volney
1931   The Ethnobotany of the Isleta Indians. M.A. thesis, Department of Anthropology, University of New Mexico, Albuquerque.

Judd, Neil M.
1954   *The Material Culture of Pueblo Bonito.* Smithsonian Miscellaneous Collections 124, Publication 4172. Washington, D.C.

Judge, W. James, W. B. Gillespie, Stephen H. Lekson, and W. H. Toll
1981   Tenth Century Developments in Chaco Canyon. In *Collected Papers in Honor of Erik K. Reed,* edited by A. Schroeder, pp. 65–98. Papers of the Archaeological Society of New Mexico, No. 6. Albuquerque.

Kaplan, Lawrence
1956   The Cultivated Beans of the Prehistoric Southwest. *Annals of the Missouri Botanical Garden* 43: 189–251.

Kershner, John M.
1984   Chronology of the Middle Vermejo River Drainage. In *Papers of the Philmont Conference on the Archeology of Northeastern New Mexico,* edited by Carol J. Condie, pp. 115–125. New Mexico Archaeological Council Proceedings, Vol. 6, No 1. Albuquerque.

Kessell, John
1979 *Kiva, Cross and Crown: The Pecos Indians and New Mexico, 1450–1840.* National Park Service, Washington, D.C.

Kidder, Alfred V.
1924 *An Introduction to the Study of Southwestern Archaeology, with a Preliminary Account of the Excavations at Pecos.* Papers of the Southwestern Expedition 1. Department of Archaeology, Phillips Academy, Andover, by Yale University Press, New Haven. (Reprinted in 1962 by Yale University Press with "A Summary of Southwestern Archaeology Today," by Irving Rouse)
1925 *Pecos Explorations in 1924.* Papers of the School of American Research, No. 11. Santa Fe.
1926 *Early Pecos Ruins on the Forked Lightning Ranch.* Archaeological Institute of America. Papers of the School of American Research 14 (n.s.). Santa Fe.
1927 Southwestern Archaeological Conference. *Science* 66:489–491.
1932 *The Artifacts of Pecos.* Yale University Press, New Haven.
1958 *Pecos, New Mexico: Archaeological Notes.* Papers of the Robert S. Peabody Foundation for Archaeology, No. 5.
1962 *An Introduction to the Study of Southwestern Archaeology,* reprint edition. Yale University Press, New Haven.

Kidder, Alfred V., and Charles A. Amsden
1931 *Pottery of Pecos,* Vol. 1, Dull-Paint Wares. Papers of the Southwest Expedition, 7. Phillips Academy, Andover, and Yale University Press, New Haven.

Kidder, Alfred V., and Anna O. Shepard
1936 *The Pottery of Pecos,* Vol. 2, The Glaze-Paint, Culinary, and Other Wares. Papers of the Southwestern Expedition, 7. Phillips Academy, Andover, and Yale University Press, New Haven.

Kintigh, Keith
1995 C14: Graphical Analysis of C14 Samples, 1995 revised version. Computer software originally produced in 1985. Available from the author, Department of Anthropology, University of Arizona, Tucson.

Kirkpatrick, David T., and Richard I. Ford
1977 Basketmaker Food Plants from the Cimarron District, Northeastern New Mexico. *The Kiva* 42 (3–4):257–270.

Kirkpatrick, David T., and Karl W. Laumbach
1984 Across the Great Plains to the Rocky Mountains. In *Papers of the Philmont Conference on the Archeology of Northeastern New Mexico,* edited by Carol Condie, pp. 3–29. New Mexico Archeological Council Proceedings, Vol. 6, No. 1. Albuquerque.

Kohler, Timothy A., and Carla R.Van West
1995 The Calculus of Self-Interest in the Development of Cooperation: Sociopolitical Development and Risk among the Northern Anasazi. In *Evolving Complexity and Environmental Risk in the Prehistoric Southwest,* edited by Joseph A. Tainter and Bonnie Bagley Tainter, pp. 171–199. Proceedings, Vol. XXIV, Santa Fe Institute Studies in the Sciences of Complexity. Addison-Wesley, Reading, Massachusetts.

Korsmo, Thomas B.
1983 Magnetic Survey, Pecos National Monument, Pecos, New Mexico. Ms. on file, Department of Sociology and Anthropology, New Mexico State University, Las Cruces.

Kramer, Carol
1985 Ceramic Ethnoarchaeology. In *Annual Review of Anthropology,* Vol. 14, edited by Bernard J. Siegel, Alan R. Bels, and Stephen A. Tyler, pp. 77–102. Annual Reviews, Palo Alto.

Lambert, Marjorie F.
1954 *Paa-ko: Archaeological Chronicle of an Indian Village in North Central New Mexico,* Parts I–V. Monographs of the School of American Research, 19. University of New Mexico Press, Albuquerque.

Lang, Richard W.
1980 Archaeological Investigations at a Pueblo Agricultural Site, and Archaic and Puebloan Encampments on the Rio Ojo Caliente, Rio Arriba County, New Mexico. Contract Archaeology Program, School of American Research, Santa Fe.
1982 Transformations in White Ware Pottery of the Northern Rio Grande. In *Southwestern Ceramics: A Comparative Review,* edited by Albert H. Schroeder, pp. 153–200. *The Arizona Archaeologist* 15.

Lang, Richard W., and Arthur H. Harris
1984 *The Faunal Remains from Arroyo Hondo Pueblo, New Mexico: Study of Short-Term Subsistence Change.* Arroyo Hondo Archaeological Series, Vol. 5. School of American Research Press, Santa Fe.

Larrick, Roy
1985 Spears, Style and Time among Maa-speaking Pastoralists. *Journal of Anthropological Archaeology* 4:201-215.

London, Marilyn
1980 Preliminary Osteological Report on Three Burials from Rowe Ruin. Submitted to National

Park Service, Santa Fe. Ms. on file, Osteological Laboratory, University of New Mexico, Albuquerque.

Longacre, William A.

1966 Changing Patterns of Social Integration: A Prehistoric Example from the American Southwest. *American Anthropologist* 68:94–102.

Mackey, James

1977 A Multivariate Osteological Approach to Towa Culture History. *American Journal of Physical Anthropology* 46:477–482.

Malotki, Ekkehart

1993 *Hopi Ruin Legends, Kiqotutuwutsi.* University of Nebraska Press, Lincoln.

Martin, William C., and C. Robert Hutchins

1981 *A Flora of New Mexico.* J. Cramer, Braunschweig, W. Germany.

Meining, D. W.

1971 *Southwest: Three Peoples in Geographical Change, 1600–1970.* Historical Geography of North America Series. Oxford University Press, New York.

Mera, H. P.

1933 *A Proposed Revision of the Rio Grande Glaze-Paint Sequence.* Laboratory of Anthropology Technical Series, Bulletin 5. Museum of New Mexico, Santa Fe.

1935 *Ceramic Clues to the Prehistory of North Central New Mexico.* Laboratory of Anthropology Technical Series, Bulletin 8. Museum of New Mexico, Santa Fe.

1940 *Population Changes in the Rio Grande Glaze-Paint Area.* Laboratory of Anthropology Technical Series Bulletin, No. 11. Santa Fe.

Mick-O'Hara, Linda

1987 Distributional Analysis: An Attempt to Unravel Complexity in Puebloan Prehistory. Paper presented at the 52nd annual meeting of the Society for American Archaeology, May 8, Toronto.

1988 Game Depletion or Selection: A Problem in the Late Prehistoric Southwest. Paper presented at the symposium on Current Research on the Late Prehistoric and Early Historic New Mexico sponsored by the New Mexico Archaeological Council.

1989 Who, What, and Where: How Farmers Hunt and the Archaeological Implications Thereof. Paper presented at the Symposium in Honor of Lewis R. Binford, Department of Anthropology, University of New Mexico, Albuquerque.

1994 *Nutritional Stability and Changing Faunal Resource Use in La Plata Valley Prehistory.* Ph.D. dissertation, Department of Anthropology, University of New Mexico, Albuquerque.

1996 The Utilization and Disposal of Faunal Remains in the Early Mesilla Phase Component at LA 457, Otero County, New Mexico. In *LA 457: An Early Mesilla Phase Occupation along North Florida Avenue near Alamogordo, New Mexico,* by Yvonne R. Oakes. Archaeology Note 180. Office of Archaeological Studies, Museum of New Mexico, Santa Fe.

Minnis, Paul E.

1978 Macroplant Remains from Pithouse Sites, Pecos National Monument, New Mexico. Ms. on file, National Park Service, Santa Fe.

1981 *Economic Organizational Responses to Food Stress by Non-Stratified Societies: An Example from Prehistoric New Mexico.* Ph.D. dissertation, Department of Anthropology, University of Michigan, Ann Arbor.

Morris, Elizabeth Ann, and Volney H. Jones

1960 Seventh-Century Evidence for the Use of Tobacco in Northern Arizona. In *Akten des 34 Internationalen Amerikanistenkongresses,* pp. 306-309. Wien, Austria.

Morrison, Kathleen D.

1987 1984 Rowe Project Site Survey: Preliminary Report. In Rowe Project: Preliminary Report, Vol. 2. Submitted to the National Science Foundation by Linda S. Cordell. On file, Clark Field Archives, Maxwell Museum of Anthropology, University of New Mexico, Albuquerque.

Naroll, R.

1962 Floor Area and Settlement Population. *American Antiquity* 27:587–589.

1970 The Culture-Bearing Unit in Cross-Cultural Surveys. In *A Handbook of Method in Cultural Anthropolgy,* edited by Raoul Naroll and Ronald Cohen, pp. 721–765. American Museum of Natural History, Natural History Press, Garden City, New York.

Nelson, Margaret C. (editor)

1984 *Ladder Ranch Research Project, A Report of the First Season.* Technical Series of the Maxwell Museum of Anthropology, No. 1. University of New Mexico, Albuquerque.

Nordby, Larry

1981 The Prehistory of the Pecos Indians. *Exploration, Annual Bulletin of the School of American Research,* pp. 5-11. Santa Fe.

1990 Small Site Survey of Pecos Monument, New Mexico. Ms. on file, Superintendant's Office, Pecos National Historical Park, Pecos, New Mexico.

Olsen, Stanley J.

1964 *Mammal Remains from Archaeological Sites.* Papers of the Peabody Museum of Archeology and

Ethnology 56(1). Harvard University Press, Cambridge, Massachusetts.

1968 *Fish, Amphibian, and Reptile Remains from Archaeological Sites.* Papers of the Peabody Museum of Archeology and Ethnology 56(2), Harvard University, Cambridge, Massachusetts.

Orcutt, Janet D.

1991 Environment Variability and Settlement Changes on the Pajarito Plateau, New Mexico. *American Antiquity* 56:315–332.

Otto, John Solomon

1977 Artifacts and Status Differences: A Comparison of Ceramics from Planter, Overseer, and Slave Sites on an Antebellum Plantation. In *Research Strategies in Historical Archaeology,* edited by Stanley South, pp. 91–118. Academic Press, New York.

Palkovitch, Ann M.

1980 *Pueblo Population and Society: The Arroyo Hondo Skeletal and Mortuary Remains.* Arroyo Hondo Archaeological Series, No. 3. School of American Research Press, Santa Fe.

Parsons, Elsie Clews

1925 *The Pueblo of Jemez.* Papers of the South West Expedition, No. 3. Department of Archaeology, Phillips Academy, Andover, Massachusetts.

Pearce, Thomas M. (editor)

1965 *New Mexico Place Names: A Geographical Dictionary.* University of New Mexico Press, Albuquerque.

Peckham, Stewart, and Erik K. Reed

1963 Three Sites near Ranchos de Taos, New Mexico. *Highway Salvage Archaeology* 4(3):1-30.

Plog, Fred

1979 Prehistory: Western Anasazi. In *Handbook of North American Indians,* Vol. 9, Southwest, edited by Alfonso A. Ortiz, pp. 108–129. Smithsonian Institution Press, Washington, D.C.

1983 Political and Economic Alliances on the Colorado Plateau, A.D. 400-1450. *Advances in World Archaeology* 2:289–330.

1984 Exchange, Tribes and Alliances: The Northern Southwest. *American Archaeology* 4:217–223.

Plog, Fred, and Steadman Upham

1983 The Analysis of Prehistoric Social Organization. In *The Development of Political Organization in Native North America,* edited by E. Tooker and M. Fried, pp. 199–213. American Ethnological Society, Washington, D.C.

Polzer, Charles W.

1989 The Spanish Colonial Southwest: New Technologies for Old Documents. *Columbian Consequences,* Vol. I, edited by David Hurst Thomas, pp

179-188. Washington: Smithsonian Institution Press.

Riley, Carroll

1987 *The Frontier People.* University of New Mexico Press, Albuquerque.

1989 Warfare in the Protohistoric Southwest: An Overview. In *Cultures in Conflict: Current Archaeological Perspectives,* edited by Diana Claire Tkaczuk and Brian C. Vivian, pp. 138–147. Proceedings of the Twentieth Annual Chacmool Conference. Archaeological Association of The University of Calgary.

Robertson, James M., and Robert H. Moench

1979 The Pecos Greenstone Belt: A Proterozoic Volcano-Sedimentary Sequence in the Southern Sangre de Cristo Mountains, New Mexico. In *Guidebook of Santa Fe County,* edited by Raymond V. Ingersoll, Lee A. Woodward, and H. L. James, pp. 165–169. New Mexico Geological Society, Thirtieth Field Conference, October 4–6, 1979.

Robertson, James M., Anton J. Budding, Frank E. Kottlowski, H. L. James, and Augustus K. Armstrong

1979 Third Day Road Log from Lamy Junction to Cowles via Glorieta, Pecos National Monument, Pecos, Tererro and Pecos Mine. In *Guidebook of Santa Fe County,* edited by Raymond V. Ingersoll, Lee A. Woodward, and H. L. James, pp. 29–42. New Mexico Geological Society, Thirtieth Field Conference, October 4–6, 1979.

Robinson, William J. and Catherine M. Cameron

1991 *A Directory of Tree-Ring Dated Prehistoric Sites in the American Southwest.* Laboratory of Tree-Ring Research, University of Arizona, Tucson.

Rogers, James B.

1987 Cultural Overview and Lithic Artifact Analysis. In *Archaeological Investigations at Los Esteros Reservoir, Northeastern New Mexico,* edited by Albert E. Ward, John D. Schelberg, and Jerold G. Widdison, pp. 29–38, 57–100. Center for Anthropological Studies, Albuquerque.

Roney, John R.

1995 Mesa Verdean Manifestations South of the San Juan River. *Journal of Anthropological Archaeology* 14:170–184.

Ruppé, Reynold J.

1953 *The Acoma Culture Province: An Archaeological Concept.* Ph.D. dissertation, Department of Anthropology, Harvard University, Cambridge, Massachusetts.

Schaafsma, Curtis F.

1979 The Cerrito Site (AR-4): A Piedra Lumbre

Phase Settlement at Abiquiu Reservoir. Contract Archaeology Division, School of American Research, Santa Fe.

Schiffer, Michael B.
1982 Hohokam Chronology: An Essay on History and Method. In *Hohokam and Patayan: Prehistory of Southwestern Arizona,* edited by Randall McGuire and Michael B. Schiffer, pp. 299–344. Academic Press, New York.

Sebastian, Lynne
1991 Sociopolitical Complexity and the Chaco System. In *Chaco and Hohokam: Prehistoric Regional Systems in the American Southwest,* edited by Patricia L. Crown and W. James Judge, pp. 109–135. SAR Press, Santa Fe.
1992 *The Chaco Anasazi: Sociopolitical Evolution in the Prehistoric Southwest.* Cambridge University Press, Cambridge.

Shepard, Anna O.
1936 The Technology of Pecos Pottery. In *The Pottery of Pecos,* Vol. 2, by Alfred V. Kidder and Anna O. Shepard, pp. 389–587. Papers of the Southwestern Expedition 7. Phillips Academy, Andover, and Yale University Press, New Haven.
1942 *Rio Grande Glaze Paint Ware: A Study Illustrating the Place of Ceramic Technological Analysis in Archaeological Research.* Contributions to American Anthropology and History, No. 39, Publication 528. Carnegie Institution of Washington, Washington, D.C.
1965 Rio Grande Glaze-Paint Pottery: A Test of Petrographic Analysis. In *Ceramics and Man,* edited by Frederick R. Matson, pp. 62–87. Viking Fund Publications in Anthropology, No. 41. Wenner-Gren Foundation for Anthropological Research, New York.

Sinopoli, Carla A.
1985 Style in Arrows. A Study of an Ethnographic Collection from the Western United States. Ms. on file, Museum of Anthropology, University of Michigan, Ann Arbor.

Smiley, Terah L., Stanley A. Stubbs, and Bryant Bannister
1953 *A Foundation for the Dating of Some Late Archaeological Sites in the Rio Grande Area, New Mexico, Based on Studies in Tree-Ring Methods and Pottery Analysis.* Laboratory of Tree-Ring Research Bulletin 6. University of Arizona, Tucson.

Smith, Watson, Richard B. Woodbury, and Nathalie F. S. Woodbury
1966 *The Excavation of Hawikuh by Frederick Webb Hodge: Report of the Hendricks-Hodge Expedition, 1917-1923.* Contributions from the Museum of the American Indian, Heye Foundation 20. New York.

Snow, David H.
1991 Upland Prehistoric Maize Agriculture in the Eastern Rio Grande and Its Peripheries. In *Farmers, Hunters, and Colonists: Interaction between the Southwest and the Southern Plains,* edited by Katherine A. Spielmann, pp. 71–89. University of Arizona Press, Tucson.

Southerland, Patrick K., and Arthur Montgomery
1975 *Trail Guide to the Geology of the Upper Pecos, New Mexico.* Bureau of Mines and Mineral Resources, Scenic Trips to the Geological Past, No. 6. Socorro.

Spielmann, Katherine A.
1987 *Inter-societal Food Acquisition among Egalitarian Societies: An Ecological Study of Plains/Pueblo Interaction in the American Southwest.* Ph.D. Dissertation, Department of Anthropology, University of Michigan.
1991 Interaction among Non-Hierarchical Societies. In *Cooperation Farmers,* edited by Katherine A. Spielmann, pp. 1–18. University of Arizona Press, Tucson.

Spielmann, Katherine A., Margaret J. Schoeninger, and Katherine Moore
1990 Plains-Pueblo Interdependence and Human Diet at Pecos Pueblo. *American Antiquity* 55:745–781.

Stanford, Dennis J., and Robert Patten
1984 R-6, A Preliminary Report of a Cody Site in North-Central New Mexico. In *Papers of the Philmont Conference on the Archaeology of Northeastern New Mexico,* edited by Carol J. Condie, pp. 188–199. New Mexico Archaeological Council Proceedings, Vol. 6, No. 1. Albuquerque.

Steen, Charles
1955 The Pigeon Cliffs Site, A Preliminary Report. *El Palacio* 62:174–180.

Stevens, Christopher
1992 Obsidian Hydration. Paper presented at the 65th annual Pecos Conference, August 13–16, Pecos National Historic Park, New Mexico.

Stevenson, Matilda Coxe
1915 Ethnobotany of the Zuni Indians. In *30th Annual Report of the Bureau of American Ethnology,* pp. 31–102. Smithsonian Institution, Washington, D.C.

Steward, Julian
1937 Ecological Aspects of Southwestern Society.

Anthropos 32:87–104.

Stubbs, Stanley A., and W. S. Stallings, Jr.

1953 *The Excavation of Pindi Pueblo, New Mexico.* Monographs of the School of American Research, 18. Santa Fe.

Stuiver, Minze, and Paula J. Reimer

1993 Extended 14C Data Base and Revised CALIB 3.0 14C Age Calibration Program. *Radiocarbon* 35(1):215–230.

Sundt, William

1987 Pottery of Central New Mexico and Its Role as Key to Both Time and Space. In *Secrets of the City: Papers on Albuquerque Area Archaeology,* edited by Anne V. Poore and John Montgomery, pp. 116–147. Papers of the Archaeological Society of New Mexico, No. 13. Ancient City Press, Santa Fe.

Swank, G. R.

1932 The Ethnobotany of the Acoma and Laguna Indians. M.A. thesis, Department of Anthropology, University of New Mexico, Albuquerque.

Tainter , Joseph A.

1995 Introduction: Prehistoric Societies as Evolving Complex Systems. In *Evolving Complexity and Environmental Risk in the Prehistoric Southwest,* edited by Joseph A. Tainter and Bonnie Bagley Tainter, pp. 1–24. Proceedings, Vol. XXIV, Santa Fe Institute Studies in the Sciences of Complexity. Addison-Wesley, Reading, Massachusetts.

Thomas, David Hurst

1971 On Distinguishing Natural from Cultural Bone in Archaeological Sites. *American Antiquity* 17:337–338.

Toll, Mollie S.

1981 A Preliminary Investigation of Botanical Remnants of Subsistence at Rowe Pueblo. Castetter Laboratory for Ethnobotanical Studies, Technical Series 33. University of New Mexico, Albuquerque.

1983 Wild Plant Use in the Rio Abajo: Some Deviations from the Expected Pattern throughout the Central and Northern Southwest. Paper presented at the Rio Abajo Area Conference on the Archaeology and History of the Socorro District, March 18–19, New Mexico Institute of Mining and Technology, Socorro.

1984a Archaic and Historic Botanical Materials from Cerrososo Canyon Sites, Northeastern New Mexico. Castetter Laboratory for Ethnobotanical Studies, Technical Series 129. University of New Mexico, Albuquerque.

1984b Taxonomic Diversity in Flotation and Macrobotanical Assemblages from Chaco Canyon. In *Recent Research on Chaco Prehistory,* edited by W. James Judge and John D. Schelberg, pp. 241–250. Reports of the Chaco Center 8. National Park Service, Albuquerque.

1985a An Overview of Chaco Canyon Macrobotanical Materials and Analyses to Date. Ms. on file, Chaco Center, National Park Service, Albuquerque. Castetter Laboratory for Ethnobotanical Studies, Technical Series 141. University of New Mexico, Albuquerque.

1985b Changing Patterns of Plant Utilization for Food and Fuel: Evidence from Flotation and Macrobotanical Remains. In *Economy and Interaction along the Lower Chaco River: The Navajo Mine Archeological Program,* edited by Patrick Hogan and Joseph C. Winter, pp. 331–350. Office of Contract Archeology, University of New Mexico, Albuquerque.

Traylor, Diane, Nancy Wood, Lyndi Hubbell, Robert Scaife, and Sue Weber

1977 Bandelier Excavations in the Flood Pool of Cochiti Lake, New Mexico, edited by Lyndi Hubell and Diane Traylor. Report from the Southwest Cultural Resource Center, National Park Service, Santa Fe, to Interagency Archeological Services Division, National Park Service, Denver.

U.S. Department of Agriculture

1974 Field Guide to Native Vegetation of the Southwestern Region. U.S. Forest Service, Southwest Regional Office, Albuquerque.

Upham, C. Steadman

1982 *Polities and Power: An Economic and Political History of the Western Pueblo.* Academic Press, New York.

1985 Interpretations of Prehistoric Political Complexity in the Central and Northern Southwest. In *Status, Structure and Stratification: Current Archaeological Reconstructions,* edited by M. Thompson, M. T. Garcia, and F. J. Kense, pp. 175–180. Proceedings of the Sixteenth Annual Chacmool Conference. Archaeological Association of the University of Calgary.

Upham, C. Steadman, and Gail M. Bockley

1989 The Chronologies of Nuvakwewtaqa: Implications for Social Process. In *The Sociopolitical Structure of Prehistoric Southwestern Societies,* edited by Steadman Upham, Kent G. Lightfoot, and Roberta A. Jewett, pp. 447–491. Investigations in American Archaeology. Westview Press, Boulder.

Wait, Walter K.

1981 The Rowe Archeological Research Project. Final Report to the National Endowment to the Humanities, RS-1144-79. Ms. on file, Southern Illinois University, Carbondale.

Wait, Walter K., and Larry Nordby

1979 Cultural Historical and Chronological Placement of Rowe Pueblo in Upper Pecos Valley Prehistory. Research design submitted to National Endowment for the Humanities.

Walker, William H.

1995 Ceremonial Trash? In *Expanding Archaeology,* edited by James M. Skibo, William H. Walker, and Axel Nielson, pp. 67–79. University of Utah Press, Salt Lake City.

1996 Ritual Deposits: Another Perspective. In *River of Change: Prehistory of the Middle Little Colorado River Valley,* edited by E. C. Adams, pp. 75–93. Arizona State Museum Archaeological Series No. 185. University of Arizona Press, Tucson.

Ward, Albert E., John D. Schelberg, and Jerold G. Widdison, editors

1987 *Archaeological Investigations at Los Esteros Reservoir, Northeastern New Mexico.* Prepared under contract CX 702970049, National Park Service, Southwest Regional Office, and contract DACW 47-78-M-0286/C-0004, U.S. Army Corps of Engineers, Albuquerque District Office. Center for Anthropological Studies, Albuquerque.

Ware, John, and Macy Mensel

1992 The Ojo Caliente Project: Archaeological Test Excavations and a Data Recovery Plan for Cultural Resources along U.S. 285, Rio Arriba County, New Mexico. Office of Archaeological Studies, Archaeology Notes 99. Museum of New Mexico, Santa Fe.

Warren, A. Helene

1970 Notes on the Manufacture and Trade of Rio Grande Glazes. *The Artifact* 8(4):1–7.

1971 Notes on Santa Fe Black-on-white and Magdalena Black-on-white. Paper presented at a conference on the Carbon-Painted Pottery of the Rio Grande Area, Museum of New Mexico, Santa Fe.

1976 Section B: The Ceramics and Mineral Resources of LA 70 and the Cochiti Area. In *Archaeological Excavations at Pueblo del Encierro, LA 70, Cochiti Dam Salvage Project, Cochiti, New Mexico, Final Report: 1964–1965 Field Seasons,* edited by David H. Snow, pp. B1–169. Laboratory of Anthropology Notes, No. 78. Museum of New Mexico, Santa Fe.

1979 The Glaze Paint Wares of the Upper Middle Rio Grande. In *Archaeological Investigations in Cochiti Reservoir, New Mexico, Vol. 4: Adaptive Change in the Northern Rio Grande Valley,* edited by Jan V. Biella and Richard C. Chapman, pp. 187–216. Office of Contract Archeology, University of New Mexico, Albuquerque.

1980 Prehistoric Pottery of Tijeras Canyon. In *Tijeras Canyon: Analyses of the Past,* edited by Linda S. Cordell, pp. 149–168. Maxwell Museum of Anthropology Series. University of New Mexico Press, Albuquerque.

Washburn, Dorothy Koster

1977 *A Symmetry Analysis of Upper Gila Area Ceramic Design.* Papers of the Peabody Museum of Archaeology and Ethnology, Vol. 68. Cambridge, Massachusetts.

Welker, Eden A.

1997 *Attributes of Aggregation at Pueblo San Marcos and Pecos Pueblo in the Northern Rio Grande, New Mexico.* Unpublished Ph.D. dissertation, Department of Anthropology, University of Colorado, Boulder.

Wendorf, Fred

1953 *Salvage Archaeology in the Chama Valley, New Mexico.* Monographs of the School of American Research, No. 17. Santa Fe.

Wendorf, Fred, and John P. Miller

1958 Artifacts from High Mountain Sites in the Sangre de Cristo Range, New Mexico. *El Palacio* 6:37–52.

Wendorf, Fred, and Erik K. Reed

1955 An Alternative Reconstruction of Northern Rio Grande Prehistory. *El Palacio* 62:131–173.

Wetherington, Ronald K.

1968 *Excavations at Pot Creek Pueblo.* Fort Burgwin Research Center Report 6. Rancho de Taos, New Mexico.

Wetterstrom, Wilma

1986 *Food, Diet, and Population at Prehistoric Arroyo Hondo Pueblo, New Mexico.* Arroyo Hondo Archaeological Series, Vol. 6. School of American Research, Santa Fe.

Weymouth, John E.

1981 Magnetic Surveying of Archaeological Sites. In *Proceedings of the First Conference on Scientific Research in the National Parks,* Vol. 2, edited by Robert M. Linn, pp. 941–947. National Park Service Transactions and Proceedings Series, No. 5.

Wiessner, Polly

1982 Risk, Reciprocity, and Social Influence on !Kung San Economics. In *Politics and History in Band Societies,* edited by E. Leacock and R. Lee, pp. 61–

84. Cambridge University Press, Cambridge.

1983   Style and Social Information in Kalahari San Projectile Points. *American Antiquity* 48:253–276.

1984   Reconsidering the Behavioral Basis of Style: A Case Study among the Kalahari San. *Journal of Anthropological Archaeology* 3:190–234.

Wilcox, David R., and W. Bruce Mass, editors

1981   *The Protohistoric Period in the North American Southwest, AD 1450-1700.* Arizona State University, Tempe.

Williams, Jerry L., and Paul E. McAllister (editors)

1979   *New Mexico in Maps.* University of New Mexico Press, Albuquerque.

Winship, George P.

1896   The Coronado Expedition, 1540–1542. In *Fourteenth Annual Report of the Bureau of Ethnology, 1892–1893,* Part 1, pp. 329–613. Washington, D.C. Reprinted by Rio Grande Press, 1964.

Wobst, Martin

1974   Boundary Conditions for Paleolithic Social Systems: A Simulation Approach. *American Antiquity* 39:147–148.

1981   Paleolithic Archaeology: Some Problems with Form, Time and Space. In *Hunter-Gatherer Economy in Prehistory,* edited by Geoff Bailey, pp. 220–225. Cambridge University Press, Cambridge.

Wolfman, Daniel

1992   Archaeomagnetic Dating. Paper presented at the 65th Annual Pecos Conference, Pecos National Historic Park, New Mexico.

Wood, Gerald L.

1963   Archaeological Salvage Excavation near Rowe, New Mexico. Project I-025-5(10)302. Laboratory of Anthropology Note 22. Museum of New Mexico, Santa Fe.

Woodbury, Richard B.

1993   *Sixty Years of Southwestern Archaeology, A History of the Pecos Conference.* UNM Press, Albuquerque.

Young, Gwen

1980   Analysis of Faunal Remains. In *Tijeras Canyon, Analyses of the Past,* edited by Linda S. Cordell, pp. 88–121. Maxwell Museum of Anthropology and University of New Mexico Press, Albuquerque.

Index